Funerals, Festivals, and Cultural Politics
in Porfirian Mexico

Funerals, Festivals, and Cultural Politics in Porfirian Mexico

Matthew D. Esposito

UNIVERSITY OF NEW MEXICO PRESS
ALBUQUERQUE

Library of Congress Cataloging-in-Publication Data

Esposito, Matthew D., 1967–
Funerals, festivals, and cultural politics in Porfirian Mexico / Matthew D. Esposito.
   p. cm.
Includes bibliographical references and index.
ISBN 978-0-8263-4883-8 (pbk. : alk. paper)
1. Mexico—Politics and government—1867–1910.
2. Mexico—History—1867–1910.
3. Díaz, Porfirio, 1830–1915.
4. Memorialization—Political aspects—Mexico—History.
5. Memorials—Political aspects—Mexico—History.
6. Legitimacy of governments—Mexico—History.
I. Title.
  F1233.5.E836 2010
  393.0972—dc22
                    2010015366

Designed and typeset by Gopa & Ted2, Inc.
Text composed in Minion Pro Regular 10.25/13.25

*This book is dedicated to my loving wife, Joy,
and our beloved sons, Nicolas and Shane.*

Contents

Illustrations

Preface and Acknowledgments

❧ ——————————————————————————————————————

THIS IS A STUDY of how rule was accomplished in the authoritarian republic of Mexican dictator Porfirio Díaz from 1876 to 1911. As such, it attempts to lay bare the sources of legitimacy and stability in one of the longest-lived, most durable states in a region notorious for its political turbulence, economic volatility, and dire poverty. The research focus is acute. The book examines how and why the Porfirian state captured the cultural realm of death ceremonials—historically controlled by traditional power centers, such as the Catholic Church, the military, and the family—and refashioned them into political statements on Mexican national history, identity, and modernity. Nevertheless, the study of state funerals, festivals of commemoration, holiday rituals, memorial building, and Day of the Dead celebrations reveals an entire constellation of power relations that has largely eluded telescopic gazes of the era. The Porfirian state's master architects and social engineers forged landscapes and mindscapes of memory from the very real materials of a shared national past and common cultural identity, the premises of which, while questioned, were never seriously challenged until 1910.

Porfirian cultural politics have never been fully deconstructed within a transatlantic context. The purveyors of all fledgling bourgeois nation-states had to appeal broadly to the masses or suffer setbacks on many fronts. After experiencing a miserable half century of war and revolution, Mexico got swept into a fin-de-siècle ethos of transformational development that dominated the Atlantic world. Although the Porfirian state was saddled with grave disadvantages at first, it found a winning formula in "reconciliation and modernization," more than "Order and Progress." The state's unifying cultural project won popular consent and enabled Mexico to compete for the political favor and foreign investment capital of advanced industrial nations. Mexico's constructed social reality as an authoritarian national state dependent on finance capital from Europe and the United States was the easiest road of many possible routes to national development. Secure in its hegemony, the state sacrificed development for growth, democracy for order, and egalitarianism for inequality. For all the effort it took to reconstruct the political realities of the era independent of the revolution that followed, this book concludes that there never was such a thing as a benign dictatorship in Mexico.

This project has drawn me into professional and personal relationships that I value deeply and for which I have incurred many debts. I owe the greatest debt to my mentor, William H. Beezley, who unselfishly devoted great amounts of time to improving this work and who allowed me to observe the craft of a pioneering cultural historian. Although his influence permeates this study, he cannot be faulted for any of its shortcomings.

I warmly thank the scholars who read early drafts of this study and offered useful suggestions that have improved it considerably. Miguel Tinker Salas, who first introduced me to the life and times of Porfirio Díaz while I was a graduate student at Arizona State University, continued to offer generous advice and friendship throughout the research and writing stages. Bill French has guided my research and challenged my assumptions as only a widely read transdisciplinary scholar can. Vince Peloso, who took a profound interest in both my subject and my career, suggested several theoretical avenues to follow. Anne Staples and Paul Vanderwood convinced me to give due attention to the continuities as well as the changes in nineteenth-century cultural practices for both the rich and the poor. Steve Vincent, Randy Hanson, Doug Richmond, Rich Warren, and Adrian Bantjes provided constructive critiques of early versions and helped greatly with conceptualization. Jaime Rodríguez O., Barbara Tenenbaum, Alan Knight, Tom Benjamin, Josefina Vázquez, Rod Camp, Tony Rosenthal, Fred Adams, Jeff Pilcher, Tom Mays, James Garza, Victor Macías, Steve Bunker, Deb Symonds, and Pedro Santoni have offered invaluable insights and assistance over the years. Professors Don Worcester, Ben Procter, Don Coerver, Mark Gilderhus, Arturo Flores, and Mark Esposito, my brother and valued colleague, have each read the manuscript and improved the writing. Editor Clark Whitehorn, Elisabeth Graves, Elise McHugh, and the editorial staff of the University of New Mexico Press once again proved that they are at the top of their game.

I am grateful to the archivists and employees at several of Mexico City's research centers. To Maricarmen Lomeli, Virginia Monzón Ríos, Alma Nely Lugo Mejía, Pedro Galván, and Gerardo Suárez Orihuela of the Hemeroteca Nacional, I owe the greatest debt. I also thank Eugenia Ponce Alcocer and Teresa Matabuena at the Universidad Ibéroamericana's Colección General Porfirio Díaz for providing specific documents from Díaz's personal papers. Elvia Morales of the Sala Porfirio Díaz at the Universidad de las Américas was consistently helpful for the same. At Condumex, Karina López, Susana Morales

Feregrino, and Violeta Sánchez were models of efficiency. I am indebted also to the staffs of the Biblioteca Miguel Lerdo de Tejada, the Biblioteca del Instituto Nacional de Antropología e Historia (INAH), and the Biblioteca Daniel Cosío Villegas at the Colegio de Mexico. At the Archivo General de la Nación, Alma Vásquez of the *fototeca* was efficient and helpful, and Juan Galván was generous with his time and knowledge of reproduction techniques. At the INAH Biblioteca Orozco y Berra, María Esther Jasso Sáenz graciously opened up the pamphlet and manuscript collections. Alberto Luna at the Archivo Histórico "Genaro Estrada," de la Secretaría de Relaciones Exteriores assisted me greatly. At the glorious INAH photographic archive in Pachuca, Hidalgo, I thank Ricardo Fernández, Rogelia Laguna García, and Olga Salgado Torres for their help with essential photographs. Paulina Michel and Sandra Peña of the Archivo Histórico Universidad Nacional Autónoma de México–Centro de Estudios sobre la Universidad reproduced photos at the Fondo Fototeca Ezequiel Chávez. Although these photographs were not all incorporated into the book, they have served as useful historical documents for reconstructing the visually stunning state festivals and funerals of Porfirian Mexico.

Librarians and archivists at the Mary Couts Burnett Library of Texas Christian University (TCU), the Nettie Lee Benson Latin American Library at the University of Texas at Austin, and the Cowles Library at Drake University contributed substantially to this project. Joyce Martindale and her staff at the Interlibrary Loan (ILL) office of TCU tracked down dozens of nineteenth-century travel accounts and newspapers that have strengthened the work. Laura Gutiérrez Witte, Carmen Sacomani, Russ Thomas, and the very generous Michael Hironymous granted me the key to the rich collections of the Benson Library. Craig Schroer, digital reproduction specialist, was an incredible ally who redefined professionalism and service. Jim Leonardo, Mark Stumme, and Kris Mogle at Drake University were so helpful in identifying electronic resources and so forbearing for renewing my lapsed ILL materials. I also wish to thank Lois Santi and Ziyu Tan of the Drake University History Department for their impressive assistance with digital imaging for this project.

Research for this project was funded by a Fulbright–García Robles grant and a Faculty Research grant and Research Materials Support grant from the Drake University Center for the Humanities. I thank Linda Goff, Vivian Antaki, Adriana Arzac, and Mary Hernández at the U.S.–Mexico Commission for providing administrative support in Mexico City. Karl Schaefer, Craig Owens, Karen Leroux, and the Humanities Center Board were always gracious supporters of my research and requests for visual materials.

I could not have completed the research without the logistical and moral support of a variety of people in both the United States and Mexico. Annie Nicolas in San Diego and the Nicolas family, Jerry and Josephine, in

Oceanside gave me a place to stay for research jaunts in southern California. Juan Manuel and Alejandra Maldonado opened their home in Colonia Las Aguilas to a complete stranger. Mark D. Barringer, a great friend and trusted colleague, pushed me along with consistent words of encouragement. My parents, Albert and Donalin Esposito, taught me to finish what I start. I would never have completed the book without the consistent encouragement of my wife, Joy.

Chronology of National Commemorations in Porfirian Mexico

Figure 1. José Guadalupe Posada's *Fiestas de la Patria*. From Roberto Berdecio and Stanley Applebaum, eds., *Posada's Popular Mexican Prints* (New York: Dover Publications, 1972).

Introduction

Memory, Hegemony, and Cultural Politics in Porfirian Mexico

> Immense sacrifices have sanctified liberty in this Nation.
>
> —BENITO JUÁREZ

IN 1902, Justo Sierra asserted that Mexico gained both national pride and its international personality during the Porfiriato. A journalist, a congressman, a historian, and Mexico's first minister of education, Sierra was the most influential intellectual of his time. Although he can be congratulated or criticized for having written the "Porfirian Bible," recent historians have agreed with his assessment that the Porfirian regime began Mexico's transformation into a modern nation.[1] Porfirio Díaz, the eight-term dictator who dominated the era (1876–1911), governed at a time of unprecedented political stability and economic growth. Not surprisingly, the Díaz era also represented the heyday of magisterial displays of state power and national wealth. Over the course of thirty-five years, the Porfirian state constructed dozens of national monuments, performed countless commemorations, and held 110 state funerals. The passing of a generation partially explains the large number of memorial acts. But the state also exhumed the bodies, repatriated the remains, and financed fourteen reburials of historical figures long consigned to tombs. In addition, the government decreed new "days of public mourning" and incorporated ceremonies honoring the illustrious dead in every national holiday program. Every death or exhumation was followed by a state funeral, a burial monument, and ongoing acts of remembrance. The Porfirian state's construction of landscapes and mindscapes of memory was the response of any modernizing nation that wished to express gratitude to heroes of the Patria.[2]

To the Mexican people, the Tuxtepec Revolt that brought General Díaz to power was the latest chapter in the jeremiad of nineteenth-century Mexican history. A suitable form of government eluded Mexico for most of the century. After independence, Mexico experimented with monarchies, republics, unconstitutional dictatorships, and provisional war governments. From 1821 to 1876, national leaders promulgated three constitutions, the presidency changed hands seventy-five times, and the average presidential term lasted eight months. One *caudillo*, Antonio López de Santa Anna, served as head of state eleven times but never completed a single term. Given the high turnover rate in the chief executive office, stable cabinet ministries proved impossible. Here, the ebb tide of crisis was the war with the United States. From 1846 to 1848, Mexico went through nine presidents, ten war ministers, twenty-three finance ministers, fourteen foreign ministers, and nineteen interior ministers.[3] Internal divisions and U.S. imperialism cost Mexico half of its national territory (Texas, New Mexico, Arizona, and California were ceded to the United States) and the temporary secession of Yucatán. The nation failed to unite in common defense against a foreign invader.[4]

After the war, anticlerical Liberals overthrew Santa Anna in the Revolution of Ayutla (1854) and defeated pro-clerical Conservatives in the War of the Reform (1858–61). In the 1860s, the Liberals rallied behind republican president Benito Juárez, triumphing over the allied forces of Emperor Maximilian, the French army of Napoleon III, and Mexican Conservatives. Juárez ended Mexico's second monarchy by executing Maximilian at Querétaro in 1867. Immortalized in French impressionist Edouard Manet's painting *Death of Maximilian*, the execution sounded the death knell of both clerical conservatism and European intervention in Mexico. This time a significant portion of the citizenry had fought and won Mexico's "second independence." Only then had Mexico "earned the incontestable right to call itself a nation."[5] The embattled Juárez reinstated the Liberal Constitution of 1857 and restored the republic. But Mexico had suffered devastating losses in lives, revenue, and property. Juárez implemented a reform program but died in office. In 1876, the nation endured yet another military coup when Porfirio Díaz, one of the foremost Liberal republican generals, overthrew Juárez's successor, Sebastián Lerdo de Tejada, and installed himself in power for over three decades. With the help of foreign capital investment, Díaz made astounding economic progress, but with social costs that caused the Mexican Revolution of 1910.

Unstable politics and fiscal insolvency in the first half of the nineteenth century were undeniable, but they also presented period historians like Sierra with a foil against which they constructed the Porfiriato as a mythical era of unabated order and progress. Likewise, historical writing since the Mexican Revolution (1910–20) left behind a distorted view of the Porfirian era as an *ancien régime* sandwiched between more progressive periods of the Liberal Reform and the revolution. It took four decades of historians since Daniel Cosío Villegas to demystify the Porfiriato by debunking myths inspired by Porfirian fables and the historiography of La Revolución.[6] Yet, even with

Figure 2. Porfirio Díaz. Portrait courtesy of the Fondo Ezequiel Chávez of the Biblioteca Nacional, Universidad Nacional Autónoma de México.

recent politically motivated attempts to rehabilitate the dictator and declare the revolution dead, Díaz remains a reviled strongman,[7] and his era is still misunderstood as static and incongruent with anything Mexican. Scholars have overlooked the continuities between Juárez and Díaz and have not linked hegemonic processes of the revolution to Porfirian antecedents. Thus, historians of nineteenth-century Mexico who read the historical literature on the Mexican Revolution note similarities in state rhetoric and national projects and question the novelty of the revolutionary and postrevolutionary states that replaced it. We are at once reminded of Benedict Anderson's inimitable metaphor: "Like the complex electrical system in any large mansion when the owner has fled, the state awaits the new owner's hand at the switch to be very much its old brilliant self again."[8] The formation of new states presumes continuity with the past, since historical actors assume control over forces that are materially unknown but which become active and operational at once.[9] Thus, generations of historians have denied the Porfirian state's rightful place in Mexican history as fluid, dynamic, and contiguous in important ways with those of the Reform and revolution.

A century after its collapse, the Porfiriato remains a blind spot in the rearview mirrors of historians and *pensadores* in another way. Historians have long recognized that authoritarian regimes need popular consent to establish rule and modernize societies.[10] Unfortunately, historical writing on the Porfiriato has restricted the reach of Díaz's conciliation efforts to political rivals, foreign nations, and the Catholic Church. A fourth pillar of popular class consent stabilized the Porfirian state; without it Mexico was ungovernable for four years, much less thirty-five. State events demonstrate the regime's greater regard for the inclusion of laboring classes in nation-building and show the Mexican people's high regard for Díaz. Electoral fraud and ruthless armies were never the only political weapons of Latin American dictatorships. Far from democratic, the Porfirian political system nonetheless involved complex cultural processes of legitimization, particularly as it related to working-class participation in public life. In the absence of free elections and equality before the law, the state redefined notions of "representation," "nation," and "citizenship" in state events designed to win over ordinary people. Díaz ruled as a popular dictator behind a mask of constitutionality, legality, and consent.[11]

The Díaz regime depended on memorialism, a form of cultural politics, for its legitimacy and survival. Memorialization, the active construction of official memory through the use of state ceremony, was a transatlantic phenomenon in the ages of capitalism, nationalism, and imperialism. As elsewhere, the Porfirian state used nineteenth-century ruling devices such as state funerals and commemorative festivals to inculcate rule and modernize Mexico.[12] Díaz only honored distinguished Liberals who fought in the mid-century wars. The very notion of the Patria had emerged from the shared memories of grim historical conflicts that left thousands of wartime dead and millions of citizens to remember them. The first seventeen state burials of the era helped Díaz (1877–80, 1884–1911) and his one-term successor, Manuel González (1880–84), restore order, gain legitimacy, and establish new relations of authority during the "Necesariato."[13] For most of this era, which should be re-periodized to 1890, the Porfirian regime greatly resembled the fraught republic Juárez restored. In May 1890, when Díaz reformed the Constitution of 1857 to allow for his indefinite reelection, the leitmotif of funerals and festivals changed from legitimization to material progress.[14] Opportunities to project images of "Order and Progress" multiplied because visible advances in Mexico's modernization process initiated by the Liberal Reform (1855–58) coincided with the deaths of Reforma Liberals during the mature Porfiriato (1890–1905). As Díaz remarked in a holiday speech in 1903: "Our people perceive with glowing clarity the practical results which the war of intervention and the reform brought to the country."[15] The regime therefore used state funerals and festivals concurrently as commemorative and inaugural events, drawing public attention to the historic deeds of great men while showcasing the latest evidence of material progress. This was possible in Mexico City, the nation's capital, which concentrated the largest population in the country and commanded over three-fourths of all federal expenditures.[16] State events were also replicated in miniature in cities and towns throughout the republic.

Indeed, keeping the dead alive in the national conscience helped the regime accomplish rule because no matter how lightheartedly commemorative festivals were celebrated, they always carried the sobering message that Díaz made political violence a thing of the past. The Porfirian peace relied on citizen awareness of the omnipresence of death both in Mexico's brutal national history and in everyday life. The thousands of memorial ceremonies drew from a vast reserve of colonial traditions, including the Roman Catholic liturgical calendar of saints' days and the Day of the Dead (November 2) religious holiday. President Juárez had founded a republican calendar with scheduled holidays on February 5 (Constitution Day), May 5 (Cinco de Mayo), and September 16 (Independence Day). Díaz modified this calendar to include observances on April 2 (Siege of Puebla), August 21 (Cuauhtémoc Day), and September 8 and 13 (anniversaries of the defenses of Churubusco and Chapultepec Castle). After 1887, the Porfirian Congress established days of national mourning for Juárez (July 18), Miguel Hidalgo (July 30), and the Niños Héroes (September 8), as well as endorsed days of national recognition for Vicente Guerrero (February 14) and José María Morelos (December 21). The state even conducted four pantheonizations during the Porfiriato, two for the Independence Heroes (1895 and the Centennial of 1910) and two others for Josefa Ortíz de Domínguez ("La Corregidora," in 1894) and Nicolás Bravo (1903). On average, ten national holidays and three unscheduled state funerals were held annually. Hardly a month passed in the nation's capital without a national commemoration or state funeral. Memorialization, like its fraternal twin, modernization, was a human construct that allowed the state to control public space, time, memory, and ultimately behavior at regular intervals throughout the calendar year.

Porfirian political culture involved a high level of cross-sectional appeal to keep all citizens emotionally invested in state initiatives. During funerals and commemorations, the state encouraged citizens to remember an official version of the past, appreciate the present, and visualize the future of their national community.[17] Government officials created and regulated "public time" and structured everyday behavior while the myriad forces of rapid urbanization, industrial capitalism, and technological change swept through Mexico. Politicians, patriotic societies, women's charitable organizations, and businessmen conducted annual marches to the graves of public leaders on the anniversaries of their deaths. The state mobilized thousands of bureaucrats, soldiers, office workers, factory laborers, and schoolchildren for ever-larger parades and processions. These patriotic groups representing the "nation" were actually the least of the state's concerns. Even in Mexico City, where industrialization was concentrated, factory workers and artisans never exceeded 16 percent of the population through 1910.[18] Of more concern to government technocrats was that one-fourth of all rural migrants ended their journeys in the capital. The era represented a seismic shift for a traditional peasantry who still used the term *Patria* indiscriminately to describe home villages, towns, regions, and the country. In 1877, 39 percent of the Mexican people still spoke indigenous languages.[19] As late as 1910, nearly 44 percent of Mexico City's population originated elsewhere.[20] Throughout the country there was a huge *población flotante* (floating population) of displaced agricultural workers, skilled artisans, and unemployed day laborers seeking wages.[21] Many of them were young newcomers unaccustomed to the rigors of urban life.[22] Largely uneducated and illiterate, these *campesinos* migrated to and from the nation's capital to become captive audiences of public spectacles and discourses that mitigated the insecurities accompanying unfettered progress. The state, represented not just by a dictator but by scholar-politicians like Justo Sierra, never stopped talking about its heroic formation. Civil servants, historians, sociologists, folklorists, novelists, journalists, statisticians, criminologists, literary critics, archaeologists, cartographers, and military scientists culled the data that proved Mexican nationhood.[23] For three decades, the Porfirian state promoted more concrete notions of national community than any previous government in Mexico. This is how citizens of marginally unified countries imagined their nations into existence. It is also how subjugated peoples imagined the mortality of states.

Hegemony

This study utilizes hegemony as a unifying concept to explain the paradoxes of the Mexican state, the *pax Porfiriana*, and nationalism. Antonio Gramsci, the Italian Marxist who originated the concept of hegemony, argued that the supremacy of any social class is asserted in two ways, through domination and "intellectual and moral leadership."[24] By hegemony, Gramsci meant the "spontaneous consent" given by the masses to the "dominant fundamental group" to direct society.[25] Powerful classes, such as an oligarchy or bourgeoisie, which occupy privileged positions and functions in the world of production, coordinate with the general interests of subordinate groups, such as the urban working class and peasantry. During its ascendancy, the interests of the dominant class prevail but fall short of narrowly corporate economic interest. Since the prevailing class cannot create the conditions for its own optimal expansion without the popular sectors, it seeks their cooperation through the exercise of hegemony.[26]

   At the pinnacle of his power in 1903, President Díaz explained in a speech before the Porfirista National Liberal Convention that the lesson he took away from the Liberal triumph of 1867 was that "our citizens will serve the country better when they concede their unlimited confidence and powerful moral support."[27] Hegemonic rule requires the dominant class to win the consent of traditional underclasses or risk social conflict that might counteract its interests. "Consent," the widespread acceptance of the principles and practices of a particular sociopolitical order, is an empirical reality evident in the conforming behaviors of the urban and rural poor. In a letter to Nuevo León governor Bernardo Reyes in 1901, Justo Sierra used the term *consentimiento* to describe the Mexican people's support for Díaz. Sierra explained that "the social dictatorship of General Díaz has in its conciliatory judgment [*juez de paz*] constituted itself in the expressed consent of a people, a consent that nobody doubts, [and] nobody discusses that which permits the President to be political arbiter without breaking a single constitutional law."[28] Specifically, popular consent ranges from collaboration to approbation to provisional tolerance of the existing order. Ruling classes manufacture acquiescence through participatory political cultures and complex national projects that keep societies within this continuum of consent. Through strategic cultural politics—memorialization of the national dead, for example—governing elites connect with the everyday experiences and traditions of the very people they subordinate in order to stabilize undemocratic regimes. The threat of officially sanctioned force still exists, but conflict is often resolved nonviolently through negotiation within a common discursive framework. Predominant classes achieve hegemony when it appears to the lower classes that some of their needs have been met.[29]

Although not one to embrace hegemony as a unifying concept, historian William Beezley called this informal mechanism of social mediation and consensus-building the "Porfirian persuasion."[30] Gramscian hegemony, like many of the episodes in Beezley's highly original and oft-cited book *Judas at the Jockey Club*, explains how power is lived in a particular context and how some regimes produce and reproduce themselves in the daily lives of individuals.[31] To date, even the best intellectual histories of Porfirian-era liberalism, positivism, and nationalism have stressed the high tides of European doctrinal influence on literate minorities without addressing relations of power. Few offer interpretations why traditional underclasses lived through the harsh realities justified by these modern ideologies. Hegemony is such a pervasive force that oppressed peoples can semiconsciously or unwittingly participate in their own victimization.[32]

Contributing to one's own subjugation is not the end of the story. The steady pressure of elite manipulation makes it difficult to accept hegemony as a process of political, moral, and cultural legitimization, unless legitimacy and authority are also contested from below.[33] Hegemony is never achieved solely on the basis of unequivocal consent. Resilient popular classes that are historically on the defensive use hegemony as an improvised shield. Subordinate classes such as urban wage laborers or rural peasants rely upon customary rights of their own, often manifested as acts of resistance.[34] As theorist Raymond Williams explains, "Alternative political and cultural emphases, and the many forms of opposition and struggle, are important not only in themselves but as indicative features of what the hegemonic process has in practice had to work to control."[35] Because the poor often know how they are being dominated and by whom, they not only develop distinct cultures and worldviews but acquire behavioral and discursive mechanisms to undermine, resist, and confront the dominant.[36] Such responses are constructed from lived experiences, performance traditions, and individual perceptions derived from interaction with dominant groups during the formation of modern colonial and neocolonial states. Historian Florencia Mallon argues that "hegemony cannot exist or be reproduced without the constant, though partial, incorporation of counter-hegemony."[37] What passes as consent from subjugated classes may actually be resistance dressed up by experts in "impression management" and "feigned performance."[38]

The applicability of hegemony to a circumatlantic world that includes Mexico fosters greater understanding of transnational processes of historical change in the late nineteenth century. Similarities exist between Porfirian Mexico and the contemporaneous "passive revolutions" of the opportunistic French Third Republic, Transformist Italy, and Restorationist Spain.[39] *Trasformismo*—the desertion of classical liberals to the Right—occurred when national bourgeoisies permanently displaced traditional aristocracies as the dominant class but now faced challenges on the Left in an era of increasing mass literacy, mass consumerism, mass media culture, and working-class politicization. Claiming to represent the nation, bourgeois regimes incorporated opponents into the state power structure in an effort to broaden the ruling class and minimize hostilities. At the same time, they effectively neutralized large-scale class conflict by constructing informal networks of power and appealing to the shared morality and principles of the popular sectors. Thus, hegemonic states are the product of historical continuity, supraregional coalitions, and class alliances.[40] The Díaz regime lacked the economic resources, military power, and national population to effect anything more than gradual acceptance of Porfirian rule. Consent was won through cultural politics fashioned by what Gramsci called the "ethical state."[41] During state events, traditional Mexican social relations and customs evolved into state-regulated obligations that granted working people participation without power. Porfirian funerals and festivals of commemoration were in fact conservative in their purposes to bring about national reconciliation, normalize class inequality, and preserve the status quo.[42]

In contrast to totalitarian states, the hegemonic state does not generally use instruments of coercion as an offensive weapon. Gramsci defined the hegemonic state as "the entire complex of practical and theoretical activities with which the ruling class not only justifies and maintains its dominance, but manages to win the active consent of those whom it rules."[43] Ruling elites tend to deploy state-sanctioned force defensively to safeguard the mediation process and maintain an acceptable equilibrium for the national good. Sociologist Stuart Hall states it this way: "Secure in its hegemony, the dominant class is spared the trouble of continually refurbishing its armoury, accommodating new elements, constructing hegemony from a selection of the materials offered by real relations."[44] In this sense, Díaz's political bosses (*jéfes políticos*), urban policemen (*gendarmes*), and rural police force (*rurales*) were the classic state-defense arms, while the professional military marched in seasonal parades. As anthropologist James C. Scott has shown, ritual displays of power became inexpensive substitutes for coercion because they economized on the actual use of violence.[45] The state also neutralized enemies through ad hoc arbitration of disputes and conventional government administration. In the early Porfiriato, Díaz relied on a national policy of conciliation. In the high Porfiriato, scientific administrators, lifetime bureaucrats, and a middle class dependent on the state held this "desktatorship" together.[46]

Hegemony and Nationalism

Recent literature on nation-state formation and nationalism emphasizes both to have been imagined and constructed by nineteenth-century elites. Nationalism's emergence was a contingent development. For consciousness to become national, nationalist movements had to connect to or collapse existing patterns of social organization through imaginative ideological discourse. Transforming a fragmented and disunited population into a coherent nationality required unifying ideologies and creative political action that combined smaller units (regional, religious, ethnic, peasant) into a larger collectivity.[47] Even at its heights, the Porfirian state was still engaged in the work of its Liberal predecessors of delegitimizing traditional organizations and solidarities to forge the imagined community of the nation.[48]

Nationalism's power to form subjects and identities suggests that it is a product of a hegemonic order. Interpretive anthropologist Claudio Lomnitz has pointed out the Mexican state's incessant references to the roots of the nation in the marketing of modernization projects. Origin stories and appeals to the historical depth of nations (claims to ancestral lands or territorial sovereignty, for example) spread feelings of kinship and comradeship among otherwise unconnected and diverse populations. Nationalism is useful to hegemonic elites because it formalizes communitarian relations that in fact do not exist.

To Lomnitz, the historical construction of "national subjects" proves that democracy, popular sovereignty, and rational government administration are never fully attainable. Citizens are constructed subjects of the state, tenuously linked together by abstract notions of shared nationality because they do not enjoy equality or even an effective vote. Therefore, the maxim of the modernizing state is to make the abstract nation and sense of national belonging concrete realities by intellectual development of a shared national space and organization of communitarian relationships to occupy that space.[49]

The formation of national identity depends on each citizen's subjective memory and a sense of belonging to a nation, just as one belongs to a family, church, or community.[50] The critical task of Porfirian nation-builders was to link individuals to the nation through the common bond of a shared history. Justo Sierra affirmed that historical memory was critical to national self-preservation: "While solidarity exists between the dead and the living, which revives the past and constantly sows the seed of the future in the womb of the present, the soul of a nation cannot expire."[51] Nobel laureate Octavio Paz later contended that a nation can only exist if its past influences it inactively through a valid historical project that animates, unifies, and transcends dissimilar spirits.[52] To this end, Porfirian officials constructed a usable past to promote national identity and produce loyal citizens.

To both Sierra and Paz, modern Mexico was born during La Guerra de la Reforma, the nation's brutal civil war. In Porfirian funerals and festivals, national leaders situated dead heroes in that epic mid-century struggle that destroyed conservatism, curbed the power of the Catholic Church, and claimed three hundred thousand lives. Delivered within a context of national reconciliation, Porfirian funeral orations and memorial speeches hearkened back to a mythical era when Liberals agreed with one another. Notable for their linearity and triumphalism, these history lessons described a unified movement that galvanized the nation against foreign and domestic enemies. Porfirian narrators identified themselves with the victors and recounted how Juárez, Zaragoza, Díaz, and the latest dead Liberal saved the Patria from certain extinction. Any evidence of ideological disagreement, factional infighting, and armed conflict, such as Díaz's rebellions against Juárez and Lerdo, was stricken from the record. Orators made no attempt to distinguish former *moderados, puros, juaristas, lerdistas, iglesistas*, or *porfiristas*. Rather than reminding citizens of political division, hegemonic discourses stressed national unity in Mexico's evolution toward inevitable progress. Funerals and festivals dramatized national community at the expense of truth.

All nation-builders efface historical memory that conflicts with their political aims. Commemorations foster not only remembrance; in their attempt to silence contrary interpretations of the past, they often encourage collective amnesia.[53] To Justo Sierra, forgetting was necessary because time evaporated the unimportant and left only the pure essence in the memory of survivors.[54] Liberal revisionism and positivist teleology turned seemingly harmless funerals and festivals into modern propaganda. Each memorial event reconstructed a suitable past that served a political purpose in the present, illustrating liberalism and positivism not as sets of exalted principles but as applied political doctrines of a hegemonic ruling class.[55] The very elasticity of liberalism and positivism proves their capacity for maintaining fluid social relations. When scholars describe Díaz's mercurial liberalism with distinct modifiers that change its meaning with every circumstance (e.g., *radical, moderate, jacobin, social, constitutional, folk, popular, patriotic, pragmatic, patriarchal, elite, Conservative, Porfirian,* and so on), they describe not only a dominant ideology but a hegemonic social reality in which a ruler has been granted informal power to subordinate principle to exigency.

Hegemony, Nationalism, and Cultural Politics

Significantly, the death of Benito Juárez in 1872 gave birth to the cultural politics of Díaz and originated the mythical discourse of the Porfirian state. The legacy of Juárez looms large in these pages, for his was the last state funeral for a sitting president in republican Mexico. Juárez himself was responsible for reestablishing the state funeral with the restoration of the republic, allocating more money for funerals than for Cinco de Mayo and Independence Day celebrations.[56] When Juárez died unexpectedly of a heart attack on July 18, his funeral proved the existence of a Mexican national community. The government declared a period of mourning for seven days, and the press placed a moratorium on criticism of the Great Republican. Nearly the entire population of Mexico City filed past his body as it lay-in-state in the National Palace. On July 22, six gray steeds pulled his hearse through the main arteries of the city, while Juárez's empty travel-worn black carriage and countless mourners followed behind. Over one hundred thousand people witnessed his magnificent procession and struggled for a place to listen to twelve orators deliver their eulogies at San Fernando.[57] If the city was a magnificent stage, it appeared that every citizen played a part. For thirty-five years, the Porfirian regime tried for encore performances of the original.

It is with good reason that Claudio Lomnitz identified Juárez and death as two out of three national totems in Mexico (the third is the Virgin of Guadalupe).[58] The genius of state funerals and commemorative festivals lies in their kinship to Mexico's cult of the dead. From the skull-laden architecture of Chichén Itzá and funerary urns of Teotihuacán to the home altars and spiritual devotion of Catholic Mexico, death has been a defining motif of the culture

206

Figure 3. Benito Juárez. Portrait courtesy of the Nettie Lee Benson Latin American Library, University of Texas, Austin.

and a constant theme in its iconography.[59] Day of the Dead practices probably have more in common with Spanish holy days than with Aztec rituals,[60] but Mexico's cult of death could be nationalized by the central state only if it had been already rooted in local popular culture. In one of his many essentialist statements, Octavio Paz remarked: "The Mexican is familiar with death, jokes about it, caresses it, sleeps with it, celebrates it; it is one of his favorite toys and his most steadfast love. True there is perhaps as much fear in his attitude as in that of others, but at least death is not hidden away."[61] This theme of communion between the living and the dead prevailed in nineteenth-century civil society's main media forms, including the newspaper columns of urban chroniclers, macabre journalistic humor, the *calaveras* of engraver and print-maker José Guadalupe Posada, *costumbrista* literature (*cuadros de costumbres*), the morbid drama *Don Juan Tenorio* by Spanish playwright José Zorrilla, and other popular Day of the Dead traditions examined in this study.[62] The Porfirian state's nationalization of the cult of the dead worked in harmony with other policies that reached out to rivals, accommodated the ruling class, and appealed to the shared values of the popular sectors.

All traditions large and small are "invented" at some point and reinvented for ever-larger social units. In Catholic nations, traditions of ancestor worship transformed into collective memory and identity when families gathered on the same day of the year, wore the same dress, recited the same prayers, codified the same gestures, evoked the dead, and invited them to eat the food of the living.[63] Since the eighteenth century, Mexican Day of the Dead activity was concentrated in urban marketplaces and along Paseos de Todos los Santos throughout the month of November. The commercial aspects of the holy day, which guaranteed income for vendors, merchants, and city governments alike, helped popularize the festival of death.[64] Newspapers during the Porfiriato tell us that Mexicans worshiped their ancestors, Catholic saints, and national heroes in continuous affirmations of faith in family heritage, Catholicism, and national identity. Nationalism is founded upon shared ancestral traditions, which transcend geographical barriers, social class, and kinship lines. When local patriots die as national heroes, the nation traces its own lineage back to the hero's birthplace.

Justo Sierra, Octavio Paz, and Benedict Anderson alike identified nationalism's abiding concern for death and immortality and uncovered its deepest cultural roots to reveal religious imaginings.[65] To Anderson nationalism is the great-grandchild of universal religions. To some extent, the Porfirian regime borrowed its rites of state from the Catholic Church. This appropriative process or "transfer of sacrality," as Émile Durkheim called it, shows how modernizing societies still depend on religion to conceive themselves as sacred. All liberal states sought to create citizens who believed that their fatherland was as sacred and eternal as Christianity. Leaders of the French Revolution attempted to transfer the emotional allegiances of people from the old order to the new and from the church to the state by deploying new symbols within a traditional framework.[66] For the hegemonic state, an effective way to develop a "secular religion" was to appropriate the familiar behaviors of Catholic life and consecrate them as civic acts. With minor alterations, death ceremonials, a sociocultural realm controlled historically by the Catholic Church, were incorporated into all Porfirian festivals. State funerals, civic holidays, public speeches, and national cemeteries served as lay counterparts of religious processions, liturgical festivals, Christian sermons, and churchyards. As such, they were modular ruling devices that commanded deep personal attachments to La Patria. Every September 16 (Independence Day), the chief executive officer of every state and local government placed a floral wreath at a monument of independence.[67] Civic orations about martyred heroes carried messianic Christian undertones. Each unveiling of a life-sized statue represented the secular beatification of a historical figure. And at cemeteries the retrospective burial monument of the classical hero supplanted the prospective marble angels of a heavenly paradise.[68] Repeated performance traditions transformed into *rasgos nacionales*: "The Mexican is the sum of his most frequent behavior: when he goes to mass, his nature is religious, when he enjoys himself on grand occasions, he is austere and ritualistic . . . when he believes in the patria he is organically nationalistic."[69] However, transforming Catholic rituals to de-Christianized liturgies of the secular state fostered such ambivalence and contention that Liberal defanatization campaigns risked the opposite effect, that is, stronger allegiances to the Church.[70]

For the Porfirian state, the hegemonic construct that mediated this process of consecrating national symbols was positivism, the bourgeois intellectual's form of nationalism and to everyone else the corporate variant of the authoritarian liberalism of yesteryear.[71] In contrast to anticlerical liberalism, positivism emphasized political order and material progress, serving as a fulcrum to maintain equilibrium between the Church and state. Díaz, a thirty-second-degree Mason, knew that Lerdo's radical persecution of the Church and expulsion of foreign Jesuits and the Sisters of Charity had backfired. Over 90 percent of Mexican citizens were Catholic. Having decided on a policy of conciliation with the Church, Díaz once told a confidante, Bishop of Puebla Eulogio Gillow: "As Porfirio Díaz in private life and head of my family, I am an Apostolic Roman Catholic; as head of the State, I profess no religion because the law does not permit me to do so."[72]

President Díaz's concordat with the Church was manifested in other important ways. Díaz regularly attended the Virgin of Covadonga festival at Santo Domingo and opened his private residence to high Church officials. He and his first wife, Delfina, encouraged their son to declare himself Catholic. After Delfina died, Bishop Gillow issued his blessing for the marriage of Porfirio, age fifty-one, and Carmen Romero Rubio, seventeen. Díaz's pious second wife attended mass, sponsored Catholic charity events, and exchanged gifts with the ultraconservative Archbishop Pelagio Antonio de Labastida y Dávalos. This former regent of the empire considered Carmen his goddaughter. When Labastida died, Díaz marched in his funeral procession. In addition, Díaz had served as a *padrino* at Gillow's consecration as bishop of Oaxaca and asked his cabinet officials to do the same when Próspero María Alarcón took possession of the archbishopric of Mexico. Many high officials attended the Coronation of the Virgin of Guadalupe in October 1895.[73] Their participation in ecclesiastical functions convinced Catholics that state mistreatment of the clergy had subsided. In fact, the federal government rarely enforced constitutional restrictions on the Church.[74]

Concessions to the Church allowed the state to expand its role as a formative educator. A public school system eluded Mexico until 1888, when the federal law of primary instruction made six years of elementary education free and obligatory for children. Historians of the Porfirian educational system all stress government initiatives to indoctrinate children in nationalism and prepare them for the capitalist workforce.[75] According to Justo Sierra, the Mexican people needed "as a means of their own preservation (a task which becomes more painfully urgent with the gigantic advances of our neighbors) to improve their elements of work to make them more productive . . . more intelligent, instruction must transform him."[76] Porfirian educators shared Sierra's belief in the educability of indigenous people and brought civics lessons out of the classrooms and into the streets. Through education, the pedagogical state could provide uniform direction for the whole of society.[77] In a largely illiterate urban society, the state deployed redundant visual and aural media to teach citizens moral discipline and civic virtue. Common educational experiences created the social cohesion necessary for national memory and identity to take hold. As with most "invented traditions," which appear ancient but are of recent origin, ceremonial routines referenced and implied continuity with the past.[78]

Unlike in the United States, where the private sector emerged as "custodians of tradition," the Porfirian government was the primary agent to promote patriotic education and national identity in Mexico.[79] Díaz believed that "all citizens of a republic should receive the same training, so that their ideals and methods may be harmonized and the national identity intensified."[80] The regime produced a "public transcript" in its intentions to spend lavishly on educational festivals while in return exacting public deference and symbolic tribute from citizens.[81] The rationale for government-supervised holidays was expressed in an annual report from the Interior Ministry: "Nothing is more natural under the rule of democratic institutions than the Government forming a partnership with the people to celebrate dynamically the anniversaries of the most notable events in the history of the Patria."[82] A government-subsidized newspaper remarked that *fiestas cívicas* imparted the memory of heroes and national glories to new generations in order to train them as citizens.[83] Another affirmed: "The cult of heroes has prodigious educational power; it raises spirits, reaffirms will, points out new paths, and opens wider horizons to national life."[84] As these statements suggest, the annual remembrance of heroic martyrs ensured generational intercommunication.[85] Although the death of a leader happened unpredictably, funerals, like civic festivals, recurred and were equally designed to educate the people.

Among the greatest pedagogical assets of the modernizing state was a capital city with a historic center that kept the past alive. Porfirian Mexico City's *centro conmemorativo*, now called the Centro Histórico, was a vital statement of official ambitions to remember the dead at great expense to the living. The cityscape was literally embedded with both human remains and official symbols of the dead. Monuments, statues, commemorative plaques, and street names may appear to be static and unchanging to a single casual observer, but their meaning is transformed with every new subjective glance. Of all the media used to perpetuate the memory of the great man, the statue was most preferred since the Enlightenment taught that vision is the most influential sense.[86] Statues more than symbolize a dead person. They alter the temporality associated with that human being, arrest the process of bodily decay, and bring the subject "into the realm of the timeless or the sacred."[87] Memorials to the dead clearly identify the dead persons and compensate for their lost lives, but they also provide a means of identity formation for surviving observers. Since the dead ostensibly stood for the same cause as the memorial builders—they died for an exemplary reason—survivors are obliged to acknowledge the sacrifice so that they did not die in vain.[88] When the state constructed a ring of twenty-four burial monuments in a popular cemetery and another thirty-six statues along a crowded thoroughfare, Mexico no longer had local landmarks but, rather, national pantheons of eternal heroes. The Rotunda of Illustrious Men and the statues of the Paseo de la Reforma brought permanence both to national heroes and to the Díaz regime. Prior to Díaz, Mexico boasted only seven such statues nationwide.[89]

The Porfirian state excelled at mapping temporality onto public space. Generally speaking, the passage of historical time moved spatially west and southwest from the central plaza of the Zócalo—where the National Palace, Grito de Dolores ceremony, and fireworks displays annually signified independence—to the Avenida Juárez and the Paseo de la Reforma, which symbolized the Mexican republic's triumph after the mid-century wars. If the Porfirian regime marketed the modern suburban *colonias* along the Paseo as the present, it never planned spatially for the future. Instead, the state modified its blueprint by overlapping new monuments adjacent to the new living spaces of prosperous families. Along the Paseo de la Reforma, Mexican history began with Columbus (1876) in the first traffic circle, Cuauhtémoc (1887) in the second, and the Column of Independence (El Angel, 1910) in the fourth. The state planned three others to Zaragoza, Juárez, and Díaz for the remaining three *glorietas* (roundabouts). But the Revolution of 1910 redrew the map.

The regularity with which the state demonstrated its grasp on power can be viewed with both admiration and trepidation. Díaz had inherited a country long on history but short on the metrics needed to prove modern nationhood to the transatlantic world. He and his scientific administrators produced maps, censuses, surveys, and histories to simplify complex realities for both citizens and foreign investors.[90] Intellectuals and bureaucrats gathered and analyzed statistics, wrote and read bulletins, conceptualized and drew up blueprints, researched history, and published texts. In fact, the Porfirian state selected the perfect term to describe the massive compilations of national data gathered in one year's time. They were called *Memorias*.[91]

The modern bureaucratic imperative to justify the state's existence is ubiquitous but often overlooked in modern political life. The scientific data that bureaucrats called "national statistics" made for convincing reading; if Mexico could be measured as a nation, then it must exist as one. But scholars can look elsewhere for evidence of nationhood. Funerals and festivals cast brilliant light on the Porfirian state's self-definition as the highest expression of the people's will. Functionaries in charge of the visual presentation of state symbols practiced statolatry—idolatrous worship of the state—and autoethnography—defining, interpreting, and performing the state before diverse audiences.[92] Funerals and festivals were so standardized and simplified by the central bureaucracy that they became powerful fictions like other second- and third-order interpretations.[93]

Refashioning state structures of knowledge and power advanced the interests of the new propertied classes, which only promoted the desirable qualities of a modern nation.[94] To no surprise, state bureaucratic rituals affected the disseminators above all others, since they had the most invested in identity construction and fervently believed their own myths. This may have been the unintended consequence of contriving a pleasant national fiction. But one of the joint functions of organized religion and official nationalism has been to provide substitutes for class consciousness among the dispossessed, with a resultant benefit to the rich. This process of displacement involves complex mechanisms of social psychology and political manipulation.[95] The same regime that allowed workers to walk in the funeral processions and parades of national leaders forbade marches of a different kind. At the National Congress of Tobacco Workers in 1903, even the mild-mannered humanist Justo Sierra warned militant labor groups that threatening to strike would provoke the full resources and arms of the government to protect a single worker's right to work.[96]

The Porfirian state derived consent to rule by manipulating concepts of family unity, patrilineal kinship, and patriarchal authority. To suggest that hegemony does not apply to the intense emotional bonds of affection, loyalty, and reciprocity that unite a family is to deny the existence of state paternalism. Relations of power are often masked by institutionalized patriarchy and deference.[97] In contrast to royal ceremonials marking births, marriages, coronations, and deaths, state funerals were the only private rites of passage writ large on the public stage in modern republics.[98] Private Catholic funerals emphasized the relationships shared among the deceased, the family patriarch, the Church, and the remaining family members. During state funerals, this web of interconnected lives and experiences was spun onto the national stage in compulsory obligations (*deberes*) shared among the dead hero, the *jefe del estado*, the state, and the nation. Díaz attended baptisms and weddings, dispensed marital advice to young spouses, and praised his elders. He conceived of himself as the father of his people and the equitable distributor of patronage. In the first burial of the era, *El Siglo XIX* remarked: "General Díaz inaugurates a period of justice, honoring valor and services rendered to the Patria wherever they are found, not as the head of a party but as the dignified leader of the great Mexican family."[99] History lessons in Porfirian primary schools stressed that all Mexicans formed a single family.[100]

Indeed, nations are sometimes perceived as peoples from the same lineage.[101] The very language of Porfirian political life took its cues from the rigidly patriarchal family; for instance, senior politicians (*padres políticos*) mentored their apprentices (*hijos políticos*). Even if relationships lacked common bloodlines or even mutual affection, fidelity came from a respectful patron–clientelist business arrangement. All subordinates felt that they owed their livelihood to Díaz's personal benevolence, and each citizen fell under his protection. "Among us," sociologist Andrés Molina Enríquez claimed, "patriotism has never been sufficiently precise and clear to serve as a bond of union among social units."[102] Personal friendships and their corollary sacrifices, as well as concepts of Mexican honor and heritage, brought men to funerals to demonstrate their fealty to Díaz.[103] Patriotic women, encouraged by custom to mourn in private rather than march in public funeral processions, nevertheless proved their virtue by comforting widows and witnessing these grand affairs from balconies, rooftops, and sidewalks. Although confined by nineteenth-century nation-builders and their gendered laws, women such as the progressive and powerful *cacica* of Tehuantepec, Juana Catarina Romero, found ways to loosen restrictions and participate in the political and economic life of the country.[104] In these ways, the affective ties that bound all members of the family were transferred to the regime. There was no more natural political base than family loyalty or alliances won through *amificación*.[105]

During this era of hero-worship, cultivating Díaz's persona through rituals of state not only extended the life of the regime but gave Mexicans what they wanted to recognize as perennial.[106] Contemporaries commented on Díaz's immense popularity and ceremonial presence: "The country wanted him; he was considered a national glory; whenever he appeared he was received with applauses. . . . He inspired pride and dignity in Mexicans."[107] In the decorative uniform of the division general, with his medals from the United Kingdom, Germany, France, and Spain, Díaz was a walking narrative of national sovereignty and international respect. His appearance at the burials of subordinates several years his younger reinforced his status as an eternal symbol of *mexicanidad*. If every reelection was portrayed as a matter of national imperative, then every state funeral proved the superior vitality of Mexico's *mestizo* ruler for life. Díaz validated his rule through a powerful combination of traditional patriarchy and modern statesmanship. In a previous era, personalism was a key component of *caudillismo*. Díaz represented the ultimate military strongman, but one whose political genius defies facile typology. He appears to be the progenitor of a ruling style that transformed into populism. His "awesome faculty of assimilation" combined with a "tenacious purpose to improve" on a personal and national level is analogous to the qualities of latter-day populists, especially those with a military background.[108] In one categorization of Mexican presidential personas as martyrs, exemplary citizens, or modernizers, Díaz concentrated all three.[109] Although Díaz rarely toured the countryside, peasants perceived him as fundamentally good, absolving him of any wrongdoing. Instead, they blamed abusive local officials, landowners, and anyone else except Díaz.[110]

To summarize, state funerals and commemorative festivals reveal government and ruling class efforts to achieve hegemony without resorting to force of arms or democratic reform. The authoritarian republic of Porfirio Díaz accomplished rule through a multifaceted form of cultural politics that placed a high premium on memorialization. Porfirian Liberal, positivist, and nationalist ideology; sacralized republican holiday traditions; state educational use of cults of the dead and public space; bureaucratic imperatives to rationalize and nationalize governance; and Díaz's patriarchal persona and patron-clientelist authority were all facets of the same gem. Hegemony offers a helpful lens to examine this gem and its flaws. To Gramsci, rule was not accomplished through the artifice of legitimating symbols and rituals. Instead, ruling groups created symbolic universes to validate and render intelligible their de facto leadership and to convey their interests to the masses. State ceremonies, like hegemony itself, were a legitimating mask over the reality of political and economic domination of one social class over others.[111] The will of the dominant class was disclosed in the political language, laws, and rituals of the state. Porfirian cultural politics involved manipulative processes that depended on a high level of social control. The same elites who extracted material taxes in the form of labor, grain, cash, and service, also extracted "symbolic taxes in the form of deference, demeanor, posture, verbal formulas, and acts of humility."[112] Too often, stylized iconographic representations of hero cults (statues), events (monuments), and ideas (Liberal republican funerals) are misinterpreted as "thanks from a grateful nation." What they symbolize is state power used to formalize inequality and oppression. To this end Díaz abused his power, and ordinary Mexicans constructed alternative landscapes and mindscapes of memory.

Figure 4. José Guadalupe Posada's *Gran Calavera Eléctrica*. From Roberto Berdecio and Stanley Applebaum, eds., *Posada's Popular Mexican Prints* (New York: Dover Publications, 1972).

Death and the Maiden of Progress 1

M EXICO COMMEMORATES its national heroes on the anniversaries of their deaths, a legacy that contrasts with the U.S. practice of remembering historical leaders on their birth dates. Justo Sierra invented the tradition during the Porfirian era. In 1880, the promising young congressman proposed that Mexico imitate ancient Greece and fill the national calendar with holidays that honored the distinguished dead. Inspired by the teachings of French positivist Auguste Comte, Sierra's civic calendar was to complement, if not replace, the Catholic liturgical calendar of saints' days, which also venerates Christian martyrs on the dates that they died. Sierra's resolution recalls the efforts of early-nineteenth-century European thinkers to codify the Enlightenment by founding a Positivist Church, Calendar, and Religion of Humanity. Sierra implored Mexicans to pay tribute to all heroes from Padre Miguel Hidalgo to President Benito Juárez on the Day of the Dead, every November 2. He further asked Congress to construct a National Pantheon, a "hymn in marble," to serve as a site for state burials, educate citizens in their national history, and give material representation to the ideals that unite all Mexicans. Commemorating the national dead would ultimately help achieve what Sierra called "the centralization of memory."[1]

The Chamber of Deputies, Mexico's unicameral national legislature, hailed Sierra for his patriotism and passed most of his resolutions. However, critical to understanding the nature of hegemonic rule is examining the parts of Sierra's bill that went unheeded. In addition to honoring national heroes, Sierra wanted to recognize the societal contributions of common people, including skilled laborers, agricultural workers, and teachers. Along with ascribing new secular meanings to old holy days, Sierra urged the government to limit its organizing role to allow for spontaneous, popular, and authentic patriotism to spring forth during *fiestas cívicas*. The congressman believed that any substitution of national sentiment for religious zeal should begin with the *pueblo*.[2] Despite the original intent of Sierra's resolutions, the government neither honored workers nor relinquished control over holidays and commemorations. For its entire history, the Mexican government rather than the private sector or civil society has served as the principal agent in constructing national memory.

Figure 5. Justo Sierra. Portrait courtesy of the Nettie Lee Benson Latin American Library, University of Texas, Austin.

Justo Sierra's congressional resolution provides just one example of how states legislate and educate official nationalisms. In order to forge the Patria and form loyal citizens willing to sacrifice their lives for it, modernizing states had to seize control of cemeteries, death ceremonials, and rituals of remembrance from traditional power centers—the church, the military, and the family. Once these were captured, the state then transformed cemeteries into national shrines and death ceremonials into modern secular events. Fully understanding this process requires consideration of three interrelated social realities in Porfirian Mexico: (1) the omnipresence of death and funerals in everyday life; (2) death as the central theme in the popular Catholic religious festival of Día de los Muertos (Day of the Dead); and (3) state attempts to separate the living and the dead through cemetery reforms, regulatory laws, and technological advances. Nation-builders like Sierra combined two inevitable phenomena—death and progress—into a powerful unifying force in state funerals and commemorative festivals.

Muerte sin Fin: Endless Death in Porfirian Mexico

To say nothing about the Aztecs and colonial times, cohabitation with the dead was part of daily life in Porfirian Mexico. For many, life was an arduous daily struggle for survival and death was a constant reminder of the brevity of life on earth.[3] Nationwide, the average life expectancy rose from an appalling twenty-five to thirty-one years of age from 1876 to 1910. When a horrendous typhus epidemic swept through the country in 1877, Mexico City's average life expectancy fell to nineteen years of age. That year, Doctor Miguel Jiménez predicted that if things did not change, "Mexico will be completely uninhabitable in 30 years."[4] Due in large part to a chronic drainage problem and contaminated water supplies, Mexico City was considered among the unhealthiest places to live in the world. The high incidence of premature death and multiplying threats of highly communicable diseases kept public health officials on edge.[5] The infant mortality rate prior to 1880 was extremely high even among the upper classes; half of all infants died within their first year. By 1900, the rate only improved to 392 per thousand live births.[6] Even the most powerful political figures of the day, including Porfirio Díaz, Manuel Romero Rubio, and Bernardo Reyes, all lost daughters at childbirth or during their infancy. From 1869 to 1878, the number of Mexico City children to die under the age of ten was 42,162. This was almost one-half of all deaths (88,416) in the same period. It is no wonder why the conscientious physician's prescription for the infirm was to "get out of the city as soon as possible."[7]

The undernourished and poor of all ages fell victim to eight deadly diseases: typhus, tuberculosis, cholera, hepatitis, smallpox, yellow fever, influenza, and syphilis. In 1892–93, when the Consejo Superior de Salubridad (Public Health Board) began inspecting houses for communicable diseases, 283 of 303 homes in the poorest quarter of the Federal District (Cuartel I) tested positive for typhus.[8] Disease spread rapidly in Cuartels I, II, and III, where communal water systems in factories, tenements (*casas de vecindad*), and slums were located. As late as 1899, the Public Health Board still dealt with cases in which entire households of dead bodies were discovered weeks after a cholera epidemic. Other main causes of death included pneumonia, alcoholism, and streetcar accidents.[9] And if that were not enough, the murder rate was higher in Mexico City than in Cairo or Calcutta, and twelve times higher than in Madrid.[10] Since death was a regular passerby, funerary rites appeared around every corner.

What everyday people believed about the omnipresence of death in Porfirian Mexico is difficult to assess. Historians investigating attitudes toward death have trouble reconstructing a subject with limited records: "We wish to write a history of death and we are faced by silence."[11] Peoples of the past were willfully mute on the subject, forcing historians into graveyards to analyze equally

soundless relics of the dead. Historians of antiquity have relied less on the written word than on iconographic and archaeological evidence. European scholars restored the silent history of death by examining eighteenth-century wills.
Claudio Lomnitz has written a compelling work on the social construction
of the Mexican death cult largely based on published accounts, City Council
records, and iconographic representations of death.[12]

Faced with a scarcity of surviving wills and testimonials, historians can turn
to ethnographic sources on attitudes toward death and funeral practices.[13] Foreigners who toured Porfirian Mexico often contributed to local newspapers
and published travel accounts in the United States, Canada, and the United
Kingdom. Whether they were foreign correspondents, Mexico City journalists,
or simply tourists, these recreational folklorists were struck by traditions so
different from their own. What native Mexicans found unremarkable and took
for granted in their everyday experiences, foreigners reported as fascinating
cultural practices. Since there was seldom a relationship between the observers and their subjects, foreign travelers wrote detailed descriptions of death,
mourning customs, and burial rites that were also geographically representative of regions outside Mexico City.[14] Other sources that documented popular
and elite culture were the romantic writings of *costumbristas* and *cronistas*, as
well as Mexican illustrated periodicals that described well-known customs to
readers "in foreign countries where they inspire[d] so much interest."[15]

This historical evidence suggests that late-nineteenth-century Mexican
people already had modern attitudes toward death. Christians in medieval
Europe who were threatened by the ever-present possibility of death acquired
an intimate familiarity with it; they expected death, accepted it calmly and
with little anguish, and were buried without pretentious funeral rites. Fore-
warned by biological, natural, and spiritual signs, they prepared themselves
for the ritual of dying, which was as important as the funeral ceremony and
mourning custom. Dying began with a "spontaneous realization" that the end
was near. People awaited death lying down facing toward heaven, a position
mandated by thirteenth-century Christian liturgists. During their final hours
they expressed personal sorrow for their condition, forgave companions, said
farewell, prayed, and received absolution from a priest. Significantly, bed-
chambers of the dying were open to anyone. Parents never shielded children
from the realities of death. Emotional distress and mourning periods were
short-lived and public, burials were collective and impersonal, and funerals
were ritualistic but not theatrical, somber but not dramatic.[16]

Over the centuries, Western peoples experienced a "turn of mind" that
engendered a new conceptualization of death. While death remained just as
pervasive, French historian Philippe Ariès noted a gradual shift of concern
from the death of oneself to the death of the other, especially a cherished

relative. He and other scholars attributed this change in *mentalité* to de-Christianization and the rise of individualism during the Enlightenment. The secularization of the last will and testament transferred the burden of death rituals from the dying, the executor, and the church to the surviving members of the family.[17] Testaments no longer prescribed masses, prayers, and other spiritual devotions to save the soul. Instead, they prearranged the legal disposition of property and possessions. Religious provisions in wills, such as the choice of burial site, payment of religious funeral services, and almsgiving, no longer appeared with the decedent's instructions for the distribution of his worldly possessions. Instead, the dying person verbally entrusted those at his bedside to fulfill his wishes. As a consequence, relatives and friends played increasingly larger roles in organizing and performing funeral rites, with predictable results: "Bystanders were no longer the passive, prayerful walk-ons of the past" but, rather, empowered to act.[18] With additional responsibilities came agency. Catholics and Protestants developed greater attachments to the dying and intolerance for separation. Their appreciation for individuality was manifested in enhanced awareness of the importance of funerals. The new mind-set, informed by romanticism and later positivism, originated the nineteenth-century cult of cemeteries and tombs.[19] In early colonial Mexico, clergy had placed dying Indians and their survivors in a funerary framework that favored outward compliance with the requirements of a Christian death.[20] This framework was retained for centuries, as ethnographic sources from the late nineteenth century provide ample evidence that Mexican people from both rural and urban areas had already embraced modern concepts of death and funeral rites.

In Mexico, the death of a loved one elicited profound mourning and extravagant funeral rites from rural peasants and urban dwellers alike. One insightful foreign traveler witnessed firsthand a poignant death scene in a small pueblo in Guanajuato. Don Modesto, silver-haired patriarch of a family of *campesinos*, had rediscovered the fabled La Providencia mine, revered in local folklore as the silver-producing equivalent of El Dorado. He and his son Juan extracted silver from dusk until dawn, while a constant drizzle drenched them both. By morning, Modesto had mined fifty ounces of silver as well as contracted pneumonia. When he returned home his trembling was a combination of vital excitement and deathly shiver. Delirium quickly overtook him, and Modesto "knew his hour had come."[21]

Modesto's family also perceived his impending death. His wife, Felipa, sent for her children, and they all surrounded the bedside, wailing and worrying that their father left no will. Several women in the room lit candles and recited death prayers; "Felipa crouched motionless at the foot of the bed, her head muffled in her black shawl." Modesto awoke and uttered the word "Juan," which meant that his eldest son would inherit all of his material possessions. With his face streaming in tears, Juan wrapped his dying father's arms in coarse white cloth, while a scribe, the only literate person in the room, recorded the revelation. Modesto signed his life's possessions away and quietly succumbed. The family's grief and concern for the last will (which contained no pious clauses) and the appearance of the scribe (whose sole purpose was to record the last wishes of the dying) suggest modern attitudes toward death.

The funeral rites accorded the *señor* confirm this as a rite of passage that reflects modern sensibilities. The fifty ounces of silver, the product of his final labors, "paid for a burial befitting Don Modesto's station; and Felipa bought yards of black calico, with which the compadres festooned the front of the house." She dressed her husband in a black suit that she had stored away since their wedding. He lay in wake for three days, a custom that divulged the family's reluctance to let go. After prayers in a humble parish on the fourth day, mourners bore his coffin to the top of a hill for a simple burial beside the grave of his father. Alongside the decorated coffin, marchers carried torches, candles, and a drum.[22] This was not the "little tradition" of eighteenth-century plebian folk but, rather, a peasant household doing what passed for modern.[23] Even the poorest families relinquished scarce financial gains for the proper burial of their dearly departed.

To foreign travelers, ordinary funerals were among the most striking features of Mexican life. Modest processions in the heart of the capital city drew the attention of every bystander. From Calle San Francisco in Mexico City, a tourist observed:

> A very humble peon was seen bearing his child's coffin upon his back, followed by the mother, grandmother, and two children, with downcast eyes, five persons in all forming the sad procession, if it may be so called. It was observed that the gaily-dressed and elegantly mounted cabalero promptly backed his horse to the curbstone and raised his sombrero while the mourners moved by, that other peons bowed their bare heads, and that every hat, either silk or straw, was respectfully doffed along the street, as the solemn little cortege wound its way to the last resting-place of humanity.[24]

At Chapultepec Park, one American was captivated by the sight of two peasants bearing a coffin followed by a "poor half-clad woman, leading a little girl with one hand, and carrying a candle in the other."[25] Another remarked: "Any day of the week one may take a car for Tacubaya, and there see the Indians transporting their dead to Dolores Cemetery." There she saw a "poor woman bearing upon her head a plain little open coffin containing her dead child, with eyes wide open and a profusion of gay flowers covering the tiny form."[26] Visitors recorded similar scenes throughout the Valley of Mexico, Pachuca, and Cuernavaca.[27]

Mexicans showed consideration for even the anonymous dead found in the most isolated areas of the republic. Reports abound of crosses, tombstones, and other grave markers that littered remote countrysides. Late in 1869, Colonel Albert Evans compared the presence of so many roadside graves in Jalisco to Apache Country in Arizona Territory, where "poor Mexican miners stay for hours, to erect a cross of stone over the remains of some victim of the relentless savages."[28] Similar scenes appeared from Coahuila to Zacatecas in the 1880s: "Here and there a simple wooden cross indicated a grave, the burial place of some lone traveler who had been murdered and robbed by banditti, and over whose body a Christian hand had reared this unpretentious emblem [where] the pious peon breathes a prayer and adds a stone to the pile, so that finally quite a mound is raised to mark the murdered man's grave."[29] Around 1900, a tourist in the state of Guerrero witnessed campesinos take off their sombreros as they gathered around a similar mound of stones: "Each threw one more stone upon the pile, crossed himself, bent his knee, and moved on."[30] Again, death had met some unknown traveler.

In stark contrast to the solitude of crosses scattered across desert landscapes was the universal spectacle of modern horse-drawn funeral tramcars in bustling Mexico City: "Almost every hour of the day, you can see the funeral cars running out to the suburban cemeteries."[31] Mexico's first horse-drawn tramways date from 1856. Two decades later people still decried prohibitive costs, opting to hire human coffin carriers. In the early 1880s livery services that included a driver, pallbearers, and a hearse car pulled by six of the District Railway's finest horses cost 120 pesos, while simple mule-drawn pauper's cars, which *capitalinos* nicknamed *cucarachas* (cockroaches), were 3 pesos. Citizens could also arrange for passenger tramcars to conduct mourners to the municipal cemetery. First-class cars for mourners rented at 12 pesos, while plain trams went for 4.[32] If these fees could not be met, the destitute could apply for a free pauper's funeral car with passage for two. This car resembled a horse trailer, with shelves to support coffins and a small second-class car for passengers attached to the rear.[33] Despite free service, the poor continued to bear coffins on their shoulders for miles, while the affluent spent up to 1,500 pesos for a dozen or more tramcars for their corteges. Such graduated pomp reflected both the hierarchical society and the polarized wealth of Porfirian Mexico.[34]

One of the reasons families maintained pedestrian modes was the awful streetcar service. Because of the great distance from the city center to Dolores Cemetery, tramcars loaded with coffins and mourners sat for hours waiting

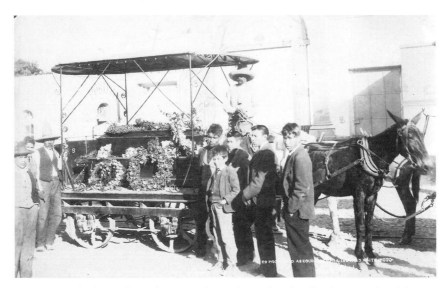

Figure 6. Mule-drawn funeral tramcar for working-class family of Mexico City. The rented services of a driver, third-class hearse, and healthy mule; the hardwood coffin; the wreaths; and the appearance of mourners dressed in their Sunday best all suggest modern attitudes toward death. Photo by C. B. Waite; courtesy of the Nettie Lee Benson Latin American Library, University of Texas, Austin.

Figure 7. Funeral hearse for affluent family of Mexico City. Towering hearses pulled by a team of six powerful and plumed black horses were used for state funerals. Photo by C. B. Waite; courtesy of the Nettie Lee Benson Latin American Library, University of Texas, Austin.

to depart in convoys. The likelihood of a breakdown or traffic accident was so high that drivers waited for multiple trams to fill and then left together to ensure mutual assistance in case of emergency. These circumstances were especially miserable during the rainy season, when the chances of derailments increased. About midway up the steep incline to the hillside cemetery, several men on horseback bearing ropes and grappling hooks would lasso the side rails of the horse-drawn tramcar and pull with their makeshift winches to supplement the insufficient power.[35]

In the 1890s, the funeral tramcar system was significantly modernized and expanded. The South African firm of Wernher, Beit, and Company entered a limited liability contract with native entrepreneurs. With government concessions and foreign investment, the Compañía Limitada de los Ferrocarriles del Distrito Federal (Federal District Railway Company) extended track to every suburb. The company converted dozens of horse-drawn tramcars into hearses and rolling catafalques called *tranvías mortuorios*. First-class hearses featured a raised bier at the center, black curtains, and a sturdy frame that was surmounted by plumes and a cross. The catafalques were usually former freight or platform cars covered with a black canopy.[36]

In the late 1890s a group of Canadian financiers, who had founded the Mexican Light and Power Company, acquired the tramway concession and began hanging lines for electric traction. Electric streetcars were designed to provide safer and more hygienic service to capitalinos since they would have regulated speeds and eliminate the bodily waste of horses and mules. The company inaugurated the first electric streetcar line from Guadalupe to San Angel in 1898, and two years later it connected the downtown area to Tacubaya. Yet, by 1906, when British entrepreneurs incorporated the Mexican Consolidated Electric Company and took over operations of the Federal District railway lines, only 90 of the 160 miles of track were operated by electric traction.[37] As could be expected, electrically propelled hearses replaced horse-drawn funeral trams. While they were decorated no differently, they ran up to thirty miles per hour.[38] By one estimate, the tramway company conducted about 90 percent of all funerals by 1906. Great progress was also made in the appearance of drivers. Funeral car motormen wore neat black "mourning uniforms" and received free haircuts and shoeshines.[39]

Despite improved service, funeral tramcar debacles persisted and frequently drew scathing public criticism. Streetcar accidents involving pedestrians occurred daily, in part because the trams were susceptible to power surges that suddenly increased their speed. In their first year of operation, they injured or killed over one thousand people. More precise figures are known for 1904 to 1906: 134 dead, 657 injured.[40] Acknowledging the high casualty rate due to unregulated voltage and driver error, capitalinos dubbed the streetcars the

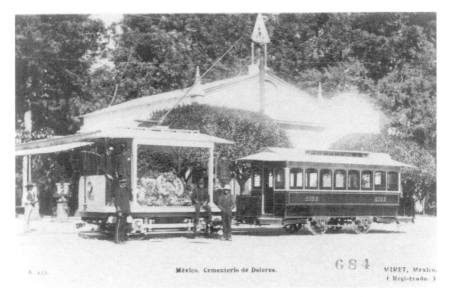

México, Cementerio de Dolores.   684   MIRET, México.
                                                        (Registrado.)

Figure 8. Electric hearse car with driver, coffin, wreaths, and an attached passenger trolley for mourners at Dolores Cemetery. Photo by Félix Miret; courtesy of the Archivo General de la Nación, Mexico City.

new "yellow fever."[41] The satiric penny press referred to drivers as *mataristas* (killers) instead of *motoristas*.[42] *El Chango*'s cartoon "Death in Electric Form" called attention to the mutilated victims of streetcars and the impersonal cruelty of mechanized death.[43] At the sight of electric trams, older residents shook their heads in disapproval and crossed themselves piously.[44] Furthermore, tracks to the suburbs were so irregular and shoddy that coffins slid off their platforms and crashed to the ground. Since there was only one set of tracks to every cemetery, derailments caused up to three-hour delays in funeral services. In 1899, six funeral tramcars got trapped behind a derailed car, forcing mourners to wait until the following day to bury their dead.[45] Likewise, electric streetcars moving along the city's bumpy roads became detached from power lines. Corteges leaving the city center at three o'clock in the afternoon were always in danger of arriving after cemeteries closed at six. As late as 1910, dozens of occupied coffins lined the streets waiting for the next available free car to pass. Families who could not afford to rent their own funeral tram loitered for hours, contributing to a most "disagreeable sight."[46] To make matters worse, superstitious commoners distrusted the electric trams not only because they maimed people regularly but because they had no visible power source. Sparks at night radiated from their roofs where the trolleys contacted overhead wires. The arcane flashes and acrid smells led to beliefs that the streetcars had satanic origins. In response to popular fears, President Díaz temporarily prohibited

Figure 9. José Guadalupe Posada's *Collision of an electric streetcar with a hearse.* From Roberto Berdecio and Stanley Applebaum, eds., *Posada's Popular Mexican Prints* (New York: Dover Publications, 1972).

trolleys using an "occult force" from carrying funeral corteges or coffins in 1900. Tradition, however, succumbed to modernization when Díaz reauthorized electric trams to conduct the dead in 1903. For the Day of the Dead, the popular engraver José Guadalupe Posada printed a broadsheet that depicted the killer trolleys bringing the dead to a cemetery where skeletons resurrected by electricity had already begun their festivities.[47]

A modern funeral industry emerged during the Porfiriato. Professional undertakers of the Agencia de Inhumaciones Gayosso assumed all of the functions related to funerals and burials. Founded and operated by Eusebio Gayosso, the agency enjoyed a virtual monopoly on mortuary services. Its locations on Cinco de Mayo, Avenida de los Hombres Ilustres, and Mariscala were all near the streetcar lines in the historic center. This made sense since law required corpses to be buried within twenty-four hours of death. Gayosso agency employees dressed in black suits and top hats. They served as pallbearers and were as conspicuous as funerals themselves. Despite cornering the market, the proprietors still advertised in the major dailies and agreed to rates fixed by the city government. Gayosso also provided services for state funerals.[48]

Although one family controlled mortuary services, coffin-making was a competitive industry. Curious visitors often stumbled across what they called "coffin street" in their downtown walking tours: "From one end of the street to

Figure 10. The Mexico City flower market near the National Cathedral did a thriving business in funerary wreaths on the Day of the Dead. Photo by C. B. Waite; courtesy of the Nettie Lee Benson Latin American Library, University of Texas, Austin.

the other you see in every door men and boys making and painting all kinds and sizes of coffins."[49] Caskets designed for adults were jet black, but those for children were elaborately painted with scrollwork and white flowers upon a black background. The eleven coffin manufacturers along this street used such decorated coffins as business signs advertising their wares.[50] Capitalinos purchased flowers and wreaths from kiosks in the Zócalo and Alameda as well as stands outside cemetery entrances.[51]

While foreign travelers frequently complimented Mexico for its reverent and picturesque funeral customs, they also found traditional practices morbid and uncivil. One judgmental tourist described the practice of renting a coffin solely for the funeral service and then returning it to the dealer for future use as "truly horrifying."[52] Suitable hardwoods were so scarce and expensive that the poor could not afford to purchase coffins. At the cemetery mourners removed the cadaver from the coffin and either placed it in a pine box or wrapped it in coarse cotton winding cloth (*manta*) for burial.[53] In reaction to this macabre custom, one woman warned, "Americans always want to go back to the States to die."[54] In San Luís Potosí, those who could not afford the coffin rental simply wrapped the corpse in a blanket, tied it to a chair, and carried it to the cemetery.[55] Another custom peculiar to foreign observers was fitting pure silver handles to expensive caskets only to remove them before burial, "as otherwise they would be dug up and stolen."[56] Frequent incidents of grave robbing obliged survivors to remove before burial any jewelry adorning the corpse.[57] Sacrilegious thieves plundered cities of the dead with impunity; they even stole and resold marble tombstones, sometimes to the very sculptors and shops (*marmolerías*) that originally sold them.[58] A reporter in Mexico City for *Harper's Magazine* wrote about the tradition of hiring professional carriers (*cargadores* or *mozos*) to bear the dead in pine coffins to cemeteries at a "jog-trot."[59] Where great distances were to be covered, corpses were placed in a litter swung between two burros.[60] Campesinos living on the fringes of the capital continued to bury their loved ones clandestinely in any open field. Persistent dogs regularly dug up makeshift coffins containing the bodies of children who had been buried in shallow graves. Children were otherwise buried in a fashion that was both dignified and peculiar to foreign observers. Mothers who lost their children to fatal diseases calmed their sorrow with the belief that God had greater need for their *angelitos*. Parents dressed their infants in white clothing, attached paper wings to their shoulders, applied rouge to their faces, and otherwise rendered them lifelike:[61] "They are carried to the grave, put into coffins in which tortillas, money, and possibly little charms have been stowed, then buried while rockets are fired to heaven by the mourners to announce the departure of the child-soul."[62]

"I wonder why women so rarely go to funerals here?" asked one curious visitor. "There is a string of men a block long, but no women."[63] Except in the rural countryside, women customarily did not attend funerals. Instead, they donned black garb and mourned privately in the home. Such practices date to colonial times but were also reinforced by patriarchy and a Porfirian cult of female domesticity. Manuals of urban etiquette prescribed that women who sequestered themselves should not receive visitors personally. During their seclusion, which could last up to one month, they entrusted their closest relatives and intimate friends to welcome mourners during *visitas de duelo*. Families that could not visit the bereaved sent letters of condolence (*cartas de pésame*).[64]

In the nineteenth century, cemeteries were popular destinations for adventurers in search of glimpses of *México viejo*. Tourists, however, criticized Mexican burial practices as dark remnants of Spanish colonialism. The centuries-old Panteón de Guanajuato replicated the grisly catacombs of the Old World. It consisted of ten acres of ground enclosed by ten-foot-high walls with hundreds of chambers into which bodies were consigned permanently or temporarily. Families paid a lump sum for their deceased to occupy a chamber for a period of five years. If a renewal payment was not made before the expiration of this term, workers removed the rapidly decaying remains and heaped them into a mass grave.[65] This extended to other parts of the republic such as the Panteón de Belén (Bethlehem Cemetery) in Guadalajara, Jalisco.[66] At the

Figure 11. Mummies of the Panteón Municipal de Guanajuato. Photo by C. B. Waite; courtesy of the Nettie Lee Benson Latin American Library, University of Texas, Austin.

Campo Mortuorio del Refugio de Zacatecas (Mortuary Park of the Refuge of Zacatecas), bodies were exhumed in a state of putrefaction in order to bury new ones.[67] Some of the alcoves in these "beehives," paid for in perpetuity, had engraved marble headpieces. More commonly, after a body was interred, the family cemented the open end and used a stick to etch an epitaph. Some niches were enclosed with sheet iron with inscriptions painted on them. These legacies of the colonial era had survived into the twentieth century.[68]

During the Porfiriato, foreigners witnessed frightful spectacles in churchyards, such as "a grinning skull [that] sat awry on a heap of earth amid a few thigh bones and scattered ribs" and cemetery employees "tossing skulls and bones about amid facetious banter."[69] To observers Mexican cemeteries were ill kept and unhygienic: "One has the feeling that fever broods there constantly."[70] In spite of the ghastly spectacle of the Panteón de Guanajuato, its main attraction was the catacombs full of preserved mummies, photographs of which appeared in many contemporary travel accounts. For a small admission fee, travelers in Aguascalientes were allowed entrance to the Church of San Diego, where they set eyes on mummies sitting on an enormous pile of skulls and bones. Tourists all "hastened away with a sense of disgust."[71] Even in the nation's capital, curiosity seekers viewed mummies from the Toltec culture exhibited off Escalerias Street in 1889.[72] But one did not have to pay to see skeletons in Mexico City. The historic center was one giant graveyard, and construction workers regularly discovered human remains during their excavations.[73] One U.S. traveler remarked that Mexicans had "a certain apathetic indifference to death, and a playful manner with its remains."[74] Another commented: "The people are no respecters of human bones."[75] On the contrary, Mexicans were deeply concerned with death, a fact most evident during Día de los Muertos.

Day of the Dead

Any discussion of Mexico's cult of the dead begins with the popular religious holiday of the Day of the Dead. Images of death appeared in Mexican art and architecture since pre-Columbian times, but this historical preoccupation did not end with the Spanish conquest.[76] Since the colonial era, Latin Americans have celebrated the Roman Catholic festivals of Todos Santos (All Saints' Day) every November 1 and Todos Muertos, Día de los Muertos, or Día de los Difuntos (All Souls' Day or Day of the Dead) every November 2. The Christian death cult never fully supplanted its pagan counterparts. In Mexico, indigenous and Hispanic traditions merged into a syncretic form of religious celebration unique to Mesoamerica. On All Saints' Day pious Mexicans from every social class pray for the Christian martyrs; on All Souls' Day they take to the streets to remember their departed ancestors, friends, and family.[77]

During the Porfiriato, rural peasants and the urban poor expended extraordinary amounts of time, energy, and money on the Day of the Dead. In anticipation of the holy day, families saved money, gathered *ofrendas* (offerings), constructed altars, and invited friends and relatives to visit their homes. Indigenous families made great financial sacrifices to buy statues of the Virgin Mary and saints, candles, copal incense, flowers, and *alimentos* (beverages and food), all of which they lovingly offered to their ancestors on home altars and at gravesites. Families living outside the city limits journeyed miles carrying armfuls of marigolds known as the *flor de muertos* or *zempasúchil* (flower of the dead). Pilgrims bore wooden crosses and etched stones, which served as new headpieces to re-mark graves that had been destroyed by inclement weather. Various foods and bottles of alcohol, the favorite items of dead loved ones, were also carried during the pilgrimage. Arriving at cemeteries on the evening of November 1, families cleaned and decorated graves, mourned, prayed, and awaited the arrival of their departed family members during the overnight vigil, called the *iluminada* or *llorada*. Even the gravesides of sinners—gamblers, gluttons, alcoholics, and thieves—were decorated with playing cards, tortillas, *pulque* (an alcoholic beverage made from fermented cactus), and various articles they had stolen. Amid the glow of flickering candles and burning embers, people prayed and reminisced throughout the night. Such behaviors show unconditional devotion to family and religious traditions and reflect complex personal relationships between the living and their beloved dead.[78]

Every November 2, cemeteries took on the appearance of public parks as

Figure 12. Indian women visiting the *campo santo* during the Day of the Dead. Poor families made huge financial sacrifices to buy wax candles, flowers, wreaths, and food gifts to celebrate the memory of loved ones. Photo by C. B. Waite; courtesy of the Archivo General de la Nación.

Mexicans invited their ancestors back to an atmosphere of revelry and mockery. Whether in pastoral countrysides or urban centers, popular cemeteries were not forbidding places to avoid but centers of social interaction: "When you arrive to the Necropolis it seems like you are at a garden to attend a splendid fiesta."[79] Lines of colorful paper cutouts strung between trees and fence posts at the cemeteries gave the impression of an impending celebration. Following the overnight vigil, prayer and remembrance often turned to gossip and drink. At the popular cemeteries, people strolled, picnicked, slept, romanced, and gambled. They flowed in and out of chapels but also made their way to pulque stands.[80] Catholic sacraments performed in cemeteries were customarily exempt from the Reform Laws, which normally prohibited any religious activities outside churches.[81]

Like other festivals such as Carnival and Holy Week, the Day of the Dead took on more commercial and mundane aspects as a recreational holiday.[82] Nineteenth-century tourists described the feast day as a citywide "carnival of death," with a mingling of sadness and frivolity.[83] Shopkeepers often closed their doors, but bakeries sold edible sugar skulls and other sweets (*dulces*), jellies (*jaleas*), and decorative sweet bread (*pan de muertos*) twisted into every conceivable shape to resemble hideous human skulls and grotesque skeletons. Stews and hot beverages simmered in clay pots. Street vendors peddled wooden and papier-mâché skulls (*calaveras*) and skeletons; puppets (*títeres*);

toys resembling coffins, catafalques, and tombs (*entierros*); rattles (*matracas*); tops bearing the names and images of saints; and miniature churches, chapels, and streetcars converted into funeral hearses. Small wooden and clay skeleton figurines (*calacas*) played fiddles and performed occupational tasks.[84] These jobs were captured in the *relatos costumbristas* of Antonio García Cubas and the engravings of José Guadalupe Posada.[85] Funereal toys like these prompted onlookers to describe the Day of the Dead as carnivalesque. Theaters opened their doors for free showings of the Spanish play *Don Juan Tenorio*. Also popular were one-act plays (*tandas*), many of which were comic skits. Churches held mass with full orchestral accompaniment. And tramcar operators practiced their usual custom of admitting more passengers than they could safely carry.

The rise of consumerism was duly ridiculed in the satirical press. The jam-packed trolleys of the Day of the Dead appear in Posada's immortal calaveras. The penny press poked fun at well-known politicians and high-society snobs by printing their mock epitaphs in playful, rhyming verse. Liberal newspapers published morbid drawings of the tombstones and mausoleums of Conservatives and the clergy. Headstones were covered with crowns and crosses with the inscriptions "RIP" and "Descanso en Paz."[86] Posada often illustrated these sardonic postmortems so that they were comprehensible to everyone. The renderings offered cartoonists opportunities to express their dissatisfaction without reprisal or censorship until the 1890s. *El Hijo del Ahuizote* humiliated the Porfirian government with its satirical death metaphors. One showed a sinister Interior Minister Manuel Romero Rubio laying to rest a female figure in a coffin labeled "Freedom of the Press." Inscribed on the tombstone was "Belén," the name of the prison where Díaz jailed his opponents. Another caricature entitled "At the Cemetery" showed a woman representing the Patria weeping as she knelt at the foot of a monument to Juárez. The sword on the ground at her side read "Hope," and she held the tattered flag of the Plan of Tuxtepec in her hands. One final example from 1886 depicted a boy "In Search of Justice" at a "Democracy Graveyard" filled with tombs labeled "Liberal Party," "Congress," and the "Supreme Court."[87] These satiric cartoons outwitted public officials and undermined the official death cult.

Mexicans from the upper class were no less devoted to remembering their dead, but they expressed their devotion differently. The gothic and neoclassical architecture of upper-class mausoleums in foreign cemeteries contrasted greatly with the flower-strewn earthen mounds found in the popular cemeteries. Two morning masses were heard at the chapels of the French and Spanish cemeteries in La Piedad. Visitors noted life-sized oil portraits of deceased relatives, but with the spread of photography, elites placed pictures on their burial monuments.[88] In 1896, a tourist described the French Cemetery as "one mass of beautiful wreaths," with some tombs hardly visible beneath the floral offerings.[89] Every Day of the Dead, reporters camped out at the Romero Rubio family vault awaiting the annual visit of Carmen Romero Rubio de Díaz, the president's wife. Since Díaz often placed the first wreath, the city arranged for a heavy police presence to preserve order.[90]

Figure 13. First Lady Carmen Romero Rubio de Díaz visiting the family vault containing the remains of her father, Manuel Romero Rubio, one of the principal architects of the Porfirian state. The tomb is in the Panteón Frances (French Cemetery) in La Piedad and shows stark contrasts with the previous image of a rural peasant's grave. Photo courtesy of Fototeca Instituto Nacional de Antropología e Historia, Pachuca.

Day of the Dead brought together Mexicans from various social classes, despite the clearly delineated boundaries of everyday life. Of all the places the holiday was celebrated, only the private space of the home limited cross-sectional socialization. The rich and the poor interacted in churches, cemeteries, markets, theaters, streets, plazas, and other public areas. Churches held special requiem masses and allowed all parishioners greater access to chapels for a better view of the sacred relics and bones of saints. Catholics placed votive offerings at the chapels of shared patron saints. Streets and sidewalks were typically crowded with carriages, streetcars, equestrians, and pedestrians. The row of stalls at the improvised market along the Avenida de los Hombres Ilustres near the Alameda brought buyers of every social class to haggle for goods. From there people walked a few blocks to lay wreaths at the Juárez memorial at San Fernando, where caretakers enshrouded the impressive marble shrine with a floral curtain. Flower sellers did a thriving business. Wealthy patrons raved over the exquisite bouquets available at the Floral Market near the cathedral.[91] The Day of the Dead was an expression of Mexican folk culture. These rare moments during the calendar year when society seemed in harmony, when festival-goers overtook the streets and disregarded the authorities for a day, often served as pressure-release valves for oppressed people.[92]

Unlike the case with Carnival and the Judas burnings of Semana Santa, the popularity of the Day of the Dead never diminished over time. But the government's unprecedented regulatory control over cemeteries changed the way people celebrated. Because incidents of violence and public drunkenness on the Day of the Dead increased annually, the city government augmented its police presence and mobilized volunteer watchmen to help patrol graveyards. Increasingly larger detachments of *gendarmes* patrolled section six, the outermost arch designated for sixth-class paupers' graves. Administrators at Dolores also limited cemetery hours from 10:00 a.m. to noon and from 3:00 p.m. to 6:00 p.m. They ultimately banned the consumption of food and alcohol within the gates. The new cemetery ordinances and operating hours were posted everywhere in the city center, on cemetery walls, and in newspapers.[93] Closing Dolores at 6:00 p.m. forced the poor to change their cultural practices and consumption patterns. The prohibition of after-hours patronage caused hundreds to camp overnight in the open fields surrounding Dolores until gates opened the next day. The new hours also obligated the poor to strip their gravesites of valuables and ornaments earlier than tradition warranted. After visits, policemen herded them into streetcars.[94] In the celebration of the dead, no one, living or dead, was favored more than the other, until modernizing elites legislated against the traditions of the city's poor. To the Porfirian ruling class, this was the inexorable march of progress.

Laws are rarely the creation of subordinate classes, even if popular behavior initiates demands for social reform from above. As historian William French argued in his work on the Hidalgo District of Chihuahua, government reforms underline the complex relationship between power and morality. The state's "language of moral reform had long afforded a cultural framework, within which it could affirm its power and advance its claim to rule."[95] Nevertheless, the *gente común* alternately resisted and took advantage of new rules devised by the *gente decente*. For one, regulations banning alcohol in the cemeteries did not prevent *pulquerías* from popping up around Dolores. Heavy drinking went from a public activity in plain sight to the closed quarters of commercial establishments. One clever barkeep named his pulquería Don Juan Tenorio en el Panteón, after the easily recognizable antihero from Zorrilla's play. The state may have driven vice from the cemetery, but the "festival of death" continued full force in the road outside, which took on the character of a street party or fairgrounds. Itinerant food vendors even made camping in surrounding hillsides tolerable.[96] Common people asserted their rights to practice traditional customs and chose to which parts of "modern civilization" they wished to belong. Like their ancestors from the late colonial era, the powerless masses never perceived their dead as a public health problem.[97] The give-and-take of the hegemonic process enabled compromises, but underclasses were always on the defensive. In 1899, the City Council shut down the pulque sellers around Dolores, even denying tavern owner Francisco Yañez's petition to continue sales.[98]

"Inevitable progress" transformed other Day of the Dead performance traditions. On All Souls' Day throughout the Spanish-speaking world, theaters invited the public to see the famous play *Don Juan Tenorio*. Written in 1844 by the Spanish poet and playwright José Zorrilla y Moral, the drama was introduced in Mexico by Emperor Maximilian and Empress Carlota. The main character and story line so captivated the ill-fated emperor that he summoned Zorrilla himself to Chapultepec Castle. There, the dramatist supervised dozens of special showings for high-society guests. After 1867, the play sold out at the National, Arbeu, and Hidalgo theaters and at Orrin's Circus, with both afternoon and night performances. These theater houses charged low prices of admission (some shows were free), and troupes performed for as long as public taste approved, often well into December. In the 1890s, the play continued to maintain a strong hold on Mexico City's elite and popular classes, who were amused by the legendary title character.[99]

Don Juan Tenorio performances offer a unique window into Mexican attitudes toward death and deviancy. The purposely absurd play chronicles the criminal acts and sexual exploits of a social deviant par excellence.[100] It opens in a lowly Seville tavern during Carnival in 1545. Two of high society's lowliest libertines, Don Juan Tenorio and Don Luis Mexia, spy one another across a table to settle a wager. One year ago, they had placed a bet to see who could kill more men and seduce more women. Surrounded by his gang, Don Juan boasts of murdering thirty-two men and engaging in amorous affairs with seventy-two women. Don Luis falls short of this number, dispatching twenty-three unfortunates and seducing fifty-six women. Evoking the wild whistles and jeers of the theater's unrestrained male audience were Tenorio's infamous lines of act 1: "From a princess to a fisherman's daughter. I've loved my way up and down the social ladder!" Audiences reveled in such clever and scandalous passages from the ill-mannered *hidalgo*. They laughed at the moral degenerate, especially when Don Juan quantified the art of seduction. He claimed that he needed just five days for each seduced woman: one to fall in love, another to win her love, a third to abandon her, a fourth to find another, and an hour to forget about the first.[101]

In spite of all his philandering, Don Juan Tenorio genuinely loves only one woman, Doña Inés, the daughter of Gonzalo de Ulloa, the Comendador de Calatrava. Unbeknownst to Juan, a disguised Don Gonzalo hears every boastful detail. At the height of the bravado, Gonzalo unmasks himself, berates Juan, and prohibits him from ever seeing Inés again. Also present is Juan's own father, Diego, who maintains his anonymity beneath a mask of his own and chastises his son for such arrogant and ignoble behavior. With total disinterest and a lack of remorse, Juan shrugs them off. He spends the rest of part 1 seducing Luis's ladylove, scaling a convent wall to kidnap Inés, and dueling with both Don Gonzalo and Don Luis. Mexican audiences reportedly howled with delight when Don Juan shouted, "Let Hell win," and killed them both: "I called unto the heavens and they heard me not/and since they closed their doors to me/for all my comings and goings upon earth/Let the heavens be responsible and not I." Tenorio inadvertently causes Inés's death from grief for her father. The cheap melodrama and spiritual flights appealed to the sentimental crowd. A strange *danse macabre* of ballet dancers closes part 1.[102]

Porfirian-era audiences found their favorite scene in the first act of part 2. Don Juan appears in a moonlit graveyard among the willows and cypresses,

Figure 14. Manuel Manilla's *Don Juan Tenorio* metal cut engraving. The image depicts main scenes from the play, including duels, the death of Inés, and her forgiveness of Don Juan. From Roberto Berdecio and Stanley Applebaum, eds., *Posada's Popular Mexican Prints* (New York: Dover Publications, 1972).

the statues and crosses, and the tombs of Gonzalo, Luis, his father Diego, and Inés. A procession of penitents wearing San Benitos and carrying torches stand in the background reciting doleful chants. Referring to the ornate family vaults of the cemetery, the remorseless Tenorio delivers the following lines: "So my good father spent all my inheritance on this. He did well. I would have staked it on a single card. You cannot complain of me, my murdered ones. If I robbed you of the good life, I repaid you with a good burial. Really it's a splendid idea, this mausoleum! And my heart takes comfort in the solitude." Tenorio utters other blasphemies and invites the dead to return. The ghosts of the murdered men appear but give way to "Captain Centellas"—Satan—who challenges Don Juan to the final duel. Ultimately perishing by the sword, Juan is destined for Hell when he is dubiously rescued by the deus ex machina—the loving and forgiving Inés. "God forgives Don Juan at the foot of my grave," she affirms: "Let the heavenly rewards enjoyed by the just begin now for Don Juan." Together they ascend to Heaven as nymphs perform a ballet for them in paradise.[103]

Despite Don Juan's aristocratic pedigree, his lines seem inspired by plebeian insolence rather than patrician manners. The miracle of his salvation, the saintly Inés descending from the heavens like the Virgin of Guadalupe, made believers of everyone ever corrupted by temptation and sin. With few exceptions, however, American tourists and Mexican theater reviewers found *Don Juan Tenorio* vulgar, criminal, "off color," and otherwise unfavorable to teach any lessons in morality.[104] They never understood why a play set in the lawless and licentious sixteenth century and deemed "a correct portraiture of the age and country" in which it was produced enjoyed such a huge following in modern Mexico. In a prosaic era and country, Juan's exploits "would inevitably have qualified him for the gallows."[105] Poor reviews never prevented the wealthy theatergoers from attending and laughing uproariously with the crowd. We know the Porfirian power elite appreciated the play enough to refer to it. In a letter to President Díaz's personal secretary, Rosendo Pineda charged Veracruz governor Teodora Dehesa as "a bad-tempered fiend who abominably abuses the good name of the President and has established bullfighter's guilds everywhere, as if he were the new Don Juan Tenorio of ill will and calumny."[106]

After the turn of the century, both the themes and the typical audience of the play fundamentally changed, much for the worse some argued.[107] One astute Mexican theater reviewer in 1902, pen-named "Pepe Rey," commented on the change in thematic presentation and style. To attract theatergoers in an increasingly competitive market, the Teatro Arbeu advertised its rendition as "everything entirely national." True to the promise, the theater production and set designer crews all hailed from the National Academy. In fact, they used Mexican materials in their stage designs, crafted recognizable Mexican settings, costumed performers in *vestida típica*, and ensured that the dialogue, music, and ballet dancers were all Mexican.[108] Pepe Rey lamented:

> Don Juan has become more modern; too modern for that. He has become imbued with the spirit of the day and he does things in a cold, mechanical way that puts one in mind of the *relentless march of an electric street car*. All the buffoonery, jesting and mummery of the old fashion setting of the play have disappeared, leaving the performance bare of what used to be so dear to the heart of the public.[109]

Tenorio lost his evil ways, his villainy, his moodiness, his devil-may-care attitude. He seemed "on the high-road to a saintly crown." He appeared to be sorry for his own wickedness, he was overly apologetic, the fates seemed responsible for his misdeeds, and he seemed fit for conversion. More specifically in the Arbeu Theater version, Don Juan Tenorio appeared in a costume that reminded some of a cross between "one of Stephenson's pirates and the conventional picture of Guatemoc." The audience never took his bravado and threats seriously. Instead of "carving windowholes in people he proved himself very pious." In 1902, the deus ex machina was quite extraordinary. Following Juan's duel with the devil, Inés descended from Heaven in an electric streetcar to carry Don Juan into eternity. The play was like the "cold, mechanical, and relentless" march of progress, recalling the moralizing projects of the Bourbons.

Since the Middle Ages, ethnographic representations of death, such as Holbein's woodcuts of the danses macabres or Zorrilla's drama, reminded common people that their daily life of hardship in the material world would improve in the afterlife. Even Posada's sarcastic calaveras suggest that death at least improves one's outlook. As a people subjected to a history of brutal conquest, demographic collapse, forced labor, colonial violence, internecine war, epidemic cycles, periodic famine, and natural disaster, Mexicans confronted the specter of death daily with both mockery and respect. Solemn rituals for the dead were not held exclusively during funerals or on the Day of the Dead. People visited family graves on the two-week, one-month, six-month, and annual anniversaries of their loved ones' deaths. Cemeteries were the destinations for thousands of processions and pilgrimages throughout the year. Church mass and Catholic liturgy commemorated departed saints and parishioners weekly. Families remembered their ancestors at grace before meals daily. The prevailing method of dealing with permanent separation was to retain the presence of the deceased person in every way. This was precisely the goal of nation-builders constructing national cults of the dead.

The Segregation of the Living and the Dead

During the colonial period in Mexico, the Catholic Church controlled burials and churchyards, preserving practices handed down from the Middle Ages. The burial site within or outside the physical architecture of the church demonstrated an individual's status within the caste society. Priests were interred in the main altars; nobles, in church chapels, naves, atria, halls, walls, and floors; commoners, in open grounds adjacent to the church; and the indigent, in burial pits left uncovered until enough corpses filled the collective grave. All cemeteries reflect social hierarchies, but class distinctions like these were spatially more pronounced before the Enlightenment.[110]

During the late-eighteenth-century Bourbon reforms, Spain's King Charles III attempted to secularize burials and relocate cemeteries from central living spaces to suburbs throughout the Americas. Both objectives clashed with the will of the Church, for the move weakened Roman Catholicism's spiritual and social dominion and desacralized the rites and sites of burial. The reforms also struck at the religious sanctification of social hierarchy reflected in lavish funerals for the aristocracy and high clergy.[111] In Mexico City, the modernizing Bourbon viceroy, the Conde de Revillagigedo, responded to overflowing and unsanitary churchyards by opening four *cementerios extramuros* (suburban cemeteries, literally "outside the city walls"). In 1818, Viceroy José de Iturrigaray appointed the eminent Spanish architect Manuel Tolsá to construct a public municipal cemetery, but ecclesiastical opposition killed the project, and the other cemeteries also failed. Mexico City inhabitants still depended on the Church for burials after independence.[112]

Mexico's successful transition from churchyard to public cemetery originated with the Liberal Reform. Since 1833, Liberals Valentín Gómez Farías and José María Luís Mora tried to reduce Church power by establishing civil registry of vital statistics and marriages, as well as opening public cemeteries. The most that became of the latter was a circular that ordered the removal of all cadavers to an unfinished cemetery at the convent of Santiago Tlaltelolco.[113] Legislation awaited the 1850s, when President Ignacio Comonfort ordered civil authorities to replace priests in recording births, adoptions, marriages, and deaths. Later, in the Veracruz Decrees of July 31, 1859, Benito Juárez authorized civil employees to inspect cemeteries and bury cadavers. The president later created the Department of Hygiene to operate all municipal cemeteries and oversee proper interments. Although Liberals eventually won "the struggle for the dead," the French Intervention postponed the implementation of new laws.[114]

Modern societies reorganize public space to accommodate both the living and the dead. To serve the growing population of Mexico City, a British firm established the first modern public cemetery during the Lerdo de Tejada administration. In 1874, Benfield, Breker, and Company received a government contract to demarcate burial grounds on the Tabla de Dolores, southwest of the city center in the suburb of Tacubaya. Lerdo inaugurated the Panteón Civil de Dolores on March 21, 1876.[115] By order of the Interior Ministry and Governor's Office, the city purchased the Dolores Cemetery in 1880 and shut down the churchyards of Santa Paula, San Pablo, Campo Florido, Los Angeles, and San Diego in the Federal District, as well as other cemeteries in Xochimilco and Tlalpan.[116] The city government and Public Health Board ordered the transfer of bodies from graves paid for in perpetuity to the Dolores Cemetery. Construction crews then converted most colonial-era burial grounds into public parks or residential sites. By the end of his second term, Porfirio Díaz carried out the most comprehensive cemetery reforms since the Bourbons.

Public health concerns, rather than the enforcement of anticlerical Reform Laws, motivated Díaz's effort to modernize cemeteries. The regime believed that death had no place in a healthy modern city. The potter's field of the capital, Dolores became the most frequented cemetery in all Mexico. By 1888, the twelve-year total number of interred dead surpassed one hundred thousand; by 1901, the figure surpassed the living population of three hundred thousand.[117] The majority were buried in the sixth-class section for free. In contrast, few could afford the first-class section from year to year. Paradoxically, the constant flow of tomb patrons, funeral marchers, and Day of the Dead pilgrims rendered the spatial segregation of the living and dead meaningless. Cultural tradition encouraged people to spend much of their lives in this city of the dead.

This fact was not ignored by the Porfirian regime. Structural engineers may have provided the blueprints for an improved Dolores landscape, but social engineers made it a memorial park symbolic of Porfirian rule. Lerdo de Tejada had reserved about forty-four hundred square meters near the Dolores Cemetery's entrance to enshrine national heroes in the Rotonda de los Hombres Ilustres.[118] In 1876, he had politicized the necropolis by burying two officers, Pedro Letechipia and Diódoro Corella, who were killed by Díaz's rebels. After overthrowing Lerdo, Díaz re-inaugurated the pantheon in 1879. Although Díaz interred leaders in other cemeteries, the Rotunda of Illustrious Men was the final destination for 27 of 110 state funerals (see Appendixes A and C). The state also reserved a separate section called the Rotonda de los Defensores de 1847 for officers who died fighting the U.S. Army. When the City Council ordered the construction of a 2.5-meter-high wall to enclose the cemetery, visitors had to funnel through the rotunda in order to reach the graves of loved ones. The state exploited the cultural tradition of gravesite patronage to present its visual pedagogy to the urban masses. On the Day of the Dead, low-level bureaucrats, factory workers, campesinos, and the urban poor alike passed the national shrine. What they noticed was always reported in *El Imparcial* as tombs covered by a veritable paradise of bougainvilleas, heliotropes, and immortelles.[119]

Figure 15. The Rotonda de los Hombres Ilustres near the entrance of the Dolores Cemetery. Hedges, trees, and sidewalks formed two concentric circles around which national leaders were buried. The rotunda was the final destination for twenty-seven state burials during the Porfiriato. Photo by C. B. Waite; courtesy of the Archivo General de la Nación, Mexico City.

During the Porfiriato each of the main foreign colonies managed a well-kept cemetery of its own. They contrasted greatly with the "ghastly cemeteries" of the rural countryside and the "potter's field" of Dolores. The French and Spanish cemeteries at La Piedad, both established during the Díaz regime, reflected the cultural affinity between Mexico and other Catholic nations. Affluent Mexicans, including a large number of Díaz's own officers and cabinet ministers, purchased plots in these exclusive cemeteries. The American and English colonies also boasted fine cemeteries in Tlaxpana but did not attract the gente decente so much as serve the needs of U.S. and British expatriates.[120]

In the 1880s and 1890s the city sent cleaning teams into neglected cemeteries such as the Panteón del Tepeyac and Panteón de San Fernando. Foreign visitors to Guadalupe were impressed with the historic monuments at Tepeyac but struck by the humility of Antonio López de Santa Anna's grave. Whereas tourists always described provincial cemeteries in negative terms, they compared San Fernando to Mount Auburn, Westminster Abbey, the Père Lachaise, and other memorial parks.[121] San Fernando never deserved such lofty praise, but foreigners accurately described the Juárez mausoleum within it as one of the world's most beautiful sculptures and an expression of "great vigor and dignity."[122] One traveler remarked, "No monumental effort in the United States tells such a story of heroic grief or so immortalizes the dignified emotion of a nation."[123]

The Juárez burial monument was the sacred centerpiece of an urban axis that Porfirio Díaz devoted exclusively to the Lincoln of Mexico in 1887. Congress had commissioned the Juárez tomb in 1873. Mexican artists Juan and Manuel Islas completed it in time for Díaz to unveil it on the eighth anniversary of Juárez's death, July 18, 1880. Beneath a stone pavilion supported by sixteen columns, a life-size marble Juárez lies on his back with his head in the arms of a female allegorical figure representing the Patria. She is crying, but with her chin facing away from the Great Republican, showing her disbelief and sorrow. Since San Fernando housed the remains of independence hero and Mexico's second president Vicente Guerrero in addition to Cinco de Mayo general Ignacio Zaragoza, it drew thousands on three holidays a year. By 1910, Juárez would have a mausoleum, major avenue, residential neighborhood, and stone hemicycle dedicated to him—all within three city blocks.[124] Porfirian monumental architecture promoted many fallen heroes, but Benito Juárez reigned supreme.

Many European contagions crossed the Atlantic and entered Mexico. "Statuomania," an affliction that resurrected public leaders in the forms of bronze statues and stone monuments, swept through Porfirian Mexico in the 1890s. The epidemic in bronzed effigies attacked the Paseo de la Reforma, while the outbreak of marble statues centered at the Rotunda de los Hombres Ilustres. In these two areas alone, the Porfirian government erected sixty-five monuments. Several heroes, including the *porfirista* General Donato Guerra, received the honor of two monuments, one at each site. Sculptural achievement in both bronze statuary and funerary art peaked during the Porfirian *bella época*. Díaz hired Mexican and Italian sculptors alike, while Congress exempted the states from paying taxes on imported marble used for monuments.[125]

Like all artwork, funeral monuments reflected the society that produced them. The sepulchral monuments of the aristocratic French and Spanish cemeteries symbolized the prosperity of Porfirian Mexico. The expensive statuary and elaborate vaults were items of conspicuous expenditure that reflected elite aspirations and showcased the social positions of families. Status was also conveyed by the hiring of eminent Italian sculptors, such as Enrico Alciati, Alfredo Ponzanelli, Cesare Volpi, Noville Navari, and U. Luisi. Distinguished Mexican sculptors Manuel Islas, Gabriel Guerra, Miguel Noreña, and Jesús F. Contreras produced magnificent works of art. For many, funeral monuments constituted their largest business. Wealthy patrons contracted Contreras's Fundición Artística Méxicana or T. Carandiente Tartaglio's Fundición Artística de Tacubaya and imported marble from Carrara and Paris for their elaborate family mausoleums. Visits to the family vault were a pleasant social event.[126]

Although access to aristocratic cemeteries was generally restricted, state funerals and commemorative festivals granted access to social groups that previously had no reason to visit the foreign cemeteries. Workers and soldiers who marched in processions gathered around the final burial grounds of a class to which they did not belong. These official visits to the foreign cemeteries by the poor reinforced social hierarchies and identities because those who observed tombs as large as mini-mansions drew conclusions about the subjects' social position and their own. Hierarchy could be observed through visual recognition of architectural styles, the size of vaults, the number of stone effigies, the name of the sculptor inscribed on the tomb, and the type of materials used to construct the edifice.[127]

Tomb patronage not only increased during the Porfiriato; after 1895 photographs of distinguished tombs began appearing in November issues of the illustrated magazines *El Mundo Ilustrado* and *El Tiempo Ilustrado*. Even the cheaper dailies, *El Imparcial, El Mundo, El Nacional*, and *El Popular*, published sketches of elite tombs on the Day of the Dead. Readers who normally never visited the aristocratic graveyards "visually patronized" the vaults. Liberal newspapers only published pictures of the gravesites of Liberal heroes. Editor of the *El Tiempo* publications Victoriano Agüeros, however, kept conservative Catholic memories alive by publishing photographs of the tombs of Tómas Mejía and Miguel Miramón side by side with those of Ignacio Zaragoza and Ignacio Comonfort. Since all four were buried within feet of one another in the Panteón de San Fernando, Agüeros implied to his readers that mortal enemies in life ended up at the same national shrine in death. Unity was to be found in cities of the dead and the kingdom of heaven.[128] The affluent also hired photographers to record the image of their family tombs for posterity. The photos were incorporated into family albums that enhanced remembrance. Memorial books for prominent people called *necrologías* or *coronas fúnebres* contained portraits of the deceased and photographs of their mausoleums. These and other commemorative publications circulated throughout the republic. Pictures of cemeteries and the Juárez tomb appeared in many travel accounts and tourist guidebooks. Photography did not offer everlasting life, but it did immortalize images of Porfirian elites and their vaults.[129]

Porfirian-era funerary art was dominated by the prospective image of death and the afterlife. In the aristocratic French and Spanish cemeteries of Mexico City, family vaults were miniature cathedrals that incorporated baroque, gothic, and *churrigueresque* architecture and shrines. Christian symbols such as Christ, the Virgin Mary, the holy cross, and androgynous angels and cherubs abounded. These easily recognizable figures were sculpted with open arms that welcomed stone figures of the deceased into the afterlife. Based on European models, the *sepulcros* looked like three-dimensional baroque paintings with a full iconographic repertoire of symbols from the Old World. Italian sculptors produced statuary that included feminine or infantile effigies mourning the loss of their loved ones. Many appeared kneeling, praying, holding flowers, or laying wreaths.[130]

In contrast to artistic representations of a heavenly afterlife, the prevailing style of government-sponsored funerary monuments was retrospective. A statue was a replica of the dead that presented the exact physical form of the deceased in recognition of his past life. Marble busts and bronze statues of dead heroes replaced Christian icons. In the same foreign cemeteries and the Rotonda de los Hombres Ilustres, political leaders appeared in military uniform or civilian dress depending on their historical contributions. For example, Contreras's equestrian monument of Ignacio Escudero in the Spanish Cemetery shows the general cautiously advancing into battle on horseback while a soldier stands waiting to sound the bugle. Female allegorical figures such as "La Patria" or "El Pueblo" accompany the leaders. The funerary monument of engineer Manuel María Contreras at Tepeyac features a grieving Mexico City, represented by a statue of a weeping matron. Female figures personified city and nation, but civic virtues as well. Four female allegorical statues—Justice, Equality, Strength, and Patriotism—surround the statue of Sebastián Lerdo de Tejada in the rotunda. Gorgeous bas-reliefs depict leaders such as Ignacio Comonfort in San Fernando or defining moments in the hero's life as seen in the famous Cuauhtemotzin Monument. These combined with neoclassical symbols such as broken columns, pyramids, obelisks, inverted torches, military trophies, weapons of war, coats of arms, and open books supplanted religious iconography and served the state as educational devices. The official mortuary art reflected both the government's concern for the secularization of society and the commemoration of great leaders. The government-financed funerary monuments could not pretend to rival the extravagant neo-gothic and neoclassical chapels of the aristocratic families, but they met the minimum standards of the French and Spanish cemeteries.[131]

Unfortunately for the state, the multiplication of lifelike statues made distinguishing one from the other exceedingly difficult. Benedict Anderson referred to this as official nationalism's logic of substitutability. Statues purport to embody someone, but they quickly become serialized replicas, not of the singular historical figures they represent, but of one another. In this sense statues can substitute for each other, and their images circulate easily on postcards, postage stamps, and currency without anyone feeling profaned.[132]

When appearing side by side in ever-larger numbers, statues on the Paseo de la Reforma or in the rotunda lost their symbolic aura and became a series of indistinguishable bronze or marble men. Eventually, they became a common part of the landscape memorable to none and invisible to all. There were exceptions. Because of distinct physical characteristics that stood out without the need for artistic embellishment, Miguel Hidalgo and Benito Juárez escaped this phenomenon of limitless substitutability. Their reproducibility was akin to that of Washington and Lincoln.

Other signposts of nationalism easily melded into cityscapes with nary a distinction. Porfirian state-builders went beyond the proper burial of the remains of the illustrious dead. They designated the places where they fell as sacred national spaces. All modern nations sanctify physical objects or edifices with commemorative plaques that carry inscriptions denoting the sites' historical significance. Porfirians stand out for their indefatigable effort to consecrate everyday living spaces with epitaphs. In 1885, José María Mata presented the city of Chihuahua with a plaque that read: "In this spot was deposited the beheaded body of the Father of Mexican Independence Don Miguel Hidalgo y Costilla shot in Chihuahua, July 31, 1811, and from this spot the remains were exhumed to be taken to the city of Mexico." Mata got the date wrong, but the placement of the memorial tablet in the chapel of San Antonio "sanctified" Chihuahua's Church of San Francisco. Hundreds of similar spatial consecrations took place throughout the republic. Citizens of Mexico City's fifth ward dedicated a plate at the Santa Veracruz Church where the remains of insurgent general Ignacio López Rayón were once entombed.[133]

The height of Porfirian aspirations to honor the dead and indoctrinate the living was demonstrated in 1903 when Díaz laid the first stone for the Panteón Nacional in the garden of the San Hipólito hospital, adjacent to San Fernando. The grand dream of the idealistic Justo Sierra came close to realization after his appointment as the new minister of education in 1905. Italian architect and sculptor Enrico Alciati drafted a five-million-peso project that may have overshadowed all other state sanctuaries. But engineer Guillermo Heredia was awarded the contract. The project failed, Heredia was reassigned to the Juárez Hemicycle, and the remains of the Independence Heroes would have to await Antonio Rivas Mercado's Column of Independence (El Angel), the mother of all Mexican burial monuments.[134]

Funerals and death ceremonials are held for the living, not the dead. Cemeteries and memorial parks are similarly designed to accommodate the emotional needs of the living. The entire death industry compensates for one of the greatest limitations of the human experience, mortality. Figuratively speaking, death was a constant companion of the Mexican people. The loss of a half million people between 1821 and 1876 in wars engendered by political pronouncements would only be exceeded by the one million deaths ushered in by the *pronuncimientos* of the Mexican Revolution. Those who survived the mid-century struggles for national existence coped with the pain of loss daily. Even so people continued to die of diseases and accidents at alarming rates during the Porfiriato. Foreign travelers provide fleeting glimpses of the suffering. Tourists could hardly complete their travel accounts without references to death, mourning customs, and graveyards. The elaborate traditions of the Day of the Dead were human and material testimonies of death's powerful reign. Death was firmly implanted in the landscapes and mindscapes of nineteenth-century Mexicans.[135]

As Mexico City government employees regulated a constant stream of patrons at Dolores, the Porfirian state controlled the endless flow of citizens through the rotunda. Early in the Porfiriato, Justo Sierra presented a legislative solution to Mexico's nineteenth-century national identity crisis. He resolved to declare days of national remembrance for Mexico's greatest heroes, disallowing the government from intervening in what should have been civil society's prerogative to construct national memory and honor heroes and working people in a manner of their choosing. Instead, the Porfirian state came to exercise hegemony over the symbolic ceremonies and sites of national commemoration. The state certainly appealed to the national sentiments of skilled workers, peasants, and urban professionals to modernize Mexico, but without ever actually honoring their labors the way Sierra had proposed. The path not taken is often the path that ruling elites work hard to prevent.

Among the most significant and frequently performed political rituals of the Porfirian era was the state funeral—the subject of the next chapter. State funerals are national burial ceremonies for great public figures initiated, organized, and financed by the government. Since they are the only rites of passage enacted by executive decree or congressional law in modern republics, state funerals are as inevitable as death itself.[136] They occurred at a time when people yearned for ways to cope with their losses, reconcile with the past, and remember their dead.

Figure 16. José Guadalupe Posada's *Rebumbio de Calaveras*. From Roberto Berdecio and Stanley Applebaum, eds., *Posada's Popular Mexican Prints* (New York: Dover Publications, 1972).

The Politics of Death 2

State Funerals as Rites of Reconciliation, 1876–89

I N 1876, THE Revolution of Tuxtepec raged in the Mexican countryside, producing more war dead for families to mourn. The timely arrival of General Manuel González on the battlefield at the hacienda of Tecoac (Tlaxcala) forced Federal Army general Ignacio Alatorre to surrender to the rebels on November 16. Without an army, President Sebastián Lerdo de Tejada went into exile, and the forces of General Porfirio Díaz entered Mexico City unopposed. Widespread melancholia continued through December. The journalist "Juvenal" (Enrique Chávarri) wrote about the gloomy outlook in the capital, where no serenades or social gatherings rang in the New Year. Instead of patronizing restaurants, people flocked to churches to pray for a better year.[1]

The nation hardly embraced *porfirista* rebels as a liberating army. Since Díaz usurped power after a decade of constitutional successions, he lacked political legitimacy. The leading English-language newspaper referred to Díaz as a "failure," his revolution as "desultory," and his movement as soon to be set to a "hasty flight."[2] He faced difficulty raising money from "voluntary" loans; the Mexico City aristocracy limped in with a few thousand pesos each, but more sizable donations came from a mysterious woman whose fortune derived from thvation to the botched hot-air balloon launches of Mexican aeronaut-in-training Joaquín de la Cantoya y Rico: "The descent of Cantoya seems like nothing compared to the decline in the public men of our country."[4] Reflecting public skepticism about his right to govern, the press referred to Díaz as *general* rather than president. Regional oligarchs withheld support for him. Cabinet officer and Supreme Court resignations proliferated. Generals Mariano Escobedo and Sóstenes Rocha rebelled in an attempt to restore Lerdo. Bandits robbed and pillaged the countryside with impunity. Nor did foreign nations instantly recognize and extend credit to his regime. In 1878, Díaz's presidential address, which traditionally highlighted the annual achievements of the republic, was among the shortest on record. He devoted the first half to the frequent difficulties with the United States and began the second with the reassuring statement: "In a nation like ours, which has been subject to frequent political convulsions, the state of the public treasury is always an embarrassment."[5] And if it has any significance as a social indicator whatsoever, the capital city was going to the dogs; police destroyed 11,627 strays in the second quarter of 1879 alone.[6]

Yet, in 1881, the chronicler who lamented the dreary mood in 1877 observed a different downtown scene. Theaters and cafés were closed, but "it seemed as if the exorbitant and compact multitude was headed for a fireworks display." People were "so joyful and content to go to the free funeral ceremony of Arista," where they could listen to the music of Verdi and Meyerbeer. Juvenal likened the nighttime atmosphere on Calle San Andrés to a *verbena*, or street party. The sounds of funeral marches mixed with the cries of food vendors who had set up peanut stands, earthenware pots of *buñuelos* (fried pastries), and tables of *tortas* (sandwiches). Thousands of citizens crowded the entrance of the Palacio de Mineria to view the funeral chapel of ex-president Mariano Arista. The writer described the multitude as

> the great bedlam, essential in such circumstances, which forms part of our national customs. . . . [W]hoever fell, fell; that ocean of human heads began to get rough; the ebb tide rose, swelled, [and] then came the thunderstorm and tempest; they pushed and knocked the señoras to the ground, they crushed and bruised them; we were, in the end, *in perfect confusion*, just as we are under the lights of El Carmen or La Merced; at the *tandas* [one-act plays]; at the fireworks displays; just like at all of these amusing places.

All social classes interacted at the Arista funeral, the sorbets of the rich with the palm sombreros of the poor: "The nation still smiles at the dead and amuses itself with the rib-bones of their poor deceased fellows." Juvenal also explained the event's popularity:

> Mineria has been the favorite *paseo* of this great capital; all Mexico has gone to visit the remains, principally in the nights, when the amusement had the added attraction of electric lights, which shined imperfectly at first and then not at all; and the other incentive [was] the modest price. . . . It is hoped that an illustrious man dies once a week in order to enjoy the pomp of these entertaining funerals which make a downcast and depressed society smile.[7]

While not weekly as Juvenal had hoped, state funerals took place every three months on average from 1876 to 1911.

It may be difficult to accept the notion that funerals entertained people during the century of lights. People do not normally look forward to funerals of any kind. But the past is a foreign country, and scholars must relinquish their false sense of familiarity with it.[8] As Juvenal understood, the popular classes interpreted state funerals as festivals that departed from their dreary daily routine. Another reporter remarked: "It seemed like people were going to the circus rather than visiting the remains of one of our illustrious men."[9] Citizens set out to the streets of their own free will. No one ordered them to socialize at state functions. There was a certain victory of social equality and harmony, as well as a triumph over rational use of public space in their spontaneous convergences. The dramaturgy of national union in Mexico, as elsewhere, required festivals to take place in vast open spaces to suggest limitless boundaries.[10] In Mexico, the open air of wide avenues, public plazas, and colonial palaces contrasted with the cloistered private quarters of people who lived in one-room huts and urban tenements. Much of life was lived on the street. Street diversions in Bourbon as well as Porfirian Mexico evoked expressions of reclaimed liberty, broke down social hierarchies, and stressed the ethical and religious equality of humans.[11]

But why did occasions designed to evoke solemnity such as funerals also provoke disorder, property destruction, and petty theft? During lyings-in-state and funeral processions, crowd behavior often oscillated between hushed reverence and wild pandemonium. Customary civil discord was evidence of the "moral economy" of the crowd, when people set aside their fears and deference to superiors to assert traditional notions of fairness during unjust times.[12] Periods of economic uncertainty incite violence, larceny, insolence, mockery, parody, noise, and subversion, all of which make perfect sense to the participants but appall ruling classes.[13] Although a foreigner at the Arista funeral saw people "behaving in a most orderly manner," a Mexican journalist reported mobs crushing the palace guards, who retaliated with blows from their rifle butts.[14] He sarcastically assigned blame, but not to the soldiers: "Those good citizens in the crowd were pleased to push up against one another and raise infernal hell."[15] Noisy streets betrayed the intentions of quiet mourning; street vendors and tavern-goers were especially obnoxious. Besides trampling one another, the one hundred thousand citizens who turned out for the lying-in-state destroyed the stone walkways of the Mining Palace. And pickpockets made away with anything of value.[16]

In the first decade of the Porfiriato, state funerals invoked transgressive behavior that reflected what Juvenal called times of "perfect confusion." The weak and divided central government had little choice but to excuse crowd misbehavior. Authorities tolerated popular indiscretions as the patriotic exuberance of citizens practicing "folk" liberalism. Unpredictable disorderly throngs had always been associated with national holidays, religious feast days, and other occasions when people of distinct social classes intermingled. Inhabitants of the "marginal" city (mostly eastern slums) converged with the "civilized" neighborhoods in the downtown area, where street markets, public events, and *pulquerías* abounded.[17] Rather than a serious threat to public order, episodic chaos was rationalized as the temporary sins of excess, moral licentiousness, and social inversion.[18] Porfirio Díaz and Manuel González risked new forms of socialization and politicization to gain adherents and popular consent to rule.

As the previous chapter demonstrates, death ceremonials were a cohesive force in a nation of citizens who worshiped ancestors on the Day of the Dead, national heroes monthly, and Catholic saints daily. Historically, funerals also have served as incomparable rites of political reconciliation for both monarchical empires and republics. In Porfirian Mexico, the government hosted state funerals to unite citizens and reconcile with the nation's troubled past. Every citizen who had suffered the loss of a loved one during wartime was invited to join in the solidarity of collective mourning and remembrance. Politicians set aside their grievances for an indeterminate time. Opposition journalists and other contrarians placed moratoriums on public criticism. Rival military officers let bygones be bygones in mutual respect for the dead. This was a major theme in the United States in the case of Abraham Lincoln's funeral.[19] Díaz and his one-term successor, Manuel González, even buried former political opponents in extravagant funerals. From 1877 to 1889, the government financed seventeen funerals. Eight individuals received major state burials: Ignacio Ramírez, Gabino Barreda, Jesús González Ortega, Mariano Arista, Ezequiel Montes, Juan José Baz, Sebastián Lerdo de Tejada, and Ramón Corona. Of these eight, only Ramírez and Montes were porfiristas. All officialdom and thousands of citizens mobilized to honor public men who "sacrificed personal ambitions" and "relinquished power" for the sake of national unity.

The Search for Historical Legitimacy and Political Regeneration

Scholars who have studied commemorative funerals elsewhere have argued that parading the dead bodies of heroic individuals enables modern states to use their biographies to reevaluate the national past.[20] Such was the case in Mexico, where, in every funeral, the state not only rewrote a usable past and reminded citizens of their shared history but emphasized Díaz's link to earlier periods. The reevaluation of the national past emphasized the common experiences of military officers who fought for distinct causes in different time periods, but it also had the effect of tracing Porfirio's historical genealogy to the nation's very birth. Two generations after independence, the Díaz regime decreed funerals for José Vicente Miñon and Calixto Bravo, the last survivors of the *treinta contra cuatrocientos* (thirty rebel commanders against four hundred Spanish royalist officers) who fought in the Liberation Wars. In 1878, Díaz visited Miñon on his deathbed, and he eulogized Bravo for serving with his brother, renowned *insurgente* Nicolás Bravo.[21] By associating himself with independence leaders, Díaz related his struggle to the nation's own. Although Díaz was born in 1830, he proclaimed himself the progeny of a national historical lineage that dated from the independence wars (1810–21). Once independence leaders died, Díaz arranged funerals for Liberal heroes of Mexico's "second independence," the Wars of the Reform and French Intervention. Thus, he found no shortage of war heroes to bury. The president's search for historical legitimacy explains much of his political behavior.

If Díaz compared his armed services credentials and exploits to the annals of Mexican military history, he expected just as much from his subordinate officers. The general required aspirants to the new ruling clique to document their loyalty to his cause and their military service to the Patria. By reviewing the armed services files of Manuel Barrón, for example, Díaz verified the officer's involvement in the war against the French. Three porfirista generals, Juan N. Méndez, Feliciano Chavarría, and Vicente Riva Palacio, confirmed Barrón's participation in the Revolutions of La Noria and Tuxtepec.[22] This evidence of direct fealty to Díaz earned Barrón a pension and a political office in the new regime. Beyond confirming a hierarchical relationship based on military rank, the review also indicates who had earned the political right to appraise the qualifications of officers in historical military campaigns—the *jefe supremo*, Díaz.

As fate would have it, the Porfirian government could not have planned for a better first recipient of major state funeral honors than the author of the very constitution Díaz swore to defend. Ignacio Ramírez, preeminent jurisconsult and cowriter of the Liberal Constitution of 1857, fought for political equality, social justice, and national education for all Mexicans. Of Tarascan descent, Ramírez attended José María Luís Mora's Instituto Literaria de Toluca and, with Ignacio Manuel Altamirano, launched the literary awakening of the Reforma era known as the Renacimiento. During the Juárez and Lerdo administrations, Ramírez mentored students who later helped construct the Porfirian state. Juan A. Mateos, Jorge Hammeken y Mexía, Porfirio Parra, and Justo Sierra all carried their lessons into the Chamber of Deputies, cabinet ministries, and government schools. They referred to Ramírez as *el sábio*, "the learned one."[23]

Ramírez stood at the center of controversy for most of his lifetime. A confirmed atheist, he once incited the wrath of the Catholic Church by proclaiming, "God does not exist." A Jacobin in spirit and cynic in temperament, he wrote hundreds of newspaper editorials under the pen name El Nigromante (The Necromancer). A diehard classical liberal, he all but parted company with everyone else. He served as a personal secretary of Ignacio Comonfort during Ayutla but spurned his old boss to join the *puros*. After a decade of loyalty, he broke with Juárez after his third reelection. For crossing Lerdo, Ramírez found himself in jail. His support of the Plan de Tuxtepec drew accusations that he betrayed José María Iglesias. As minister of justice under Díaz, Ramírez exhorted other cabinet officials and resigned after one month.[24] While his political criticism was always meant to be constructive, he remained blasphemous to the end. On June 15, 1879, he defiantly rejected the last rites and "accepted death with a sardonic smile and outstretched hand as if it were a friend awaiting him."[25]

Funerals were authorized by presidential decree during Díaz's improvisational first term. In Ramírez's case, President of the Supreme Court Ignacio Vallarta requested that the state pay all funeral expenses, provide a pension for the family, and offer protection to Ramírez's two sons. "Protection" came in the form of government scholarships to pursue professional degrees at national schools.[26] It also meant political patronage. When Military Zone Commander José Guillermo Carbó died, political protection was already in place when Carbó's brother asked Díaz not to abandon them.[27] Executive decrees were publicized on street-corner posters and in official mortuary announcements (*esquelas*). In Ramírez's case they requested all citizens to honor "one of the most illustrious sons of the Republic and one of its most loyal and dignified servants."[28]

The lying-in-state for Ramírez was subdued, compared to the restive funeral ceremony. A quiet public shuffled past his coffin during the twenty-four-hour exposition in the Chamber of Deputies. On June 18, dignitaries sat through a torturous three-hour ceremony that included thirty-five orations and poems. Ireneo Paz, editor of *La Patria*, reprimanded the organizers: "If *El Nigromante* could have escaped from the imprisonment of his coffin, he would have shouted 'That's Enough! That's Enough!' after the first half-dozen speeches."[29] The lengthy program took its toll on the irritable audience, which whistled and catcalled during the funeral oration of the unpopular Protasio Tagle. Politicians rarely expressed their disfavor so openly during funerals, but this event resembled a raucous legislative session.[30] The conservative Catholic newspaper *La Voz de México* later berated the government for allowing Masons to memorialize Ramírez in the Chamber of Deputies.[31]

After the ceremony, Supreme Court justices bore the casket to a magnificent hearse outside. Since 1823, republican heads of state always rode at the end of funeral processions, distant from the hearse at the front. Presidents Guadalupe Victoria and Vicente Guerrero had established the "people first" practice of linking the dead hero and the president with a human chain of bureaucrats and citizens to emphasize political equality and popular sovereignty over social hierarchy.[32] Juárez carried on this tradition in the funerals of Ignacio Zaragoza, Manuel Doblado, and Miguel Lerdo de Tejada. Likewise, Sebastián Lerdo de Tejada appeared last in the Juárez procession of 1872. In contrast, Díaz led the march on foot and occupied the *sitio de honor* (place of honor) directly behind the hearse for the Ramírez funeral. Funerals stressed his political leadership and personal relationship with the deceased. After a forty-five-minute tramcar journey through the city, the cortege reached Guadalupe, where Ramírez was buried next to his wife in the Panteón del Tepeyac.[33] Observers compared the procession to the splendid funerals of Europe: "The combined movement of the trams [was] worthy of a European city. . . . [T]he capital of the Republic already has the means to handle those indispensable necessities of all civilized countries today."[34] A Mexican journalist summarized the event with a local saying: "The government threw the house out the window" to honor Ignacio Ramírez.[35]

In funeral orations and obituaries, Ramírez was portrayed as a savant worthy of universal comparison, his historical legacy for a nation searching for international acceptance. Humanity, Liberty, and Science were in mourning. Mexico had lost its own Aristotle, Galileo, and Humboldt combined into one, exclaimed Ignacio Altamirano.[36] Other orators likened him to Voltaire as "our chief in every battle against intolerance and fanaticism" and a "poet, historian, [and] philosopher, who enlarged the human spirit and taught men to be free."[37] Porfirio Parra placed him in a long line of dissenters since Erasmus and Luther.[38] *Diario Oficial* counted him among the few radicals who contributed to national regeneration.[39] References to Greek and Roman antiquity, Renaissance humanists, French *philosophes*, and Mexican Liberals disassociated Ramírez from feudalism, monarchism, colonialism, conservatism, and Catholicism. Orators gave status to Ramírez, Mexico, and themselves in the great performance tradition of funeral orations since Greco-Roman times.[40]

The effort to situate Ramírez within the whirlpool of a Western intellectual tradition complemented another intention. Although Díaz and González buried fellow army officers, the funeral for Ramírez de-emphasized the military to project the image of civilian rule to foreign powers. Seeking foreign recognition and credit from 1877 to 1889, the regime hosted more state funerals for politicians and men of letters (ten) than for high-ranking officers (seven), despite the fact that more officers passed away.[41] To valorize civilian professionalism over militarism, the regime created new occupational categories for

state burials. Honors historically reserved for presidents and division generals were now rendered to great cabinet officials, jurists, diplomats, educators,
musicians, and even doctors.[42] Funerals were devised to convince the Western
powers that Díaz brought an end to palace coups and placed Mexico on the
path of modern development. For these reasons, the army was not called out
of its barracks to escort Ramírez's coffin.

Despite his qualifications, Ramírez was a risky choice for the fledgling
Porfirian state. The fact that Liberals united at the coffin of this independent
agitator augured well for Díaz's attempt to lay to rest a turbulent century. As
a scathing critic of the political machines of Comonfort, Juárez, and Lerdo,
Ramírez had made enemies; as coauthor of the Constitution, Liberal reformer,
influential publicist, *juarista*, and porfirista, Ramírez earned respectful mourners. Only after death can such an incendiary personality be used to medi-
ate conflicting and oppositional forces. In addition, not only did his lifetime
coincide with the nation's historical evolution from promulgation to Porfirio
(1857–77), he personified the transition from Juárez to Díaz (1867–77). In the
twilight of his life, as well as in death, Ramírez helped legalize a regime born
of rebellion and tainted with illegitimacy.[43]

National sympathy for Ramírez paled in comparison to that expressed for
President Díaz when his wife, Delfina, and his newborn daughter, Victoria,
died from childbirth complications in April 1880. Díaz had married Delfina
Ortega, his niece, in 1867. She and Porfirio had suffered the harshest tragedies of
losing four children during their infancy, due in no small part to consanguin-
ity. In 1880, few could remain indifferent after learning of the intense physical
pain Delfinita endured before succumbing. Nearing the end of his first term,
Díaz received letters of condolence from all parts of the republic.[44] Even "the
enemies of Díaz extended their hands in common emotional support."[45] Delfina's burial was not a state funeral because the government neither authorized
nor paid for it. What distinguished state funerals from private ones was the
absence of any symbol of Christian religiosity: no churches, priests, crosses,
or candles. All abounded at the Catholic funeral for Delfina. Díaz may have
secretly arranged religious services for her at Guadalupe and even renounced
the Reform Laws in a private letter to the Church so that his pious wife could
receive the last rites.[46] But comparing her funeral and those of the archbishops of Mexico to state burials reinforces the notion that nation-builders call
upon a repertoire of religious theatricality to sanctify the nonsacred.[47] Large
crowds entered Díaz's home to view the body and sign the visitors' book. Those
who could not left cuttings of crepe paper with their names written on them
outside the house. Her burial at Tepeyac struck an emotional chord with the
people, who joined the president in mourning the loss of a pious wife and loving mother.[48]

In honor of his pledge to uphold the principles of effective suffrage and no reelection, Díaz stepped down after his first term. The constitutional amendment prohibiting reelection became effective in 1878. Public memory of the manufactured reelections of Juárez and Lerdo, and of Díaz's own campaign promises, was too strong to gamble away his future. Withholding support for politicians who might prevent his return to power, Díaz convened a secret junta of governors in October 1879 and endorsed his old comrade-in-arms, Minister of War Manuel González.[49] Never one to feel indebted to anyone, Porfirio at least credited his Tuxtepec victory to the providential arrival of González's troops at Tecoac.[50] Severely wounded at the engagement, González suffered through a painful second amputation of his stump, which required an extended period of rehabilitation.[51] He once stated to Díaz: "If with my blood a single one of your sorrows could be avoided, I would gladly shed it; and if my poor life were needed in order to preserve your life for my unfortunate country, I would sacrifice it."[52] For his loyalty and sacrifices on the field of battle, González was awarded the presidency in 1880.

González governed the nation much like Díaz, even if his personal history and political style were sufficiently dissimilar to invite undue criticism. One important distinction between the generals stood out during state ceremonies. Originally a Conservative officer during the Reform, González switched sides when the French invaded in 1862. This fact was drowned in the accolades that González earned since his conversion to liberalism, but he could not attend every state event. He had fought with distinction alongside Zaragoza and Díaz. Juárez appointed him as governor of the National Palace and commander of the Federal District and First Army Division. González joined two porfirista revolts and served as governor of Michoacán and minister of war. But since his Liberal credentials were impeachable, he often surrendered the limelight to his former superior officer.[53]

The González cabinet uniformly opposed scientific positivism, which had gained many ideologues by the 1880s. A student of Auguste Comte, Gabino Barreda introduced the philosophy and political doctrine to Mexico in his famous Civic Oration of 1867. Barreda later founded the Escuela Nacional Preparatoria (ENP; National Preparatory School), where he directed a generation of students through a positivist curriculum. In 1878, porfiristas asked Barreda, who had close ties to Lerdo, to resign as director of the school. Minister of Justice and Public Instruction Ezequiel Montes, Minister of Foreign Relations Ignacio Mariscal, and the new director of the ENP, José María Vigil, were all doctrinaire puro Liberals who wanted to preserve the gains of the Reform and the Constitution of 1857. Another group, the young intellectuals who wrote for *La Libertad*, such as Justo Sierra, Francisco Bulnes, Jorge Hammeken y Mexía, and Pablo Macedo, advocated scientific politics, positivist education, a stronger national government, and constitutional reform. The two factions quarreled over faculty appointments, the curriculum, and textbook adoptions at the ENP.[54] But before the storm of debate broke out, Barreda died on March 11, 1881. Like Ramírez, Barreda did not hold a public office at the time of death. But members of the scientific and literary community asked the president to decree a state funeral anyway. González rose above factional politics and responded definitively: "It is necessary that the country show its appreciation for this wise and good man."[55]

Since Barreda had established the ENP, organizers held the lying-in-state at the school's library. After three days of steady visitation, Francisco Díaz Covarrubias hosted a record four-hour funeral ceremony. In their orations, positivists Sierra, Parra, and Juan de Dios Peza expressed that Barreda's spirit would live on at the ENP. After the ceremony, a long train of mourners accompanied the hearse to Dolores.[56] Like the funeral of Victor Hugo in France, the state funeral for Gabino Barreda enlarged the category of those who could receive such honors to great men of letters. Although González did not attend the funeral, he recognized Barreda as one of the premier intellectuals of the century and allowed opponents to speak freely about Barreda for three days. Crowds were not treated to the popular spectacle of a military escort, but they turned out in great numbers to view a procession of dignitaries in black top hats and frock coats.

General Jesús González Ortega Renounces Power Again

If the Barreda funeral increased goodwill among Liberal factions, the state funeral for Mexico's leading anticlerical general ended speculation that González still harbored sympathy for the Conservatives. In 1881, Mexican citizens learned that Liberal *caudillo* Jesús González Ortega was critically ill. After a prominent but contentious career, González Ortega had retired to Saltillo, Coahuila, where he lived in poverty and obscurity. Minister of War Gerónimo Treviño asked President González to restore him to his former rank "as a debt of gratitude to the military leader of the Reform and to the heroic defender of his country's soil against the foreign invader."[57] González Ortega passed away on February 28 and received funeral honors befitting a division general.

Benito Juárez had appointed González Ortega as the supreme commander of Liberal forces during the War of the Reform, but they later became political enemies. As civil war loomed, González Ortega had assumed military control of Zacatecas. He won tide-turning engagements against the Conservatives at the hacienda of Peñuelas (Aguascalientes) and Silao (Guanajuato). On December 22, 1860, he destroyed Miguel Miramón's army, thus earning the epithet "Victor of Calpulalpan" and ending the civil war.[58] In 1861, González

Ortega ran for president and lost to Juárez. He briefly served as war minister but resigned after accusing Juárez of withholding support for his campaigns against Conservative guerrillas. The general eventually crushed the reactionaries with the aid of a young Oaxacan colonel, Porfirio Díaz, and their service together carried over into the war against the French. After Ignacio Zaragoza's death, González Ortega fortified Puebla, endured a heroic sixty-two-day siege, and surrendered to Forey in 1863.[59] Imprisoned in Veracruz, he and Díaz escaped to rejoin the republican army. When Juárez's term expired in 1864, González Ortega cited Article 82 of the Constitution, which provides for the president of the Supreme Court (González Ortega) to succeed him. Juárez justified his continuation in power on the grounds that the nation was at war, but González Ortega denounced him as a dictator. In 1867, Juárez ordered his arrest. After a one-year prison term, the bitter general retired from public life.[60] During the González Ortega funeral this adversarial relationship with Juárez was completely effaced in favor of promoting reconciliation and a myth of national unity against the French.

Upon news of his death, both his native state of Zacatecas and the federal government claimed his remains. On March 1, Trinidad García de la Cadena, president of the Zacatecas state legislature, declared González Ortega a *benemérito*, decreed a period of mourning, closed public offices, and prohibited all forms of licensed entertainment for three days. Zacatecans set flags at half-mast, tied black ribbons around their arms, and fired cannon salvos every fifteen minutes. The state government even authorized a funeral ceremony and the construction of a burial monument.[61] President González nevertheless ordered Zacatecas governor Jesús Aréchiga to modify the program: "Fulfilling the duty of patriotism, I have arranged for the federal treasury to assume all the necessary costs for the transfer, embalming, and funeral for the precious remains of General Jesús González Ortega. . . . [T]hey must rest beside the illustrious men of the Nation [in Mexico City]." The president enlisted Aréchiga, War Minister Treviño, Interior Minister Carlos Diez Gutiérrez, and Coahuila governor Evaristo Madero to hold a national funeral "of the best possible brilliance." Aréchiga promised to "open a new epoch in honoring great men."[62] Treviño ordered a brigade of soldiers to render military honors in Zacatecas and escort the body to Mexico City, where it was to be buried in the Rotonda de los Hombres Ilustres. Lost were the wishes of the González Ortega family. They originally declined the offer of a national burial but relented after private conversations with Governor Aréchiga. Meanwhile in Saltillo, Madero rendered honors to González Ortega and predicted that his remains would reach Zacatecas in one week.[63]

Something remarkable happened in Zacatecas when the carriage bearing González Ortega's coffin arrived at the city limits. A group of civilian residents detached the horses and pulled the vehicle through town on the strength of their own shoulders. While the newspapers in Zacatecas and Mexico City concluded that these citizens simply wanted to show their patriotism, the act represents what James C. Scott calls a "hidden transcript" that critiqued centralized power behind the public transcript of the official story.[64] Zacatecans acted in concert with the preemptive efforts of García de la Cadena to claim and retain the body for Zacatecas state and subvert federal authority. Without advanced notification to the Federal Army, the citizens altered the protocol of the military escort, pulling the carriage through the principal streets to the governor's palace and later reluctantly loading the coffin onto a train heading south. Since Mexico did not have a uniform rail system, the funeral train traveled slowly; stopped at railroad stations in León, Guanajuato, and Querétaro; and finally arrived one month after González Ortega's death.[65]

Through the use of visual symbols, lyings-in-state always highlighted the principal reasons for the national glorification of heroes. Over one hundred thousand citizens viewed González Ortega's body overnight at the Mining Palace from March 31 to April 1. Ironically, the chapel designer, Ramón Rodríguez Arrangoity, had served in the court of Emperor Maximilian. The chapel scene was clearly an homage to González Ortega's military career, rather than political persona. The architect hung black and white curtains behind the coffin to accentuate the symmetrically arranged flags, military trophies, rifles, sabers, cannons, and pyramids of cannonballs that surrounded the bier. Along with the stone columns of the palace's architecture, these items served as symbols of stability. The absence of items commonly placed for politicians, such as classical stone statuettes, tomes, and flora, discloses intentions to de-emphasize his roles as presidential contender, president of the Supreme Court, and legal successor of Juárez. At the center of the display sat the general's black and silver casket topped with the symbols of the division general: a plumed hat, sword, and cane. The presentation of national artifacts combined the sacred and the mundane. Items were kept at a distance from the crowd to suggest the eternal, but they belonged to that category of public property readily observable at the National Museum.[66]

Even in death, González Ortega rivaled Juárez, but his funeral procession was also a Napoleonic display of Porfirio Díaz's power. Díaz and Treviño organized the funeral march to reenact González Ortega's triumphal entry into Mexico City (1860) but scheduled the event to coincide with the anniversary of Díaz's capture of Puebla (April 2, 1867). Consequently, the procession was the "most imposing seen in this city since that of President Juárez."[67] Six caped and plumed black horses drew the hearse through a compact crowd. Old soldiers who had fought for González Ortega walked alongside, holding black cords tied to the casket. Several division generals led the cortege, which also

Figure 17. Lying-in-state of General Manuel S. Rivera. This photograph illustrates the combination of military themes (represented by trophies of war) and republican iconography (statues and floral crowns) found in Porfirian-era state funerals. Division General Mariano Escobedo, another high-ranking officer, and two infantrymen serve as honor guards. Photo courtesy of the Fototeca Instituto Nacional de Antropología e Historia, Pachuca.

incorporated service horses, carriages, and special tramcars. An immense crowd enjoyed what amounted to a festive military parade, as marching bands mixed martial hymns and funeral dirges with entertaining *polkas* and *danzas*.[68] Citizens watched Díaz, astride his battle horse, lead an army division on April 1 and read articles about his Puebla siege on April 2.[69] One newspaper reported: "The armed forces that provided the service attracted public attention for the ease with which they executed all their movements."[70] President González did not participate that day. He could not because he fought for the Conservatives under General Miguel Miramón. His conversion to liberalism postdated González Ortega's heralded military victories. Reportedly in bed with bronchitis, the president did not count himself among the exclusive fraternity of officers who marched in the procession and wept during Vicente Riva Palacio's funeral oration.[71]

After the funeral, a bitter struggle over national memory ensued. The conservative Catholic daily *La Voz de México* complained that people "did not go there to pray for the soul of the deceased, but to look for entertainment and satisfy their curiosity. We consider this profane."[72] Catholics chastised González Ortega as a self-proclaimed enemy of the Church. During the Reforma War, he had accused the clergy of using their pulpits to incite reaction, branded them hypocrites, and persecuted them mercilessly. Terrified priests christened him with a different nickname: "The Devil Preacher."[73] Funeral orator General José Montesinos remarked that González Ortega "broke the hard head of the Catholic clergy with his sword."[74]

Catholics passed judgment not only on González Ortega's anticlericalism but on the government agenda to manipulate memory of him. An anonymous writer in a Catholic weekly began a polemic over the "villainous attempt to deceive Zacatecanos." The editorial alleged that the opportunistic government sought to resuscitate a man who had been discarded years ago: "Liberalism is in mourning because of the death of one of its caudillos, Jesús González Ortega, who the same liberalism banned, nullified, and killed." Victimized by Liberal intrigues and "fearful of poison or the dagger," González Ortega took refuge in Saltillo. His very "executioners" now declared him a benemérito and held an elaborate funeral for him: "Perfidious friends sold him out, abandoned him, forgot him, and counted him among the dead while he was alive. . . . [N]ow dead, they count him among the living."[75] Following its denunciation of the government, the open letter disparaged González Ortega: "How many hospitals did he found? How many workshops did he establish? How many orphanages? What number of schools? How many colleges? Which houses of charity did he open and support for the benefit and advancement of the youth of the town?" The letter accused González Ortega of plundering the Hospital de San Juan de Dios, the Instituto Literario, libraries of the Colegio de Guadalupe, the Convent of San Francisco, and the baptismal font in which the children of Zacatecas were baptized. The author further admonished the Liberal general for promising prosperity, a return of the baptismal font in gold, and land redistribution. According to the writer, he instead gave Zacatecans prison chains, mock elections, the *ley fuga*, onerous taxes, and "the hateful draft tickets of the national guard." The heated editorial concluded: "Zacateca-nos the day of memory has arrived."[76]

Mexico City newspapers interpreted the letter as an assault on the nation and launched spiteful counterattacks. *El Monitor Republicano* retorted: "the eternal enemies of conscience and the Patria. . . . Barbarians in the midst of progress in the final third of the century of lights, carry their hatred beyond the tomb, pretending to destroy the glorious deeds of the hero of the reform and our independence with their favorite weapon, calumny."[77] *La Libertad* chastised it as "filthy anonymous libel" from those reactionary, intransigent men "who represent neither the ideas nor the sentiments of illustrious Catho-lics." According to *La Libertad*, such attacks on González Ortega's character highlighted President González's magnanimity in granting a former adversary absolution to accommodate the sympathies of the Mexican people.[78] Notwithstanding the ardor with which the Zacatecan letter attacked González Ortega, the Hospicio de Niños in Guadalupe de Zacatecas celebrated the memory of its founder on the fourteenth anniversary of his death in 1895. Officials inaugurated a $35,000 equestrian statue of the general on the avenue in Zacatecas that bore his name into perpetuity. Sculptor Jesús F. Contreras forged the four-ton monument in the workshops of the Fundición Artística Mexicana in Mexico City. During the Centennial of Mexican Independence in 1910, González Ortega was hailed as one of the great heroes of Mexico's "second independence." The juxtaposition of portraits of González Ortega and Porfirio Díaz on artful postcards invites historians to examine their professional relationship for a confluence of political styles.[79] Both were National Guardsmen, both served together during La Reforma, both opposed and pronounced against Juárez, and both renounced power (1862, 1880). Comparisons were not lost on the press.

What is striking about the funeral discourse is the candor of officials and the press toward all but one aspect of González Ortega's career. Orators and journalists did not efface memory of him as an anticleric or invent an explanation for his reclusive retirement. General Montesinos stated plainly that "González Ortega fled with his glory and his laurels to hide himself, sad and deceived, in the capital of Coahuila," where he "suffered a premature forgetting."[80] That the sitting president, Manuel González, once went to war against the Liberal stalwart was of little concern. Spokesmen retold the military histories of Calpulalpan and Puebla without hyperbole.[81] Yet the exception to full factual disclosure was the heated rivalry with Juárez. This would have contradicted official myths about Liberal unity and the Juárez hero cult, as well as reminded citizens that González Ortega, Porfirio Díaz, and Manuel González had all pronounced against Juárez at one time or another.[82] Instead, the regime portrayed González Ortega as a Cincinnatus who rose to defend his country and then laid down his arms in greater regard for national unity. The general became the first in a series of men idolized by the Porfirian state for renouncing power to preserve order. Hegemonic discourses have greater political purposes than upholding historical truths. The editors of *La Libertad* professed: "Before the pomp and austerity of this death, honorable men must take off their hats and show today's children and youths . . . how heroic countries conduct to their final resting place those who overcame, sacrificed their tranquility, interests, lives, and even their posthumous fame for the sake of the fatherland."[83] One Zacatecan never learned from González Ortega's example. Anti-reelectionist Trinidad García de la Cadena launched an unsuccessful rebellion against Díaz and was assassinated in 1886.

The Dead Render Services

In contrast to the González Ortega fanfare, which drew large crowds to bid farewell to a popular hero in a national event, the repatriation of former president Mariano Arista's remains resurrected an obscure president within an international context. During the churchyard closures of the 1880s, city workers stumbled upon the neglected tombs of many historical figures. The City Council worked with the national government to exhume their remains and rebury them in state funerals. Most Porfirian reburials took place in the 1890s and are the subject of chapter 6. However, the first period reburial for Arista is more instructive when examined in its historical context in 1881. It illustrates the power of state funerals as propaganda tools of dominant political elites. The unprecedented level of cooperation in government circles and international waters was out of proportion with Arista's historical significance until the regime gave Mexicans something to cheer about. It started in the pro-Díaz Liberal newspaper *La Libertad*, which printed an article entitled "The Dead Render Services." The editors claimed that state funerals strengthen fraternal relations between nations through, among other things, telegrams of condolence. They further argued that funerals advance the domestic political agendas of ill-fated martyrs themselves, since sympathetic successors implement the policies of the victim to defeat the very enemies responsible for their demise. This makes the dead powerful public servants.[84]

Arista clearly lacked the credentials of González Ortega. A *creole* from San Luís Potosí, he originally served the Spanish crown until joining Iturbide's Trigarante Army. Promoted to brigadier general, he fought the French during the Pastry War, marched with Santa Anna during the Texas revolt, and engaged the U.S. Army at the Battle of Palo Alto. After the war, Arista served in various cabinet positions until Congress named him president in 1851. He held the dubious distinction as the first chief executive to come to power peacefully since 1828, but his presidency lasted only one year. His attempts to reform the army, end corruption, and reduce the national debt provoked congressional opposition. His refusal to accept payments from the United States in recognition of Article 11 of the Treaty of Guadalupe Hidalgo won him a legion of admirers but one unfortunate adversary. Santa Anna forced his resignation in 1853. When Arista's supporters encouraged him to defend his reforms, he chose exile instead, living out his years in Seville and Lisbon. Destitute, he died on a Portuguese vessel en route to France in 1855.[85]

This is where the morbid details begin. Arista's heart was extracted, passed from associate to associate, and eventually delivered to Mexico; meanwhile, his cadaver was buried in the Eastern Cemetery of Lisbon. Learning of Arista's sad death, President Ignacio Comonfort declared him a *benemérito de la*

Patria (illustrious benefactor of the nation) in 1856, but the nation soon forgot Arista.[86] Twenty-five years later, the Porfirian regime resurrected him as a martyr of democratic institutions, a guardian of republican virtue, the personification of law, and the incarnation of patriotism.[87] Now cast in the mold of Juárez, the return of his remains was perceived as an act of historical vindication similar to the return of Napoleon's ashes. Rather than embroiling his country in another ill-fated civil war, Arista had stepped down from office voluntarily, having "chosen the punishment of leaving his bones in a foreign land."[88] Prominent Porfirian Liberals asserted that this was Arista's greatest deed, and on the eve of Porfirio's own waltz off the political stage![89] *La Libertad* stated: "He could well have kept himself in the presidential chair; but knowing that such conduct would be attributed to personal ambition, he made the greatest sacrifice rather than fuel civil war."[90] The story on Arista was immediately followed by, what else, election news.

Díaz ordered the repatriation at the end of his first term, but the funeral took place under González. After five years, Congress was finally granted a significant role in organizing a state event. In October 1880, the Portuguese family that had entombed Arista offered assistance to the Mexican Consulate in Lisbon. Díaz authorized Vice-Consul Luis Breton y Vedra, Foreign Relations Secretary Julio Zárate, and congressional deputies from Arista's native state of San Luis Potosí to repatriate the remains. Since Congress was concerned about expenses, Potosino deputy Francisco J. Bermúdez promised that Arista's remains would be returned "in a way commensurate with the sad state of the national treasury."[91]

In their congressional speeches, intellectuals drew comparisons from European history. Joaquín Alcalde noted what he believed resulted from such affairs:

> The first act of the Orleanist dynasty after the fall of Charles X was to . . . bring the remains of Napoleon from the Island of St. Helena in order to place them under the dome of the Invalides, and this deed which *has served the purpose of unifying many points of France, also brought great respect to this dynasty. Those who honor the dead, deserve the respect of the living.*[92]

Mexican politicians and intellectuals who received educations in Europe and the United States often drew historical parallels into their political speeches. Such comparisons carried authority in an age when Mexico sought to become a part of the modern transatlantic system. Arista and Napoleon held little in common, but proponents of the "ethical" or "teaching" state (*estado docente*) had overriding concerns of national legitimacy, unity, and reconciliation.

National legislators were also concerned with legality in September 1881. Congress declared the nation in mourning for three days once the remains touched Mexican soil, named a eulogist, chose the Rotonda de los Hombres Ilustres as the burial site, and ordered the construction of a monument.[93] But one year after Justo Sierra resolved to limit government participation in national commemorations, Félix Romero proposed to send congressional delegates to Veracruz to accompany the remains back to Mexico City. This violated laws dating from 1824, which prohibited congressmen "to attend, collectively or individually, a public function outside its palace." José S. Arteaga and Juan A. Mateos believed that Congress should enact, not attend ceremonies. Romero defended his proposal with an example from the French Revolution. When the Constitutional Assembly learned of the death of Benjamin Franklin, Mirabeau had urged France to declare fifteen days of mourning and render honors to the illustrious American. Romero argued: "What did Franklin, an American citizen, have to do with France and Mirabeau? Absolutely nothing; but that is how great men are honored." Poet-nationalist Guillermo Prieto brought unity to the forum. Arteaga was correct to uphold congressional rules since "the law has no heart," but "all men who love law should honor Arista." He suggested that Congress nullify the law, send a delegation to Veracruz, advise governors to observe days of public mourning in their states, and ask them to send state representatives to the capital for a national funeral. When President González authorized Congress to coordinate the funeral with the Interior and War ministries, public servants from all branches of government and officials from outlying states attended. These developments appeared to support an all-inclusive event, but they took shape as a bureaucratic monopoly. When the working-class newspaper *El Socialista* requested that the government invite former officers of the National Guard to honor Arista, González rejected it, reserving the duty exclusively for the professional army. Congressional deputies tried to locate the few survivors who served in Arista's administration. They found only two former treasury ministers, Manuel Payno and Guillermo Prieto.[94]

Mexico had ample time to prepare because the transatlantic voyage that repatriated Arista took over a month. Breton y Vedra verified the remains in Lisbon, and the Portuguese government sponsored a military ceremony. On August 18, the *El Oficio* conveyed the casket to Cádiz, Spain, where it was transferred to the postal steamship *Coruña* bound for Havana. After a naval ceremony in Cuba on September 19, the Spanish warship *Blasco de Garay* led a fleet of twenty-one ships to Mexico. Arista was the only Mexican honored with a transoceanic procession. At least one U.S. ship, the *City of Alexandria*, sailed with Spanish and Mexican vessels. The Mexican gunboat *La Libertad* met the fleet and escorted it into Veracruz harbor.[95]

The city of Veracruz and Ministry of War had prepared a hero's welcome for

Arista. Houses, public buildings, and plazas had been customarily decorated. Cannon salvos from the fortress of San Juan de Ulloa announced the arrival of the ships. All businesses closed their doors, and dockworkers were excused from their labors. Wearing their finest Sunday dress, Veracruzanos packed into the main plaza, but a health inspection delayed the disembarkation ceremony for eight hours. Many had already returned home when the casket was finally transported to the Municipal Palace.[96] War Minister Treviño had sent General Ignacio Revueltas to escort the remains to Mexico City. Revueltas had planned to hold a "dance and demonstration of joy" for the Spanish naval officers, but Treviño deemed this "inappropriate, given the circumstances, [and] liable to be ridiculed if the demonstrations were not mournful and extremely serious."[97] Treviño ordered Revueltas to invite the Spanish sailors to Mexico City, pay for their expenses, and treat his guests with honor befitting their military ranks.[98]

As Juvenal mentioned, thousands came to the Mining Palace to see the small wooden box containing Arista's remains, the martial decorations that encircled the ex-president, and the new electric lighting of the palatial facade. A foreign traveler recorded his impressions of October 6–7: "For the entire two days and two nights countless multitudes of people streamed up the staircase and round the corridors, gazing down upon the gorgeous and impressive scene below."[99] Referring to the palace, which headquartered the Ministry of Development, eulogist José Ceballos pronounced: "The temple of science is transformed into an altar of sincere patriotism, honor, and profound respect for the law."[100] Those who attended early on the first day saw Porfirio Díaz standing guard over the remains, alongside Generals Berriozábal, Pacheco, Pradillo, Sánchez Ochoa, Mejía, and Alatorre.[101] Just five years earlier Mejía, Lerdo's minister of war, and Alatorre, the *lerdista* commander at Tecoac, fought against Díaz. Now former enemies appeared together at a public event. Thousands waited in three-hour lines to witness living proof of national reconciliation.

By allowing the remains to lie-in-state for three days, the government delayed the funeral procession until a Saturday, ensuring greater attendance. Díaz and Treviño drew up the itinerary and established the order of march. Conspicuous for its impracticality, the procession took a circuitous route through the principal downtown streets. Rather than heading directly west and then on a southwestern trajectory from the Mining Palace to Dolores, mourners walked east to the Zócalo and wove their way back along Calle Plateros and San Francisco. The cortege extended for three city blocks, but the march was well regulated.[102] The procession was composed of public clerks, civil employees, army generals and high public officials, city councilmen, diplomats and secretaries of state, *jefes políticos* and military officers, the hearse, survivors, a military band, the presidential carriage, troops, and private carriages.[103] In Arista's funeral the hearse and presidential carriage were found at the rear of the march, just before the military escort. In contrast to the Ramírez funeral in 1879, when Díaz had reversed the processional order, González upheld the republican tradition of riding last behind forty horse-drawn streetcars. Strangely, no one reported seeing the president, only a closed carriage.

Funeral processions in the 1880s contained a heavy bureaucratic and military component but also incorporated "invited countrymen and those who wished to take part." Like the religious processions of Corpus Christi, all believers in the new civic religion could participate in this inclusive event. The government typically reserved a place for anyone to join at the end of the march, right before the military escort. This often resulted in thick, compact lines that extended for blocks. People clogged downtown arteries and then joined the procession. It was an informal way to measure popular sentiment. Urban workers and peasants who assembled in the city streets surely began as detached spectators, but there was promise of a future of self-representation, political equality, and fraternal solidarity with each enjoined march.

Such unguarded moments of popular nationalism never last. By 1889, funeral corteges articulated positivist social organization in physical space by highlighting vocational groups. More than just flow charts of government structure, it became de rigueur for corteges to incorporate up to forty specialized labor organizations and workers' associations, without improvised informal participation.[104] In this sense they resembled Mary Ryan's definition of an American parade as "a collective movement through the streets . . . with separate marching units, each representing a pre-established social identity."[105] If léperos, day laborers, or rural migrants did not belong to a workers' society, they were not recognized as contributors to Mexico's material development. Thousands of unrepresented people formed their social identities in reaction to those marchers representing "the nation." Other restrictions based on race, class, and especially gender applied. Women had no place in the tableau vivant of the procession. A man's life, retraced in the different marching sections, was apparently devoid of any female influence. Such gendered state events served to reinforce gender inequality, as the funeral became a site where male/female binaries and power differentials were clearly and publicly articulated.[106]

War Minister Treviño's reservations about marring a somber occasion with frivolous fetes for the Spaniards were no longer a concern after the funeral. The government honored the sailors with a splendid banquet at the Municipal Palace. Mexican officials and Spanish officers exchanged toasts in the great dining room lined with portraits of leaders from Hernán Cortés to Porfirio Díaz. Presenting himself as both diplomat and nationalist, Díaz toasted the Spanish army and Captain General Juan Prim, the Spanish liberal whom Mexicans admired for opposing European intervention in the 1860s. The banquet confirmed Mexico's friendly relations with its former metropole. After sailors dined, they attended an extravagant ball hosted by the Spanish Casino.[107]

Compared to Juárez and González Ortega, Mariano Arista was an uncelebrated figure until the government took extraordinary measures to restore national memory of him. Thereafter, the Ayuntamiento of Tacubaya sponsored a literary event in his honor. In 1887, public officials dedicated a plaque at the house where Arista once lived in Mexico City. The city of San Luis Potosí named both a district and a plaza after him. Italian sculptor Nicoll produced a bust of Arista in Rome and shipped it in time for Díaz to unveil it as a burial monument in the rotunda in 1901. Twenty years after the reburial, Antonio Ramos Pedrueza compared Arista to Aristides, another classical hero who stepped down from power rather than plunge his country into war. Such thematic continuity survived a generation after the state funeral that rescued Arista from historical oblivion.[108]

Like Díaz, González demonstrated a willingness to pardon enemies and reconcile Liberal factions. Despite increased foreign investment in land, commerce, and railroad development, his political opponents were not as compromising. Allegations that González used his office for his own self-enrichment, charges of corruption, and the reduction of bureaucratic salaries severely weakened his support base. In 1883, González overcirculated nickel coinage, deepening an economic recession that severely marred his presidency. His unpopular decision to recognize the English debt coupled with ugly divorce proceedings with his wife turned public opinion against him. His scandal-ridden term cleared the way for Díaz to return in 1884.[109]

For his part, Díaz served briefly as minister of development in the González cabinet before taking power as governor of Oaxaca. During the González interregnum, he remarried and spent his honeymoon in the United States, where he was championed in major cities. His young second wife, Carmen, was the eldest daughter of Manuel Romero Rubio, a leading lerdista who had returned from exile. The matrimonial union cemented a political alliance between adversarial factions exemplified by Díaz's appointment of Romero Rubio as minister of the interior and architect of the policy of conciliation. In 1885, when General Bernardo Reyes encountered an armed uprising in Nuevo León, Romero counseled him to "deploy a conciliatory policy and inspire trust in all men of worth from the opposition so they do not turn against the good of the State." Romero Rubio further directed Reyes to exercise prudence and diplomacy to attract them to the armed forces with guarantees and support so that they retire to their homes, preferring peace over violence and revolution.[110]

Díaz's second term (1884–88) was an amazing period of nationalistic fervor. For better and for worse, workers drove the final spikes on two rail lines that connected the nation to the United States. State governors who faced bankrupt treasuries nonetheless financed a splendid statue to Father Miguel Hidalgo at Dolores. In 1887, Díaz ceremonially unveiled the glorious monument to Cuauhtémoc, the last Aztec emperor, on the Paseo de la Reforma. Such symbolic acts provided Díaz with enough political capital literally to bury his enemy Sebastián Lerdo de Tejada, as well as reform the Constitution to allow for his indefinite reelection.

The Posthumous Return of Lerdo de Tejada: Judge. Jurisconsult. Justice. President?

Few events during the "Necesariato" provide a greater example of Díaz's policy of reconciliation than the state funeral of his archnemesis. After thirteen years of exile, Lerdo died in New York on April 21, 1889. The U.S. government supported the repatriation of his body to Mexico. Colonel Albert Zabriskie, an American reporter for the *Tucson Star*, accompanied the funeral train from El Paso to Mexico City and described the events of May 13–14:

> The obsequies of Lerdo de Tejada were grand and imposing. The body lay in state at the House of Representatives for two days. Immense crowds viewed the remains. Eulogies were produced on behalf of the different departments and then the remains were interred with great pomp. Amid the booming of cannon in front of the National Palace the solemn cortege proceeded along the main line of one of the street railroads.
>
> A magnificent funeral car conveyed the body and then came 32 cars containing relatives, friends and citizens. All the drivers of these cars were dressed in deep black with tall silk hats and a black rosette on the left side of each hat. They all wore white gloves. In the rear marched the military, consisting of Infantry, Cavalry and Artillery. Each Infantry battalion was preceded by a drum corps of 24 drummers.
>
> All the drums were encased in black, leaving only a space on top about the size of a pie plate for the drummers to strike. They marched along by the simple tap, tap, tap.
>
> Then came the infantry bands on foot, and the Cavalry bands mounted. The Cavalry buglers would sound the taps and retreat, and then the band would take up the echo and carry on the sad refrain. It was a most imposing spectacle, and well worthy of the occasion. . . . [Sebastian Lerdo de Tejada] will live in the annals of his country as one of her greatest sons.[111]

Zabriskie proved to be a better reporter than prophet. Lerdo was overshadowed by both Juárez and Díaz.[112] He nevertheless received the largest funeral since that of Juárez, ironically from the very general who overthrew him.

Sebastián was the younger brother of Miguel Lerdo de Tejada, author of the Reform Laws against corporate landholdings. A lawyer by training, Sebastián served as foreign affairs secretary, minister of justice, and congressman from 1857 to 1869. He was one of the *inmaculados* who accompanied Juárez to Paso del Norte during the French Intervention. As president of the Supreme Court, Lerdo legally succeeded Juárez after his death on July 18, 1872, and won reelection in October. He had gained control of the electoral machinery and defeated both Díaz and José María Iglesias in the presidential election of 1876. Iglesias annulled the elections and claimed the presidency for himself. Díaz pronounced the Revolution of Tuxtepec. Porfirista rebels defeated Lerdo and turned their rifles on Iglesias. Although Lerdo's family remained in Mexico City and Veracruz, he rejected the proposition of living in a country run by generals.[113]

Lerdo nevertheless "came back to life through death."[114] Manuel Romero Rubio, his former ally and now Díaz's father-in-law and interior minister, asked the Lerdo family for permission to return his body to Mexico City. In his letter of condolence, Romero Rubio emphasized that Díaz had initiated the demand for funeral honors and that the state would pay all transportation and funeral costs.[115] The family agreed without conditions. Romero Rubio then notified Mexican Ambassador to the U.S. Matías Romero and the New York consul, Juan Navarro, to have the body embalmed. Díaz ordered other former lerdistas, including General Mariano Escobedo and several high-ranking officers, to depart for New York and escort the cadaver to Mexico.[116] *Diario del Hogar* observed that any elegy made in Lerdo's honor "will be interpreted as a rapprochement among those who have survived on the Mexican political scene."[117]

To Mexicans, the U.S. government response testified to an emerging friendship. A U.S. Army brigade welcomed the Escobedo delegation and escorted the body by train from New York to the Pennsylvania Railroad Station in Jersey City. There, diplomats from eleven European and Latin American nations joined the Mexican dignitaries for a brief funeral ceremony. The casket was then placed in an elegant Pullman car that flew the Mexican flag. The railroad journey from New York to Mexico City underscored the international link. Mexican Americans in U.S. cities along the route said good-bye to Lerdo much as citizens had met Lincoln's funeral train in 1865. The steam-powered procession called attention to the progress of the Mexican railway network. Completed in 1884, the nearly two thousand kilometers of Mexican Central brought the coffin from Ciudad Juárez (Paso del Norte) to the Valley of Mexico. Romero Rubio ordered the train to stop for a half hour at each depot along the route so citizens could pay their last respects. On May 10, schoolchildren from Ciudad Juárez crossed the U.S.–Mexican border and marched with a military band alongside the locomotive as it slowly approached Mexican territory. When the train ground to a halt, schoolgirls placed wreaths by the casket and orators delivered speeches. The train then journeyed across Chihuahua, the largest state in the union. Whenever it reached a new station, local jefes políticos boarded and rode with the coffin. Major stops included Chihuahua City, Zacatecas, Aguascalientes, Encarnación, Silao, Irapuato, Celaya, Querétaro, and Tula.[118]

Lerdo's repatriation drew together the "imagined community" of the Mexican republic.[119] The railroad made possible the symbolic repetition of patriotic acts that encouraged state formation, centralization, and integration. The shared experience of officials and citizens honoring heroes in state capitals and towns along the line helped promote national memory and identity. At each stop, citizens who never met one another or never visited other capital cities now performed ceremonial acts together and could imagine others doing the same at the next depot and the stop after that. Political officials and regional elites recognized their jurisdictional limits more routinely than ever. Loose familiarity with local topography grew to greater knowledge of Mexican geography and a politically delimited terrain. Their obligations to the state and nation were carried out in a train ride from one city or district to another, where they manifested their respect for the limits placed on their authority by conferring responsibility for the coffin to another. These political rituals had eluded Mexico until the Porfiriato. Bureaucratic officials who personified the state disseminated claims to political legitimacy through such ceremonial obligations.

Although the government expected the body on the weekend, the train did not roll in until May 13, a Monday. The city suspended its normal routine. Freed from their daily labors, people walked not only toward the train depot and congressional building to get a glimpse of Lerdo but also to San Fernando Cemetery to view Juárez's memorial. Their tomb patronage proves that people never forgot the historical connection between the two men. Carriages and wagons could not pass through the congested streets. At the Buenavista train station, a crowd squeezed together and pushed in accordance with national custom. At the corner of San Andrés and Factor, surging masses impeded the movement of the tall hearse, and the interior minister called in the 21st Battalion and city police to provide crowd control.[120] Arriving at the Chamber of Deputies, General Escobedo announced that he had returned Lerdo's body to fulfill the wishes of the nation. Romero Rubio remarked that the government had risen above past differences to honor the "illustrious patriot."[121] When rain fell at night, citizens waiting to see Lerdo's body shoved one another and fell victim to *rateros*. At dawn, people still stood in line, for rumor had it that the lying-in-state was the most spectacular ever seen.[122]

Congressman Ignacio Bejarano and an army of laborers had transformed the Chamber of Deputies into an altar for patriotic worship. Workers hung three thousand yards of fine black draperies to serve as a theatrical backdrop for the scene. At center stage, the coffin sat on an inclined plane for easy viewing. Decorators blanketed the vestibule with an improvised flower garden and wired over 150 light bulbs and thirty candelabras to cast brilliant light into every corner. Strategically placed mirrors reflected the lights to heavenly effect. In the streets outside the congressional building, functionaries hung flags, black crepe, white lace, and tricolored ribbon and bunting. Lining the processional route were huge pedestals surmounted by burning torches that emitted a green glow and the scent of rich perfumes.[123]

Entire delegations of mutualist societies and workers' associations were prohibited from entering the congressional building. Frustrated over their slim chances of viewing the body at a decent hour, members arranged their own gatherings throughout the city. In these *veladas fúnebres* workers remembered Lerdo's refinement, respect, deference, and gratitude toward the workingmen and -women of Mexico. Veterans of the Society of Tailors told a reporter from *El Siglo XIX* that President Lerdo had attended their anniversary ceremony, intermingled with workers, and offered his words of encouragement: "He enjoyed lunch with them and interacted with them without pretense. He shared the cigarettes that he smoked." Lerdo had toasted the workers many times, affirming with each raised glass his support for democratic ideals. The textile workers had applauded joyously because they sensed sincerity in his words. They also recalled that Lerdo donated money to various mutual aid societies and always generously returned favors. Working-class memory of Lerdo had survived, and his funeral threatened to subvert authority when popular memory conflicted with official versions.[124]

These hastily arranged wakes in honor of Lerdo provide a lucid example of a "hidden transcript," or political and cultural hegemony from below.[125] Although the regime established the official forum, procedures, and means to honor Lerdo as a great statesman, workers operated within this context and organized memorials of their own outside the state's formal surveillance. Rather than force their way into the Chamber of Deputies or demonstrate in the streets, mutual associations acted within a common moral and cultural framework that recognized power differentials, even as they contested or accepted as legitimate their exclusion from the official event. Workers replicated in miniature the prescribed form of expression (the *velada*) in a different setting, complementing the goals of the state; however, the style and content of their expression resisted state domination.[126] Why this specific case conflicts with official discourse is found in both the language workers used to remember Lerdo and the fact of its publication as testimonials in the independent press. The workers' repertoire of narrative example and personal anecdote—so common in oral traditions—depicted a generous and warm Lerdo that contradicted the cerebral shell of a man that the state promoted.[127] As we shall see, the most deviant discourse was their reference to Lerdo as *president* of Mexico.

For with one exception, official speeches delivered between Lerdo's death on April 21 and his burial on May 14 deliberately omitted his role as constitutional president.[128] In Congress, Guillermo Prieto spoke of the "preeminent jurisconsult." At the funeral ceremony, Genaro Raigosa recounted Lerdo's services during the darkest hours and described him as an "incorruptible patriot and inveterate foe of imperialism." Joaquín Casasus traced Sebastián's support of anticlerical reforms and his involvement in the Wyke-Zamacona Treaty. Again, Lerdo's legacy ended with the restoration of the republic in 1867. Manuel Lozano stressed his role as president of the Supreme Court. At the cemetery, Alfredo Chavero again passed over Lerdo's presidency, while Agustín Verdugo focused exclusively on his legal expertise.[129]

The Porfirian state substituted Lerdo the judge for Lerdo the president in the selective use of public space and statuary. In 1876, Díaz had campaigned against Lerdo with the slogan "effective suffrage and no reelection." In 1889, elections were still a farce, Díaz had just been reelected for his third term, and the Constitution of 1857 was all but dismantled.[130] Rather than remind citizens of old campaign promises, the regime ruled out the National Palace in favor of the congressional chamber for the lying-in-state. Even Lerdo's burial monument in the Rotonda de los Hombres Ilustres stressed his career as lawyer, juarista legislator, and Supreme Court justice. A lifelike statue of Lerdo is surrounded by four allegorical statues representing Justice, Law, Strength, and Patriotism. It embodies in marble the crafted words of Porfirian eulogizers with very selective memories.[131]

One funeral oration in the Chamber of Deputies did address the Lerdo presidency. As usual, the irrepressible iconoclast Francisco Bulnes took it upon himself to "express the new relationship between the motherland, its history and one of its favorite sons." Despite his authority, Lerdo never spilled his blood in defense of the Patria, never dominated public opinion, and did not start the Reform. Bulnes asserted that he fell from power for ignoring the welfare of poor citizens:

> Lerdo placed the Constitution and the Reform laws equally high but the tattered rags never fell from our bodies and the tables continued to be empty! . . . He had only two choices: to succumb to a dictatorial act or collapse with his era! He preferred to submit to democracy. The cannon fire of Tecoac called 200,000 workers to

lay 10,000 kilometers of railway lines. Bread began to be the inseparable companion of peace.[132]

The funeral oration provoked an astonishing response. Every period was interrupted by deafening applause in what some consider the polemicist's best speech.[133] It glorified both Lerdo and Díaz. Romero Rubio orchestrated the entire event, but Díaz felt it politically unjustifiable to attend. The ruling elite's euphoric reaction represented the strongest mandate for the absent president. Workers could not challenge blatantly false statements, such as Lerdo ignoring public welfare and submitting to democracy. Like González Ortega, Lerdo was portrayed as a principled politician who selflessly stepped down and enabled Díaz to bring peace, democracy, and bread.

In preparation for the gigantic procession of May 14, *gendarmes* formed a strong cordon intended to hold back "crowds of people such as are seen only on great national holidays like the 16th of September and the 5th of May."[134] Despite some plebian excesses, public security was well organized, and no incidents disturbed the occasion. The cortege formed at the corner of Factor and Santa Clara streets. Six black horses pulled the towering hearse. Men representing workers' societies flanked the hearse and carried the colorful standards of their associations. A platoon of mounted policemen and forty-five curtained trams proceeded slowly up Calle Tacuba, crossed Empedrillo to Constitution Plaza, and moved on to Refugio, Coliseo, Independencia, and the Paseo de la Reforma to Dolores. Former lerdista officer Sóstenes Rocha, whom Díaz had just promoted to division general, led the army division. It took the funeral procession one hour to pass any given point. There was an end to the procession but no end to the crowd. Citizens lined the route from the Zócalo to the Paseo de la Reforma. Pedestrians followed the streetcars up the long hill to the cemetery. Over five thousand attended the burial ceremony at the rotunda.[135]

After the official event, students of national schools gathered in the Teatro Nacional. Authorities approved their literary program in advance, but the historical allusions in one of the poems were lost on the government censor. Under state surveillance, the evening proceeded without incident, until shouts were heard for "González" to speak. The young Gabriel González Mier took center stage and read a poem entitled "Ode to Athens." The poet called upon "Mother Athens" to awaken from her slumber and remember one of the last "giants of patriotism." González Mier referred to Lerdo's lifeless body as "covered in crepe/plundered, stripped of words/greatness, splendor and glory." He assured listeners that "the imposing silence speaks loudly of this death" and implored Mother Athens to revive her faith and mission, break the chains of oppression, and cast out "Xerxes." The *pueblo*, he predicted, will mobilize and end his tyranny. In a code of classical references González Mier exalted Lerdo and ridiculed Díaz (Xerxes) for disgracing the Patria. Before he could finish, police stormed the podium. Surrounded by a protective wall of students, the orator escaped arrest, but the police detained the poem's coauthors, Joaquin Clausell, Inés Vásquez, and Julio Posada, and imprisoned Tomás Cote on charges of inciting rebellion.[136] Porfirian reconciliation had its limits; freedom of expression extended only to those invested in the Reform. Political dissent that had been tolerated in the early 1880s was increasingly prohibited in 1889. Jilted at the public altar, workers and students remembered Lerdo differently in their own evening gatherings. Although they operated within a common discursive framework endorsed by the state, the discourse itself contested state authority.[137]

While the Tuxtepec Revolt was short-lived and the Díaz regime was hardly revolutionary, the subsequent decade of Porfirian reform altered the relationship between the state and the people. Prior to 1890, the regime scarcely resembled a dictatorship, so much as the distressed republic that Juárez and Reforma Liberals restored.[138] Funerals showed a high level of popular participation in the political culture of the state, generally free and open public discourse, and an energetic national polity in search of its place in the world. As the primary agent in promoting national identity and state formation, the Porfirian government adopted a directive role much like its predecessor. The regime's growing monopoly on rites of commemoration reflected its greater purpose to rule by mediated consent, rather than the democratic process.

State funerals therefore reflected the accomplishments and shortcomings of the Porfirian state. On one hand, they helped bring order and promote national unity. On the other, they sowed deep concerns about an increasingly centralized authoritarian regime. Díaz convinced citizens and foreign observers that he was the rightful heir of Liberal republicanism rather than the latest exemplar of militarism. By sponsoring the solemn burials of former juaristas and lerdistas, his government repeatedly declared its ideological continuity with previous Liberal regimes. Citizens came to understand his claim to legitimacy through state events that encouraged their participation. Díaz's reelection in 1888 culminated over thirty years of struggle: ten years to expel foreign invaders (1857–67), ten years to dispatch domestic rivals (1867–77), and ten years to reconcile with all other opposition (1877–87). Since he devoted half his life to coming to power, he would never again relinquish it.[139]

Funerals were unmatched as political rites of reconciliation. From death to eulogy and burial, the public dialogue of a man's life and legacy was shorn of divisive controversy. As hegemonic political discourses, funerals smoothed out the rough edges of contentious history to harmonize realities in the present. The heroes selected for national burials all passed a litmus test of sorts:

Could the subject be portrayed as a man who sacrificed personal ambition to ensure national unity? Indeed, men who vociferously represented different ideological factions in life—Ramírez, Barreda, González Ortega, Arista, and Lerdo—were forced into a homogeneous mold after their deaths. The state hailed their timely renunciations of power and deployed their dead bodies to promote an enduring myth of Liberal unity and reconcile with a troubled past. Most evidence suggests that common people embraced state funerals, even if their subjective reasons for doing so varied individually. Officials arranged funeral programs, but commoners created the festival atmosphere, enjoyed the music, waited hours in line, and shoved their way into spectacular chapels. They pulled hearses through the streets of Zacatecas and joined the grand processions of Mexico City. Many walked the long route uphill to Dolores and visited the tombs of heroes. Citizens saw division generals in person, read stories about heroic remains crossing the ocean, and heard tales of coffins conducted by railroad from Veracruz or New York to Mexico City. They imagined the journey over national territory while the international community rendered homage to their leaders. State funerals honored great men on unscheduled and unforeseen dates. Mobilizing the nation for an extravagant burial within forty-eight hours made state funerals impulsive outpourings of grief and sometimes causes célèbres.[140]

Yet the contours of the authoritarian republic became visible in 1889. Festival organizers aim for spontaneity but install so many precautionary restraints that they always prohibit some from joining the community.[141] In Mexico, significant exclusions of light industrial workers, soldiers of the National Guard, students, day laborers, and above all, women fostered the formation of distinct identities and alternative memories. Díaz and González abided no challengers. When state control over discourse broke down, it resorted to surveillance, censorship, and other coercive means. The Liberal and official press attacked Catholic naysayers who contradicted state propaganda. President González denied the request of *El Socialista* for former National Guardsmen to participate in the Arista funeral. The Porfirian regime barred delegations of workers from attending the official funeral for Lerdo in the Chamber of Deputies. Students who tricked the government censor were summarily punished. Over time, minor factual omissions turned into blatant falsehoods. The state hosted funerals of reconciliation to heal old wounds but inflicted new injuries in the process. On May 10, 1890, a year after Lerdo's funeral, Congress ratified a constitutional amendment allowing successive reelection of the president and state governors. It was at this point in the era that Díaz crossed the line from reelectable president to interminable dictator. Operating beneath a veneer of constitutionality, Díaz had forged a durable hegemonic state and brought unprecedented stability to Mexico.

Figure 18. José Guadalupe Posada's *Storybook Illustrations of 5 de Mayo*. From Roberto Berdecio and Stanley Applebaum, eds., *Posada's Popular Mexican Prints* (New York: Dover Publications, 1972).

Reviving the Dead 3

Holiday Commemorations in Porfirian Mexico

The firing has begun! People come running up the street. The Indians are hurrying back to their villages in double-quick trot. As we are not in the centre of the city, our position for the present is very safe, all the cannon being directed towards the palace. All the streets near the square are planted with cannon, and it is pretended that the revolutionary party are giving arms to the léperos. The cannon roaring now. All along the street people are standing on the balconies, looking anxiously in the direction of the palace, or collected in groups before the doors, and the azoteas, which are out of the line of fire, are covered with men. They are ringing the tocsin—things seem to be getting serious.

—FRANCES CALDERÓN DE LA BARCA, *LIFE IN MEXICO* (1840)

The firing of cannon yesterday morning, announced the dawn of the Fifteenth of September and aroused the sleeping city to . . . the 82nd anniversary of the Nation's Birth.

. . . [T]he civic procession, which accompanied by military bands and bearing lighted torches, marched through Avenida Juárez, San Francisco, Plateros and Mercaderes streets until it arrived in front of the National Palace. . . .

Precisely at 11 o'clock President Díaz appeared upon the central second story balcony under the illuminated portrait of Hidalgo beneath the clock, and repeated the "grito" or cry for liberty given forth by the patriotic Cura de Dolores late at night September 15, 1810. At this moment, the azoteas of the buildings surrounding the plaza were illuminated with Bengal lights, and groups of firemen produced similar illuminations all over the Zocalo. At the same time sky-rockets, bombs, the playing of the National Hymn by the bands and the ringing of the bells, announced that the Mexican people were celebrating . . . their

Independence Day. Fully 20,000 people were present in the plaza, and the uproar at 11 o'clock was deafening.

—*TWO REPUBLICS*, 16 SEPTEMBER 1892

R EADING NINETEENTH-CENTURY accounts of Mexican life, one is struck by the similarity between holiday celebrations and the palace coup. Frances Calderón's report of an actual revolt resembled descriptions of Independence Day and Cinco de Mayo celebrations. The comparison goes beyond the disruption of everyday time and space. Holidays heightened spirits, intensified behaviors, and temporarily collapsed social hierarchies. Every September 16 and May 5, thunderous cannon awoke citizens at daybreak and continued at half-hour intervals. Church bells chimed, and buglers sounded their instruments. Soldiers grabbed rifles, left their barracks, formed columns at the citadel, and marched to military reviews, artillery demonstrations, and war games on the Anzures Plains. Detachments of *gendarmes* galloped on horseback with drawn sabers, while the *rurales* in distinctive *charro* outfits rode fit horses that chipped the cobblestone beneath them. The great generals appeared in full dress uniform at the head of the mobilized army, commencing an exhibition of martial force as horses pulled artillery and ammunition through the main arteries of the city. Excited citizens poured onto balconies and rooftops and into streets, their eyes directed toward the National Palace. There, the *jefe supremo* occupied the central balcony, signifying his control of palace, city, and nation.[1]

Porfirian holiday celebrations acted as historical reenactments of the war-torn Mexico of yesteryear. Porfirio Díaz did not create the republican calendar of civic festivals, which evolved alongside the ideological genesis, struggle, and triumph of liberalism. Instead, he codified the calendar, added holidays to it, and placed military parades, memorial services, and commemorations at the center of every holiday program. Dramatizing rituals of war and reenacting the historical acts of great men enabled the regime to present a favorable interpretation of history to the Mexican people. Through *fiestas cívicas*, the state also re-created the nation and reconstituted the republic at consistent intervals throughout the year. Every holiday, President Díaz marched and rode at the head of parades. He listened to memorial speeches and national hymns. He decorated war veterans and dedicated wreaths at the tombs of the illustrious dead. Public orations and the inaugurations of monuments heightened citizen awareness of the terrible sacrifices that had been made to preserve nationhood. These performances provoked a defensive nationalism from audiences that reflected the paradoxical marriage between anticolonial sentiment and the modern neocolonial state.[2]

Hence all Porfirian holiday commemorations were political *acts* in almost

Figure 19. *Rurales* with drawn swords riding in formation during a Porfirian-era holiday parade. Photo courtesy of the Nettie Lee Benson Latin American Library, University of Texas, Austin.

every meaning of the word. They belonged to that species of government-led performance event that could be judged as patriotic transaction or false pretense. Holiday programs complemented the enormous state production of "knowledge" that had specific uses for those in power. As examined in the previous chapter, the state reconstructed historical figures to possess characteristics and goals similar to those of the modernizing state. On holidays, state historians linked and likened Díaz to national heroes he never knew, depicted him as a loyal associate of heroes he contested, and portrayed him as the natural product of a preordained past. At some ceremonial events, Díaz himself became a surrogate for Hidalgo, Morelos, Juárez, and Zaragoza. Commemorative festivals collapsed past and present, uniting political officials with national heroes of the immemorial Patria. The combination of national myths and creative interpretation provided a foundation of historical knowledge upon which the modern nation-state rested. Díaz's control over this mythico-historical discourse for thirty Independence Days and thirty Cinco de Mayo holidays (1877–1910) stressed a single incontrovertible fact: after his own revolution, Díaz rendered war a thing of the past. His era gave historians good reason to use a Latin term commonly attributed to stable historical epochs, the *pax Porfiriana*.

This chapter does not provide a comprehensive history of Porfirian-era holidays. Citizens pursued many forms of holiday entertainment. An entire volume could be written about Mexican *verbenas* (street parties), *zarzuelas* (musicals), *jaripeos* (rodeo-like exhibitions of lassoing and bull riding), circus performances, flower wars, and other forms of popular amusement. Much of the festivities took place in the precincts and suburbs rather than downtown. To draw citizens to the city center and enliven the festival atmosphere, Mexico City officials often hired performers and granted booth licenses to food vendors. But they also frowned upon frivolities that undermined state objectives. Acrobats and clowns were prohibited from performing in the Zócalo and Alameda. Díaz banned bullfights in the Federal District. The City Council even denied the request of Joaquín de la Cantoya y Rico to ascend in a hot-air balloon on Cinco de Mayo (1885) because the stuntman suffered epileptic seizures and an embarrassing riot had ensued when his aerostatic lift-off failed on Díaz's birthday in 1878.[3] This chapter instead examines state narratives of power and progress during the most popular holiday events: the Gritos de Dolores, military parades, civic processions, and memorial services for Zaragoza and Juárez. Civic festivals were occasions when the state delved into national origins and presented its own genealogical views of itself.[4] Official commemorations of the national dead also cemented the imagined community of Mexicans. Political legitimacy and authority were won not through democratic processes, well-developed political institutions, and free elections but through organized civic parades, popular processions, and mass gatherings that passed as informal plebiscites for the state.

Simulacra and Surrogation on Independence Day

The confluence of past and present was most pronounced on Independence Day, a holiday that the Porfirian government took great pains to revitalize after a half century of ambivalence. In the decade prior to Díaz, Cinco de Mayo drew greater crowds for understandable reasons. National memory of the Mexican victory over the French at Puebla on May 5, 1862, remained strong. In addition, the republican holiday was never subjected to the calendrical hopscotch that Conservatives and Liberals had played with Independence Day. During the First Empire, Congress had decreed September 27, the day Agustín de Iturbide entered Mexico City in 1821, as the moment when Mexico won its independence from Spain. After Iturbide abdicated, republicans transferred the holiday to the date Father Miguel Hidalgo y Costilla issued the famous Grito de Dolores, the Cry for Independence, on September 16, 1810. Historical narratives since Carlos María de Bustamante's *Cuadro histórico de la revolución mexicana* depicted an integral independence movement that began with the heroic achievements of Hidalgo, Ignacio Allende, and José María Morelos. Even so, Liberals at mid-century such as José María

Luís Mora and Lorenzo de Zavala never chose between Hidalgo and Iturbide as founding father of the nation. Independence Day celebrations lost prestige after Mexico's humiliating defeat by the United States. Emperor Maximilian duly recognized September 16, but celebrations lacked popular participation until Benito Juárez revitalized them in 1867.[5]

The shift of Independence Day from the date of achievement back to the day it began implied to citizens that Hidalgo's revolution continued and that the nation must remember and preserve its independence into the infinite future.[6] The change to date of origin parallels commemorative trends in the United States and France, which celebrate independence on the days that the revolutions were initiated not consummated.[7] Even so, the United States did not officially recognize July 4 as its Independence Day until its first centennial in 1876, and France did not announce the first official anniversary of Bastille Day until 1880. Republics such as Mexico, which withstood repeated challenges to their very existence, were compelled to reflect upon what their original independence meant throughout the nineteenth century. No wonder that protecting national sovereignty was the key message of Mexican Independence Day speeches. Impressively enough, Liberal republicans aligned the start of the political year with Hidalgo's rebellion. Díaz convened the first session of Congress annually on September 16. This had propaganda value since newspapers published the president's State of the Union message alongside the indispensable front-page portraits of Díaz and Hidalgo. Recasting Independence Day as the premier *fiesta patriótica* necessitated reinvention of national origins and rehabilitation of Hidalgo and other insurgents to make their sacrifices relevant to modern life. Accordingly, the government simultaneously inaugurated historical statues and new buildings every September 16.[8] Like their original acts, festivals captured the exhilarating sense of beginning anew as well as the intoxicating spirit of innovation.[9] So followed street nomenclature. By 1908, downtown streets that had different names with every new block were now lengthy thoroughfares called Calle de la Independencia and Avenida del 16 de Septiembre.

Díaz restored Independence Day as the leading national holiday for self-serving reasons as well. The president enjoyed the great historical fortune of celebrating his birthday and saint's day (September 15) in conjunction with the nation's own (September 16).[10] Whether genuine coincidence or astute temporal positioning, the regime capitalized on it as if God planned it that way. From Paris, Ambassador Gustavo Baz informed Díaz that Mexican and French functionaries celebrated September 15 as a double anniversary.[11] In Baja California, the *jefe político*, Rafael García Martínez, added a banquet in honor of Díaz's birthday to the September program in compliance with such a request from the minister of development.[12] The celebration of the dictator's birthday was thus inextricably intertwined with the commemoration of national heroes. In 1891, Félix Romero offered this birthday toast to Díaz: "[We] congratulate not only the warrior but the able administrator, whose name, in conjunction with those of Hidalgo and Juárez, signifies victory, patriotism and the integrity of our national territory."[13] Like Hidalgo and Juárez, Díaz was the "living personi-fication of La Patria," a compliment offered during the September holidays.[14] The Círculo de Amigos del Sr. General Porfirio Díaz elected officers whose sole responsibility was to celebrate his birthday in a way that compared Díaz to the forefathers.[15] Díaz reciprocated by decorating and promoting his officers on September 15 so that their date of promotion to brigadier or division general and Díaz's birth date were one and the same.[16] In this way, the date itself signi-fied not just Díaz's birthday but a symbolic temporal union between men.

The fact that independent Mexico was only nine years older than its dicta-tor reinforced Díaz's permanence, and government officials understood that to memorialize Hidalgo was to promote themselves. Commemorations rein-forced the public's acceptance of the dictator, who in turn extended politi-cal favors to his loyal subordinates. One only has to read the reports of jefes políticos and high-ranking military officers to understand how deliberately the September holidays were used to insinuate Díaz into public commemora-tions. In Chihuahua City, General Juan Hernández dedicated the month of September 1895 to memorializing the exploits not of the Independence Heroes but of Díaz and his loyal porfiristas. "The fiestas we prepared in your honor," he began, "included fireworks with magnificent illumination of a giant portrait of General Díaz," a civic march to the Plaza de la Constitución, concerts, and war games that simulated the assaults on Puebla and Querétaro in 1867. "Reviewing my troops," Hernandez wrote, "I permitted myself to speak on your behalf and recount your glorious achievements of directing our national forces to recap-ture the beloved soil of our Patria."[17] On September 19, Hernández invited jour-nalists of the newspaper El Progreso to report on the ceremony he organized at the tomb of "unforgettable" porfirista general Donato Guerra. "It seemed like every social class manifested their condolences" for the general killed in battle during the Tuxtepec uprising. It was "the spontaneity of the Pueblo Chihua-huense that provides evidence of their sympathy for the acts of the Supreme Government . . . to honor patriots." Hernandez thanked Díaz for sending the artillery battery, "which rendered solemnity to the funeral honors."[18]

At times, programs for the dictator's birthday rivaled the splendor of Sep-tember 16, even if events did not go as planned. Adoring followers held elabo-rate banquets and expensive fireworks displays for Díaz. Small fortunes went up in smoke on September 15. In the words of General Bernardo Reyes, Don Porfirio's birthday "was a grand hymn of congratulations sung in all parts of the Republic."[19] In 1899, residents were treated to a magnificent parade arranged for Porfirio's sixty-ninth birthday. Díaz rode from the Paseo de la Reforma into town, passing through triumphal arches and lines of rurales. Confetti and flowers rained down upon his open coupe, while trumpeters announced his arrival at the National Palace. Díaz, scores of officials, diplomats, and foreign capitalists watched a convoy of parade floats devoted to Mexican modernity pass before them, seemingly without a hitch. The true story of the Porfirian dictatorship was hidden from view in the allegorical floats that never made it. The float representing the national schools got entangled with electric lines. The wheels of the infantry's float became submerged up to their hubs in enormous potholes in the streets. Roman legions could not have budged the cavalry's titanic float. And the float representing the grocers' association collapsed under its own excessive weight of food and wine and was looted by spectators. In contrast to the polished illusion at the National Palace stood a capital city and its parade floats in need of fine-tuning.[20]

Since Díaz descended from the Liberal republican bloodline, he carried forth its ceremonial traditions. Rather than signal a sharp break with the past, he enhanced Independence Day programs gradually to maintain historical continuity, promote national reconciliation, and transfer citizen allegiances from the Church to the state. He also democratized political rituals such as the famous Grito de Dolores to garner popular support. Strictly speaking, the Grito ceremony was not a Porfirian innovation, but it acquired its modern form and function as an "invented tradition" under Díaz. Modern states in Europe, for example, used symbolic state rituals to inculcate values and prescribe behaviors through repetition and claims of continuity with the past, even though the rituals were in fact of recent origin. Manufactured traditions multiplied during eras of rapid transformation and mass politics (1870–1914), when political elites needed new devices to rule.[21]

Consistent with other nations in the transatlantic world, the Porfirian regime promoted the Grito as a tradition with primordial origins. The original historical act happened sometime between midnight and dawn on the morning of September 16, 1810. Informed that the royal government knew of his conspiracy to launch a revolt, Father Hidalgo hurried to his parish in the village of Dolores, Guanajuato, rang the bell that called the village to mass, and with a *grito* or "cry" for independence incited villagers to join his revolution against Spain.[22] From 1867 to 1886, official ceremonies of September 15 resembled literary events. Programs that included music, patriotic speeches, and poetry readings culminated at 11:00 p.m., when President Juárez or Lerdo delivered the Grito in imitation of Hidalgo and waved the flag before a select gathering in the National Theater. While the president cheered before restricted audiences, citizens ambled through the streets shouting, "Viva México!" (Long Live Mexico!). By the early 1880s, the ceremony had already become quasi-democratic.

In 1883, when President González delivered the Grito, people in the streets outside the theater heard the audience within echo the president and spontaneously responded with *vivas* of their own. This came at a time when thirty thousand tourists from exterior states and foreign nations had flocked to the capital for the national festivities.[23]

The historical reenactment moved outdoors and took on its popular democratic character during Díaz's second term. In 1887, City Councilman Guillermo Valleto suggested that the government transfer the ceremony from the exclusive venue of the National Theater to the Zócalo (Constitution Plaza). The historic central plaza is the largest public gathering place in the capital and the sacred heart of the republic. It is framed by grand symbols of authority, including the National Palace, Municipal Palace, and National Cathedral. When Díaz agreed, city employees transformed the plaza into a huge stage for a national theatrical drama. A colossal painting of Hidalgo was unveiled in front of the National Palace. Workers draped the entrance of the cathedral with an enormous Mexican flag. Tricolored lights and bunting, triumphal arches, and flags appeared in all public areas.[24] On the night of the 15th, any citizen willing to bear a torch met at the entrance of the Paseo de la Reforma to enjoin a gigantic torchlight procession through the city to the new festival ground. This solemn reenactment of the masses flocking to Hidalgo's cry for independence ended beneath the National Palace's central balcony and the illuminated bell towers of the National Cathedral.[25]

What came next was performed annually by President Díaz for twenty-four consecutive years (1887–1910). The ten acres of Constitution Plaza became a teeming mass of humanity. At 11:00 p.m., ten thousand lights flashed on and Díaz waved the Mexican flag before the people. Díaz then called out *his version* of Hidalgo's war cry: "Mexicanos! Viva la Independencia! Viva la República!" The modern state had no use for Hidalgo's original curse, "Death to the Spaniards and Bad Government!" Moments later, trumpets, drums, cannon fire, bells, and fireworks seized the senses; thousands milled around the plaza shouting patriotic slogans, professing national loyalty, and raising bloody hell. Slowly they filed into the adjoining streets with whistles, horns, flags, and liquor bottles in their hands. Citizens shouted, "Viva el Cura Hidalgo!" and, "Viva el Presidente!" The ceremony reinforced Mexican identity and provoked anticolonial nationalism, illustrated by the shouting of "Mueras" (Death to) to Spaniards and other foreigners. For many celebrants, holidays were less a time to celebrate Mexican nationhood than an excuse to vent their frustration with Europeans and *norteamericanos*. The national press always lamented the destruction of Spanish-owned property in September, but any unlucky soul could be victimized.[26] In 1901, an unfortunate *pelado* committed the fatal error of shouting "Muera México!" and was promptly stabbed to death.[27]

The Grito de Dolores ceremony incited the masses in ways that violated the sensibilities of the very state-builders who invented it. The Hispanophobia, anti-American sentiment, and violence against foreigners and foreign-owned businesses manifested on Independence Day place in relief a central contradiction in Porfirian nationalism. The whole argument for sovereignty from foreign powers was undermined by a state whose goal was never to restore Indian Mexico so much as modernize the motherland through European and U.S. investment.[28] Doubly troublesome was the fact that foreign capital investors and a small *creole* business class profited most from the national economy just as Mexican national identity began to coalesce. It seems entirely consistent with popular historical memory for the underclasses not to be enamored with the foreign presence in Mexico and to express their frustrations with the neocolonial arrangement by casually destroying the most visible foreign property on Independence Day. As representational behavior, were these not reenactments of the Hidalgo phase of the Independence Wars? The annual reproduction of Hidalgo's rebellion in the Zócalo every September 16 created a "habitus," or socially structured space that motivated negative social behaviors based on popular perceptions of Hidalgo's insurgency.[29] The relative decline of crimes that specifically targeted foreigners on Independence Day from 1888 to 1910 illustrates the state's success in reconstructing a more convenient Hidalgo and authenticating the "national" rather than the anti-imperialist aspects of the holiday.[30]

To this end, Porfirian officials focused on acquiring more unifying symbols of Hidalgo's insurgency. In 1896, a presidential election year, the federal government further authenticated the Grito by transferring the very bell that Hidalgo rang from Dolores to Mexico City. Interior Minister Manuel González Cosío commissioned police investigator Gabriel Villanueva to determine if the bell in the west tower of the parish church of Dolores was the one Hidalgo sounded on the morning of September 16, 1810. Fearing government appropriation, the diocese of Guanajuato and Dolores residents issued false reports that the real Independence Bell had been recast into cannon long ago. But Villanueva's study of the west tower bell confirmed its authenticity. Satisfied, Díaz sent General Sóstenes Rocha with a light cavalry company and a team of engineers to remove the bell safely and escort it back to the Federal District.[31] A Guanajuato state official later admitted, "[Although] the people of Guanajuato were at first unwilling to give up the great historical bell, they are now convinced that it is better to have it transferred to this city and honored by all Mexicans, since it is not a state but a national relic."[32] Upon its arrival in June, the army rendered the bell full military honors and placed it in the National Artillery Museum. Eminent Mexican composer Ernesto Elorduy wrote a march entitled "La Campana de la Independencia" in time for the holidays. President Díaz consulted with City Councilman Guillermo Valleto and an architect about the possibility of hanging the bell from the National Palace. On September 14, the bell was the centerpiece of an allegorical parade float. When it arrived at the Zócalo a band struck up the National Hymn and officials released a thousand doves wearing tricolor neckbands.[33] In a short speech, President Díaz promised that the Independence Bell would be "rung every year to recall the example of heroes of the past, to encourage the people of Mexico to defend their independence, and to continue the work of national regeneration of which the struggle for independence was the preface."[34] Here in a telltale statement Díaz regards Hidalgo's revolution as a prelude to his own labors.

With the bell installed just above the central balcony of the National Palace, Díaz added a bell ringing to his Grito performance. Only certain technological enhancements were permitted thereafter. In 1899, electric lights in the shape of a star surrounded the bell, and they flashed on brilliantly when Díaz tugged the cord.[35] The City Council also spent 14,500 pesos on twenty-seven hundred green, white, and red incandescent lights to illuminate the facade of the cathedral.[36] The Grito ceremony in Mexico City has remained unmodified. In observance of the sesquicentenary of independence (Año de la Patria) in 1960, thirty-two replicas of the original Independence Bell were cast, one for every state of the republic. Each was placed over the main entrance of the state palaces for governors to repeat the act.

The Grito ceremony had its detractors. The conservative Catholic press tried to expose the Grito as an "unfounded custom" and a "crude invented excuse."[37] In 1908, the editors of *El Tiempo Ilustrado* sarcastically described this "firmly established and deeply rooted custom" as a contrived fantasy dreamt up by polemicist Carlos María de Bustamante. Catholics denounced the original Grito as a hastily arranged plea made by a desperate Hidalgo that took place at 5:00 a.m. on September 16, not at 11:00 p.m. on the 15th. They argued further that Hidalgo never used the phrases "Viva la Independencia" or "Viva México," which Díaz always yelled. Conservative editors admitted: "It will be difficult to uproot this established custom of celebrating independence at that hour since it dates from almost a century ago, but we must try to do it, and if every year the reasons are repeated, the historical truth will triumph." Conservatives asked: "Why do the music and the enthusiastic gritos of the masses on September 16 fall silent on September 27, the date when independence was achieved? We must ask the men who have been in power for more than forty years this question."[38]

The Grito has survived to the present day not because of its historical accuracy but because of its function as a powerful unifying myth. It has captured the national imagination and captivated tourists for over a century. Its performance temporarily collapses everyday hierarchies and eliminates distinctions in an immense plaza that seems to accommodate the nation at large. To joyous revelers, the open air and lack of boundaries convey social equality, shared liberties, and endless possibilities. Even young men and women from "good station" wore *petate* hats, drank tequila, and otherwise performed Mexicanness by becoming one with the undulating masses.[39] The Grito ritual achieves three overlapping goals of both invented traditions and hegemony: social cohesion, legitimization, and redefinition of relations of authority. It is among the greatest examples of how state power is replicated through routine cultural politics and how power is lived by citizens of a national culture.[40]

Even before the Díaz regime, Independence Day was commemorated like a Memorial Day and Veterans Day combined. During the Second Empire, Maximilian decorated veterans of the liberation wars and dedicated a statue of Morelos in the Plazuela de Guardiola.[41] Juárez awarded service medals to aging soldiers, Lerdo de Tejada dispensed with the tradition to de-emphasize the military, and Díaz revived it in 1878.[42] Despite some misgivings about portraying his government as a military regime, Díaz knew that soldiers honored publicly had vested interests in the continuation of the regime. The president's role appears ceremonial, but the state kept veteran rosters, paid pensions on time, and invited long-forgotten soldiers to receive official recognition. Whenever Díaz presented veterans with medals or monetary gifts, he reaffirmed the government's commitment to the survivors and to the cause for which they fought. Proceeds from the sale of holiday commemorative albums also went to war veterans.

State political rituals retold the history of independence with due attention to spatial and temporal structure. Every morning of September 16, Díaz marched with veterans from the National Palace to the Alameda. Orators and sometimes the president himself read aloud the original text of Mexico's Act of Independence issued at the Congress of Chilpancingo in 1813. If Díaz stood in as Hidalgo for the nighttime performance of the Grito, he did his best impersonation of José María Morelos in declaring the Acta. In combination, the Grito and the Acta retold the Hidalgo and Morelos phases of the independence movement in distinct places and times. War games, artillery demonstrations, and the military parades that followed collectively represented the third triumphal phase.[43] How interesting that the captivating (and expensive) fireworks displays coincided with Hidalgo's cry, not Iturbide's victorious occupation of Mexico City. Conservative Catholics complained that the "Liberator of Mexico," Iturbide, and September 27, the day of triumph, were both condemned to a "most unjust oblivion."[44]

Even as veterans of the Independence Wars passed away, the state simply began celebrating the memory of those who fought during the Reform and French Intervention. Independence Day speeches at the Alameda or San Fernando tied both liberation movements together. In 1899, Díaz decorated five *ancianos* "of the modest class" who fought under his command at Puebla (April 2, 1867). A year later he presented gifts to a dozen Indians who assaulted Querétaro (May 15, 1867). He even decorated Generals José Vicente Villada and Bernardo Reyes with the Condecoración de Constancia (Cross of Constancy), apparently for their peacetime service as governors of modernizing states. And officers in the Indian campaigns of Yucatán also received medals. Beginning in 1900, the government moved September 16 ceremonies outside the historic center to the Anzures Plains in La Vaquita so the audience could view army maneuvers that followed. After 1904, services found a new home in the Monumental Tribune at the foot of Chapultepec Castle, Díaz's summer residence. These changes in commemorative space symbolized the shift of glory from Hidalgo and his soldiers to Díaz and his generals.[45] But even as late as 1908, young men and women from the national schools still enjoined torchlight parades downtown. In the dead of night two thousand of them shouted *Vivas!* to their favorite independence leaders, while citizens in the second- and third-floor balconies sounded, "Vivan los estudiantes!"[46]

On Independence Day, the state also paid tribute to nonmilitary figures. In 1901, Díaz invited to the capital Jaime Nunó, the coauthor of Mexico's National Hymn. Nunó had married an American woman and moved to Buffalo, New York. He agreed to return to Mexico and lead an official performance of the national anthem on Independence Day. An emotional Nunó directed the Himno Nacional and shed tears after being honored with heartfelt applause. He later wrote the epic march entitled "Porfirio Díaz" before dying in Queens, N.Y., in 1908. The regime also rendered posthumous honors to Nunó's collaborator, Francisco González Bocanegra. The Mexican poet who authored the lyrics of the National Hymn had died of typhoid fever in 1861. During the *fiestas patrias* of 1901, the government held an *homenaje* at Bocanegra's San Fernando tomb and later moved his remains to the Rotonda de los Hombres Ilustres. Although the event received widespread publicity, his urn was not interred in the rotunda until 1932.[47]

In an effort to promote historical consciousness and defensive nationalism, public orators used metaphors of death with great rhetorical power in Independence Day speeches. Emeterio de la Garza's oration of 1896 taught that the French *philosophes* "tumbled the eighteenth century into its grave." He continued, "[That century] expired in the dreadful convulsions of epileptic exhaustion." The death of the old ushered in the moral resurrection of mankind under Washington in the north, Bolívar in the south, and Hidalgo in Mexico. What Hidalgo failed to do in life, he accomplished in martyrdom: "His remains are the loadstone of our veneration. . . . When that body fell inanimate, the soul took refuge in the national conscience." De la Garza describes the nineteenth-century wasteland: "So many have died for the country that Mexico is one huge cemetery where the bones and ashes of our fathers rest. . . . [I]t is holy ground"; "We are no longer liberals or conservatives; in the presence of the heroes of independence we are Mexicans. We are the Republic." Like most sermons, his ended with an invocation: Union, Homage to Progress, Vindication of the Past.[48]

To elevate Padre Hidalgo as the Father of Mexican Independence the government sponsored popular workingmen's parades and deployed historical artifacts that belonged to him as visual aids in Independence Day events. From 1883 forward, workmen's guilds, laborers, water carriers, porters, and schoolchildren preceded government bureaucrats and the military in Independence Day parades. The U.S. consul remarked that the cotton shirt and straw hat gentry-for-a-day seemed to "enjoy their dignity highly."[49] Of course, the state's very inclusion of working-class representatives denied other members of the same associations a place in line or the possibility of initiating their own parade.[50] The Porfirian government referred to unauthorized gatherings as mob demonstrations. Chapters 5 and 6 examine the creation of Hidalgo Day and the state's use of the actual skulls and skeletal remains of Hidalgo, Morelos, and other heroes. For now, relics of a different kind will be the focus. It was one thing to present artificial replicas of consecrated items on allegorical parade floats, and yet another to present the genuine artifacts to the people. On Independence Days, the state displayed four items of particular relevance to national origins and the Hidalgo cult: the aforementioned Mexican Independence Bell, the Virgin of Guadalupe flag, Hidalgo's war cannon, and his baptismal font.

In 1895, Díaz launched two initiatives to transport historical artifacts from the exterior to the capital where they could be exhibited for national and foreign audiences alike. He had learned the value of this aspect of national preservation not during his military travails but in his tenure as development minister under González, when he directed Mexico's exhibit at the New Orleans World's Industrial and Cotton Centennial Exposition (1885). To prepare for the Congress of Americanists meeting in October, Díaz named Tlaxcala governor Próspero Cahuantzi as head of the Antiquities Commission. The committee was authorized to requisition pre-Columbian and colonial-era artifacts from every state and place them on permanent display in the National Museum.[51] Díaz's second order was for governors to send every historically significant cannon, rifle, war trophy, and battle flag in the republic to the National Artillery Museum in the Mexico City Citadel.

The nationalization and preservation of relics was another effort to resuscitate the national dead and centralize memory, but it had mixed results. The state of Michoacán immediately complied with the decree by sending a flag that Morelos lost to Agustín de Iturbide in the Battle of Puruandino. However, Nuevo León governor Bernardo Reyes refused to relinquish three rifles used to execute Maximilian, Miramón, and Mejía (Reyes exclaimed: "Let us keep these rifles!").[52] Reyes did hand over one of Iturbide's swords and tried unsuccessfully to recover the flag that Santa Anna stole from the U.S. Army. According to Díaz, Santa Anna gave it to the state legislature of San Luis Potosí only for it to be sequestered by General Santiago Vidaurri.[53] During the Independence Day holidays, the war minister announced that General Mariano Escobedo had donated the sword Maximilian surrendered to him at Querétaro.[54] Such announcements brought more people to museums. Public spending on the National Museum grew tenfold from 1877 to 1910, and the annual number of visitors surpassed 230,000 by 1897. Foreign scientists still dominated the technical field of archaeological excavation in Mexico, but the government strictly prohibited them from exporting the national patrimony.[55]

In this context, the federal government forcefully appropriated Hidalgo's war banner from the Catholic Church. Hidalgo had adopted the Virgin of Guadalupe as a symbol of Mexican identity. Her image appeared on the battle flag that his peasant army carried in their campaigns. It is no coincidence that the government confiscated it from the clergy just after its use in the Coronation of the Virgin ceremony in October 1895. Díaz and his cabinet sought to de-emphasize its religious symbolism, imbue it with secular meaning, and promote the Hidalgo cult. Despite unanimous Church protests, the War Department entrusted jefe político and future Federal District police chief Eduardo Velásquez to acquire the flag. The Guadalupe parish surrendered it without incident, and Velásquez deposited it in what he thought was a safe location but later admitted that the flag disappeared like the apparition of La Virgen herself. Velásquez ordered detectives to search for the stolen relic, while the highly publicized theft shocked the nation. To everyone's relief, police investigators found the banner at the home of Archbishop Próspero María Alarcón, who admitted to taking it. Minister of the Interior Manuel González Cosío later authenticated the flag, and museum curators placed it in a foremost position in the National Artillery Museum. Díaz could now issue the grito and wave the real artifact from his balcony every Independence Day.[56]

Sharing national treasures with the people allowed the state to educate citizens and compare modest origins to advanced technology. The process involves the public comparison of antiquities from national museums to their modern counterparts. In the Independence Day parade of 1898, the War Ministry rolled out the historic cannon that Hidalgo used in his military campaigns. It appeared as an unimposing peashooter alongside the Mondragón, Hotskiss, Bange, and Nordenfield artillery pieces. The juxtaposition of the historical artifact and modern machinery of death showed all observers how far Mexico had advanced. German and Austrian military attachés were duly impressed with the parade of soldiers and guns in 1903.[57] Years later, the national government acquired Hidalgo's sacred baptismal font from Guanajuato. During the Centennial of Mexican Independence (1910), the font came to symbolize the birth and baptism of the Patria and the reanointing of both Hidalgo and Díaz (elected to his eighth term). Over one million nationals and foreigners participated in the Fiestas del Centenario, confirming that Independence Day pageantry was second to none.[58]

Figure 20. A Mexican artillery battalion displaying horsemanship and a cannon as crowds look on from the street corners and sidewalks. Photo courtesy of the Nettie Lee Benson Latin American Library, University of Texas, Austin.

For centuries, the Catholic Church used material objects infused with religious symbolism, such as the holy Eucharist, the cross, or personal belongings of the saints, in its processions and pilgrimages. Nation-states similarly imbued relics with symbolism and deployed them as the centerpieces of parades in hopes of producing loyal citizens with deep personal attachments to the Patria. Unique to Mexico was the fact that many of the objects of veneration had religious significance, from Hidalgo's Dolores church bell and Virgin of Guadalupe banner to the baptismal font he used to christen newborns. Mexico's historical reality of an independence movement initiated by parish priests facilitated the Porfirian state's efforts to sacralize the relics that once belonged to the national dead. This process included the sanctification of human remains, similar to the bones of saints, a topic further explored in chapter 6.

Military Maneuvers: Mexican Victory on Cinco de Mayo

Since its inception under Benito Juárez, Cinco de Mayo celebrated a great military victory as well as glorified Ignacio Zaragoza, the young Liberal republican commander of the Army of the East. Zaragoza was just thirty-three when he defeated the French at the Battle of Puebla on May 5, 1862. Tragically, he died of typhoid fever just four months later on September 8. As much as the outcome of the battle, it was his death that captured the hearts and minds of Mexicans. Those who knew him described his passing as an irreparable loss for the fatherland. A shocked Francisco Zarco lamented: "His death snatched him from us when we needed him most." In his funeral oration José María Iglesias admitted his anguish: "Yesterday he was our hope, today he is the cause of our sorrow."[59] Zaragoza became the first martyr of the republican cause he championed.

The way public officials and citizens responded to Zaragoza's death sheds light on the overlapping processes of creating heroes, festivals, and the nation in republican Mexico. It also shows how Díaz modeled his own behavior after Benito Juárez. President Juárez ordered Colonel Mariano Escobedo to transfer Zaragoza's body from Puebla to Mexico City for a state funeral. Congress declared him a *benemérito de la Patria* and resolved to inscribe his name in gold lettering in the congressional building; promote him posthumously to division general; rename the city he defended "Puebla de Zaragoza;" rename two streets in Mexico City "Zaragoza" and "Cinco de Mayo"; raise a monument to him on Guadalupe Hill, the site where the battle took place; name Zaragoza's only child a "daughter of the nation" and provide her with both an annual pension and 100,000 pesos of expropriated property; and offer generous pensions to Don Ignacio's other female relatives.

Even before these resolutions were publicized, citizens demanded that the government declare May 5 a national holiday. On September 13, 1862, Juárez accompanied citizens in a funeral procession from the National Palace to the Panteón de San Fernando, where Zaragoza was laid to rest. Governors, municipal presidents, and private individuals from communities as far removed from one another as Michoacán and Alta California planned monuments and christened streets, parks, and public squares after Zaragoza. Citizens donated money to the general's survivors. Patriotic associations and benevolent societies adopted his name. Juárez decreed Cinco de Mayo a national holiday on February 16, 1863. Both the triumph over the French on May 5 and the national outpouring of grief for Zaragoza convinced Juárez that the country would unite behind the republic.[60]

Official Cinco de Mayo programs sustained national memory of both the Puebla battle and Zaragoza, but they did not acquire a predominantly military

character until the Porfiriato. The charter program of 1863 called for the firing of cannon salvos, the unfurling of flags, the decorating of veterans, the
unveiling of an enormous painting of the battle, and the delivery of speeches
at the bust of Zaragoza in the Alameda. From 1864 through 1867, celebration
of the republican holiday was reduced to isolated acts of resistance to the
imperial government, especially in Puebla. After the expulsion of the French,
Juárez built a stone memorial to Zaragoza at San Fernando. The City Council
exhumed and reburied the general's remains prior to the inauguration of the
burial monument on May 5, 1868. Justo Sierra, Guillermo Prieto, José María
Iglesias, and Alfredo Chavero all delivered orations. The Juárez government
even circulated special commemorative medallions featuring a portrait of
Zaragoza on one side and the liberty cap on the other. Calle Cinco de Mayo
officially opened. One year later, the state of Coahuila renamed itself Coahuila
de Zaragoza. Other villages and towns followed suit. Nationalist poet and novelist Ignacio Manuel Altamirano reported that the Mexican people celebrated
the holiday of May 5, 1870, more enthusiastically than ever before. Although
Mexicans continued to celebrate Cinco de Mayo, the official Zaragoza commemoration at San Fernando vanished during the Lerdo years.[61]

Since the Battle of Cinco de Mayo also brought fame to Porfirio Díaz, who
served under Zaragoza at Puebla, he wantonly exploited the holiday to advance
his political program and personal prestige. Díaz capitalized on a political
culture that wanted to believe in a common triumphal military history that
united all classes under the umbrella of national sacrifice.[62] Beginning in 1877,
letters poured in congratulating the officer who "ground to dust the vain and
proud French Army" and became president on the day of Mexico's greatest
victory.[63] Díaz took power for the first time on May 5. The anniversary was
intended to calm anxiety over the political transition. In a circular dated the
following day, Díaz appealed to the patriotism of public officials to join him
in his work "to restore the integrity of the fatherland" and "build all the good
works that it deserves."[64]

The following year the government scheduled a public reading of the constitutional amendment prohibiting presidential and gubernatorial reelection.
Díaz promised no reelection and effective suffrage in his Plan de Tuxtepec, and
he fulfilled the promise by having the new legislation publicly proclaimed on
May 5, 1878. Díaz, his cabinet, public functionaries, the military, and thousands
of citizens assembled in front of the National Palace to hear a clerk recite the
law. For a moment the ceremony brought nationwide attention to his forth-
rightness, but the political act (in both senses of the word) was ephemeral: the
public reading of the no-reelection law never recurred. In 1879, it was replaced
with the official reading of Zaragoza's battle report. Díaz used the Cinco de
Mayo holiday in subtler ways. During his second term, Díaz imprisoned

General Miguel Negrete for rebelling against his government. Negrete was the officer who repelled the main French attack and ensured victory for Zaragoza at the Cinco de Mayo battle. As Negrete grew dangerously ill in prison, the public began to show sympathy for him. Díaz released Negrete, restored him to division general, and invited him to march in the Cinco de Mayo parade in 1887. Such calculated magnanimity was repeated a decade later when the president awarded Negrete with a state funeral.[65]

On Cinco de Mayo, Díaz showcased the army, decorated loyal officers, and otherwise promoted the military. To promote the military was to promote the idea that Mexican citizens must be willing to lay down their lives for the Patria. The president laid the first stone of the memorial to Cuauhté-moc, the last Aztec emperor and symbol of the defense of Tenochtitlán, on May 5, 1878. The federal and city governments combined resources and spent nearly 5,000 pesos on martial holiday decorations.[66] Official programs always included parades, troop reviews, war games, artillery practice, fireworks, and evening serenades performed by military bands. The celebration of 1885 was especially militaristic due to the war scare with Guatemala. Díaz ordered thousands of troops to the city, bringing the parade total to twenty-one thousand men, the largest force assembled since the siege of Querétaro. Military bands belted out "Military Honor," "Cinco de Mayo," the "Zaragoza March," and the National Hymn. Up to one hundred thousand cheering people witnessed the imposing parades annually.[67] Cinco de Mayo celebrations dramatized state power, reminding all that the president exercised full control of the republic. One observer of the 1887 parade warned: "The military display yesterday must have convinced those soreheads who dream of revolutions, that the overthrow of the present government is more easily imagined than realized. . . . [T]here is not the faintest probability that the prevailing tranquility will be disturbed."[68]

Among the great spectacles of Cinco de Mayo programs were the war games of La Vaquita on the Anzures Plains. After 1900, tramcars designed for twenty-five passengers provided round-trip service for three times that number. Citizens of the accommodated classes always complained of the moving sardine cans, but thousands gathered to view artillery demonstrations, assaults on fixed positions, infantry movements, and cavalry attacks. Upon Díaz's arrival, citizens from all classes shook their hats in the air, applauded, and belted out vivas to the president.[69]

The Porfirian government scheduled two memorial ceremonies that paid homage to Díaz's former commander: an official laying of a wreath at Zaragoza's tomb in the San Fernando Cemetery and the public reading of his official report of the Battle of Puebla in the Alameda. Introduced in 1878 and 1879, these two ceremonies remained in the program throughout the Porfiriato.

Figure 21. The view from Díaz's open parade coupe. The president's bodyguard wore decorative parade uniforms with helmets that brought height, formality, and pomp to the imposing march. Photo courtesy of the Nettie Lee Benson Latin American Library, University of Texas, Austin.

Every May 5, patriotic societies turned Zaragoza's burial monument into a giant military trophy arrayed with swords, cannon, shot, and, in later years, even machine guns. Government officials and civic clubs gathered at the tomb to hear the stirring orations of distinguished ideologues José María Gamboa (1887), Gustavo Baz (1888), Emilio Rabasa (1890), Justo Sierra (1891), and Eze-quiel Chávez (1899). High-ranking officers who fought under Zaragoza dedi-cated wreaths with the president. Following the requisite artillery salutes, Díaz led marches to the Alameda and decorated survivors of the Battle of Puebla. In 1883, it was particularly fitting for President González, who lost an arm in battle, to present monetary gifts to five badly wounded veterans of Cinco de Mayo. In other years, Díaz presented the same "mutilated" veteran soldiers with commemorative gold pieces, medals, and money gifts of 50 pesos. As it became more difficult for the remaining soldiers to ascend the platform with each passing year, appreciative audiences applauded them with greater enthu-siasm. After these moving ceremonies, citizens listened to readings of Zara-goza's account of the Puebla conflict.[70]

Zaragoza commemorations were described as the "most impressive and dignified ceremony of the day."[71] Outstanding nationalists sang praises for the Puebla defenders, offering eternal glory not only to the commander but also to "the rank and file, those who bore the heat and burden of the day, who sleep silently, unknown martyrs of duty, unrecognized heroes."[72] Selfless martyrs were recognized in other ways. During his presidential tour to Puebla in 1901,

Figure 22. A Cinco de Mayo trophy of war dedicated to Ignacio Zaragoza. Artists reconstructed an Aztec floating garden on a pool of water. Mexico rises triumphantly among organic ferns and plants, covered with flags, wagon wheels, bugles, swords, and bayoneted rifles. An eagle with outspread wings and a snake in its beak symbolizes the foundation myth of Mexico. Photo by C. B. Waite; courtesy of the Nettie Lee Benson Latin American Library, University of Texas, Austin.

Díaz inaugurated the Franco-Mexican Tomb of Unknown Soldiers, which honored soldiers from both nations who sacrificed their lives at Puebla.[73] The tomb was built by the French colony in Puebla years before Europe's Great War would immortalize the cult of the Unknown Soldier. These deliberately empty tombs and cenotaphs have no precedents in earlier times, but they are "saturated with ghostly national imaginings."[74] Ultimately, President Díaz sought solace for May 5 services and moved the speeches and poetry readings to the Monumental Tribune of Chapultepec.

Despite efforts at national healing, Cinco de Mayo speeches stimulated defensive nationalism from orators who still resented the foreign invaders. Maximilian was a favorite whipping boy. Speaker Emeterio de la Garza, fond of anticlerical rhetoric and necrological metaphors, described the emperor's domain as "that ridiculous, improvised, priest-ridden Empire, with its prodigality and scandals, with its sham titles, its mirth-moving vestments, crosses, decorations and mitres. It was a Dantesque monstrosity which momentarily revivified the corpse of conservatism."[75] In 1899, General Manuel Flores read from the glorious pages of Mexico's military history against "imperial barbarians of the conquest, Independence, the North American Invasion, and French Intervention."[76] Here Flores plainly categorizes the Spanish, Americans, and French as foreign aggressors. After listening to these orations, schoolchildren, delegates of workers' associations and patriotic societies, and women's charitable organizations held their own civic processions to and from Zaragoza's tomb. Díaz distributed prizes to students for their prose, poetry, and artistic renditions of the Cinco de Mayo victory.

Memorialization of Ignacio Zaragoza and the national dead on Cinco de Mayo took on other forms. Manuel González inaugurated the Hipsographic Monument to cosmographer Enrico Martínez on May 5, 1881. Between 1889 and 1900, Díaz uncovered eight statues on the Paseo de la Reforma on Cinco de Mayo holidays.[77] Coahuila and Puebla state governors immortalized Zaragoza's image in huge bronze equestrian monuments forged by Contreras and approved by Porfirio Díaz. In the late 1890s, the Mexican Navy vessel *Zaragoza* carried the hero's name and the Mexican flag across the globe.[78] The spread of Cinco de Mayo celebrations to the U.S.–Mexican borderlands and beyond (including Des Moines, Iowa, and New York City) testifies to its importance as a date worth remembering.

Rites of Spring: The Anniversary of the Siege of Puebla

"Companions in arms! I wish to be the first to pay tribute to your heroism. The entire nation and posterity will perpetuate your glory.

You have inscribed another memorable date in the city where Zaragoza immortalized his name and the fifth of May. The second of April of 1867 will henceforth be registered in the calendar of our national glories."[79]

National commemoration of the siege of Puebla on April 2, 1867, was nonexistent before Díaz assumed power. This official holiday celebrated the successful assault on one of three imperial strongholds during the French Intervention. Republican troops of the Army of the East under the command of General Díaz swept through Oaxaca and stormed both Puebla and Mexico City. Díaz routed Maximilian's forces at Miahuatlán, La Carbonera, Oaxaca, and Puebla. These victories all but ensured the fall of the Second Empire and contributed morally and materially to the capture and execution of Maximilian at Querétaro in May and June. Díaz regarded his action at Puebla as significant in the annals of Mexican history. In his political speeches he referred to the glorious dates of April 2, May 5, and May 15 (fall of Querétaro) in the same breath. Always cognizant of the significance of calendar dates, Díaz at age thirty-six married his twenty-year-old niece, Delfina, on April 2, so that his wedding anniversary coincided with his greatest victory. Porfirio named his second and third daughters Luz Aurora Victoria and Victoria Francisca (the child who tragically died at birth) after his military triumph at Puebla. In 1903, Minister of War Francisco Z. Mena negotiated with muralist Francisco P. Mendoza to paint two of President Díaz's favorite historical scenes of battle. Díaz chose the defense of Chapultepec by the cadets of the Military College (the Niños Héroes) and his own siege of Puebla. In fact, Mendoza had already completed a painting for the National Palace that depicted Díaz making his triumphal entry into the central plaza of Puebla. Díaz and Mena ordered an exact reproduction of that painting installed at Chapultepec. Mendoza obliged and later presented Díaz with his interpretation of "The Battle of Miahuatlan" as a gift on April 2, 1906.[80]

As one might expect, the holiday glorified the president and brought national recognition to the many officers who had served him at Puebla.[81] In one holiday speech, Congressman Juan Mateos compared Díaz's taking of Puebla with the exploits of Wellington at Waterloo, Grant at Richmond, Moltke at Sedan, and Oyama at Mukden. He recited for his audience the "genealogical tree of victory"—the officers who fought at Puebla: Alatorre, Mena, Carbó, Terán, and Pacheco.[82] Minister of Development Carlos Pacheco, who had lost an arm and a leg during the attack, received the highest accolades. After Pacheco's death, military officers met at his tomb in the Rotonda de los Hombres Ilustres every April 2. The generals could not visit his grave according to custom because the anniversary of Pacheco's death was the same as Díaz's birthday, September 15. For his many victories, Díaz became the sole recipient of the Cordon of Military Merit in 1906.[83]

Perhaps due to the annual success of Independence Day and Cinco de Mayo, Díaz never felt compelled to reenact his exploits of April 2. There were no annually repeated state rituals to enhance remembrance. Instead, the holiday was observed by dedicating public works and congratulating the "indefatigable champion of the Republic."[84] On April 2, 1878, Díaz inaugurated railway lines to Toluca, Celaya, and Guanajuato. The high-officer corps and congressmen visited or dined with the president and arranged for military bands to serenade him. Programs to honor Díaz were organized by various exclusive groups, including the Asociación Patriótica Mexicana; Sociedad de Amigos del Presidente (renamed the Junta Central Porfirista in 1891); Club Central Porfirio Díaz, Comité Central Porfirista; Círculo de Amigos del General Díaz; Círculo Nacional Porfirista; and Unión Liberal Nacional. But veterans' organizations, mutual societies, and students also supported the popular *caudillo*. In 1892, agricultural workers from outlying villages drove their oxen up the Paseo de la Reforma to manifest their appreciation for Díaz. Beginning in 1898, Díaz hosted public receptions with veteran soldiers that lasted hours. In 1899, the president decorated and exchanged embraces with veterans, all of whom were overcome with emotion.[85] The Círculo Nacional Porfirista organized a great procession from the Paseo de la Reforma to Constitution Plaza in 1903. Most delegations in this parade carried their banners, but the workers of El

Buen Tono cigarette factory hefted large black umbrellas with sashes that read "Constitution of 1857." Díaz also dedicated ten of the statues along the *paseo* in conjunction with April 2 programs. Occasionally, he scheduled tours to the exterior, where he was received with triumphal arches and grand parades. In 1891, he inaugurated a new penitentiary in Puebla and proclaimed the abolition of capital punishment in the state.[86]

In his reception speeches, the president always paid tribute to the heroic dead and encouraged surviving officers and soldiers to lead by example: "Comrades! May those memorable dates, the 5th and 15th of May and the 2nd of April, ever remain in the memory of our people as sources of patriotic inspiration and of a determination to imitate the example of the men who shed their blood in defense of the country."[87] Never known for his high oratory, Díaz nevertheless improvised a toast or a statement of gratitude every Dos de Abril. His speeches always contained a populist rhetorical quality that downplayed his role and emphasized horizontal camaraderie, rather than vertical hierarchy. Referring to his campaign, the general praised the *pueblo* for their valor, sacrifices, and patriotism in a "tremendous and unequal contest." When referring to his government, he claimed that he was nothing more than "a directing influence aided by those who by their talent or activity have achieved the success of my administration."[88]

Another important aspect of the April 2 holiday was that it fell one day after Congress opened its second session. Like the coordination of the dictator's birthday, Independence Day, and the first session of Congress (September 16), news of Díaz's opening of Congress appeared in the national press on April 2, beside pictures and articles about General Díaz's command at Puebla. Past and present converged in the columns of official newspapers and in other media as well. In 1900, the audience watching military maneuvers from the grandstands near San Lázaro read printed copies of Díaz's original April 2 address to his victorious troops.[89] Díaz's annual reports to Congress published by *El Imparcial* always contained a section on the latest weapons acquired by the War Department. In 1901, he noted the arrival of thirty-two small-caliber machine guns, nineteen thousand Swiss entrenching tools, the steamship *Stanford*, and three other naval vessels for use in the Yucatán Indian campaigns.[90] Likewise, in his September 16 message to Congress he announced receipt of three million bullets and forty-six hundred cavalry sabers. Díaz also noted that Mexico began building its own ammunition and gunpowder factories in 1902. The force of such arms was often demonstrated on the Anzures Plains every April 2. Two gunships, the *Bravo* and the *Morelos*, powered into Veracruz on April 2, 1905.[91] The act of reading about the president's dual roles as famous general and commander in chief reinforced his authority. Eventually, formal Dos de Abril ceremonies were moved to the same Monumental Tribune in

Chapultepec Park where citizens commemorated the military on Cinco de Mayo and September 8. State governors decreed civic festivals on April 2, promoting Díaz as a living legend.[92]

April 2 lacked the popular festivity of other holidays. Rather than shower blind adulation upon the dictator, commoners often celebrated Holy Week by burning Judas effigies of rich businessmen and public officials in a popular Catholic death ceremonial that poked fun at the ruling elite.[93] Referring to Díaz's public reception on April 2, 1896, one observer noted, "Owing perhaps to the fact that the day was a great religious one for the Church, the reception did not have all the splendor of former years."[94] The fusion of April 2 with the national political calendar also backfired, exposing the flaws of the personalist dictatorship. In late March 1901, bad health forced the seventy-year-old Díaz to Cuernavaca to recuperate from what many thought was a life-threatening illness. The April 2 program was cancelled. Mexican stocks and bonds dropped eleven percentage points, political enemies attacked him as too old to lead the country, and *científico* supporters cited his poor health as reason to create the office of vice-president before the 1904 election. The illusions of political strength and economic prosperity worked only if the irreplaceable dictator was healthy.[95]

Cinco de Febrero: Constitution Day and Violation of the Constitution Day

During their first administrations, Díaz and González officiated at Cinco de Febrero ceremonies to draw attention to their elections by constitutional means. The holiday observance commemorated the promulgation of the Constitution of 1857, the national charter that was completely unsuitable to Mexican realities. A battle-hardened pragmatist, Díaz invoked the sacred document at will but never bound his state to its lofty principles. The Constitution provided for the formation of a federal republic based on liberal democratic principles, representative government, universal male suffrage, the protection of individual rights, the separation and balance of powers, and of course the anticlerical provisions of the Reform Laws. In actuality, Díaz could not have governed a more traditional society of *hacendados* and peasants, rural indigenous communities, and hierarchical corporate bodies such as the Church and military, which were anything but modern.[96] He was to perceive the Constitution as a national fiction except when its periodic revision reinforced the patron–clientelist structures of state hegemony and helped him centralize power. Only the amended constitution became sacrosanct to Díaz. He certainly never expected that wage earners in Chihuahua would use the Constitution or Juárez's good name against him. Nor did he predict that its translation to Nahuatl would empower indigenous groups in their anti-Díaz campaigns of 1910.[97]

Traditional and modern society competed for the very date that the state commemorated the anticlerical Constitution of 1857. The holiday's temporal placement on February 5 was problematic for coinciding with Candlemas and the feast day of San Felipe de Jesús. Archbishop of Mexico Pelagio Antonio Labastida y Dávalos had canonized San Felipe and beautified the shrine of the saint in the National Cathedral. Every Cinco de Febrero, Catholics held religious pilgrimages to worship San Felipe. Although prohibited by law from appearing publicly in their clerical vestments, priests took advantage of the government's rapprochement by leading evening candlelight processions through the streets. Even as Constitution Day was fast assuming larger proportions as a national holiday, Church officials had priorities of their own. In 1886, Labastida invited Doña Carmen, the devout wife of the dictator, to dedicate the Church of San Felipe de Jesús on Calle San Francisco. There, clergy decorated the temple with both flowers and Mexican flags, signaling an effort to reduce Church–state conflict. Perhaps the Mexican people could be both pious and patriotic on San Felipe Day and Constitution Day.[98]

Constitution Day stood as a civilian version of Independence Day because common citizens used the holiday to exalt Benito Juárez. In contrast to the military parades and war games of other holidays, Cinco de Febrero organizers downplayed militarism in favor of popular liberalism, civilian rule, and the primacy of law, three ideals that Juárez embodied. Beginning in 1885, the Constitution of 1857 Club and the Association of Democratic Propaganda deployed the standard commemorative devices: civic marches through decorated streets, parades of allegorical floats, inaugurations of monuments, and memorial exercises. Procession itineraries were the reverse of Independence Day parades. Instead of mobilizing in the Zócalo, citizens assembled at the Alameda or San Fernando Cemetery, marched to Constitution Plaza, passed in the shadows of the Municipal and National palaces, and then walked back to the Alameda once again until they reached the San Fernando Cemetery. There, public officials eulogized heroes and laid wreaths at the tomb of the greatest defender of the Constitution, Juárez.

Constitution Day ceremonies also lauded both the living and the dead signers of the Constitution of 1857, collectively known as the *Constituyentes*. One-third of the ninety-three signatories were still alive in 1885. Most served in public office, and a few occupied the highest political positions in the land. Interior Minister Manuel Romero Rubio; Foreign Relations Ministers Ignacio Vallarta, José María Mata, and Ignacio Mariscal; Justice Minister Justino Fernández; senior congressmen Guillermo Prieto and Juan José Baz; and Supreme Court Magistrate Félix Romero were all signers of the Constitution.[99]

On February 5, the Asociación Patriótica Mexicana and the Gran Congreso Obrero sent congratulatory notes to every living signatory and placed wreaths at the graves of each signer who had passed away. Constituyentes marched in processions, unveiled statues, delivered eulogies, and joined Díaz in placing flowers at the Juárez memorial. While they were alive, Díaz bestowed awards and political office upon them. After they died, he granted them magnificent state funerals.[100]

A foreseeable problem with Constitution Day was that only educated elites possessed the knowledge to appreciate Mexico's magna carta as a legal document. These *letrados* constituted a tiny fraction of a nation that was only 20 percent literate. As a consequence, the state tried to make Constitution Day marches truly democratic workingmen's parades to inculcate the laboring classes with civic education and patriotic values.[101] Such parades continued to exclude women until large numbers joined the manufacturing and clerical workforce in the high 1890s. City councilmen coordinated with patriotic societies and labor organizations to invite everyone from government employees and mutual societies to factory operatives, students, and even *cargadores* (professional carriers).

Unfortunately, the Interior Ministry also reserved the right to cancel the mammoth parades. In 1886, the government suddenly called off the civic procession due to "gloomy weather." But the independent press knew that it was because opposition congressmen had published statements urging people to vote for their own legislative candidates in upcoming elections and "planned to make use of the procession for purposes of agitation."[102] Díaz had his own slate of candidates. Attempts at democratic participation in the commemorative arena were as abortive as the political one, as citizens were denied both formal and informal means of political expression. Ironically, on Constitution Day the government forbade its rivals from exercising their constitutional right to free speech during the workingmen's parades. Mexico's magna carta may as well have been a dead letter.

Congressional legislation ultimately changed the celebrations of Constitution Day dramatically. In 1887, Congress decreed July 18, the anniversary of Juárez's death, a national holiday. The declaration of Juárez Day displaced February 5 as the great day for solemn civic processions to San Fernando and memorial services for Juárez (see chapter 5). Thereafter, the government did little more than inaugurate monuments and public works on Constitution Day. Programs also shifted from the historical center (the politically charged spaces of the Alameda and San Fernando) to the Paseo de la Reforma, reflecting the extension of commemorative space in a southwestern direction toward Chapultepec Castle. The event that marked this transfer was the inauguration of the memorial to Cuauhtémoc on the paseo in 1887. On Constitution Days, Díaz unveiled the statues of Leandro Valle and Constituyente Ignacio Ramírez. Federal District Governor Rafael Rebollar dedicated the statue to insurgent heroine Josefa Ortíz de Domínguez in the Plaza of Santo Domingo. Furthermore, the military began appearing in force on Cinco de Febrero, eclipsing the original intent to keep the holiday a civilian affair. It became commonplace for Díaz to review troops on the paseo, urging them to defend their Constitution.[103] Reduced city budgets and declining participation of patriotic societies diminished Constitution Day.[104] The holiday was a temporal dead zone until anti-reelectionists used it to demonstrate against the Díaz government. After years of protest, the Flores Magón brothers, Paulino Martínez, Camilo Arriaga, Santiago de la Hoz, and Juan Sarabia organized an anti-Díaz *velada* in Laredo on February 5, 1904. Their Club Liberal de "Ponciano Arriaga" used the same ritual structure to criticize the dictator for violating the constitutional rights of Mexicans. That year Congress amended the Constitution once again to extend the presidential term from four to six years and to create the office of vice-president.[105]

The contested nature of holiday celebrations was more prevalent outside the Federal District. The popular classes celebrated holidays in the nation's capital enthusiastically, but indigenous communities used holidays to protest against state regulation of their traditional religious festivals. In 1885, for example, natives of villages surrounding Toluca refused to send representatives to the city's official Cinco de Mayo celebration because the government forbade them from participating in Holy Week processions. This counterhegemonic resistance, secession from an official event, qualifies as one of James C. Scott's "weapons of the weak" and deserves systematic empirical study.[106] Similarly, pious Catholics clung to their own religious celebrations, occasionally clashing with agents of the state. In 1895, Catholics in Zacatecas who were denied permission to ring church bells during the Coronation of the Virgin of Guadalupe celebration of October 12 scaled the stairs of a local temple intent on sounding the bells. Police arrested them for trespassing, but on the way to jail the group incited a riot, which police crushed.[107] State governors often asked for federal forces to reinforce local detachments of gendarmes during religious festivals or national holidays.[108] Jefes políticos and state governors also informed Díaz of demonstrators who made use of holidays to protest against governors or arm themselves against the state.[109] And no matter how many missives Díaz sent out, "cold and indifferent" Michoacanos did not immediately flock to the idea of memorializing the Liberal martyrs of Uruapan.[110] The monument to Arteaga, Salazar, Díaz, Villagran, and González, all of whom were executed by the imperialists in 1865, was not inaugurated until 1893.

Turn-of-the century Mexico could boast of powerful holiday traditions because the Porfirian state engineered them to serve those in power. Agents of the state used national holidays as political mechanisms to unify the nation in ritual celebration and remembrance. Independence Day and Dos de Abril rekindled national sentiment at the same time Congress reconvened the political life of the nation. It just so happened that Congress opened within days of the dictator's birthday in September and one day before the anniversary of his greatest military victory in April. Cinco de Mayo also appealed to the imaginations of citizens who knew their president was the highest-ranking officer in the nation and had once served under Zaragoza. National glory, the national dead, and the national leader were inseparable. Constitution Day followed in the same pattern from 1877 to 1887, as government officials commingled with commoners and Constituyentes to honor the national charter, as well as the champions who upheld it. There was initially no more democratic representation in Mexico than a workingmen's parade, even though women were still excluded from marching. Facing political dissent that called attention to the violation of constitutional principles, however, the regime reduced its commitment to the Cinco de Febrero holiday, reflecting its greater disregard for the Constitution of 1857. Chapter 5 examines the state's construction of Juárez Day as a safer alternative for the ruling elite. The Porfirian state never democratized the political system to bring electoral procedures in line with constitutional principles and provisions. Instead, it won popular consent through mass mobilization of the citizenry, which substituted for free elections and representative government.

Independence Day and Cinco de Mayo celebrations were also historical reenactments of Mexican military victories. Soldiers and civilians no longer died in the battlefields, but military activity that simulated war restored popular memory of the worst of times. The implication was that Díaz pacified Mexico and the people now lived in the best of times. The president's holiday inaugurations of material works and historical statues attempted to prove national progress. Ceremonies and parades educated citizens about the tremendous cost in lives that the country paid for its national sovereignty. A Cinco de Mayo speech from 1898 encapsulates the themes of duty, sacrifice, and martyrdom, the prerequisites of nationalism:

> It was the period when the fulfillment of duty led the way to death through hecatombs of corpses and lamentations, when the soil trodden by the invaders reeked with blood, when the traitor had trampled his country's banner in mud and when the patriot doomed to the scaffold asked only where lay the ashes of his father or his children, that he might fall beside them. . . . Then sacrifice

was the general lot, reward was victory or a glorious ascent in the luminous scale, from combat to heroism to martyrdom, from martyrdom to immortality.[III]

This poetic segment illustrates that foundational discourses depend on the dramatic reinterpretation and selective remembrance of historical figures and events. A cultivated version of the past was incorporated into the official calendar and grafted onto the national consciousness through incessant memorialization of the martyrs who gave their lives for the Patria.

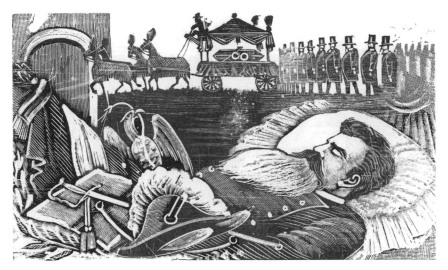

Figure 23. José Guadalupe Posada's *Arrival of the Body of Citizen-General Manuel González.* From Roberto Berdecio and Stanley Applebaum, eds., *Posada's Popular Mexican Prints* (New York: Dover Publications, 1972).

The Only Show in Town 4

State Funerals in the Heyday of Modernization, 1890–1911

W ITH THE EXCEPTION of Benito Juárez, no person in history had a more sustained influence over the Mexican people than Porfirio Díaz. Central to his political survival was selling the legitimacy of his regime to the world community and convincing Europe and the United States that Mexico was a safe place to visit and invest. By 1890, the regime had turned a corner, having won the consent of the propertied classes, middle sectors, and urban working class. A manipulative consensus politics emerged from the exclusion, marginalization, and repression of dissenting opinion. The politics of bureaucratic expansion and management was cogently expressed in the telltale phrase *poca política y mucha administración* (less politics and more administration) attributed alternately to Díaz or President of the Supreme Court Ignacio Vallarta. During the high Porfiriato, state hegemony enabled the regime to concentrate capital and modernize significant areas of the Mexican republic. In the turn-of-the-century decades, the major theme of most state events was no longer reconciliation but material progress.[1]

State funerals reached their height of pretension at the turn of the century. While each national burial was unique, the regime performed them all in accordance with legal provisions (state funeral legislation), military protocol (Honras de Ordenanza), and cultural traditions (lyings-in-state and processions) that recognized the event as the final rite of passage in an individual's life.[2] To subject a small sample of funerals to serial analysis would risk redundancy and reveal little about their overall function and meaning. Instead, this chapter examines in historical context the two state funerals that set the tone for the mature Porfiriato and then situates others within a framework pioneered by historian of the French Third Republic Avner Ben-Amos.[3] State funerals proceed through the same three stages that characterize all rites of passage: (1) separation, (2) transition, and (3) incorporation. Analyzing the structure and performances of state funerals from deathbeds through commemorations reveals a series of *political* acts that constituted a powerful repertoire and rhetoric of rule.[4]

Material Progress in the Porfirian Belle Epoque

The economic reforms of the 1880s set the stage for impressive economic growth in the mature Porfiriato. In his first term, Díaz mended relations with Europe and the United States, improved the nation's credit rating, and removed obstacles to private investment. During the presidency of Manuel González, Congress authorized private companies to survey public lands for future sale. It then enacted a new mining code that permitted speculators to purchase extensive property for commercial development and subsoil mineral extraction. With the completion of railroads, these reforms increased real estate values, as well as agricultural and mineral production. To encourage exports, Minister of Development Carlos Pacheco granted monopolies, concessions, subsidies, tax exemptions, and tariff protection to land developers and mining enterprises. Pacheco also formed joint-stock companies to concentrate foreign and native capital. Mexico faced a recession in 1884, but chronic economic collapse was a distant memory.[5]

With foreign capital and technology, the regime modernized transportation and commercial infrastructure. Between 1884 and 1888, U.S. capitalists completed the Mexican Central Railroad connecting Mexico City and El Paso and the Mexican International, which ran from the Valley of Mexico to Laredo. In 1888, Finance Minister Manuel Dublán restructured the foreign debt and invited European financiers to establish banks in the Federal District. The sale of bonds to British and German interests consolidated Mexico's liabilities, counterweighed U.S. influence, and secured additional credit at favorable interest rates.[6] Finance Minister José Yves Limantour made no secret of his intentions: "Our doors must be open . . . to foreign capital, or we will never evolve beyond our stagnant and sickly way of life."[7] He abolished the *alcabala* (interstate tariff), reformed the Commercial Code, established new monetary laws, and created a national banking system. Mexico showed its first budget surplus in 1895, when its annual budget exceeded 100 million pesos. The export boom allowed the national economy to grow at an average rate of 8 percent per year. Between 1877 and 1910, total national income doubled and foreign trade grew 900 percent; the value of exports and imports increased from 50 million to 488 million pesos from 1876 to 1910. By 1906, Limantour had adopted the gold standard and acquired the majority of shares in the Mexican Central Railroad. He reduced foreign debt payments from 33 percent of revenue in 1904 to 28 percent in 1909. Despite a three-year global recession (1907–9), Mexico boasted a metallic reserve worth 80 million pesos and a budget surplus of

29 million pesos in 1910. By this year, direct and indirect investments in mining alone reached 3.4 billion pesos.[8] The problem of the Mexican belle epoque was not sluggish growth but unequal distribution of the product of unparalleled growth. In this sense, Mexico's "good old days" resembled those of Europe and the United States. Díaz was unapologetic: "I am convinced that I have been able to govern successfully, to preserve peace and to secure some progress for Mexico, because I have availed myself of the help of foreign capital."[9]

Foreign investment also helped finance public works in the nation's burgeoning capital. From 1877 to 1910, Mexico's population almost doubled from 8.7 to 15 million. During the same period, Mexico City grew from 230,000 to 471,066 inhabitants. This growth compelled city planners to improve urban health and safety standards. Persistent flooding shortened business days, damaged property, and spread communicable diseases. Foreign companies built new drainage and sewage systems, repaved streets, repaired sidewalks, and replaced hydrogen gas and oil lanterns with electric streetlamps. Interior Minister Manuel Romero Rubio issued the nation's first health codes in 1891 and 1894. Municipal services improved with the construction of new penitentiaries, hospitals, orphanages, and electric streetcar lines.[10]

Along with creating a healthier city, Díaz and his francophile cohort renovated the capital to project a positive image to foreigners. Self-conscious about their aesthetically displeasing capital, elites altered public space to fit their vision of a cultivated city. Civil engineers and architects completed a plan to replicate Haussmann's Paris in the Federal District. They redrew district boundaries for Frenchified *colonias* and Italianate *villas*. They broadened avenues to accommodate trolleys. Construction companies demolished buildings, gutted palace interiors, and installed new marble floors, staircases, and statuary. The National Palace, Municipal Palace, Mining Palace, and Chapultepec Castle all received makeovers. As for new construction, the government granted tax exemptions on imported building materials and forgave property taxes. By 1900, foreign-owned businesses dominated the downtown area. The banks of the financial district alone held a national monopoly on credit disbursement. One-fourth of the nation's retail sales were conducted in the commercial zone between the Zócalo and Alameda.[11]

Reorganizing urban space also reflected the trend to reform society through education. Díaz enhanced the *centro histórico* with new monuments to Benito Juárez and the Chapultepec Defenders. Key to the city's physical transformation and pedagogical function was developing the Paseo de la Reforma, the graceful boulevard resembling the Champs Elysées that extended from downtown, southwest to Chapultepec. The giant equestrian statue of Charles IV marked the entrance. In 1877, railroad magnate Antonio Escandón donated another reminder of the Spanish legacy, a statue of Christopher Columbus, for the first *glorieta* (traffic circle) of the *paseo*. In the second, Díaz dedicated the monument to the last Aztec emperor, Cuauhtémoc. Architects planned memorials to Zaragoza, Juárez, and Hidalgo for the last three circles on the paseo, but these projects lost momentum. Instead, Díaz honored Zaragoza with a statue at the San Fernando Cemetery, Juárez with a Hemicycle in the Alameda, and Hidalgo and other insurgent heroes with the Column of Independence. Thirty-six additional bronze statues of Liberal reformers lined the paseo's sidewalks in a spatial representation of the Porfirian version of history. Carriages and pedestrians traveled from Columbus's discovery to the last defender of the Aztec Empire, skipped the colonial period entirely, and picked up with Hidalgo at independence. Liberals punctuated the journey just as they had the historical timeline in a state effort to graft temporal sequence onto public space. Like Mexican history, the paseo was to end with an equestrian statue of Porfirio Díaz designed by Italian architect Adamo Boari, but the avenue terminated instead at the presidential residence, Chapultepec Castle.[12] Significantly, the dictator situated himself not just at the end of the *Liberal* continuum but at the terminus of *all* national heroes. His regime was presented as the culmination of an immemorial past, a history lesson repeated with every parade and procession down the paseo. Beyond Díaz and Chapultepec lay the sacred grounds. The Rotonda de los Hombres Ilustres in the Dolores Cemetery served as the National Pantheon where the state enshrined its heroes.

The nation now had its ceremonial city, but modernization only rewarded traditional landowners and new capitalists. Conjoined through marriage and alliance, this aggressive business class formed partnerships with foreign investors who toured the capital with increasing regularity. The native elite depended on both a prosperous image and a cooperative workforce to preserve their status in an arrangement that tied everyone's livelihood to foreign markets. *Empleomania*, the manic quest for government jobs, left 70 percent of Mexico City's salaried professionals and bureaucrats dependent on the regime.[13] Along with these "accommodated classes," a growing pool of factory and service-sector workers relied on government patronage. But "well-being" extended only to those with official connections. Newly arrived *pelados* of mostly indigenous heritage had no affiliation and performed day labor for menial wages. Constantly displaced by urban reorganization, they starved in eastside shantytowns of adobe huts and wooden shacks.

Ruling elites knew that national progress was inconceivable without the cooperation of the working class. Popular consent is constructed historically through the evolution of forms, routines, rituals, and discourses that reiterate to subjects or citizens the moral values on which state authority rests. Urban reforms that promoted morality, industry, and sobriety suggest that the aspiring middle class was the least of the state's concerns since it identified squarely with the progressive regime and disassociated itself from the "unredeemed" masses. Porfirian state theater was performed for "the people." First-wave industrialism had rounded up the usual suspects: dangerous factory workplaces, declines in real wages, worker alienation, squalid living conditions, rapid spread of lethal diseases, systemic injustice, and rights violations. The dissemination of leftist ideologies threatened to politicize workers and destabilize the capitalist regime. Although the government alternately co-opted and repressed the laboring classes, it crafted a semiparticipatory political culture that minimized overt coercion. Porfirio Díaz was always more than a military general. He had acquired legal training, legislative experience, and an education in lawful swindling from Justo Benítez, Protasio Tagle, and Manuel Romero Rubio. Díaz revised the Constitution and violated laws whenever public opinion was on his side. He also gained control of the military, the bureaucracy, the press, labor organizations, and the "captive public" of schoolchildren.[14] Just as the regime capitalized on heightened public spirit during holidays, so did it exploit national solidarity with state funerals.

The Honest, Loyal, and Distinguished Friend of Commerce

From the restoration of the republic in 1867 to the fall of the Díaz regime in 1911, Mexico mourned the passing of only one sitting president, Benito Juárez in 1872.[15] The optimum occasion for a nation to unify through the collective mourning of its head of state never presented itself during the Porfiriato. Indeed, the bell tolled for everyone except Díaz, who survived his regime and died in Paris (1915). Moreover, the four former presidents whom Díaz interred were not celebrated public figures. Mid-century political chaos obscured the legacies of Mariano Arista and Manuel de la Peña y Peña. The accidental discovery of Peña y Peña's bones in a decaying churchyard resulted in a reburial featuring an eloquent panegyric by Justo Sierra but not much else. The *porfirista* vilification of Sebastián Lerdo de Tejada transformed overnight into glorification at his state funeral. Manuel González also suffered character assassination for allegedly enriching himself during his presidency, but his 1893 funeral briefly restored his reputation. Nuevo León named him a *benémerito*, and Matamoros raised a monument to perpetuate his memory. Despite these posthumous resurrections, Díaz profited above all.[16]

Although the Porfirian state never buried a popular president, it interred controversial cabinet ministers with the same pomp accorded to heads of state. Minister of Finance Manuel Dublán hailed from the southern state of Oaxaca. He studied law, served in Congress, and advised Juárez. When Dublán died on May 31, 1891, press obituaries omitted his service to Emperor Maximilian, reflecting two informal rules: the suspension of all public criticism during state funerals and the government's policy of reconciliation. The moratorium suited Díaz, who once condemned Dublán the Imperialist to death in 1863, only to appoint Dublán the Republican as his finance minister in 1884.[17] Dublán nevertheless earned a reputation as a financier with "few peers and no superiors in modern times."[18] News of his death prompted British Ambassador to Mexico Sir Spencer Saint John to end an evening ball in honor of Queen Victoria's birthday. Investors in New York, London, Paris, and Berlin sold their Mexican securities. Valentin Uhink, head of the Industrial and Commercial Confederation and the Chamber of Commerce, asked downtown business owners to close their doors "as a tribute of respect to the memory of the renowned statesman, and honest, loyal, and distinguished friend of Commerce."[19] Bankers, retailers, and restaurant owners hung black crepe in their windows and closed shop for two days.

The theme of economic progress permeated the Dublán funeral. On June 1, his body was transported to the National Palace, which overlooked Constitution Plaza, or the Zócalo. For the public lying-in-state, the Ambassador's Ballroom was converted into a chapel ablaze with new electric lights. Formally attired politicians, bankers, and industrialists guarded the coffin while ninety-six thousand citizens quietly filed past.[20] On June 2, "the nation" marched in a huge procession. To convey Dublán's coffin, the Federal District Railway Company rolled out the same towering hearse used in the funeral for Archbishop of Mexico Pelagio Antonio de Labastida. Transporting the anticlerical Dublán in a hearse reserved for the highest men of the cloth irritated Catholics.[21] Flanked by Ambassador Saint John and Foreign Relations Minister Ignacio Mariscal, Díaz led a cortege of three thousand notables through the city. A Division of Three Arms escorted in formation while military bands performed the funeral march of Chopin. Over one hundred thousand citizens stood along the sidewalks, making it impossible to move one step. At the Alameda mourners boarded 242 streetcars and carriages in a horse-drawn procession to the distant French Cemetery.[22]

At the burial, orators praised Dublán, Díaz, and material progress in the same breath. In his melodramatic eulogy, Congressman Luis Labastida depicted the 1884 recession as a national crisis and credited Dublán for saving the republic from sure disaster: "Bankruptcy, with its cold and ominous presence, threatened the National Treasury. Implacable creditors sapped national income, industry agonized from anemia, and commerce closed its doors before the public misery." General Díaz "reappeared miraculously and showed the most praiseworthy evidence of patriotism by facing such a distressing situation." The president called upon "Juárez's friend," Manuel Dublán, to reorganize the national economy: "Under the protection of the patriotic and honored Government, [Mexico] began its rapid and secure march on the road to progress." At the end of his oration, Labastida referred to Dublán's tomb as an "altar of immortality." An embodiment of Porfirian excess, the $20,000 family mausoleum was a fitting termination point for the lavish funeral.[23]

The Dublán funeral testified to the respect he earned within exclusive circles. *La Patria Ilustrada*, a weekly magazine published by Díaz sympathizer Ireneo Paz, printed a memorial edition with drawings of the mortuary chapel and hearse. The artist's rendition of the ballroom and crowded streets showed modern gentlemen in suits and top hats, not the barefoot *indígenas* in tattered rags and palm sombreros who also attended. The sketches could have been drawn in any European capital.[24] Moreover, the popular character of the funeral procession was truncated with the forty-five-minute carriage ride to the gated foreign cemeteries of La Piedad. Certainly, over three thousand guests and a division of tired soldiers witnessed the burial, but their participation contrasted greatly with the one hundred thousand citizens who saw Juárez buried at the centrally located Panteón de San Fernando in 1872. Letters of condolence that Díaz received from *políticos* and businessmen all expressed sympathy for Díaz's "irreparable loss" but also praised Dublán for saving the public treasury, improving the nation's credit, joining Díaz's powerful and patriotic march toward progress and national regeneration, or a combination thereof.[25] Miguel Ahumada, a military commander in Chihuahua and future governor of the northern state, ordered his soldiers to dress in mourning for nine days. Congressman Simón Parra invited Díaz to a service for Dublán sponsored by Mexico City's Masonic lodges. And Yucatán governor Daniel Traconis recounted a splendid memorial service at the Municipal Palace in Mérida.[26] The Dublán funeral stood for those with a stake in society. The only acknowledgment of popular participation was a special edition of the *Gaceta Callejera* featuring engravings by Posada. More typical of government-subsidized newspapers was the publication of Juan de Dios Peza's elegy: "He whose brilliant intellect/One day improved the credit of Mexico/And opened the free, easy, and wide path/Of commerce for my patria."[27]

Funeral Crepe over the Holiday Program

Months later, Independence Day 1891 promised to be a splendid national festival. Díaz and the nation were again to celebrate their birth dates. The Círculo de Amigos del Presidente, headed by former minister of development Carlos Pacheco, hired caterers and musical bands for the dictator's sixty-first birthday. For the nation's seventieth anniversary, the holiday program included the typical fanfare. The *círculo* even invited municipal presidents from throughout the republic to celebrate the fiestas in the capital, so they could return to their towns as propagandists for Díaz's reelection in 1892. But on September 15,

Pacheco died in Córdoba, Veracruz, and Díaz postponed his banquet. Publicist Ireneo Paz remarked, "The death of this great patriot has come to spread funeral crepe over the holiday program." A distraught Díaz told a foreign reporter: "We have lost a hero in war, a champion of progress."[28]

The dictator grieved because Carlos Pacheco had proclaimed for him during the Tuxtepec Revolt and fought bravely under his command. Born in 1839 to a poor family in Parral, Chihuahua, Pacheco enlisted in the militia at age nineteen. He sided with the Liberals, took orders from Díaz against Maximilian, and lost an arm and a leg in the Siege of Puebla (April 2, 1867). After his recovery, Pacheco could ask Díaz for anything. Brief stints as a federal deputy, governor of Morelos, minister of war, and governor of the Federal District strongly support this, but it was Manuel González who appointed him as minister of development. After serving ten years, poor health and the Tehuantepec Railroad scandal forced his resignation on March 21, 1891. But the president still promoted him to division general.[29] In April, they congratulated one another on the anniversary of Puebla. Pacheco saluted Díaz: "I can now die with a clear conscience, satisfied, after receiving these distinctions and honors from the man who has been my only ideal in war and politics." Díaz returned the gesture: "I will preserve your letter in my trophy case along with other caring expressions that have captured my heart."[30]

In a celebrated essay, historian Leslie Byrd Simpson satirized the Age of Santa Anna (1832–55) by highlighting the only continuity in this era of domestic crisis, foreign war, and fiscal insolvency: Santa Anna's missing leg in the national headlines. "Santa Anna loved his wound with pathological intensity," never allowing the fatherland to forget his leg and even burying the grisly relic in a national funeral.[31] Nor was the nation to forget the sacrifices of Liberals. Porfirista Generals Pacheco, González, and Luis Mier y Terán all lost limbs or their mind in the struggle for nationhood.[32] Pacheco "had the advantage of carrying on his body the visible imprints of his military career."[33] A high-profile public figure, he hobbled about painfully on a rickety crutch. As one obituary claimed: "Half of the body of General Pacheco was buried in Puebla on April 3, 1867; within two days his companions in arms will bury the other half, that which contained a great spirit."[34] Graphic press descriptions generated sympathy for the "indefatigable fighter" and "heroic mutilated one." One morbid statement read: "The cadaver of General Pacheco was embalmed in Motzorongo. When we say cadaver we are using a metaphor; we should say half-body because he already sacrificed the other half on the altar of the Fatherland, during our great contemporary epic." Pacheco "incarnated our autonomy and progress."[35]

While no one made light of Pacheco's disabilities, Daniel Cabrera, irreverent publisher of the virulent antigovernment satirical weekly *El Hijo del Ahuizote*, disagreed with this last assessment. He criticized Pacheco for compromising Mexican autonomy, ruining access to international credit, and presiding over other fiascos, including

> the drainage of the Valley of Mexico, Italian colonization, ostrich breeding, the colonization of Baja California, the innumerable expired railroad contracts, the sterile scientific explorations, the extravagant official competition of Mexico in the recent Exposition of Paris; the identification, survey, and partition of lands that have given rise to so many unnecessary protests and that have caused some public disturbances; the squandering of the Tlahualilo waters to farmers, the works at the ports of Tampico and Veracruz, where [the government] is spending so much money, [but] today it remains barely visible what this sacrifice will bring; the irritating tolerance of domineering railroad companies that control trade and agriculture, the plundering of lands, etc. etc.[36]

Pacheco was a gambler, often found at the roulette wheel in the Jockey Club at the Casa de Azulejos. He imbued his ministry with this personal trait. More important to Díaz was that Pacheco gambled on the *Tuxtepecazo*. Charges of favoritism, risk-taking, and selling out the nation hardly redefined Porfirian business ethics. As with the amputee politicians after the U.S. Civil War and World War I in France, Pacheco's sacrifices gave him the right to stick around for the great payoff. And Cabrera spent another term in Belén Prison, where he later contracted typhus and died. There was no elaborate state burial for this former porfirista, but he would be remembered.[37]

His shortcomings aside, Pacheco's lying-in-state was an homage to modernity. On September 17, Díaz received the body at the Buenavista Station of the Mexican Railway and escorted it to the Ministry of Development in the Mining Palace. For the public exposition, decorators arranged trophies of war, science, and industry throughout Pacheco's old stomping grounds. Encircling the casket and bronze bust of Pacheco were items that championed science and progress: a barometer, a monocle, modern agricultural tools, and mining equipment; models of a locomotive, a lighthouse, a bridge, and a monument to independence leader Miguel Hidalgo; and a map of Mexico. The chapel simulated a technology exhibit at an industrial museum or world's fair. For citizens who waited in three-hour lines, the government presented in one dramatic scene three institutions of nation-building: the census, map, and museum. By virtue of their attendance, people counted themselves as citizens of the republic, filed past the display of the nation, and imagined the modernization of their country through science and art. Like museum exhibits and other tableaux, lyings-in-state revealed the infinite reproducibility of state regalia for citizen-consumers.[38]

The procession of September 18, a Saturday, drew a colossal attendance. For the first time in Mexican history a telephone coordinated a state event. When Díaz arrived at the Mining Palace at 9:00 a.m., railway administrator Francisco Peón del Castillo voiced directions over the phone for employees to line up fifty tramcars along Independence Street. The timing was perfect, and the telephone's role promoted the new Ministry of Communications. In funerals for division generals, riderless parade horses often trotted behind the hearse to emphasize the loss of the *caudillo*. For the Pacheco funeral, organizers rolled out his vacant landau to emphasize his role as development minister. Over 120,000 tourists (visiting for Independence Day), professionals, industrial workers, and expatriates living in the foreign colonies witnessed the event. *Gendarmes* barely restrained the restive crowd, but as pallbearers placed the coffin on the hearse the mass of onlookers doffed their hats. Díaz rode in the tramcar immediately behind the empty coach, symbolizing his proximity to Pacheco while presiding over the state ceremony.[39]

Funeral orations and commemorative acts incorporated Pacheco into collective memory. Even after death, the praetorian regime apportioned the spoils of war. Díaz reserved a place for him in the Rotunda of Illustrious Men, where eulogists acclaimed his progressive thinking. After the burial, the states of Chiapas, Sonora, Tabasco, Chihuahua, and Morelos all named Pacheco a *ciudadano* (Great Citizen) or benemérito. Mexico City renamed the Candelarita Plaza after him. The steamship *Carlos Pacheco* brought his name to ports throughout the Caribbean. Jacinto Moreno composed a funeral march for him. Public dignitaries, such as Pacheco's successor as minister of development, Manuel Fernández Leal, led annual pilgrimages to Pacheco's tomb. When Morelos governor Jesús Preciado contracted Gabriel Guerra to produce a bronze statue in 1895, American railroad entrepreneur Colonel J. H. Hampson shipped it free of charge from Mexico City to Cuernavaca, where it was unveiled in the garden of the Palacio de Cortés. In 1896, Díaz unveiled a burial monument that showed Pacheco wounded but standing triumphantly, like the modern republic for which he fought.[40]

While Díaz immortalized his loyal followers for posterity, the deaths of two important cabinet ministers had a weighty impact on national politics. The loss of Dublán and Pacheco empowered a ruling clique that revolved around Interior Minister Manuel Romero Rubio. A foreign relations minister under Sebastián Lerdo de Tejada, he had grown influential with the dictator ever since Díaz married Romero Rubio's oldest daughter, Carmen, in 1881. Romero Rubio's own presidential aspirations ended with the constitutional revision of 1890, which allowed for Díaz's indefinite reelection. Nevertheless, he engendered a notable legacy as the *padre político* of the *científicos*. During the González interregnum, these lawyers, engineers, and economists met at the Romero Rubio home to discuss public policy and debate theories of governance. As positivist technocrats, they secured power with the appointment of José Yves Limantour as finance minister in 1893. Thereafter, state funerals differed from the Dublán and Pacheco archetypes only in their magnified scale and opulence.

Separation: Deathbed Scenes and Famous Last Words

In the 1890s, newspaper reporters and artists went to great lengths to reconstruct a public leader's "exemplary death," the opening act in the state funeral drama.[41] Rather than the final stage of a public career, the manner of a national hero's death begins the rite of passage known as separation. Journalists were deeply moved when they saw General Mariano Escobedo, the Victor of Querétaro who defeated Emperor Maximilian, weeping at the bedside of his dying comrade-in-arms, General Sóstenes Rocha. One headline read "The Agony," and editors authenticated the incident by publishing the names of all witnesses.[42] In 1889, Jalisco governor Ramón Corona fell prey to a deranged assassin in Guadalajara. Newspaper correspondent Manuel Caballero provided excruciating detail of the murder and even hired a boy to dip his hand in red ink and stamp each front page of the November 11 edition as if it were the bloody hand of the killer. This sensationalism horrified *tapatíos*, but they turned out in huge numbers for Corona's funeral.[43] When Manuel Romero Rubio underwent brain surgery in 1895, periodicals lamented that chloroform rendered the highbrow of the government comatose.[44] Whenever the state exhumed a national hero for reburial, the press took great care in describing the deplorable physical state of the remains. Such was the case for the "bullet-perforated skull" of ill-fated patriot Melchor Ocampo and the "disintegrated craniums of the Independence Heroes after years of church neglect." Liberals howled, "History protests against this sacrilege," but sad stories of emotional breakdowns, sensational murders, and neglected remains stoked the fires of the national imagination.[45]

Turn-of-the-century Mexicans also developed an obsession with famous last words. General Sóstenes Rocha, who had fought for the Liberals in one hundred engagements over a forty-two-year span, identified an unvanquished adversary on his deathbed: "Yes, this is the final march Eduardo [Velásquez], not in retreat but in front of the enemy, clericalism."[46] In 1902, Mariano Escobedo's last words aided the state: "The new generation follows in the footsteps of the old in creating citizens who will defend the integrity of our territory, and because they are already so enlightened they will do more than what we did, converting hoes into rifles and church bells into cannon." Before passing, he delivered a final dramatic phrase: "respect to the authorities."[47] Whether genuine or apocryphal, this was a proverb originally attributed to Benito Juárez, instructing citizens to obey authority.[48]

Meaningful to citizens was whether a priest performed the last rites. Many leaders were militant anticlericals and Freemasons, who spent lifetimes reducing Church influence only to see it resurge under Díaz. Roman Catholic doctrine permitted sinners and nonbelievers to be saved if they repented, confessed, and received the last sacraments on their deathbed.[49] Speculation always arose whether Liberals entered the hereafter free of all mortal (and political) sins. Implacable reformer Ignacio Ramírez, who drew the clergy's ire with his infamous phrase "God does not exist," died an atheist.[50] In 1891, a Catholic newspaper expressed concern for Dublán's soul: "We do not know if Mr. Dublán had abjured his masonic beliefs and received the last rites of the Catholic religion in his final hour, [but] we hope that this was the case."[51] El Tiempo proudly stated that General Mier y Terán, expelled from the Masons after the Veracruz executions, returned to the maternal protection of the Church. A huge debate erupted over the alleged deathbed conversion of Manuel Romero Rubio. His personal secretary, Rosendo Pineda, testified that after surgery, Don Manuel never even regained consciousness, much less converted. In contrast, when Guillermo Prieto faced death he received the final sacrament. When the Catholic El País insinuated that Mariano Escobedo received the last rites from his brother, a priest, who stood beside his bed, Diario del Hogar retorted that the entire family was there to console him, not convert him in his final hours.[52]

The government often hired a professional artist to form a plaster of paris death mask to preserve the image of the deceased subject's face for eternity. Although the custom of producing a mascarilla originated in medieval Europe, it took on political overtones in republican Mexico. Death masks served as three-dimensional models to produce statues, busts, and sepulchral monuments long after burial. Porfirian sculptors only took the aspect of great Liberals, politicizing the act of artistic reproduction by ensuring that only their visages were immortalized. Likenesses of Juárez sprouted up throughout Mexico because his mascarilla preserved the image of the "Great Republican" for posterity. The state exhibited the Juárez mask at the National Museum, and a reproduction was given as a gift to Díaz during the Year of Juárez in 1906.[53] The Italian Enrico Alciati and renowned Mexican sculptors Miguel Noreña and Gabriel Guerra produced death masks for politicians and generals.[54]

Government-sponsored artists, workshops (talleres), and schools dominated the production of public art in Porfirian Mexico. Díaz took pride in the work of Jesús F. Contreras, who "studied with the best European teachers under the protection of the government."[55] Contreras was attached to the

Mexican delegation at the Paris Universal Exposition of 1889. He carried a government stipend and letters of introduction from President Díaz and Justice Minister Joaquín Baranda, impressing the great masters in the workshops of France and Italy. As an apprentice of Miguel Noreña, he produced the bas-reliefs for the Cuauhtémoc memorial but is best known for *Malgré Tout*, his sublime marble masterpiece of a chained woman. Díaz entrusted Contreras with the death mask of his father-in-law, a bust of the archbishop of Mexico, and dozens of statues.[56] The president also helped Contreras establish the Fundición Artística Mexicana. If Mexico's official sculptor was unavailable for funerary art, the regime enlisted his apprentices at the *fundición* or the Escuela Nacional de Bellas Artes.[57]

Transition: State Appropriation of the Body, Lyings-in-State, and Processions

With the body heavily guarded at the home, the government prepared the funeral event with all of its technologies of power and social control. The dawn of the information age and transportation revolution turned newsworthy stories into national media events. By 1890, every Mexican government ministry had a telegraph office. News of a public leader's death traveled as fast as electrical currents and locomotives.[58] Historian Luís González y González explains that trains brought city dwellers and country folk together in San José de Gracia: "Don Gregorio Pulido brought back tales from the capital of the republic. . . . He was the one people looked to for descriptions of Don Porfirio and the magnificent processions in the capital."[59] An imagined community sometimes prevailed over the geographical and social dislocation of eight million rural agrarians.[60]

Cloaked in the patriotic rhetoric and paternalistic style of its architects, the Porfirian state *stated* how days of public mourning were spent.[61] Suspending birthday parties for Queen Victoria and President Díaz during the funerals of 1891 was merely proper etiquette compared to state decisions that changed everyday life. Functionaries closed public offices and suspended national schools, but bureaucrats and schoolchildren were expected to participate in the obsequies. The government mobilized armed personnel to provide security and escort the hearse. Citizens regularly watched troop movements through the streets. Street-corner advertisements the size of bullfighting posters placarded the colonnades along the Zócalo. Official mortuary announcements (*esquelas oficiales*) compelled the private sector to attend. Although Mexican law required burial of cadavers within twenty-four hours of death, processions were postponed up to three days to guarantee a large weekend crowd.

For ordinary people, state funerals were intrusive. *Capitalinos* knew

Figure 24. The coffin containing the body of Mariano Escobedo, the "Victor of Querétaro," leaving his residence in the suburb of Tacubaya. Soldiers guard the entrance to the home. Officers, infantryman, and the employees of the Gayosso Agency serve as pallbearers. A police escort awaits. The sable trappings of the division general top the casket. In the background, women peer down from the rooftop. Photo courtesy of Fototeca Instituto Nacional de Antropología e Historia, Pachuca.

Figure 25. José Guadalupe Posada's *Arrival of the Cadaver of General González a esta capital*, from the *Gaceta Callejera*. This illustration shows the train decorated *en luto* (in mourning) as it pulls into Mexico City. The twin towers of the National Cathedral appear in the background. The army escort reunites with their general. Umbrellas, the woman in her *reboso*, and the doffed hats of the rich and poor show the respect of the Mexican people. Photo courtesy of the Hemeroteca Nacional.

someone had died when the War Ministry ordered salvos of cannon fire discharged from the Ciudadela every thirty minutes from dawn until dusk. Word spread by messengers, house-to-house rumor, coffeehouse chat, and newspaper hawkers.[62] Although funerals cut into profits, private businesses responded favorably. Merchants closed their doors. Railroad and streetcar schedules were modified, and passenger fares were reduced. Musical bands in the Zócalo and Alameda disappeared. Promenades remained deserted. The Arbeu, Hidalgo, and Principal theaters canceled performances. Staging a *zarzuela* (a picaresque musical comedy) or *tanda* (popular one-act play) may have provoked a negative response from authorities. Orrin's Circus and the Peralvillo Race Track rested their animals. Casinos stored away the dice and playing cards. National lotteries were rescheduled. Holiday fireworks, the spring Flower Wars (Combate de Flores), and even charitable events were postponed. State funerals were the only show in town.[63]

Meanwhile, the president decreed or Congress passed funeral laws whereby the nation assumed all expenses. After an impassioned speech by a congressman, the Chamber of Deputies voted funds. The Senate, often caricatured as a "Political Cemetery" of old cabinet ministers and military officers, reviewed resolutions. Passage of a funeral bill was automatic, but the provisions of each law disclose government intentions and the political status of the fallen leader. For example, friends and political protégés of the deceased lobbied Díaz and Congress for pecuniary aid for surviving family members. After the death of Ignacio Ramírez in 1879, Díaz granted his sons scholarships to national schools.[64] Influential publicist Rafael Reyes Spíndola asked Díaz to honor the "great wish" of General Mariano Jimenez by employing his twenty-one-year-old son.[65] Upon the death of Manuel González, his subordinates requested immediate audience with President Díaz to ask for his political protection.[66] Guillermo Prieto's plea for Congress to pension the widow of Altamirano further demonstrates state paternalism: "We cannot turn our backs on his *compañera*; the Chamber, in the name of the Patria, must say 'we protect you because you loved him.'" The reward for lifelong companionship was 100 pesos monthly.[67] There was no statute of limitations on government pensions, as the daughter of Donato Guerra and the granddaughter of Miguel Hidalgo both received them.[68]

Widows of the illustrious dead had a powerful ally in the first lady of Mexico. In the event that legal hurdles proved insensitive to the immediate needs of widows, a private entreaty to Carmen Romero Rubio accelerated the process. Josefa Fernández de Jimenez did not know Doña Carmen well prior to the death of her husband, General Mariano Jimenez. But when she asked Carmen to name her the executor of her husband's will to speed up the distribution of her husband's wealth in the courts, Carmen replied, "I have the great pleasure of granting your wish. . . . I spoke to Porfirio about the issues you raised and he will resolve them in the best way possible." Presidential intervention in this case involved transferring executorship from one Lara Jimenez to Josefa, negotiating with family lawyers, and navigating through the logjams of court proceedings in Oaxaca. Josefa Fernandez de Jimenez knew the Oaxacan legal system all too well: "Business here only advances when they are favored by some superior recommendation or by the intervention of persons protected by power."[69] Given the volume and variety of personal requests of the first lady, Carmen Romero Rubio was by her early thirties the most influential woman in Mexico. The records are mute about what became of General Jimenez's will. But it is reasonable to assume based on Díaz's record of paternalism that Carmen's wishes were granted.

While passage of a funeral resolution was guaranteed, state appropriation of the body was not. In 1891, Congress authorized a funeral for José María Iglesias, Díaz's electoral opponent and disgruntled political enemy, but the family flatly rejected the offer. When an official delegation visited the home, Iglesias's son Fernando turned them away: "Following the line of conduct adopted by my father of complete withdrawal and never accepting the present order of things, we have decided that only the family has the right to organize the funeral."[70]

Congress usually determined the site for the lying-in-state and burial, the two coordinates linked by the funeral procession. While several palaces served for public visitation, the choice of burial grounds was limited to the private aristocratic French Cemetery or the *rotonda*. The regime chose sites that captured the essence of the hero, accommodated family wishes, and met Díaz's approval. The lying-in-state of Juan N. Méndez, second-in-command during the Tuxtepec Revolt, took place at the War Department to emphasize his loyalty, patriotism, and military record. Press obituaries emphasized his service with Zaragoza at the Battle of Cinco de Mayo (1862) and with Díaz when Méndez led a porfirista force of twenty-six thousand into Mexico City (1876). In 1894, the War Ministry organized the funeral to reenact the capture of the city.[71]

If family wishes were not a consideration, the government chose the Panteón de Dolores over the aesthetically pleasing French Cemetery because the vitally important rotunda drew larger numbers of impressionable citizens. Between 1897 and 1900, Díaz authorized the exhumations and reburials of three *Constituyentes*: the ill-fated martyr Melchor Ocampo, Foreign Minister to the U.S. José María Mata, and federalist lawyer Ponciano Arriaga.[72] Citizens may or may not have viewed Ocampo's remains, visited Mata's funeral train, or attended Arriaga's state reburial.[73] But customary pilgrimages to the popular cemetery of their nation's capital meant that they leisurely filed past their burial monuments throughout the year. The next generation did the same.

Arriaga's eulogist, Félix Romero, commented: "With these manifestations of national gratitude you educate the people in civism and prepare the infinite future of the Republic."[74]

Once the departure point and final resting place were known, the interior minister planned the funeral itinerary to travel through the wealthiest downtown boulevards. Corteges formed outside the Legislative Palace at Factor and Vergara streets and headed east along Tacubaya or Cinco de Mayo toward the Plaza de la Constitución, or Zócalo. Although the Zócalo was the axis of nine intersecting streets, processions followed the same route. Mourners walked to the plaza, passing the National Cathedral and National Palace, before turning west down San Francisco and Plateros streets (now Francisco I. Madero) to Avenida Juárez, which fronts the Alameda. They passed in front of impressive baroque, *churrigueresque*, and neoclassical colonial palaces that housed international banks, department stores, the Jockey Club, and cafés. It was a route of power and prestige, exclusivity and privilege. But funerals created a time and space for the uninvited commoner, whom police might have forced away during a normal business day.

To add grandeur to the spectacle, wealthy capitalists and small business owners alike offered their assistance to the state. In 1893, English-born railroad tycoon and president of the Banco de Londrés y Méjico, Thomas Braniff, donated his private coach to transport Ignacio Altamirano's remains. For the 1903 reburial of independence hero Nicolás Bravo, affluent families loaned their carriages to the city for use in the procession. Family coats of arms and initials identified the owners of each stately Victoria. Extra coaches were even parked along the processional route to add decor. City businesses decorated their facades in both black crepe and the national colors. After 1902, electric trolleys conveyed mourners, and the Mexican Valley Railroad occasionally interrupted processions. The surprise locomotive reminded onlookers of national progress.[75]

Delays due to international transport were expected if a statesman died overseas. But funerals also strengthened binational relations. The French government transported Altamirano's remains from San Remo, Italy, to Paris for a service at the Père Lachaise.[76] On New Year's Day 1899, U.S. president William McKinley attended the funeral for Matías Romero at St. Matthew's Cathedral in Washington, D.C. In 1905, President Theodore Roosevelt ordered the U.S. Navy cruiser *Columbia* to repatriate the body of Ambassador Manuel Aspíroz. After the voyage, Díaz invited the American sailors to march behind the hearse and asked their band to perform at the burial ceremony. The splendid funeral seemed out of proportion with Aspíroz's historical significance, but the navy personnel later banqueted with President Díaz and cadets from the Chapultepec Military College. The government also scheduled two sporting

Figure 26. Porfirio Díaz, Ramón Corral, and a host of public officials receiving the coffin of a distinguished figure, Juventino Rosas (1909) or Ignacio Mariscal (1910), at the National Railway Station. State funeral hearses stood over ten feet tall with feathered plumes, artistic scrollwork, and a decorative wreath emblem. They looked like stages of a Victorian theater, complete with raised platform and drawable curtains. Photo courtesy of Fototeca Instituto Nacional de Antropología e Historia, Pachuca.

events that represented national pastimes: a Mexican bullfight and a baseball game between the sailors and a Mexican team. In 1847, U.S. armed forces had stormed Chapultepec, killing many of the defending cadets of the Military College. In 1905, American sailors fraternized with them and performed free concerts at Chapultepec Park. Even Filomena Mata, the valiant opponent of *porfirismo*, admitted that U.S.–Mexican relations were never so good.[77]

Officials hosted lyings-in-state in the most impressive palaces in the City of Palaces. The public expositions of famous bodies were deliberately staged events. As a rule, presidents, cabinet ministers, and generals lay-in-state at the National Palace; congressmen, in the Chamber of Deputies; governors, at the Municipal Palace; and magistrates, in the Supreme Court building. The choice of venue spoke about the hero's career but also revealed what parts of the person's past the regime wanted to emphasize most. The chapels for lyings-in-state (*capillas ardientes*) were decorated with items that symbolized selected achievements. Whereas Emperor Maximilian's architect, Ramón Rodríguez Arrangoity, festooned the catafalques of early Porfirian funerals, civil and military engineers took over after 1890. They typically wrapped coffins in the national tricolor and placed them on an inclined surface for easy viewing. Coffins featured transparent crystal lids for the people to see the

Figure 27. Lying-in-state of Alfredo Chavero in the Chamber of Deputies (1906). This image captures the evocative brilliance of electric lighting, natural floral wreaths, and public speech. Here civilian leaders serve as the honor guard as Díaz presides. Photo courtesy of Fototeca Instituto Nacional de Antropología e Historia, Pachuca.

upper torso and face. For González, a special $1,200 casket was constructed from a design originally used for the son of the Prince of Wales. *Ingeniero* Ignacio Bejarano ordered González to be dressed in military uniform and surrounded with martial emblems and the regalia of a thirty-third-degree Mason. For Guillermo Prieto, he placed a golden lyre and two open books, *History* and *Law*, near the casket. Gilberto Luna transported the contents of the National Artillery Museum to the National Palace for War Minister Berriozábal. Rifles, bugles, drums, and shovels were placed in the infantry section; swords and antique lances in the cavalry section; and cannon and shot in the artillery section. The navy was underrepresented in art as in life, with a sole anchor. When the public filed past, they were inundated with soldierly images, including the battle flags of the republic. For the Independence Heroes, the city converted the San José Chapel in the National Cathedral into a secular altar.[78] Officials removed candles, which they felt represented the Church, and installed chandeliers that cast brilliant light. To round out the multisensory experience, full string orchestras performed classical requiems and dirges and were instructed not to play Church hymns. In fact, chapels were devoid of any Catholic symbols, except for the occasional holy cross, a concession to families. Militant Liberals complained if a single crucifix appeared. Similarly, the overbearing presence of Masonic emblems infuriated Catholics.[79]

The twenty-four-hour lyings-in-state were quintessential Porfirian stage-craft, but they drew huge crowds and elicited genuine respect. Newspapers published the rotation of honor guards who held overnight vigil. Popular attendance ranged from several hundred to over one hundred thousand citizens. Poor weather or the late arrival of the coffin discouraged attendance; the two factors in combination ruined obsequies for General Donato Guerra.[80] Citizens turned out to pay their respects to leaders, satisfy their morbid curiosity, and see Díaz, González, Escobedo, and Bernardo Reyes serve as sentries. People dressed as custom warranted, maintained silence as they approached the catafalque, and took off their hats. Filing slowly past the coffin was a deeply personal but also communal experience. When reaching the body, each mourner had a moment to cope with private memory and grief, but not without realizing that strangers in line before and after them were doing the same.[81] At that point strangers became fellow citizens in mourning. Public grief for Manuel González was phenomenal. Hundreds of urban poor passed the coffin with tears streaming down their faces. Overwhelmed with emotion, one *señora* fainted at the bier. González had pardoned her husband, who was sentenced to be shot at the military prison.[82]

The government tried to preserve tranquility by stationing policemen at cramped entryways, but pushing often led to fistfights, riots, and petty theft. No one was safe from hooliganism, but the targeting of authorities suggests that larceny constituted resistance. During the González lying-in-state, gendarmes barely controlled the tightly packed crowd. Pickpockets stole General Francisco Troncoso's watch, Colonel Juan Vega's ornamental tie tack, Captain Castañeda's pistol, and the hats, jewelry, umbrellas, shawls, and canes of everyone else.[83] A journalist at the Independence Heroes debacle outside the National Cathedral witnessed the crowd "precipitating an avalanche that the police had difficulty containing, even making use of their arms."[84] Another reporter blamed policemen for clubbing indiscriminately, cursing obscenities, and otherwise mistreating citizens. The crowd retaliated by unhorsing and beating a patrol officer. In response to these aggravations, Díaz ordered the 21st Batallion to guard the Independence Heroes urn overnight. Undeterred, thousands forced soldiers through the cathedral door after midnight. The following morning of July 30, the anniversary of Father Miguel Hidalgo's death, a huge crowd committed the customary misdemeanors that were evolving toward felonies. The hats of well-to-do women were torn from their heads and trampled or stolen. One woman lost her petticoat, her hat, and a shirt sleeve to the frightening riot and covered her face with a handkerchief in shame. When Díaz arrived, a wave of human flesh surged in his direction, prompting the dictator to place his wreath and quickly escape through a side door. The governor's shouts of "Order!" and "Move back!" had no effect on the disobedient

mob. Engulfed, soldiers and policemen unsheathed their weapons and fever-
ishly delivered blows. From his vantage point in one of the church towers,
Federico Gamboa saw several people brutally assaulted. To view Romero
Rubio's body in October 1895, crowds broke through a line of sixty gendarmes
and forcibly occupied the theater boxes of the Chamber of Deputies. When
soldiers opened the National Palace for the Berriozábal lying-in-state, three
thousand people rushed the entrance, causing the worst confusion and a most
disrespectful scene.[85] Such incidents embarrassed a government trying to con-
trive an urbane event.

After the lying-in-state, the government sometimes held a short official
ceremony, but the main event was the grand procession. Gigantism reigned
as American- or English-built hearses towered over participants. Drivers in
top hats, black plumes, and golden angels added verticality to the visual effect.
Not unlike miniature Victorian stages, hearses had drawable curtains and an
elevated platform for the casket. Wreaths, flags, and crepe were visible, but
nothing ever obstructed the view of the coffin. Audiences of this street theater
sympathized with the loss only if they saw it. Six powerful coal-black horses
with rich capes draped over their backs pulled the heavy structure. The spectacle and sound of enormous and spirited horses stepping through a silent cor-
ridor of uniformed men inspired awe among a people accustomed to dodging

Figure 28. José Guadalupe Posada's print of Manuel González lying-in-state
(1893), from the *Gaceta Callejera*. Caskets often had transparent glass or crystal
lids so that citizens could properly view the fallen hero. Image courtesy of the
Hemeroteca Nacional.

Figure 29. State funeral for Mariano Escobedo (1902). This scene from the Zócalo shows the ritual structure of all Porfirian state funerals. People from all social classes lined the streets, but only dignitaries marched. Soldiers formed a double line to honor the deceased and to contain the crowd. Prominent families loaned their carriages to frame the procession and add to its visual appeal. Photo courtesy of Fototeca Instituto Nacional de Antropología e Historia, Pachuca.

smaller carriages drawn recklessly by undernourished horses.[86] Adding to the impression of the horses' beauty and strength were the six groomsmen who each held a horse's bridle. For Berriozábal, the Federal District Railway Company tested the first hearse with double-wheeled traction. It rolled along cobblestone streets on one set and then switched to narrow-gauge rails at the paseo.[87]

On special occasions, railroad platform cars and gun carriages, commonly used for holiday parade floats, replaced or supplemented the imported hearses. For the 1894 pantheonization of Josefa Ortíz de Domínguez, the Hercules, Purísima, and San Antonio textile factories in the state of Querétaro built an allegorical float to conduct her remains. The urn was presented with a backdrop of the national emblem (an eagle with outspread wings), war trophies, and floral wreaths. After a lengthy tug-of-war, Mexico City surrendered "La Corregidora" to Querétaro, but Doña Carmen oversaw the construction of a surrogate, a monument to her in the Plaza de Santo Domingo. During the state funeral for Manuel Romero Rubio, a railroad car conveyed five hundred wreaths to the cemetery, including one from Guanajuato governor Luis González Obregón made entirely out of silver.[88] For the Independence Heroes reburial, two patriotic societies, "La Gran Familia Modelo" and "Junta Patriótica Hidalgo," blan-

Figure 30. State funeral for Ignacio Mariscal (1910). This photograph provides a close-up view of the tall hearse "staging" the casket for the crowds. Vice-President Ramón Corral and city fathers escort the remains. Photo courtesy of Fototeca Instituto Nacional de Antropología e Historia, Pachuca.

keted a platform car with black velvet and red roses. Two life-sized statues of Hidalgo and Juárez guarded a case containing the skulls of four insurgent leaders. In 1903, an urn containing the remains of caudillo Nicolás Bravo was placed on a rolling gun carriage.[89]

In all processions, the ruling elite formed a linear sequence that reflected the political order and social hierarchy. The González cortege unraveled in a typical order: gendarmes as armed escorts, hearse, riderless horse, Díaz, cabinet members, diplomatic corps, Supreme Court justices, congressmen, generals, line officers, the Federal District governor, city councilmen, public employees, and private guests. An army division formed a rear guard. Elites and bureaucrats formed the cortege, while public security confined the popular classes to the sidewalks. In a city where it was easy to determine one's class based on outward appearances, the state prohibited the downtrodden to detract from the event. Streetcars were fitted with *letreros* (nameplates) indicating who sat where on the way to the burial site. Others walked or went home. The introduction of electric streetcars disallowed pedestrian access to the *carro completo*.[90]

The participation of workers' associations was limited until the Independence Heroes funeral of 1895. As thousands underwent first-wave factory discipline, their role in state ceremonies steadily increased. The industrial census

Figure 31. Díaz marching on foot flanked by his cabinet ministers in the state funeral of Ignacio Mariscal (1910). Funeral processions were always manifestations of political power during the momentary weakening of the state after the death of one of its members. Photo courtesy of Fototeca Instituto Nacional de Antropología e Historia, Pachuca.

of 1902 listed fifty-five hundred manufacturing industries nationwide, mostly in the production of light consumer goods such as textiles, shoes, and cigarettes. Delegations were invited to fly their banners in processions, but most working-class men and women gathered along the customary parade route and concentrated at the Alameda. This marked the entrance to the popular Avenida Juárez and the transitional point from the march on foot to the streetcars. Less congested than sidewalks, the Alameda offered commoners a place to socialize and reinforce their identity vis-à-vis the tramcar passengers. On occasion, the park also served as the rallying point for protesting students and workers. It was their last downtown refuge, sandwiched between the panopticons of Church and State in the Zócalo and the rich colonias along the paseo.[91] With this spatial concession, the state indoctrinated workers in the catechism of modernity and encouraged them to "vote with their feet." Popular behavior generally suggests acceptance of the social order and even complicity with the dominant ideology. Although the ruling class engineered the very standards by which its rule was evaluated, working people enjoyed the diversion from normal time and a day off.[92] No evidence surfaced of the late-colonial aristocracy's practice of hiring *monigotes* (professional mourners, usually street denizens who needed the income) to walk in processions.[93] However, the enormous representation of low-level bureaucrats and city workers (all on the government payroll) ensured impressive corteges.

Far from the solemn and orderly rituals the state envisioned, funeral processions were sometimes interrupted by unruly crowds. A reporter witnessed "a most indecorous scene" at the Dublán procession when policemen thrust their swords at the crowd, which "countermarched, pushed, whistled, and shouted, as if they were at a bullfight."[94] Beginning in 1893, an escort (*descubierta*) of fifty mounted gendarmes cleared the way for processions. Soldiers, who once served a decorative function, now formed a wall to contain the crowd. The enhanced presence of armed men exacerbated tensions, as soldiers frequently used their rifle butts to open passageways through walls of people. Surging masses broke through security lines at the Romero Rubio procession. Hundreds were pushed into the procession or scaled carriages parked along the route to escape the crushing wave of human flesh. The arms of authoritarianism responded with characteristic cruelty. Mounted *rurales* used their clubs freely to clear the streets. One of Díaz's closest friends, Bishop of Oaxaca Eulogio Gillow, lost an 800-peso watch to a *ratero*. Isolated incidents perpetrated by a few rabble-rousers evolved into greater discord caused by abusive policemen and transgressive masses. Given their organic view of society, positivists interpreted any sign of disorder as a disease capable of poisoning the whole social body. The ruling elite expected dereliction from the "degenerate masses," but not during state ceremonies.[95]

Porfirian modernizers hoped that constructing a National Pantheon downtown would reduce unnecessary face-to-face encounters with the rural poor. Indeed, the technocrats' grand state funeral framed by a modern city always transformed as processions headed south into the bucolic area approaching the French Cemetery of La Piedad. *Campesinos* watched from the rooftops of ramshackle houses and tree branches. Barefoot children, stray dogs, and chickens dodged the streetcars. Here the rural poor played unrehearsed roles, and the image of wealth, power, and prestige lost its potency. Any sensible person might have pondered the urban–rural divide, social inequality, and rural neglect. In this contact zone, even the differences between moderately dressed urban proletarian wage earners and sparingly clad peasants were pronounced. The hegemonic process required negotiation between modernization and tradition, *los de arriba* and *los de abajo*, but the ruling elite made no effort to hide their disdain for peasants.[96]

Other unrefined scenes and disgraceful incidents embarrassed Porfirian "wizards of progress." This is historian Mauricio Tenorio-Trillo's term for the organizers of Mexican exhibits at international expositions. The era produced a guild of wizards who brought Europe home with them after the world's fairs. But for every three dozen wizards manipulating the national image in the name of progress, there was always one Dorothy willing to draw the curtains and expose their charlatanism through satire and puns.[97] Opposition journalist

Daniel Cabrera, for example, was known to hang a black cloth from the balcony of his office to mourn the death of press freedom.[98] During one state funeral in 1894, soldiers returning downtown after the grueling march from Dolores Cemetery passed out from heat exhaustion. As their superior officer castigated them, local women cried abuse: "Poor boys, they have not eaten! Let them rest!" The women sympathized with the foot soldiers and assigned blame to the army for their nutritional deficiency. The press carried the story but derided the soldiers for drinking *pulque* before the funeral.[99] Moralists blamed this alcoholic beverage derived from the maguey plant and a staple of the popular-class diet for every social problem.[100]

Processions were so standardized that deviations from the norm invited criticism. In 1900, a new government ordinance called for soldiers to converge at Dolores to prevent the obstruction of streetcar lines. Filomena Mata accused the government of sacrificing the spectacle of marching soldiers for the display of well-regulated modernity: "People who attend a burial know they are not at a fiesta but fulfilling a distressing obligation, and they expect the customary nuisances; so we find it unjustified that the character and solemnity of a military burial is eliminated for the comfort of mourners." Mata also insisted that the march on foot for Dublán was more dignified than the tramcar procession for Felipe Berriozábal.[101] Electric trolleys created as many problems as they solved. In the funeral of Mariano Escobedo in 1902, President Díaz and a long train of mourners boarded the trolleys at the Calzada de Tacubaya and traveled down the Paseo de la Reforma at an impressive pace. Climbing the hill to Dolores, the procession slowed to a crawl and eventually a dead stop due to insufficient electrical power. Technicians scrambled to detach the stalled trolleys at the end of the convoy so those at the front could continue. Moving each car up the hill one at a time delayed the funeral service. Pedestrians arrived punctually, but tramcar passengers reached the cemetery one hour into the burial ceremony. Technological innovation, the heralded solution to all ills, diminished the splendor of this state event.[102]

Incorporation: Burial Ceremonies and Commemorations

The state funeral represents the zero anniversary of a leader's death, but its impact continues as long as memory is preserved. Funeral orations always praise the dead and convey the significance of individual lives to contemporaries and for posterity. As political speeches, they were incomparable documents that resonated with state pedagogy. They recurred so often during "national time" that they became ritualized lessons like the singing of a national anthem or the recitation of a popular poem or prayer. Similar to the Liberal sermons published in newspapers, funeral orations upheld the national dead as models of civic duty and pride, taught a code of ethical behavior, and censured poor conduct.[103] Eager to embrace modernity, the cultured middle class responded with gratitude. The state's inculcation of working class discipline, a capitalist work ethic, and civic virtue received mixed responses from the popular classes. Nevertheless, state ideology permeated obituaries, symbolic imagery, and above all orations.[104]

While detailed analysis of funeral orations lay outside the parameters of this study, memorial addresses for Manuel Romero Rubio typify the state formula. Senator Apolinar Castillo opened the ceremony with a telling statement: "The present is bound to the past by memory. When a public man dies, he continues to be useful to humanity[, and] his fellow citizens are called on to pass sentence on his character." Castillo then situated Romero Rubio in the continuum of national heroes: "Nations justly revere all their great men. We see in Hidalgo the creative force which brought forth Morelos and Guerrero . . . in Juárez the creative force of Miguel and Sebastián Lerdo de Tejada, Ocampo, and Zaragosa, and in Porfirio Díaz . . . the many able men who have worked and are still working with him for the aggrandizement and peace of the Republic."[105] This timeless triumvirate of Hidalgo–Juaréz–Díaz, referred to as "the exalted trinity of our national religion," was officially codified in the 1890s to pay homage to the past and congratulate the present.[106] The next speaker, Congressman José María Gamboa, predicted the future: "The present generation will transmit its admiration of Romero Rubio to its children." And científico lawyer Joaquín Casasús sent everyone home with the moral of this fable: "Peace has rested on three solid foundations: material improvements, popular education, and order."[107]

If this formula was typical, General Bernardo Reyes delivered the Porfirian funeral address par excellence for Mariano Escobedo. Three scholars who later wrote histories of the Porfiriato, José López-Portillo y Rojas, Rafael de Zayas Enríquez, and Rodolfo Reyes, also spoke at Escobedo's funeral, but it was the elder Reyes who stole the show. Before national delegations in the congressional chamber, Reyes pronounced on May 22, 1902:

> The nation mourns; a patriot has expired; a hero has returned to dust, a giant gladiator, who began his epic struggle in 1847, who combated tyranny, who labored unflaggingly for the triumph of our political constitution, whose victorious sword flashed in the titanic battles of our second independence is stricken by the hand of death.
>
> Deposit his body, then, like a relic in the bosom of the earth and let his memory live on gloriously in our consciences.
>
> The national flag, the emblem of the people's deeds of greatness and sacrifice, in which the illustrious deceased took a heroic part;

that glorious flag, with its august folds, shelters him; and History, even now, as he succumbs amidst the full swell of the trumpets of Fame, entones a hymn in immortal verse to him.

Running through its thunderous strophes one seems to hear the roar of cannon, the bugle's blast, recalling the isolated, brave deeds of the tremendous national defense in 1847, in whose combats of sacrifice, Mariano Escobedo, full of the enthusiasm of youth, took a part. The epic notes of that hymn bring back the struggle of liberty against obvious tyranny; they evoke the image of Escobedo in the legions of the north, fighting by the side of Zuazua, Zayas and Zaragoza until they finally waved aloft the victorious flag of Ayutla. In that tumultuous lyric we hear the shouts of those who, with Escobedo, fought until they won the Great Charter of 1857, whereupon the republic is based; we hear the enthusiastic harangues of the triumphant leaders of the Reform. . . . [Escobedo,] the frontier chieftain, the thunderbolt of the North when he strikes and lays low the enemy at Santa Gertrudis and San Jacinto. They seem to give the order for the advance; we see the band of warriors sweep impetuously over the plain, until they surround the imperial army, with the emperor at its head, in the city of Querétaro; they sound the signal for the attack and the awe-striking blasts are repeated until, while the world looked on in amazement, the so-called emperor and empire were, on May 15, 1867, forever buried beneath the ruins of that heroic city; and until, later on, on June 21 of the same year, the conqueror of the east, the immortal hero of April 2, now the ruler of the nation, after the siege and capture of the city of Mexico, planted once more on the battlements of the national palace the glorious flag of the republic, the flag that enfolds the bier of the heroic dead at this solemn moment when History, amidst the full swell of the trumpets of Fame, entones a hymn in immortal verse to him.

. . . [Escobedo] stands forth as an example for the new generation of our soldiers eager to tread the brilliant if painful path, of glory. Peace to his ashes! Honor to his name! To his memory everlasting glory![108]

The peroration received wild applause. Reyes lionized Escobedo like a classical military hero. Reference to patriotic symbols (flags and the hymn) stirred emotion. The speech was historical and alliterative; Reyes moved through time, linking his protagonist to other Liberals who defended the nation (Zuazua, Zayas, and Zaragoza). The lesson recounted glorious events (the capture of Querétaro) and omitted disputes (Escobedo was Lerdo's minister of war and rebelled against Díaz in 1878).[109] And Escobedo served as an exemplar for future soldiers. Ultimately, the oration brought glory to "the conqueror of the east, the immortal hero of April 2, now the ruler of the nation," Porfirio Díaz, whose status as living legend surpassed all others. The past and present converged because the historical Díaz was very much alive. Funeral orations, like state funerals in general, memorialized great heroes and events on one hand, and exalted Díaz and modern Mexico on the other.

Like any public speech, funeral orations were not always received with compliments. Eulogists who were excessively ingratiating to foreigners incited the most virulent attacks. Filomena Mata berated Foreign Relations Minister Ignacio Mariscal for his statements: "The Minister, whose principal duty consists in maintaining the best harmony with foreign representatives, not only passed over [Berriozábal's] services against the American invasion, but he said that *we must forget the War of '47*." Mata implored Mexicans to remember that the National Guard at Churubusco and military cadets at Chapultepec preserved the country's honor after the North Americans routed the professional army: "International hatred must be avoided but the lessons of history must never be forgotten."[110] Eulogists avoided controversies, revised harmful facts to benefit the republic, and, if all else failed, issued the presentism disclaimer: "His [embattled President Manuel González's] government will be judged by history some day. We are too close to him: the judgments of contemporaries are uncertain and incomplete. . . . History needs to meditate free of present concerns and with impassionate analysis, channeling its judicious reasoning through exaggerations invented in the light of legend."[111]

After funerals, the state promoted national memory of the fallen. Manuel Romero Rubio survived as long as public officials throughout the republic commemorated him. Telegrams and letters expressing the deepest sympathies to Díaz and praising the fallen statesman poured into the National Palace.[112] In one letter to President Díaz, the Mexico City Council described the funeral as a spontaneous outpouring of respect and sympathy from all people, regardless of nationality, social class, or condition.[113] Chihuahuans and Tamaulipans held literary events in Romero Rubio's honor at their spacious state palaces. Governor of Tamaulipas Alejandro Prieto declared nine days of public mourning and invited 250 of Ciudad Victoria's leading citizens to attend the ceremony.[114] Abstaining from the Coronation of the Virgin of Guadalupe, the editors of *El Partido Liberal* deposited a copy of their newspaper wrapped in black crepe along with a bundle of flowers at his tomb on October 12.[115] On the Day of the Dead, November 2, 1895, "the monument that called the most attention to itself was the *sepulcro* of Don Manuel Romero Rubio."[116] Four hundred students of the Industrial School for Orphans had covered his tomb with wreaths and flowers picked from the school grounds.

The eleven-year-olds delivered speeches, recited poetry, and otherwise post-humously thanked Romero Rubio for his protection of the school. The following day employees of the Interior Ministry joined delegates from the state of Michoacán in a tribute to Díaz's father-in-law, celebrating the one-month anniversary of his death. Special streetcars were provided to transport them from Constitution Plaza to the French Cemetery. Meanwhile, in San Luis Potosí, Governor Carlos Diéz Gutiérrez decorated the forum of the Teatro de la Paz with pyramids, one of which was crowned with a portrait of Romero Rubio.[117] And one hundred members of the Lawyers College and the Mexican Academy of Jurisprudence and Law marched to his tomb on November 4.[118] One year later, the process of remembrance began anew with an invitation to render tribute to Romero Rubio on the first anniversary of his death.[119]

President Díaz enlisted his highest-ranking generals to memorialize great caudillos in bronze and stone. This often meant federal government intervention in stalled state projects. From the time of General Ramón Corona's assassination, the Jalisco delegation of Congress and interim governor Mariano Bárcena worked diligently to raise funds for a memorial. But knowing from experience that it took men of national stature to complete such projects, Díaz enlisted General Bernardo Reyes in 1891. The Nuevo León governor met with Corona's widow and won her approval. Reyes collaborated with Díaz, War Minister Felipe Berriozábal, and Jesús F. Contreras to immortalize the "hero of la Mojonera." In 1895, public officials inaugurated the statue of Corona in Guadalajara, followed by several other Liberal republican generals in Mexico City.[120] The discerning Reyes took this duty seriously. In letters to artists, he quoted from Vicente Riva Palacio's historical compilation *México á través de los siglos* about the physical appearance, stature, and clothing of Mexican heroes. With admirable thoughtfulness, he wrote two-page descriptions of what attitudes should be conveyed through the art. For example, Servando Teresa de Mier was to be portrayed as a vigorous agitator who had endured long prison sentences and the Inquisition. General Juan Zuazua should adopt "a martial posture with a grave countenance and alert gaze."[121] When presented with sketches he disliked, Reyes criticized "the drawings [that] bear no resemblance to the subject" or complained that "the lower half of the General's arm is united with the body."[122] The clay model of Zuazua looked so "unnatural" that Reyes ordered General Juan Guerra to have the artists stagger the sculpture's legs to convey an "attitude of revolution." Disappointed with the paseo statue, Reyes even wrote to Zuazua's widow for any information about the general that could be used for a second monument.[123] To preserve the memory of Reforma heroes, statues had to be lifelike replicas that captured the essence of the subjects' character as well.

Mexicans commemorated their leaders in other unique ways. Theaters all over the republic held memorial services. Artists offered to paint portraits of heroes to hang in government buildings.[124] Gravesites were visited on the anniversaries of deaths, as well as on the Day of the Dead (November 2). In 1894, partisans placed a color portrait and three hundred wreaths on the grave of Manuel González. His sons wrote a poignant inscription for their father's tomb: "You had only one arm/but one of iron/and only one hand/but that of a friend." In 1902, the señoras of the Leona Vicario patriotic society of Zitácuaro joined students in a pilgrimage to Escobedo's grave. Cities in every northern state were renamed Ciudad Escobedo, and Mexican matador Cuatro Dedos (Four Fingers) held bullfights to raise money for an Escobedo monument. Liberals had their names imprinted on the city landscape with iron commemorative plaques and street signs. The Mexico City government renamed the Villamil Plaza and Santa María de la Ribera Park after Altamirano. Oaxacan composer José Alcalá wrote a funeral march in his name. Human remains were incorporated into sanctified buildings such as the National Cathedral. Cemeteries became stone cities of the dead, exemplified by Miguel Angel de Quevedo's $5,000 monument to civil engineer Manuel María Contreras at the Panteón de Tepeyac. Survivors published memorial books called *coronas fúnebres* (funeral wreaths). A friend or protégé compiled funeral-day ephemera and hired a family press or newspaper to publish 500 to 1,000 copies to be issued as memorabilia. All contributed to an ideology formulated by modernizing elites who never distinguished national interests from their own.[125]

Deconstructing state funerals from deathbeds through acts of commemoration discloses the cultural politics that reinforced the Porfirian dictatorship at its peak. Although only a small fraction of nearly eighty-three hundred porfiristas were honored with state funerals, the tireless hegemonic state succeeded in elevating the statures of cabinet ministers and military generals posthumously in national funerals that resembled those held for dead presidents.[126] This was accomplished through the state's declaration of a national mourning period, the thoughtful presentation of emotionally provocative discourses, and the artful display of nationalist imagery to the public. Nothing else competed for the nation's attention. Porfirian officials used every technology and media source at their disposal to educate citizens in their national history, promote nationalist sentiment, and maintain the illusion of a powerful modern state. The combination of all these factors made state funerals transcendent national cultural events. Extravagant and time-honored, the funerals implored Mexicans to compare the painful past with the peaceful present and to think about the close relationships between illustrious men and Porfirio Díaz, the powerful leader who buried them all.

Figure 32. José Guadalupe Posada's *El Motín de los Estudiantes*. From Roberto Berdecio and Stanley Applebaum, eds., *Posada's Popular Mexican Prints* (New York: Dover Publications, 1972).

"The Exalted Trinity of Our National Religion" 5

*The Memorialization of Juárez, Hidalgo, Díaz,
and Other Mexican Heroes*

A FUNNY THING HAPPENED on the way to national hegemonic order in Porfirian Mexico. The revolutionary who launched an armed rebellion to overthrow President Benito Juárez in 1871 now found himself immortalizing him in 1887. Previous chapters have shown the process by which Díaz enshrined his former political enemies. He controlled public memory and discourse about their lives during their deaths, state funerals, and commemorations. His state spent lavishly on their burial monuments and memorial statues. In similar fashion, Porfirio's subordinates downplayed his Revolution of La Noria against Juárez and reconstructed a more useful national memory of their adversarial relationship. One example is found in a petition to Díaz to be first subscriber to a monument for the "eminent statesman whose political life is intertwined with your own" as a "sign of your friendship with the Hero of the Reform."[1] Thus began the conjoined processes of falsifying the Juárez–Díaz confrontation as a minor political quarrel and requisitioning Juárez's towering image for state purposes. In truth, Juárez and Díaz were anything but friends.

On the fifteenth anniversary of Juárez's death in 1887, the Porfirian government announced a new form of national observance, the Day of Public Mourning (Día de duelo público). With memory of Juárez's funeral of 1872 still alive and his body entombed at San Fernando, the regime held "funeral festivals" for the greatest leader in Mexican history every July 18. Days of public mourning were always announced upon the death of a renowned figure. Juárez Day, however, belonged to a new variant of national commemoration that simulated funerals, except without the bodies. Whereas citizens of the United States recognize historical figures on their birth dates or commemorate their wartime dead on the last Monday in May (Memorial Day), Mexicans remember their national heroes on fixed dates in the calendar year to recognize the date they died, regardless of which day of the week the holiday falls on.

Figure 33. Burial monument of Benito Juárez at the Panteón de San Fernando. Photo by C. B. Waite; courtesy of the Nettie Lee Benson Latin American Library, University of Texas, Austin.

The practice has Old World Catholic antecedents since saints were venerated on the very dates they became martyrs.[2]

On days of public mourning for Juárez, the Porfirian state never scheduled the jubilant parades, public works inaugurations, fireworks, or flower wars that marked other holidays and anniversaries. Instead, Juárez Day brought somber and reflective memorialization at a statue, bust, plaque, or even framed image of the Great Republican in the Federal District, major cities, and small towns all over the republic. Memorial days differed from other holidays in another significant way. The Porfirian state harnessed the immense popular love for Juárez and other national heroes to mobilize the working-class and democratic nation. According to *El Imparcial*, the *pueblo* could not deduce on its own the practical results of the noble deeds of great historical figures. The official newspaper's frequent references to the *tribuna popular* suggests that memorial programs served the needs of public education and proxied for inclusive forms of democratic representation.[3] One error in Mexican historiography is that somehow "popular" or "mass" politics disappeared during the Porfiriato.

Juárez Day enjoyed such immediate success that the state inaugurated days of national mourning for Miguel Hidalgo y Costilla (July 30), Cuauhtémoc (August 21), and the Niños Héroes (September 8). The regime also endorsed annual observances for José María Morelos (December 22) and Vicente Guerrero (February 14). Incorporating these dates into the national calendar and constructing monuments as spatial reminders of heroic lives were steps toward the permanent inclusion of heroes in the Mexican pantheon. Prior to the Porfiriato, the only republican hero that the state recognized was Ignacio Zaragoza on Cinco de Mayo.[4] By 1910, the Porfirian state inserted six additional historical figures into the calendar, urban geography, and national memory of Mexico. Each of the nineteenth-century republican hero cults survived the revolution and appeared in Mexico's National Civic Calendar in 1940.[5]

The Juárez and Hidalgo hero cults were motivated by the state's need to co-opt industrial workers, day laborers, wage-earning women, and peasant migrants. In the 1880s and 1890s, radical liberalism, social Catholicism, socialism, and anarcho-syndicalism all sprouted roots in Mexico. Working-class newspapers such as *El Socialista, La Union de los Obreros, El Ancona, La Justicia, El Obrero Mexicano*, and *La Internacional* sought to defend workers' rights. Whereas the First Workers Congress declared itself apolitical in 1876, it supported political candidates in 1898. Modernizing states undergoing late industrialism in Europe and the Americas adopted reforms that deflected serious challenges posed by leftist ideologies, organized labor, and the politicized Left. Labor reforms coincided with Pope Leo XIII's encyclical *Rerum Novarum* (1891), which called attention to the deplorable labor standards and wretched living conditions of the working class as a means to counter the growth of revolutionary movements. But Mexico never bothered to reform its political system or labor laws until after 1904. The regime successfully divided an already segmented working class. Porfirian "reforms" often favored management. Workers had no effective vote or the rights to unionize, strike, or collective bargain for higher wages, a shorter workday, or better working conditions. Article 50 of the Penal Code stipulated, "Anyone attempting to raise or lower his wage will be considered subversive."[6] State efforts were directed instead toward gradual inclusivity of the people in the political rituals of the nation. Mexico's days of public mourning and national hero cults demonstrate how hegemonic processes come to pervade cultural systems, conventionalize social behaviors as norms, and present a constructed social order of inequality and domination as if it were a natural order of equality and reciprocity. In essence, they illustrate how inequality becomes a lived cultural reality without ever referring to the original intent to dominate.[7]

Juárez Day

As a symbol of Mexico's heroic struggle for nationhood, Juárez provided the Mexican republic with a unique opportunity to forge a nexus of nationalism in one person. Like Abraham Lincoln in the United States, Juárez is an iconic figure in Mexican history and still stands as the nation's greatest president. As for most wartime presidents, his time in office was not without controversy, but his stature grew with the passage of time. During the Porfiriato, the characteristics of a mythical Juárez clearly overshadowed the facts of his controversial presidency. He fell under fire for decisions to execute Maximilian (Juárez refused to commute his sentence after condemned by a military court), expropriate Church property, liquidate peasant communal lands, build an unbeatable political machine, manipulate elections, and seek reelection to a fifth term. Yet, since Juárez's unexpected death of coronary failure on July 18, 1872, Liberals honored the Hero of the Reform. In 1873, Congress decreed Juárez a *benemérito de la Patria*. A resolution called for the inscription of his name in gold letters in the congressional building, a burial monument at his grave, and a 50,000-peso national memorial by May 5, 1874. The Cinco de Mayo inauguration date reveals the fact that July 18 did not yet capture the national imagination.[8]

Porfirio Díaz and his state governors derived a huge amount of political capital from Juárez's postmortem career because these congressional acts stalled under President Sebastián Lerdo de Tejada. After ousting Lerdo, Díaz dedicated the Juárez sepulchral monument in 1880. In Juárez's natal state of Oaxaca, *juarista* governor Mariano Jiménez had contracted engineer Francisco G. Cosío and sculptor Miguel Noreña to raise a statue in the city in 1873. It was not completed until *porfirista* governor Luís Mier y Terán unveiled the monument in 1885. Even plans to convert Juárez's former home into a national historic site were delayed until Díaz's second term. Still, national ambitions to honor Juárez grew as time passed and Mexico prospered. The original stone memorial for which Congress had budgeted 50,000 pesos later resulted in a 1,650-ton Juárez Hemiciclo that cost nearly 400,000 pesos. Inaugurated during the Centennial of Mexican Independence in 1910, the Hemicycle's size and cost achieved the proportions of Juárez's historical stature in Porfirian Mexico.[9]

The Juárez memorial stands as a hemicycle of hegemony when one considers the troubled relationship between Juárez and Díaz. At age thirty-six, Díaz was a national hero for having vanquished the imperialists in Oaxaca, Puebla, and Mexico City. Juárez, who led an older generation of *puro* Liberals, never showed favor for Porfirio and was wary of his popularity as a military leader. Their estrangement originated with the dissolution of the wartime coalition in 1867.[10] With civilian and military support, Díaz grappled with the president for control of Oaxaca and the national electorate, but Juárez won every power struggle, including the presidential elections of 1867 and 1871. Juaristas blocked Díaz's ambitions to win governorships in the states of Morelos and Mexico and showed little respect for the provincial, unpolished, and inarticulate Díaz while he served in Congress. Weakened in national politics, Díaz pronounced against Juárez's government. The abortive La Noria rebellion resulted in the violent death of Díaz's brother Félix, and Porfirio was still a fugitive when

Figure 34. The Juárez Hemicycle of Mexico City's Alameda. Built in 1910, this 700-ton "Hemicycle of Hegemony" symbolized the consent-building conciliatory policies of the Porfirian state. Photo courtesy of the Nettie Lee Benson Latin American Library, University of Texas, Austin.

Juárez died. Amnestied by Lerdo, he moved to Tlacotalpan, Veracruz, to grow sugar and practice carpentry on his hacienda of La Candelaria. When he overthrew Lerdo, he achieved what Juárez had denied him for a decade.

Thus Díaz's promotion of the Juárez cult was neither automatic nor natural but, rather, came as part of a conciliatory agenda that appealed to all classes. If official goals to perpetuate national memory of Juárez were realized at a slow pace, they at least enjoyed the probability of completion. This could not be said for the countless unfulfilled plans to extol Juárez that originated with private citizens, civic organizations, and the independent press. In 1885, the Convención Radical de la República Mexicana, a Mexico City workers' association, solicited every citizen in the republic to donate 10 centavos for a Juárez monument. Donations were to be collected locally by mutual societies and plantation owners.[11] The Liberal press proposed a similar scheme to build a Juárez monument at the Shrine of Guadalupe so that Indian pilgrims could render homage to the Virgin and Juárez at the same time. Liberals believed that Juárez deserved secular veneration for his role as savior of the nation, even deeming the men who fought for Juárez as "Apostles." Generals Pedro Hinojosa and Sóstenes Rocha directed two different *juntas* to raise capital for the interminable project.[12] In some cities, patriotic citizens held bullfights and other fund-raising events for a Juárez memorial. It practically took an act of Congress to render tribute to Juárez.[13]

As explained in chapter 3, citizens memorialized Juárez on Constitution

Day, Cinco de Febrero. Two federal laws gave rise to Juárez Day as its official replacement. The first was the constitutional amendment of 1887 that allowed the president to serve one additional term. Opposition deputies in the chamber interpreted the bill as a dictatorial act and later condemned the law for undermining constitutional government. Dissenting lawmakers and the independent press had also encouraged citizens to vote for their own candidates for public office and organized antigovernment demonstrations on Constitution Day. In response, the regime canceled Constitution Day parades and enlisted the City Council to schedule "democratic workingmen's processions" on July 18, 1887. In November, a second congressional resolution decreed July 18 as an official day of national mourning.[14]

The original bill for Juárez Day found little congressional opposition, but legislators criticized it for not detailing a commemorative program. Congressman Rodolfo Sandoval proposed that federal law follow Oaxaca state law, which obliged public functionaries to solemnize July 18 in the same way the nation honored Juárez when he died. Congressman Rafael Herrera argued that national holiday laws always contained specific provisions and that Congress should compel citizens to memorialize Juárez in the same manner that Padre Hidalgo was honored on September 16 and other heroes were honored on Cinco de Mayo.[15] In combination Sandoval and Herrera believed that Juárez Day should fuse state funeral legislation (Oaxaca state law) and national holiday laws. The Mexico City Ayuntamiento later called Juárez Day a "funeral festival."[16] The calendar date of July 18 found a secure niche temporally equidistant between May 5 and September 16.

Senior congressmen Gustavo Baz and Juan A. Mateos defended the bill in its original form but for different reasons. The resolution's only article read, "July 18 of every year, the anniversary of the death of the great citizen Benito Juárez, *benemérito de la Patria*, is declared a day of national mourning."[17] Baz, the author of the resolution, had been at Juárez's side when he died. He insisted that the president rather than Congress should determine the way the nation remembered Juárez. In contrast, Mateos believed that the government should not regulate days of mourning at all: "[Juárez Day is] the only popular fiesta, during which manifestations have been absolutely spontaneous throughout the republic." Mateos warned that if the government mandated the way this holiday was celebrated, it would diminish the enthusiasm that citizens have for the memory of Juárez.[18]

Guillermo Prieto then delivered a decisive speech. The beloved national poet who once saved Juárez's life was the final arbiter in most questions of patriotic duty. Prieto earned the title of *inmaculado* (immaculate one) for accompanying Juárez on his arduous flight to Paso del Norte (now Ciudad Juárez) during the nation's worst hour. The honor refers to the few patriots who never tarnished themselves by residing in territory subject to Maximilian's rule. Prieto also wrote a textbook on national history for use in public schools. In the Chamber of Deputies, Prieto spoke: "I think that solemnities like the one we are considering must have a highly moral purpose for the people; they must provide testimony of great deeds to serve as lessons to future generations, they must be presentations of this model citizen so that our children rush to follow him and adopt the example of his virtues and patriotism." Using vivid imagery, Prieto called Juárez the national savior and a rock in the days of misfortune, who "stood at the edge of the desert with our torn flag and said 'We have a Fatherland, let us move ahead, we will triumph.'" Prieto implored the government to leave the commemoration of Juárez to the people, even if they worship him in a different manner: "This might mean the spilling of flowers, the singing of liturgical hymns, and venerating his memory in public revelry[, but] it will be the best apotheosis of the benemérito and immortal Juárez. . . . faith, not decree; faith, not *aguilitas* [tiny eagles, the government emblem], drums, and bell ringing; faith and belief." With Prieto's support, the bill passed into law by a vote of 103 to 21, and Juárez Day was to be commemorated by the people.[19]

There was no debate over whether or not July 18 would become a day of national mourning. Differences of opinion centered on the oft-repeated question of how the government and the people should commemorate Juárez. Some legislators wanted to impose official mourning customs. Mateos and Prieto counseled that leaving the holiday to the will of the people would evoke more sincere remembrance and patriotism. Prieto himself had changed his opinion on this very issue. In 1881, he resolutely urged Congress to take part in the obsequies for Mariano Arista; now Prieto hoped that public officials would preserve Juárez as a man of the people by not intervening in remembrance of him. Although Prieto carried the day, Gustavo Baz predicted the era: the president was the one to determine the public demonstration of mourning.

Or was he? An undeniable pattern found in the letters of Díaz's presidential archives is his hands-off but affirmative reactions to the initiatives of loyal subordinates who were once juaristas and therefore maintained greater interest in recognizing the merits of their former *jefe*. It was politically expedient for Díaz to allow the Juárez cult to flourish without his direct attention or personal advocacy. His cultural politics depended on the use of the state as a cat's paw to achieve positive outcomes such as reconciliation, unity, and progress. In one of his administration's first symbolic acts to honor Juárez in 1887, Finance Minister Manuel Dublán, the former imperialist, dedicated a commemorative plaque in the National Palace that marked the exact spot where Juárez died while working at his desk. At the dedication ceremony, Dublán expounded: "Fifteen years ago in the room in which we are all gathered, one of our most outstanding men ended his glorious career of perseverance and patriotism: President Juárez, memory of whom will be eternal so long as a single Mexican exists." Dublán concluded with a coded reference to Díaz's lack of involvement in the all-too-common adulation that connected the president to Juárez: "I have done no more than second your sympathy for the illustrious republican, whose death we commemorate this day, along with your lofty objectives for the liberty of the Mexican people."[20] In late 1888, when foreign sculptors offered to build statues of Juárez for the Mexican government, Díaz replied that the Juárez memorials were not federal government initiatives. Instead, the government was to complete monuments of heroes "in historical order" beginning with Hidalgo.[21] Three years later, the task of resurrecting Juárez in bronze again fell upon Manuel Dublán. Not long before his own death in 1891, the finance minister dedicated the Juárez monument that still resides in the National Palace. The bronze statue was cast from cannons used by Conservatives and the French during the intervention, but again President Díaz had no direct hand in the project.[22]

Díaz did not play a visible organizing role on Juárez Day because his surrogates could be counted on to perfect every program, reflecting the expansion of the state. The Ayuntamiento decorated the procession route. City councilmen requested residents and businesses to adorn their houses and establishments with flags and pictures of Juárez. Politicians, bureaucrats, and business owners often participated through their membership in Masonic lodges. Other principal agents included the Liberal press, the Oaxacan colony in the capital, and the Mexican Patriotic Society. The press sent out invitations, advertised the programs, ran articles about Juárez, and reprinted public orations. The Mexican Patriotic Society was led by José Vicente Villada, a former *lerdista* general, founder of the government-subsidized newspaper *El Partido Liberal*, and the future governor of Mexico state. President Díaz served as honorary president even after the society renamed itself the Patriotic Liberal Committee in 1891. After Villada died, *Constituyente* and Supreme Court Justice Félix Romero took over as active director. A Díaz confidante, Romero had always coordinated the Juárez Day activities of the Oaxacan colony. The astute leadership of Villada and Romero, not Díaz, gave Juárez manifestations civilian credibility. In fact, whenever the president had to leave Juárez ceremonies early, Villada or Romero sat in his place. After 1900, the membership of Romero's Patriotic Liberal Committee grew to over five hundred members. In 1902, the patriotic society named thirty-four committees just to invite dignitaries and government employees to Juárez Day events. The membership even helped underwrite the costs of Juárez monuments in Veracruz and other states.[23]

These politicians faithfully structured Juárez Day to resemble the 1872 state funeral. The ceremonial reenactments of funerary rituals in the same sacred urban axis resurrected the Hero of the Reform from year to year. Juárez was the first Mexican leader granted an entire axis (*eje*) of his own. If the nation-state represents the highest effective level of spatial integration, the Juárez Axis in downtown Mexico City was the gathering place of popular nationalism.[24] The Zócalo or Constitution Plaza was always the official heart of Mexico for its centralized panopticons of Church and State in the National Cathedral and National Palace, respectively. Eight blocks west, the elite spent leisure time in the Alameda and were joined by the working classes during weekends and holidays. Running alongside the northern border of the central park was the Avenida de los Hombres Ilustres. Parallel along the Alameda's southern border was the major thoroughfare newly christened Avenida Juárez (1887). Continuing along Juárez Avenue, tramcar passengers and pedestrians traversed past the Juárez burial monument to the south at San Fernando and ultimately reached the Paseo de la Reforma, the broad boulevard named after one of the Great Republican's defining achievements. In 1900, the city inaugurated the Colonia Juárez just south of the *paseo*.

Figure 35. Avenida Juárez adjacent to the Alameda in the 1880s. This is the entrance of the Juárez Axis or "Eje," which branched off to the Juárez sepulchral monument at San Fernando, Colonia Juárez, and the Hemicycle. Photo courtesy of the Nettie Lee Benson Latin American Library, University of Texas, Austin.

Even more important was the role of Avenida Juárez as a contact zone, or integrated social space for the interaction of members of distinct classes with different political views.[25] While the gente decente read newspapers and socialized in the Alameda, working-class leaders, university students, and other rabble-rousers often congregated in the popular central park. In addition, the offices of long-standing Liberal newspapers and the short-lived oppositional press lined Avenida Juárez. Unity and reconciliation were not always the top priority of editorial staffs, labor organizers, and students who often invoked Juárez's jacobinism. On Juárez Day 1895, the editors of the anticlerical newspaper *El Combate* stretched a banner across the street that bore the quote of French firebrand León Gambetta: "The priesthood, there is the enemy."[26] On Juárez Day 1901, rumors spread that students had organized anticlerical demonstrations to take place in front of the churches of San Francisco and San Felipe and the National Cathedral. Perhaps it was the organizing committee's name, the Comité Patriótico Anticlerical, that tipped the government off. When twelve thousand people turned out at San Fernando, the government mobilized seventy-five hundred troops to preserve order.[27] A year later on Juárez Day in Guadalajara, crowds shouted, "Death to the Clergy!" and harassed priests until the police dispersed the "revoltosos."[28]

Every July 18, Mexico City shut down as if Juarez's famous black carriage would appear in the distance. Of course this never happened, but the Museo Nacional did offer free admission to see the carriage Juárez once rode to Paso del Norte as well as his personal belongings and death mask. City officials hung portraits of Juárez in office windows. Businesses posted signs that read "Closed for Juárez Day." Flower sellers flocked into the city center with wreaths and floral arrangements. Patriotic citizens carried them in the civic procession and deposited them at Juárez's tomb. Processional banners show the incredible diversity of corporate associations that honored Juárez: public and private schools, literary and scientific societies, neighboring towns, Masonic lodges, mutual and workingmen's societies, foreign colonies, the Mexico City press, the City Council, state governments, state newspapers, Congress, companions of Juárez from 1863 to 1867, veterans of the Reforma War, and the immaculate ones. If 1904 was representative, fully 126 different civic groups walked in the procession and placed wreaths at his tomb. Spectators watched a biography of Juárez pass before their eyes. Although most processions included only men, women marched on July 18. Women from the normal schools and El Buen Tono cigarette factory poured into Guerrero Plaza at the San Fernando Cemetery, sat beneath a canvas pavilion, and listened to orations and poetry.[29]

Annual commemoration of Juárez became spatially diffuse in the high 1890s, reflecting the day's growing popularity and resulting in greater citywide regulation. As Mexico City's population surpassed 329,000 inhabitants in 1895, the size of Juárez Day crowds exploded. Organizers modified processional itineraries to accommodate more marchers and prevent disruptions of the streetcar service. Participants at the heads of processions often encircled entire city blocks and ran into the processions' tails, thereby blocking multiple intersections. The accordion effect slowed the pace, prompting marchers to

Figure 36. Relics of Juárez in the National Museum. Photo by C. B. Waite; courtesy of the Nettie Lee Benson Latin American Library, University of Texas, Austin.

fraternize with everyone except the police who shouted, "Move ahead." Compact crowds became such a challenge that the residents of particular neighborhoods were asked to assemble in their own precinct plazas at 7:00 a.m., march as groups to the Zócalo, and converge for a citywide parade. As participation increased, the masses had to be further disaggregated; for example, the City Council asked schoolchildren to assemble in the Santo Domingo Plaza. At the plaza students unfurled their banners and competed against one another in screaming the loudest *vivas* to Juárez. Masonic lodges led evening torchlight processions of eight thousand people to the Juárez memorial. The multitude caused disruptions at the Panteón de San Fernando. In 1899, soldiers drew their swords and beat back a "human avalanche." President Díaz rose from his seat, signaled the police to stop, and earned vivas and applause from the crowd. Before long, Juárez Day parades grew so unwieldy that police had to escort at the front and a military division brought up the rear.[30]

Public orations at San Fernando portrayed Juárez in ways that were consistent with the period's best scholarship. The intellectuals who spoke also wrote the historical works extolling him. Juárez mythmakers Justo Sierra, Emilio Rabasa, Genaro Raigosa, Guillermo Prieto, Porfirio Parra, Francisco Bulnes, Rosendo Pineda, José Zayas Enríquez, José Manuel Gutiérrez Zamora, Juan de Dios Peza, and Manuel Sánchez Marmol all held political office. Soon their protégés delivered orations. The sons of Congressman Juan A. Mateos and General Bernardo Reyes delivered orations in 1899. Rodolfo Reyes, a student at the national law school, spoke of Juárez as a symbol of Indian Mexico. He articulated a new social conscience, imploring Mexicans not to consider indigenous people as a dead race: "Educate them; help them." Reyes understood his charge: "To render tribute to Juárez is to render tribute to modern Mexico."[31]

Congressman Rosendo Pineda's Juárez Day speech of 1902 exemplifies the structure and intent of Porfirian discourse. Pineda had been the personal secretary of Díaz's father-in-law, Manuel Romero Rubio, and was now a *científico* power broker in the capital. He remarked that "the flag waves in mourning all across the Republic, evoking sorrow in our souls in memory of Juárez." Members of the Mexican family will exalt the great deeds, high virtues, and triumphs of the "distinguished plebeian." Pineda's was an appeal to shared nationality: "Songs of victory palpitate from lips, rays of hope shine in eyes, and faith fills hearts on this day as the pueblo becomes scene for the apotheosis of the victorious Republic." Pineda, a native of Juchitán, Oaxaca, retraced the steps of Juárez's life in the secularized parable of the orphaned Indian shepherd who descended from the hills of Oaxaca to triumph over the Conservatives, the French, and Emperor Maximilian. In his concluding remarks about why Juárez did not persecute his Conservative Catholic enemies once he restored the republic, the orator projected state hegemony:

> The high mission of the Government consists precisely in promoting cohesion, to conciliate through its institutions all legitimate interests and sound aspirations. For this reason, the President of the Republic is a conciliator, and this will be one of his glorious stamps on history. . . . The Reform is assured in the sentiments of the people and sustained in the hands of the current Government. We have faith in the future and confidence in our cause. . . . [O]ver the tomb of Juárez we call for concord and forget our disgraces and grudges. Only then will we consolidate Peace and the serene and just rule [*imperio*] of the Republic.[32]

Pineda's oration may as well have been titled "The Porfirian Peace" for the way it manufactured a President Juárez remarkably similar to President Díaz.

During most July 18 commemorations the living descendants of Juárez were given places of honor, thereby enhancing the political legitimacy of the Díaz regime. Despite his electoral and armed opposition to Juárez, Díaz won the support of Benito Juárez Maza, a son who served in Congress, and Ramón Prida, an in-law who edited the government-subsidized newspaper *El Universal*. Both Juárez Maza and Prida sat near President Díaz during Juárez ceremonies. So did other prominent *capitalinos* who had married into the Juárez family. Before and after the orations, everyone from the president to the humblest *campesino* exchanged embraces with the Juárez family.[33] The family never publicly objected to Díaz's manipulation of the Hero of Guelatao. Their presence reaffirmed Manuel Sánchez Marmol's words: "Juárez showed us how to be free; his successor is teaching us how to be great."[34]

What Juárez symbolized to citizens is revealed in the messages attached to the funeral wreaths that were deposited at his tomb. Only wealthy individuals could afford expensive floral and porcelain wreaths available at the flower markets. But working-class associations, municipal corporations, and patriotic societies often purchased wreaths collectively. Ribbons attached to the wreaths not only identified the family or organization placing them but carried short dedicatory messages that reveal Juárez's universal appeal. In 1899, wreaths read: "To the Consistent Upholder of the Rights of Man," "To the Heroic Champion of Reform," "To the Great Citizen of the Republic." These titles became lasting epithets for Juárez. Ribbons also bore the principles for which he stood: "Liberty," "Constitution of 1857," and "Order and Progress." And they were inscribed with his immortal words: "Liberty as the Means," "Order as the Basis," and "Progress as the Aim." In 1902, a banner read "Respect for the rights of others is peace." For those who could read, the ribbons offered short captions that complemented the scene of Juárez's tomb. The spectacle of Díaz's deference spoke to everyone else.[35]

The Juárez Mausoleum was never a large enough structure to contain the massive number of wreaths dedicated on Juárez Day. Since it was customary for families of the dead to pick up floral crowns after a week on display, the Juárez family soon noted the impossibility of moving, much less storing, over two hundred giant wreaths per year. This number does not account for the hundreds sent directly to the Juárez family or the mausoleum's exquisite base of flowers designed annually by the *floricultores* of Ixtacalco. The Juárez family gave the wreaths made of silver to the National Museum. In 1892, Nuevo León Governor Bernardo Reyes proposed that the government build a library to Juárez near San Fernando so that citizens could donate new books and money in Juárez's name instead of wreaths. Rafael Chousal, Díaz's personal secretary, liked the idea and presented it to the president.[36] But patriotic custom and grand solemnity prevailed when the Patriotic Liberal Committee took over the responsibility of preserving and storing porcelain and artificial floral wreaths, unpacking them and decorating the mausoleum with them annually as if they were Christmas ornaments in the United States. By 1906, Juárez was receiving six hundred wreaths per year, bringing the grand total to ten thousand in 1908.[37]

Juárez Day was not solely a Mexico City phenomenon. Citizens throughout the republic formed patriotic societies, marched in processions, and pledged themselves to carry out Juárez's work. The people of San Pablo Guelatao, Juárez's birthplace, held annual commemorations on his birthday and death date.

Villagers dedicated a truncated column of marble symbolizing how Juárez's life was cut short. State authorities later replaced the cenotaph with a monument taken from the Paseo de Nezahualcoytl in Oaxaca City. In Zacatecas, the "Benito Juárez Grand Liberal Alliance" dedicated itself to promoting the Liberal Party and Reform Laws. It pledged not to participate in local or national politics but to establish auxiliary committees throughout the state. In Campeche, two thousand schoolchildren sang patriotic hymns to Juárez every July 18.[38]

The Liberal and positivist intelligentsia united at Juárez's tomb in part because partisan naysayers continued to attack the controversial president. Conservative Catholics shunned Juárez Day in favor of requiem masses that commemorated the death of Agustín de Iturbide on July 19.[39] Inspired by the writings of Prince Salm-Salm, Italian historian Cesar Cantu revived the false charge that Juárez demanded a ransom from the Austrian emperor in exchange for the body of his brother, Maximilian. In defense of Juárez, the Díaz government published a pamphlet containing Juárez's diplomatic correspondence with Austria. Maximilian had asked General Mariano Escobedo to deliver his body to his physician for transfer to Austria. Juárez refused to hand over the corpse to anyone who did not officially represent the Austrian government or imperial family. Cantu also promoted the falsehood that Maximilian's corpse suffered mistreatment by the republicans. The pamphlet retorted that Juárez spent 6,000 pesos to embalm the vigilantly guarded emperor.[40] Perhaps the worst offender of the Juárez myth was positivist iconoclast Francisco Bulnes. In 1904, the publication of his book *El verdadero Juárez y la verdad sobre la Intervention y el Imperio* set off a polemic that brought Liberals from all quarters rushing to Juárez's defense. Francisco Cosmes retaliated with his work *El verdadero Bulnes y su falso Juárez*.[41] Even the president called the author into his office to "clarify" facts about Juárez based on Díaz's "first-hand knowledge as actor in the great struggle."[42]

Spokesmen for the regime believed Juárez was the leading Mexican candidate for hemisphere-wide veneration. Liberal journalists perceived the massive Juárez Day demonstration of 1888 as a paean for freedom, liberty, and republicanism throughout the world. In its invitations to foreign colonies, the Press Association announced that the Mexican people will commemorate one who "unselfishly devoted all his life to the advancement of truth, the public good and all other principles that are beneficial to humanity." The text implored all free men to present a token of gratitude or remembrance at Juárez's grave and reminded the members of the foreign colonies that "Juárez considered any honest, hardworking and useful foreigner as a son of his country hence his memory should be revered by the citizens of all countries." Juárez appealed to the foreign colonies in Mexico, especially to Americans and Cuban émigrés, who helped promote him as the *benemérito de las Américas*. The Indian Shepherd was to reside among the greatest benefactors of mankind.[43] The American émigré population readily compared Juárez to Washington and Lincoln. They noted on Juárez Day that anti-American sentiment diminished in favor of the denigration of Spanish colonialism and French pretensions of empire. Cuban exiles formed the Juárez and Martí Club to raise funds for Cuban independence.[44] Standing before the Juárez Mausoleum, an American tourist exclaimed: "Here lies the noblest Roman of them all."[45]

From its very origins during Constitution Day, the apotheosis of Juárez was a vehicle for social unification even though the mythico-historical Juárez meant different things to different people. The joint participation of urban professionals, bureaucrats, the nascent proletariat, working-class women, and foreign colonies shows the effectiveness of hegemonic rule in mobilizing the masses behind a well-crafted national myth. During the "Year of Juárez," the mythical Juárez put a benign face on a morally indefensible dictatorship. He was a symbol of justice in an unjust society, a lesson on respect for the law and the rights of others in a state that routinely violated both, and an icon of democracy in an undemocratic country. Patriotic manifestations culminated in the nationwide centenary celebration of Juárez's birth on March 21, 1906, when few predicted the surprising return of Rome's ruling mechanisms of "bread and the circus."[46] General Bernardo Reyes coordinated a mammoth civic procession in the capital and ordered military bands from all over the country to converge on Mexico City.[47] The Federal District government sponsored a public meal at Porfirio Díaz Park at Anzures, consisting of 11,000 loaves of bread, 80,000 tortillas, 16 cattle, 20 sheep, 3,000 pounds of fish, 700 kilograms of rice, 1,000 liters of beans, and 5,000 pastries. The Cervecería de Toluca donated ten thousand bottles of beer to wash it all down.[48] The *pan y circo* distracted attention from growing labor strife and deteriorating economic conditions.

No other nineteenth-century hero rose so meteorically as Juárez in the Porfiriato. Constitution Day, Juárez Day, the Juárez Mausoleum, his Axis and Colonia, statues in the Palacio Nacional and scattered throughout the republic, the "Year of Juárez," and the Hemicycle all symbolize the Porfirian state's relentless promotion of the greatness of two men. They memorialized a president whose heart gave out after a lifetime of hard-fought victories over adversaries, including the Conservatives, the Church, foreign imperialists, regional *caudillos*, and Díaz (if memory served). Only a man of Juárez's historical stature could give Díaz his standing. Promotion of one was propaganda for the other in mutual reinforcement of modern Liberal triumphs but also myths. By 1906, Juárez became a transcendental icon that helped justify Díaz's rule.[49]

Hidalgo Day

For most of the nineteenth century the *creole* priest who launched Mexico's first independence campaign against Spain remained a contentious figure. In Lucas Alamán's evaluation, Padre Miguel Hidalgo y Costilla was an irresponsible man of the cloth, a poor leader, and a bloodthirsty warrior with little regard for human life.[50] Conservatives denounced him for inciting the massacres of Spanish soldiers and civilians in his military campaign (1810–11). Liberal theorists, such as José María Luís Mora, whose family property was damaged by Hidalgo's peasant army, were reluctant to accord him the status of founding father, like George Washington or Simón Bolívar. The Mexican republic named a state after Vicente Guerrero (1849) long before conferring the honor on the controversial Hidalgo (1869). One could not find a single statue of Padre Hidalgo in the nation's capital until 1910. Until learning of President Díaz's wishes, few governors regarded Hidalgo highly enough to donate money for a monument to the insurgent priest in the states of Hidalgo or Chihuahua.[51]

Historians since Carlos María de Bustamante gradually restored Hidalgo's reputation as a revolutionary, but it was Porfirian hagiographers who rehabilitated Hidalgo as the Father of Mexican Independence.[52] Díaz and his minister of development, Carlos Pacheco, put the full weight of the federal government behind Hidalgo's national enshrinement. Díaz had restored Independence Day, reenacted the Grito, appropriated Hidalgo's sacred relics, and conveyed them ceremonially to the nation's capital, where they were incorporated into political rituals to promote Hidalgo as the foremost independence leader. The federal government also underwrote the production of historical scholarship that cast Hidalgo in a positive light. Vicente Riva Palacio's *México a través de los siglos* and Justo Sierra's *México su evolución social* are two important examples.[53] Nationalist discourses that connected the present (Díaz) to the past (Hidalgo and Juárez) always teetered on the brink of the sermon: "With the blazing star of Juárez and of the immortal Hidalgo shall be found that of Díaz, forming the exalted trinity of our national religion."[54]

Critical to elevating Hidalgo's historical status to "Father" of Independence was to identify him with the holy mother of Mexico, the Virgin of Guadalupe. The National Artillery Museum's Salón Hidalgo looked less like a citadel than a chapel guarded by the *santísima María*. The Virgin of Guadalupe banner that Hidalgo took from the Sanctuary of Atotonilco in Dolores on the morning of September 16 hovered over the collection of national relics. For the most part, the museum showcased the sidearms and swords of the insurgents along with significant battle flags from the Independence Revolution and Reform periods. But some of the items from the museum's 1910 inventory illustrate how the state crossed the line from the mundane to the sacred in its display of the personal effects of "national saints." None of Hidalgo's personal vestments survived his execution, but the museum exhibited fragments of Nicolás Bravo's uniform (taken from his bodily remains), a syringe used to inject the dying Ignacio Zaragoza, and a piece of the coat that Ramón Corona wore at the time of his assassination. The implication was that the Virgin protected these personal belongings just as she offered her maternal embrace to Mexico's heroic martyrs.[55]

Porfirio Díaz's attachment to Hidalgo was manifested in other symbolic ways. The dictator granted pensions to his descendants and presented statues and busts of Hidalgo to various institutions. Acknowledging the grace of such a donation, the San Nicolás College of Morelia unveiled its new statue on the president's birthday. Díaz was also the recipient of sculptures of the insurgent priest, sometimes from foreign artists.[56] More than this, the image of the dictator always appeared juxtaposed with Hidalgo's in commemorative posters and period memorabilia: in newspaper photos and sketches, in special Independence Day publications, and on parade floats, postcards, medallions, and other trinkets from the Centennial of Independence in 1910. The link between Father Hidalgo and Porfirio Díaz became all the more obvious because the dictator's visage rarely appeared beside that of any other caudillo. The national trinity of Juárez, Hidalgo, and Díaz was as sacred, immortal, and indivisible to the Porfirian state as the Holy Trinity was to the Church.[57]

Díaz's personal interest in promoting the Hidalgo cult was embodied in his determination to build a monument to the patriot priest in the city of Dolores, Hidalgo, where the military campaign for independence began. Dolores was the consecrated location of the famous Grito in 1810. Minister Pacheco awarded the $40,000 contract to sculptor Miguel Noreña. A law passed under the González administration on October 3, 1884, requested states to fund the project. President Díaz traveled to Dolores to lay the first stone on September 15, 1885, and ordered the free and unobstructed passage of Italian marble from Veracruz port to Pachuca.[58] But collecting money from state governors proved difficult. Larger states had to contribute a greater share based on proportional representation to Congress. Each legislator paid $176.21. With its twenty-one federal deputies, Jalisco was presented with the figure of $3,700.41, a sum that Governor Ramón Corona could not pay in one installment. Judging by the six years it took reluctant *tapatío* officials to comply (tragically Corona was assassinated in November 1889), it appears that Jalisco reluctantly forgave Hidalgo for his forceful occupation of Guadalajara.[59] Falling behind on payments to the engineers in January 1886, Pacheco had to appeal to Governor Bernardo Reyes of Nuevo León to send in his donation at once. Months later in May, Díaz reiterated Pacheco's request, urging Reyes to send "sufficient funds to continue its construction for it would be truly lamentable if the work came to a standstill." With Díaz's intervention, Reyes delivered the amount within a month. Even so, the monument was not unveiled until 1890.[60] Pacheco later opened a competition for the best architectural design of a Hidalgo memorial for the fourth *glorieta* of the Paseo de la Reforma in Mexico City. Díaz inaugurated the Column of Independence during the Centenario of 1910.[61]

It pleased President Díaz when state governors raised statues to Hidalgo in their state capitals. Díaz encouraged them to replicate Hidalgo's image in every central plaza throughout the republic. Governors from the northern capitals of Chihuahua City, Monterrey, and Saltillo kept Díaz well informed of their progress. Enrique Creel and Lauro Carrillo spearheaded the effort in Chihuahua; Bernardo Reyes, in Nuevo León; and Francisco Arispe y Ramos and Miguel Cárdenas, in Saltillo. In 1888, Carrillo lamented to Díaz that for lack of initiative and resources a monument marking where the martyrs of independence died in Chihuahua City was never built. Díaz later sent two cabinet ministers to the northern capital city to unveil a monument to Hidalgo.[62] Díaz recommended his "national sculptor," Jesús F. Contreras, to forge a bronze statue of Hidalgo for Nuevo León, but Governor Reyes had already signed a contract with Salem artist W. H. Mullins. Reyes later satisfied the president by negotiating with Contreras's Fundición Artística Mexicana for two statues on the Paseo de la Reforma.[63]

Although workingmen's associations and patriotic societies commemorated Hidalgo on the anniversary of his death, there was no official presence at the modest demonstrations of July 30. Even on the seventy-fifth anniversary of his martyrdom in 1886, manifestations were low-key and poorly attended. In April 1888, prominent capitalinos and workers' guilds petitioned Congress to follow the example of Juárez Day and decree July 30 a day of national mourning. General Francisco Ramírez and a handful of congressmen founded the Junta Patriótica Hidalgo and began organizing annual programs that included a procession from the Alameda to the Plazuela del Carmen, where participants listened to music, speeches, and poetry readings and then placed wreaths at a small bust of Hidalgo. In 1891, the "Miguel Hidalgo y Costilla" Mutualist Society of Ironsmiths petitioned Díaz to declare July 30 a national holiday, but congressional sponsorship came slowly. The City Council allocated just 30 pesos for Hidalgo Day programs, the memorial services garnered little attention, and citizen turnout paled in comparison with the Juárez commemorations of the same month.[64]

Duplicating patterns established by Cinco de Mayo and Juárez Day, the Porfirian government decreed July 30 a day of national mourning in 1895. Just as the deaths and funerals of Zaragoza and Juárez shaped the way Cinco de Mayo and Juárez Day were celebrated, a collective funeral for the

Figure 37. General Francisco Ramírez, Commander of the Rurales, helped establish the Junta Patriótica Hidalgo, which promoted the Hidalgo cult. Photo courtesy of the Nettie Lee Benson Latin American Library, University of Texas, Austin.

Independence Heroes that year forever imprinted Hidalgo Day on the national festival calendar. Minister of the Interior Manuel Romero Rubio, the Federal District government, the city press, and patriotic societies planned an impressive program. Congress declared Hidalgo Day a national holiday just two weeks before the state reburial. Hence, the first grand event scheduled on the anniversary of Hidalgo's death was a state reburial that marked his permanent entry into the National Pantheon.

The reburial of Hidalgo and the Independence Heroes in 1895 is fully examined in the next chapter. The pantheonization not only marked the memories of Mexico City residents, it gave them a terminus for Hidalgo Day processions far superior to the tiny bust in the Plaza del Carmen—the National Cathedral. Crucial to advancing the Hidalgo cult was excavating the remains of the independence leaders from beneath the cathedral's Altar of the Kings and moving them a few hundred feet within the church to the Chapel of San José. Although anticlerical Liberals complained about the location—"let us unite to wrest from the clergy these venerated remains"—the bones of the caudillos of independence occupied a privileged national space that was accessible to the Catholic nation.[65] Opening up the gated Chapel of San José brought the pueblo to the National Cathedral by the thousands. Hidalgo and the other martyrs of independence were presented as national saints in one of the largest and most spectacular cathedrals in Latin America.

Hidalgo Day organizers paid attention to the relationship between the passage of historical time and public space. Processions started at the equestrian statue of King Charles IV to signify Spanish colonialism and wound up at the National Cathedral. Díaz marched with citizens, attended memorial services, and laid wreaths on the crystal urn that made visible to everyone the mortal remains of the Independence Heroes. The president's ceremonial image was enhanced by the presence of Hidalgo's only surviving granddaughter, Guadalupe Hidalgo y Costilla, and the century-old soldier Don Zenobio Acevedo, who had served the *generalísimo* in 1810. At first, patriotic societies invited only the governors in the "cradles of Independence"—Querétaro, Guanajuato, and Chihuahua. Over time, the official presence grew to encompass delegates from every federal office, each state government, the departments of the Federal District, the City Council, police precincts, the military, and national schools. With the right formula, new traditions could be invented overnight.[66]

Since its declaration, Hidalgo Day provided the government with an opportunity to join hands with labor to promote industry and hard work in the capital. During the *fiestas pátrias* of September 1895, Díaz professed that "Hidalgo has a right to immortality because as a man he cultivated the earth and developed industry, as a priest he preached the religion of love and the rights of fraternity, and passing on to his brothers he transformed an enslaved country into an independent and free nation."[67] Outside the capital city, state government authorities and company managers used paternalism, festivals, and mutual aid societies to mold miners into a disciplined and obedient workforce and inculcate the capitalist work ethic. In the Parral mining district of Chihuahua, for example, holiday rituals in Porfirio Díaz Plaza cultivated paternalistic bonds and made workers servants of the state.[68] Since Hidalgo died in Chihuahua, the state government promoted remembrance of him, conserving the tower where he was imprisoned, laying commemorative tablets where his decapitated body lay, and raising a three-story monument of the *insurgente* in Hidalgo Plaza.

The musical and literary events (*veladas*) held at Orrin's Theater or the Chamber of Deputies promoted Hidalgo as an industrious leader of a hard-working people. The ceremony in 1903 was especially illustrative. The chamber auditorium was adorned with an allegorical composite of agricultural, mechanical, and industrial tools. Another grouping presented a traditionally dressed campesino working a plow and a mechanic operating a "very curious apparatus." Industrial workers, artisans, soldiers, and school kids carried banners in the procession to the National Cathedral. Associates of the Círculo Nacional Porfirista observed the placing of wreaths approvingly, but marchers were too numerous to enter the cathedral.[69]

Like the immortal visage of Juárez, the image of Father Miguel Hidalgo y Costilla was imprinted onto Mexican national memory during the Porfiriato. By 1910, there were more statues of Father Hidalgo than of any other hero in Mexico. In Antonio Rivas Mercado's Column of Independence, an angel ascends to the heavens, but the flag-bearing Hidalgo occupies center stage in the statuary group. Other than Juárez, he was the only historical person who drew public school children out of the classroom on the anniversaries of both his death and his birth (May 8).[70] To Mexicans he became Immortal Hidalgo. Traveling beyond the realm of political and social utility, Hidalgo became an idol of worship no less than a patron saint. As one Mexican campesino related to a foreign traveler: "We were subjects of Spain, and Hidalgo started the revolution that made us free. Therefore, he was canonized and became our patron, and now we pray to him when we want favors."[71]

The Civic Commemorations of Cuauhtémoc and the Niños Héroes

Despite obvious differences, the last Aztec emperor, Cuauhtémoc, and the Niños Héroes of the U.S.–Mexican War had much in common as subjects for national glorification. They were soldiers and officers-in-training who answered the call of duty and bravely defended their country against foreign invasion. They garrisoned the last bastion of resistance in Mexico City (Tenochtitlán and Chapultepec) and faced impossible odds in their final stand. They sacrificed their lives in adolescence, symbolizing the victimization of young empires and nations by powerful foreign aggressors with sizable military advantages. The wartime loss of national youth remains one of the harshest tragedies endured by humankind, but symbolic fatalities fortify postcolonial nationalism.

Colonial-era Jesuit scholars Manuel Duarte, Carlos Sigüenza y Góngora, and Francisco Javier Clavijero originated the Cuauhtémoc hero cult in their ideological reappraisal of the Aztec people. Their studies portrayed the Aztecs as a dignified and accomplished people, connected native religious cults to those of Christianity, and compared the once-great empire to the most advanced ancient civilizations. The reassessment of Mexico's pre-Hispanic past aided the development of a distinct American identity that historians term *creole nationalism*. Subsequent *criollo* propagandists, such as the Dominican priest Servando Teresa de Mier and the lawyer Carlos María de Bustamante, denounced the Spanish conquest altogether and demanded redemption of the Patria. Creole nationalism fueled the independence revolts. At the Congress of Chilpancingo in 1813, Bustamante and José María Morelos evoked images of a nation that existed before the Spanish arrived. Both patriots championed Cuauhtémoc and other Indian leaders as authentic forefathers of the sovereign Mexican nation. The image of the last Aztec emperor, who valiantly defended Tenochtitlán against the soldiers of Hernán Cortés, proved useful to patriots trying to cast off the yoke of their Spanish

Figure 38. Equestrian statue of Charles IV (El Caballito) marking the entrance of the Paseo de la Reforma. Prior to the inauguration of the Cuauhtémoc memorial, every statue in Mexico City symbolized Mexico's Spanish heritage and legacy. Photo by Alfredo Briquet; courtesy of the Nettie Lee Benson Latin American Library, University of Texas, Austin.

oppressors. The myth of the noble Aztec became entrenched in nineteenth-century liberal political thought.[72]

Despite the triumph of liberalism, a systematic effort to promote Cuauhtémoc as a national hero did not emerge until the Porfiriato. For two generations the cult was not manifested beyond the scattered texts of Liberal polemicists, the oral traditions of various indigenous groups, and Maximilian's efforts at *neo-Aztequismo*. Although Juárez sanctioned the commemoration of Cuauhtémoc by erecting a bust of the Aztec leader at La Viga on August 13, 1869, celebrations left much to be desired.[73] Prior to Díaz, the only significant historical monuments in the Federal District were reminders of Spanish hegemony: the equestrian statue of Charles IV (already popularly renamed "El Caballito"), the hipsographic monument to cosmographer Enrico Martínez (the engineer who provided the blueprints for Mexico City's original drainage system), and the Columbus monument on the Paseo de la Reforma (donated by Hispanophile Antonio Escandón). The August 21 inauguration of the 100,000-peso Cuauhtémotzin memorial dramatically rectified this paradox.

The selective romanticization of Mexico's Indian heritage during the Porfiriato is best understood as proto-indigenist since it neither became state educational policy nor was consistently espoused by those in power. High government officials appreciated Mexico's indigenous past, even as they failed to solve the "Indian problem" in the present. In 1884, the government named two new naval steamships *Xicontencatl* and *Guatimotizin* (Cuauhtémoc).[74]

Figure 39. Statue of Columbus donated by railroad magnate Antonio Escandón (1874). Traveling down the Paseo de la Reforma, passengers and pedestrians passed the monuments to Charles IV and Columbus before arriving to the Cuauhtémotzin memorial in the third traffic circle. The Column of Independence came to occupy the fourth. Photo by Alfredo Briquet; courtesy of the Nettie Lee Benson Latin American Library, University of Texas, Austin.

Figure 40. Monument to Cuauhtémoc on the Paseo de la Reforma. It was the first significant national memorial to honor Mexico's indigenous past. Photo by Alfredo Briquet; courtesy of the Nettie Lee Benson Latin American Library, University of Texas, Austin.

Minister of Development Vicente Riva Palacio, who opened the competition for the best architectural design for the Cuauhtémoc monument, exalted the last Indian emperor and the Aztecs in his historical writings, public speeches, and novel *Martín Garatuza*. Justo Sierra extolled several Aztec leaders but identified Cuauhtémoc as the bravest of all. President Díaz, a *mestizo* with Mixtec blood, once advised a subordinate to "pay close attention to the consideration which the Indians deserve, for they have been the cannon fodder on which we have based our efforts to change the moral and political situation of the country."[75] When Federico Gamboa, diplomat, journalist, and author of the renowned novel *Santa*, disparaged the indigenous character in a speech, the president privately voiced his displeasure and publicly snubbed him for the next year.[76]

On balance, dead Indians of national lore fared better than those living in Porfirian Mexico. Even the best-educated linguists and educators of the era described Mexican "People of Corn" in negative terms and as inferiors to European "People of Wheat."[77] While the state actively constructed the Cuauhtémoc cult, it persecuted, enslaved, or massacred the Yaqui, Mayo, Apache, and Maya Indians. Cuauhtémoc, the last sovereign ruler of the Aztecs, chose to see his city destroyed rather than accept abject slavery.[78] But Porfirian Liberals saw no living Cuauhtémocs in Cajeme, Tetabiate, Gerónimo, Victorio, or any other contemporary indigenous leader. Díaz proved as shortsighted as his Liberal predecessors when it came to improving the miserable living conditions of the indigenous poor. In his State of the Union address, the president found no contradiction whatsoever in reporting evidence of progress in the "persecution of rebellious Indians," "the pacification of Yaqui and Mayo tribes," and the "inauguration with solemn festivity of the monument in memory of Cuauhtémoc."[79]

The Porfirian state nevertheless inaugurated both the monument and an annual commemoration of Cuauhtémoc in 1887. Anticipating the dedication of the statue, city councilmen debated the most appropriate date to hold the event. They settled on August 21, the anniversary of Cuauhtémoc's torture, over the traditional date of August 13, which marked the fall of Tenochtitlán. The actual date when the last Aztec emperor died at the hands of Cortés's men has been lost to history. When the first Cuauhtémoc Day arrived, public officials and loyal citizens repeated the rituals of the first major Juárez commemoration, which took place in July. In the second traffic circle of the Paseo de la Reforma, a large audience listened to speeches and poetry recitals and placed floral wreaths at the monument. Vicente Riva Palacio, Alfredo Chavero, Francisco Sosa, and Francisco del Paso y Troncoso—Porfirian forerunners of the revolution's *indigenistas*—spoke eloquently on the legacies of Indian Mexico.[80] In the 1890s, W. W. Wheatly, general manager of the Mexican Electrical Tramways Company, offered free transit to all participants. The City Council's Festivities Commission sought to authenticate the ceremonies and celebrate Mexico's Indian heritage by inviting indigenous groups to dress their children with Aztec feathered headdresses, shields, coats of arms, and war clubs. The Milpa Alta municipality of Tlalpam, for example, sent huge delegations of ornately dressed "descendants of Emperor Cuauhtémoc." They and other indigenous groups from the surrounding states arrived on the night of August 20 and camped at the monument overnight. Linguists read compositions in Nahuatl on August 21. Children sang the National Hymn in the language of the Aztecs. The programs otherwise united President Díaz, Governor of the Federal District Guillermo Landa y Escandón, workers' organizations, schoolchildren, and indigenous groups for a day.[81]

President Díaz rarely missed the annual commemorations of the Battles of Molina del Rey and Chapultepec honoring the soldiers who sacrificed their lives defending Mexico against the invading U.S. Army of Winfield Scott in

September 1847. Memorial services took place every September 8 at the monument that Díaz inaugurated at the foot of Chapultepec Castle in 1880. To attract citizens, itinerant merchants were invited to set up their stands at the park entrance. Officers of the Asociación del Colegio Militar (Military College Association), who arranged for martial music, patriotic speeches, artillery salvos, and twenty-one gun salutes, also took their artistic tasks seriously. For the *cincuentanario* of 1897, members decorated the ceremonial stage as a defensive fortification, fully armed with cannon, swords, muskets, and coats of arms. Because spectators could not see Chapultepec Castle through a canopy of verdant trees, the association hung a huge painting of it to provide an imposing backdrop for the ceremony. Brigades of soldiers formed double lines to add martial symmetry to the affair. Although memorial exercises honored all soldiers who died in combat, speakers eulogized the six brave cadets of the Military College, the Niños Héroes, who died defending the castle on September 13. About one hundred cadets died at the Battle of Chapultepec, but the Porfirian state concentrated on six of them: Vicente Suárez, Agustín Melgar, Juan de la Barrera, Juan Escutia, Fernando Montes de Oca, and Francisco Márquez. In period speeches, orators compared the young martyrs to the Spartan defenders of Thermopylae and to the heroes of Troy, retelling the glorious episodes of "their Iliad" to attentive cadets of the Colegio Militar. Obviously, speakers never equated the boys to the defenders of the Alamo, even if American-owned Mexico City newspapers did. Ceremonies always ended with Díaz, widows and mothers, and veterans of 1847 depositing wreaths at the monument.[82]

The Military College Association issued invitations to its commemoration of the Boy Heroes but also allowed crowds to gather around the ceremonial site. Audiences began to exceed five thousand people after 1895. The restoration of the former palatial residence of Maximilian, the extension of the electric streetcar system, the growing popularity of the forest, and the increasing admiration for the Boy Heroes brought more people to what was originally designed as an exclusive military ceremony. In 1897, Minister of Hacienda José Yves Limantour and Director of the Military College General Juan Villegas opened a competition for the best architectural design for an outdoor auditorium to be used during the annual September 8 event. The prize went to Nicolás Mariscal, a student at the Escuela Nacional de Bellas Artes, for his proposal of a Greek-style amphitheater that sat encircled by the lush forest of cypresses. Construction began in 1899, and everything but the sculptures for the semicircular venue was completed in 1902. The Hellenic hemicycle, described as a "jewel of architectural art," provided a resting place for park visitors to contemplate the beauty of the forest landscape.[83]

The Tribuna Monumental, more popularly known as the Rotonda del

Bosque, became a leading site for official commemorations. After 1902, electric streetcars carried hundreds of well-to-do citizens to Chapultepec for the solemnities. For the ceremony of 1905, over one hundred students of the Miguel Lerdo de Tejada primary school sang patriotic hymns and presented an allegorical scene in which a slain cadet covered with blood and lying face to the heavens was being mourned by a young girl dressed like an angel representing La Patria. Graphic visual dramatizations of death helped promote the Niños Héroes and the military.[84]

Involving Federal District schoolchildren in the September 8 programs was a Porfirian innovation that rapidly popularized the Niños Héroes cult. In previous incarnations, memorial services honored soldiers who fell in three different engagements: Churubusco, Molino del Rey, and Chapultepec. Díaz, however, had no interest in promoting other valiant defenders, especially National Guardsmen, who also gave their lives in the war against the United States. Historian Pedro Santoni explains it this way: "Real flesh-and-blood heroes with their divergent experiences and divisive political opinions could hardly be integrated into the patriotic myths being constructed by the Porfirian enterprise."[85] Along with the Boy Heroes, period newspapers only listed the names of other cadets killed or captured by U.S. forces, among them a young Miguel Miramón. But since Miramón later joined the Conservatives during the War of the Reform, commanded armies for Maximilian, and faced the firing squad alongside his emperor at the Hill of the Bells (Querétaro), Liberals demonized him.[86] In the final decade of the Porfiriato, military officers handed over the program's organization to civilian educators, who did no better telling national truths. The Military College and public schools flew flags bearing the names of the six Niños Héroes, and the annual event at the Monumental Tribune increasingly took on the character of a national fable for generations of Mexican students receiving K–6 educations. In 1908, two professors from the Normal School held their National History and Civic Instruction class at the Chapultepec ceremony. They recounted the bravery of the Boy Heroes to students who listened with "religious attention" in the presence of President Díaz.[87] Annual retelling of the last stand of the Niños Héroes restored glory to the Patria: "Children [of the Patria] can, through love of her, transform defeat into an epos, disaster into glory and the darkness of death into the refulgence of light."[88]

Commemorations of Guerrero and Morelos

Unlike his contemporaries, Vicente Guerrero survived the Independence Wars and was elected Mexico's second president in 1828. To save his beleaguered presidency from armed Conservatives, Guerrero entered the field of battle when an Italian sea captain in the pay of Anastasio Bustamante betrayed and captured him in 1830. Bustamante ordered his execution by firing squad in Cuilapam, Oaxaca, on February 14, 1831. For Liberal nationalist historians such as Vicente Riva Palacio, Guerrero's grandson who also inherited his name, the immortal *suriano* (southerner) represented a crucial link in the contiguous campaign for independence. Following the execution of Morelos and capture of Nicolás Bravo, Guerrero had been the only insurgent still active in the field, forming the essential connection between the failed first phase of 1810–15 and the consummation of independence in 1821.

Guerrero was considered a national hero since his execution. On April 13, 1833, the state of Oaxaca transferred his body from Cuilapam to the Church of Santo Domingo in Oaxaca City. In November, Congress declared Guerrero a benemérito de la Patria, later renamed Cuilapam Ciudad Guerrero, and christened the region where the insurgent fought as the state of Guerrero. On December 2, 1842, Guerrero's remains were conveyed to Mexico City and reburied in the Santa Paula Cemetery during the interim presidency of fellow southerner Nicolás Bravo.[89]

Vicente Guerrero was a popular working-class hero, and the manifestations of Catorce de Febrero, like Juárez Day and Hidalgo Day, reflected this. In addition, the Catholic press viewed Guerrero in a positive light for his cooperation with Iturbide in bringing about the break with Spain.[90] During the official manifestations of February 14, artisans, factory laborers, city officials, and delegates from the states gathered at the Municipal Palace and marched to Guerrero Plaza adjoining San Fernando Cemetery. A high-level government functionary usually officiated at the ceremony; Subsecretary of Public Instruction Justo Sierra presided in 1904. Following the customary memorial services, wreaths were placed at the tomb of Guerrero. From 1898 to 1902, Francisco Arce, former governor of Guerrero and founder of the Círculo Patriótico del Martir de Cuilápam, organized more ambitious programs honoring Guerrero. Labor leader and city councilman Pedro Ordoñez also served as an officer of the patriotic society. General Arce commonly led civilians, detachments of soldiers, and military bands in processions from the San Fernando to the Municipal Palace and to Orrin's Theater for lengthy memorial programs.[91] On the anniversary of Guerrero's birth in 1908, state governor Damián Flores dedicated a monument, park, and library to the "immortal suriano." He then led a civic procession to Guerrero Park in Tixtla.[92]

Padre José María Morelos y Pavón, the warrior priest who led the independence revolt until executed in 1815, was designated a benemérito with a dozen other independence heroes in 1823. In honor of Morelos, the state of Michoacán changed the name of his birthplace of Valladolid to Morelia, and the federal government created the state of Morelos in 1862.[93] The Porfirian state perpetuated his memory every Independence Day, but on December 22, the anniversary of his execution, the Ayuntamiento of San Cristóbal Ecatepec and the Club Político Morelos organized commemorations at the church where he was shot by firing squad and buried. Although this was attended by governors of the Federal District, Vice-President Ramón Corral sent a representative, and the War Ministry ordered a military band to render homage to the insurgent general in 1904. Normally, two hundred capitalinos joined hundreds of residents of San Cristóbal in processions to the Morelos monument. After ceremonies, public officials dined and scrawled short notes in memorial books kept at Morelos's former residence.[94] Governor Rafael Rebollar's inscription praised the patriot in the following words: "Morelos is to our history what the highest peak of the Himalayas is to universal geography."[95] In 1891, Porfirio Díaz inscribed his thoughts about an alternative history for Mexico if only Morelos survived:

> If Morelos had lived to the year 1821, Iturbide would not have been able to take control of the national insurrection; and the nation would not have passed through a half century of shameful and bloody revolution which caused it to lose half of its national territory. Today it would be the powerful republic which we would have expected from seventy years of development initiated by the courage, the abnegation, prudence, and political skill, of which that extraordinary man was the model.[96]

What a difference one man could have made in the imagination of Porfirio Díaz.

Congratulating Don Porfirio

State control of the calendar was never limited to annual holidays or memorial days. There were five months in the Porfirian calendar devoid of a national holiday or memorial observance—January, March, June, October, and November—but it is wrong to assume periods of inactivity during these months. State funerals or any other improvised state event were just as likely to be held in these months as in any others. Moreover, commemorative events such as the Centennial of Juárez's Birth (March 1906) or the Pan-American Congresses (October) took place between major holidays. Impromptu gatherings of impassioned citizens littered the national calendar. During a war scare with Guatemala in January 1895, some twenty-five hundred students of the capital gathered at the National Palace to pledge their lives to their commander in chief. Palace security and teachers encountered much shoving and shouting as students vowed to their president that they would be the first to defend their country. Federico Gamboa noted their "forceful cheers, honest youth, [and] indispensable worship," concluding: "May God preserve for us this love of country."[97]

Likewise, the month of June was reserved for presidential campaign activity. In 1896, a mammoth meeting of four hundred prominent merchants, bankers, politicians, and professionals convened in Mexico City with the purpose of supporting the reelection of Díaz. Members of political clubs throughout the republic embraced one another and shared cigars at the Casino Nacional. The Junta Central del Círculo Nacional Porfirista held the colossal "party convention of Díaz." On June 21 bells pealed and cannon salvos awoke citizens, rockets soared from all parts of the city, military bands dispersed, and eight thousand supporters met at the Alameda and marched to the National Palace to greet the president. There, Díaz was presented with a handsomely bound album filled with 531,577 signatures. According to one report, the committee spent $15,000 canvassing the nation for over four weeks in search of literate male voters and four thousand sympathetic foreigners. The so-called Book of Gold carried the words "Peace, Progress, Morality, and Good Credit" in laurel wreaths on the leather cover. In the Zócalo, citizens watched as thirty thousand balloons ascended into the sky. At a certain height cords were pulled, and from each balloon a photograph of Díaz fell like confetti to the crowd below. It was the biggest presidential inauguration festivity in the history of nineteenth-century Mexico.[98]

Some June events met with too much success for Díaz's comfort. In 1898, when Congress amended the Liberal Constitution of 1857 to make military service obligatory, General Bernardo Reyes solemnized the occasion by ordering an army division to parade through the streets and called on all loyal Mexican civilians to form a Fifth Column downtown. In June 1902, after his promotion to war minister, Reyes issued a call to mobilize a civilian militia or Second Reserve of twenty thousand men. The invitation inspired one hundred thousand citizens nationwide to flock to Reyes's flag. Among those who volunteered was Francisco I. Madero, the revolutionary leader who later toppled the dictator. In response to the unforeseen popularity of Reyes's act, Díaz had to not only disband the Second Reserve, which approached the size of the professional army, but force Reyes to resign. Díaz reappointed Reyes as governor of Nuevo León but later reassigned him to a military mission in Europe, a kind of informal exile for politicians whom Díaz perceived as potential challengers.[99]

By 1903, the Porfirian state had achieved such a level of permanence that it committed few acts of overt coercion and even withstood internal criticism. Friends of the president held the U.S.-style Porfirista National Liberal Convention in May and June. Díaz was nominated for reelection "in the form and by the date prescribed by law" and then delivered an acceptance speech infused with his memories of the Reform and French Intervention: "It was the pueblo that responded to my extraordinary demands for energy to sustain a war effort without shelter, bread, funds, and weaponry except for the arms we took from the enemy; and in hindsight all they were promised was an obscure and tragic death." Díaz remarked on his collaboration with the "great Juárez" and in the language of hegemonic rule explained the lesson he took away from 1867: "Our citizens will serve the country better when they concede their unlimited confidence and powerful moral support."[100]

Tours to the exterior and presidential inaugurations often brought Díaz or at least his image to thousands of citizens from October through January. In the winter months, the tireless Díaz embarked on presidential visits to Puebla (1886), Oaxaca (1892), Querétaro (1896), Nuevo León (1898), México (1900), Guanajuato (1903), Guerrero (1904), Veracruz (1905), Yucatán (1906), and Chihuahua (1909). The president always arrived to cheering crowds and triumphal arches. In the age of empire they were not unlike royal visits to the colonies. Another way to view Díaz's image was to receive postcards, which littered the republic and foreign countries like so much state propaganda. During election years, citizens flocked to capital cities to participate in *fiestas presidenciales*. Michoacán celebrated Don Porfirio's 1896 reelection with a parade of campesinos from the outskirts of Morelia. They wore red shirts reminiscent of the *chinacos* who fought for independence and the Liberal Reform, but instead of marching to war they walked beside an allegorical parade float bearing the message "Peace."[101]

Historical cavalcades of Independence, Reform, and Peace also ushered in Díaz's seventh term from December 1 to December 5, 1904. An estimated three hundred thousand people witnessed the civic parade downtown. The float representing "Peace" cost nearly $6,000. The minting of commemorative gold medallions and printing of complimentary postcards cost the same. At night, the gente decente attended banquets, serenades, dances, operas, and gala balls. But on day five of the program, Mexicans of all social classes enjoyed a *féria popular* on the Anzures Plains. The Circulo de Amigos spent tens of thousands of pesos on carnival booths and free food for five thousand people, balloon ascensions and outdoor film projections, tightropes and greased poles, and fireworks and charitable *fiestas infantiles* for the poor children of the capital. The Seventh Inaugural had the character of a national retirement party for Díaz but actually served as a dress rehearsal for both the Centennial of 1910 and his reelection to an eighth term.[102]

Landscapes and mindscapes of memory formed when states coordinated spatial and ideological activities to recur often enough for citizens to embrace them as national traditions. In Mexico, the state directed the process of

Figure 41. Three period postcards of Porfirio Díaz. They served as political propaganda in their widespread distribution in Mexico and to the exterior. Private collection of the author with thanks to Randy Hanson.

constructing national memory from the broken fragments of a troubled history that had even pitted Liberals against Liberals. President Díaz enlisted an army of state bureaucrats to present a sanitized official history that downgraded his armed conflict against Benito Juárez to a slight disagreement. Before long, Don Porfirio rose to the eminent status of Juárez's successor. Díaz was so preoccupied with his political legitimacy that he once requested congressional authorization to wear on Mexican soil Prussia's Ribbon of the Red Eagle, which conferred German knighthood.[103] Such behavior confirms the belief of *El Imparcial* that Mexicans and foreign nations showered upon Díaz an "Apotheosis in Life."[104] His eight-term presidency came at a time when the entire Western world worshiped Great Men.

The Porfirian concept of nationhood depended on the ideological construction of a national space built upon the blood and bones of its greatest leaders. Through days of public mourning, the ruling class used popular hero cults and mass participation to connect with the cultural values of the very people they subordinated in order to stabilize a system that normalized inequality. Political officials tapped deeply into the well of popular culture, associated themselves with shared traditions, and drew support from common people.[105] Memorial days for Juárez, Hidalgo, Cuauhtémoc, the Niños Héroes, Guerrero, and Morelos ultimately resonated with citizens who rightfully placed a high premium on tragic martyrdom and heroic sacrifice in the face of national crisis. Perhaps nothing was so tragic as what became of the Mexican Independence Heroes, the topic of the final chapter.

Figure 42. José Guadalupe Posada's *Continuación de las manifestaciones anti-reeleccionistas*. From Roberto Berdecio and Stanley Applebaum, eds., *Posada's Popular Mexican Prints* (New York: Dover Publications, 1972).

Heroes Laid to Rest, the Past Exhumed   6

Pantheonizations of the Independence Heroes

> History says that the bloody cruelty and stupidity of Calleja in conjunc-
> tion with the infamous treason of Elizondo at Norias de Baján, ended
> with the horrible executions of the first martyrs of Mexican Indepen-
> dence. Their heads were severed from their trunks and carried in iron
> cages to the walls of the Castle of Granaditas, where they waited ten
> years for historical vindication to arrive finally under the victorious
> banners of liberty and the Patria.
>
> On the triumphal day, those skulls, whitened by the sun and worn
> by the hurricanes, were collected by the people as relics of the martyrs
> and deposited in the crypt of the Altar of the Kings in the Metropolitan
> Cathedral.
>
> Seventy-two years have passed and those relics remain forgotten. . . .
> History protests against this sacrilege.
>
> —CONGRESSMAN AND HISTORIAN JUAN A. MATEOS, MAY 1893

THE PORFIRIAN STATE contrived its legitimacy and hegemony by appro-
priating religious and cultural traditions, incorporating fallen leaders
stripped of their ideological distinctions into a pantheon of national heroes,
and reinterpreting the past to serve needs in the present. In no other activity were these cultural-political strategies for nation-building more evident
than in state funerals for heroes long consigned to the vault. Modern nations
have been notorious grave robbers. It was not enough to recognize the political careers of public men from the cradle to the grave; the state reached its
powerful hands into the crypt, extricated skeletal remains in various states of
decomposition, and thereby exhumed the past. The modernizing state dug up
forensic evidence and factual details to substantiate its extraordinary claims
during memorial acts. Based on state expenditure alone, one easily concludes
that the human bones of distinguished men and women have a high market

value as national property. The state effectively nationalized the remains of the illustrious dead for its own purposes.

State pantheonizations—the exhumation, reburial, and incorporation of premier Mexican heroes into the National Pantheon—were the most successful national media events in Porfirian Mexico. Their magnificence was rivaled only by the Roman Catholic Church's 1895 Coronation of the Virgin of Guadalupe in Mexico City or the funerals for Archbishops Labastida and Alarcón. Digging up the remains of independence heroes gave President Díaz a quasi-religious aura, which enabled him to graft his state onto an immemorial Patria.[1] After all, the state crossed a sacred barrier in disturbing the graves of mortals laid to rest long ago. Since the Porfirian intelligentsia doubled as congressmen and cabinet ministers, they colluded in associating Díaz with every national struggle. Díaz was portrayed as the heir of all causes from Cuauhtémoc's defense of ancient Tenochtitlán to the liberation movements of Hidalgo and Morelos and from the triumph of Reforma Liberals to the expulsion of the French. Over time, it became difficult for citizens to know a national past without Díaz situated squarely within it.

How could constructed subjects of the state—that is, citizens—envision modern Mexico without its dictator? How could turn-of-the-century Roman Catholics imagine Mexico without an archbishop or a world without a pope? For reasons grounded in Mexico's Catholic tradition, the pantheonizations elicited the kind of fanatical street-level devotion expressed during the crowning of the Virgin or Día de la Virgen pilgrimages every December 12. President Díaz and his governors recognized the power that the Church still wielded, even at the expense of state initiatives. In a thoughtful letter to President Díaz, Governor of Guanajuato Joaquín González Obregón cautioned against administering the 1895 national census in October since thousands of Mexicans from all over the republic would embark on pilgrimages to the capital for the crowning of the Virgin. Díaz replied that "the unfavorable timing has occurred to us."[2]

To pious Catholics, the history of Mexican independence resembled the violent history and intense suffering of religious martyrs since the days of John the Baptist, Mary, and Jesus Christ. In fact, the Porfirian state promoted such comparisons. Mexico's foremost heroes and martyrs were one and the same. Leading independence heroes—Hidalgo, Morelos, Matamoros, and Abasolo—were all Catholic priests before they were executed or jailed. Porfirian state media created a metanarrative of independence that described Christ-like saviors suffering excruciating torment and summary execution for the people. According to historian Lyman Johnson, the Catholic Church used the exemplary deaths of saints "to inculcate Christian virtues and demonstrate to the faithful the power of God acting in this world."[3] Both Church and state enshrined bodies, preserved bones as relics, and guarded the personal effects of "patron saints." These corporeal reminders of the grace and goodness of men and women were located in sites fully accessible to the masses. Catholic teachings stressed the sacrifice of Christ and the saints for humanity; Liberal and positivist treatises stressed martyrdom for the Patria. Churches displayed paintings and sculptures of Christ with gaping wounds and blood streaming down from a crown of thorns as he suffered on the cross. Political discourse retold in vivid language the traumatic deaths of secular saints. Epithets multiplied but retained the religious term *martyr*, sanctifying independence leaders while recording the sites of their deaths. Vicente Guerrero was "the martyr of Cuilápam," and José María Morelos was "the martyr of San Cristóbal de Ecatepec." What does the title *benemérito de la Patria* represent if not the secular beatification of a historical figure? In the quotation that started this chapter, Juan Mateos describes bones as the "relics of the martyrs" and their neglect as "sacrilege."[4] *Sacer*, the thirteenth-century Latin root of *sacrifice* and *sacred*, means "holy" or "something consecrated as holy."

There is no question that turn-of-the-century intellectuals were conscious of the sacralization process as a prerogative of nation-builders. Take, for example, the Independence Day speech of Rodolfo Reyes in honor of Father Hidalgo: "The worship of heroism is to the patriot what the worship of the saints is to the believer, a channel through which he may adore something abstract, which needs to be incarnated, to be related to the honors of the altar; and the fatherland, who like God has its saints, reveals itself to us through them." Thus, according to Reyes, Hidalgo "ceased to be, in order to eternally be; he found his end, in order to become endless; he left behind him this mortal life, in order to become the immortal essence of a loving nation."[5]

From the perspective of late-nineteenth-century politicians such as Mateos, the recovery of bodily remains, no matter how decayed, vindicated those heroes who gave their lives for the nation. This urgent demand for historical reparation stemmed from a fundamental need to rectify the horrible desecration and improper disposal of precious corpses. To be sure, both sides committed atrocities during Mexico's liberation wars. Hidalgo's uncontrolled mobs brutally massacred Spanish civilians. Morelos cruelly put to death hundreds of royalists. But since the victors wrote history, polemicists since Carlos María de Bustamante had demonized Spanish *jefes realistas* such as Viceroy Francisco Javier de Venegas and General Félix Calleja.[6] In a Chamber of Deputies speech (1881), Congressman Félix Romero praised the repatriation of Mariano Arista's remains with the following words: "After a long exile the consecrated relics have finally touched the soil of the Fatherland. . . . in fulfillment of a glorious reparation."[7] Julio Zárate, author of the volume on the Independence Wars in the five-volume government-subsidized historical work *México a través de los siglos* (1889), discussed the funeral of the Independence Heroes in 1823: "The hour of reparation sounded: one of the first acts of the free and independent *patria* was to consecrate the memory of the martyrs and reward the efforts of its loyal sons."[8] Such works by Congressman Zárate informed the state reburial of the Independence Heroes in 1895. The funeral was to make amends for all of the pain inflicted on the *santos* of Mexican nationhood.

State Funerals for the Independence Heroes, 1823–95

And suffer they did. Ambushed and apprehended by Spanish troops near Monclova, Coahuila, on March 21, 1811, rebel insurgents Miguel Hidalgo, Ignacio Allende, Mariano Jiménez, Mariano Hidalgo, Juan de Aldama, and Mariano Abasolo were placed in irons and forced to ride hundreds of miles on horseback to Chihuahua. The long painful journey, described by Justo Sierra as a *via crucis*, broke them physically and spiritually.[9] Crowds and guards cursed, mistreated, and ridiculed the rebels as agents of Napoleon. Death came dilatorily for each. Three months after his capture, cavalry officer Allende was led out of his prison cell into the courtyard of a former Jesuit college in Chihuahua. Facing a bullet-ridden wall with his hands bound behind him, he paid the supreme penalty for treason. A firing squad shot him through the back on June 26. The other nonclerical revolutionaries also fell by fusillade. A few insurgent priests were later executed in Durango. Abasolo, the rebel curate and militia officer, evaded execution and was shipped to the fortress prison of Santa Catarina in Cádiz, Spain, where he died in 1816.[10]

Father Miguel Hidalgo, the leading conspirator and *generalísimo*, endured greater humiliation. Canon law required that a high Church official excommunicate and defrock him under the auspices of the Holy Office of the Inquisition prior to his civil trial. Spanish officers waited four months for the ailing bishop of Durango to reach Chihuahua, only to grow impatient and name a substitute. Hidalgo's ecclesiastical degradation was debasing. On July 29, guards led him into a large room, removed his chains, and took off his prison uniform. He stood calmly as priests dressed him in clerical robes and stripped him once again before his inquisitors. Wearing only a penitential sackcloth tunic, Hidalgo was then forced to kneel, as Church officials pronounced the death sentence. The disheartened insurgent faced the firing squad on July 30, 1811. His request to be shot in the chest instead of the back was granted. All but one bullet from the first volley missed Hidalgo. The second burst of fire ended his life.[11]

Royalist soldiers placed Hidalgo's corpse beside the rotting cadavers of Aldama, Allende, and Jiménez in a nearby stable. They decapitated the four insurgents, buried their corpses beneath the Chapel of San Antonio in the San

Francisco Convent in Chihuahua, and loaded the heads onto a wagon bound for Guanajuato. Their flesh had decomposed almost beyond recognition by the time it reached the city. The skulls were placed separately in four metal cages and then mounted on the four corners of the Alhóndiga de Granaditas, where the rebels committed their treasonous acts. There the skulls signified the decapitation of the insurrection itself and served as an abject lesson to other insurgents. When Mexico achieved independence, the skulls were transferred to the San Sebastián Monastery in Guanajuato.[12]

After Hidalgo fell, the list of Mexican martyrs who died horribly and whose cadavers were subjected to similar cruelties grew longer. Insurgent leader Leonardo Bravo was imprisoned, tortured, and publicly garroted in 1813. The Spanish caught and imprisoned his son, Field Marshal Miguel Bravo, in Chila but executed him a year later in Puebla. Hidalgo's successor, mestizo priest and guerrilla warrior José María Morelos, agonized over the loss of two more of his best officers in 1814. The indefatigable Mariano Matamoros was captured, bound, and exhibited in the public plaza of Pátzcuaro. Royalists subjected him to countless indignities en route to Valladolid (Morelia), Michoacán, where he too was defrocked and summarily shot to death on February 3. Royalist troops killed Morelos's other lieutenant, Hermenegildo Galeana, in a clash on June 25. A Spanish dragoon discharged his musket into Galeana's chest and then promptly beheaded him. Galeana's head was placed on a pike and paraded around as a war trophy in the central plaza of Coyuca. Spanish officer Julian Aviles became so indignant when royalist sympathizers abused it, he had it buried in the local church. Two of Galeana's soldiers returned for his mutilated corpse and buried it at the site where he fell. Since they were killed two years later, the exact location has been lost to history.[13]

Morelos endured an ordeal of "solitude, helplessness, moral torture, complete lack of free will, relentless harassment, and endless adverse circumstances" before he was cut down by firing squad.[14] Outside Tenango, royalist officers forced Morelos to watch the execution of twenty-seven of his men. He later withstood two grueling trials. In a public *auto de fé* held in Mexico City on November 27, 1815, the archdiocesan court denounced Morelos as a heretic, atheist, deist, materialist, hypocrite, enemy of Christianity, and traitor to God who had forsaken his vows and fathered three children. Priests defrocked him while chanting *misereres*. In a separate interrogation, the bishop of Oaxaca made him wear penitential robes.[15] Calleja had more than public humiliation planned for Morelos. The new viceroy wanted the insurgent executed at the citadel, after which his head and right hand were to be severed from the body. The first was to be displayed in Mexico City's Plaza Mayor (Zócalo), and the second, in Oaxaca's central square, "to remind everyone of what will happen to rebels."[16] Only the intervention of the archbishop of Mexico prevented the

mutilation of Morelos's corpse. To avoid public execution of a popular insurgent in a city full of sympathizers, Calleja removed Morelos to the small village
of San Cristóbal de Ecatepéc. On December 22, 1815, two volleys—four shots
through the front and four shots to the back—silenced Morelos forever.[17]

The year 1817 produced two more martyrs. Cornered at the Rancho del
Venedito, insurgent Pedro Moreno refused a Spanish order to lay down his
arms. Spanish musketeers lowered their sights on the machete-wielding
giant and shot him at point-blank range. His body was buried at the Church
of La Merced, but royalists displayed his head on a pike in Guanajuato for
three months. Moreno's comrade, twenty-nine-year-old Spanish firebrand
Francisco Javier Mina, was shot in the back on Bellaco Hill (Guanajuato) on
November 11.[18]

Undeniably, the protracted and sanguinary liberation wars against Spain
exacted a heavy price. Mexico, however, reasserted its independence by vow-
ing to recover the remains of the independence martyrs. On July 19, 1823,
Congress passed a resolution that declared thirteen insurgents as beneméritos de la Patria—Hidalgo, Allende, Aldama, Abasolo, Morelos, Matamoros,
Galeana, Jiménez, Mina, Moreno, Victor Rosales, and Leonardo and Miguel
Bravo. The law authorized the government to inscribe their names in gold,
erect monuments where the heroes fell, and rebury their mortal remains in
Mexico City.[19] Amid great confusion, state delegations conveyed the insurgents
to the Villa de Guadalupe in September. Chihuahuans reunited the skulls and
skeletal remains of Hidalgo, Allende, Aldama, and Jiménez. From Guanajuato
came the bones of Mina and Moreno. Valladolid proudly returned Matamoros. Indigenous peasants from the San Cristóbal de Ecatepéc parish played
uplifting spiritual music while they marched the precious cargo of Morelos's
remains to Guadalupe on September 15. Bustamante wrote: "These sons of
nature produced a chorus with sweet harmony that would entertain the ear
of the hero of the South . . . and he would rejoice upon seeing those natives,
whom he loved so much in life."[20] Authorities never located the remains of
Leonardo and Miguel Bravo, Galeana, and Abasolo, but it was not for lack
of trying.[21]

On Independence Day 1823, the collected remains were placed in five urns
and marched to the Santo Domingo Church. A hearse led a procession that
included cavalry detachments and soldiers, public officials and municipal corporations, and seventy carriages of civilians. Enormous crowds fixed their eyes
on the magnificent display. It comes as little surprise that in the evening an
anti-Spanish mob attempted to desecrate the tomb of *conquistador* Hernán
Cortés in the Hospital de Jesús Nazareno. To prevent the act, Conservative
Lucas Alamán hid the remains, averting what he considered would have been
a disastrous historical injustice.[22] At dawn on September 17, a requiem mass

was held for the martyrs. Vicente Guerrero led another march of public officials, cavalrymen, horse-drawn cannons, confraternity members, and priests
through the main thoroughfares to the National Cathedral. The allegorical
carriage that bore the urns carried four Roman statues symbolizing the sovereignty of the nation and a frontispiece that read: "The march of death, one's
sacrifice to the country at the scaffold, is the march of the hero who walks to
the temple of immortality." Bustamante observed melancholy crowds with a
great many tearful people.[23] At the cathedral, officials placed the urns atop an
elaborate catafalque for public display and subsequently buried them beneath
the Altar of the Kings.[24] The sculptor Patiño created two statues for the altar,
but their placement was interrupted by successive revolutions. The inscription
for the statues read: "To the honorable remains of the magnanimous and fear-
less caudillos, fathers of Mexican liberty and victims of perfidy and despotism,
the tearful and eternally grateful Fatherland erected this public monument, in
the year of 1823."[25]

Historians and politicians of Mexico City perceived the original burial of
the Independence Heroes as a glorious national event. Many had read Bustamante's classic account of the original burial, which also mentioned that the
bones would remain buried in the crypt of the viceroys under the Altar of the
Kings *until the nation erects for them the pantheon they deserve, and which we
want to see*."[26] Since the 1840s early national leaders such as Lucas Alamán and
José María Andrade had visited the crypt beneath the Altar of the Kings, but
the initiative to transfer the remains of the heroes originated in the City Council. In 1881, Pedro Lascurain presented a motion to move the bones from the
altar to the Rotunda of Illustrious Men, pending the construction of a monument. He also called for the bones of Agustín de Iturbide and Santa Anna to
be transferred to the rotunda but not united with the others.[27]

An article in *El Universal* by Angel Pola propelled the project in 1893. Archbishop Próspero María Alarcón permitted Pola, several journalists, and the
administrator of the Dolores Cemetery, Ricardo Benfield, to examine the
remains of the Independence Heroes. Their report called attention to the rapid
deterioration of both the crypt and the skulls, prompting Mateos's demand for
resolution of the historical injustice.[28] Mateos admonished: "Ask the American
Union if the remains of Washington are like that. Ask the other America about
the remains of Simón Bolívar! They will respond that they guard those saintly
relics in a gold urn. The skull that once thought up Mexican Independence [is]
tossed away like an object without history. The skull of Morelos, like the nest of
the eagle, guarded the genius of war!" The congressman demanded new urns,
resuscitated Justo Sierra's plan to build a National Pantheon, and disregarded
the rotunda because anyone could be buried in the public cemetery that surrounded it.[29]

Following patterns established with the foundation of Juárez Day, patriotic societies and citizens collaborated with the national government to preserve the remains. In 1894, Francisco Torreblanca and the members of the Gran Familia Modelo mutualist society toured the crypt beneath the Altar of the Kings. The society raised funds for a silver and gold urn that featured a golden eagle perched atop its lid and a velvet cushion inside.[30] Minister of the Interior Manuel Romero Rubio hired Ernesto Iriarte y Drusina of the Compañia de Mármoles Mexicanos to construct a mausoleum for the urn inside the Chapel of San José. For the platform and steps, Drusina ordered marble from Orizaba and the Borrego quarries, but he sculpted the statue representing La Patria from imported Carrara marble.[31] In addition, the City Council converted the Chapel of San José, among the simplest chapels on the western side of the National Cathedral, into an altar befitting the insurgents. In order to hold a civic procession, the remains had to lie-in-state at the Municipal Palace. Workers hefted in great quantities of potted plants, roses, wreaths, lights, lamps, flags, crepe paper, and blocks of ice to preserve an agreeable temperature. Businesses and public employees decorated the city. The news spread quickly: the Caudillos of Independence were to appear on Hidalgo Day, July 30, 1895.[32]

It is curious to learn the lengths the modern state will go to verify and authenticate national origins in the name of science. A government commission of medical doctors and anthropologists exhumed the remains from the crypt. After scientific measurement and evaluation, the bones were dusted off and set out in the sun for three days of bleaching. At first only the skulls of Allende, Abasolo, Jiménez, and Hidalgo—encoded with the initials "A," "Ab," "X," and "H," respectively—could be positively identified, causing some anxiety. *El Gil Blas* speculated that one set of bones was so large they must have belonged to the large-framed Viceroy Juan O'Donoju, whose remains got mixed up with those of the Independence Heroes. To calm fears, scientists declared them to belong to the giant insurgent Pedro Moreno. Anthropologist Leopoldo Batres identified each skull, but bones were never attributed to their respective owners.[33] Batres also took care to maintain separation between the skulls of the insurgents of the Hidalgo phase of independence and those who fought and died under the leadership of Morelos. A second urn contained the remains of Morelos, Matamoros, Moreno, and Mina (no reports accounted for the remains of Aldama, Rosales, and Bravo). Yet another would be devoted to the ashes of Nicolás Bravo, who served with Morelos but survived the Independence Wars. Descriptions of the overall condition of the remains depended on the political views of each newspaper reporter. Liberals claimed that the skulls had rapidly disintegrated into a deplorable state within the humid Church-neglected crypt. On the contrary, the Catholic newspaper *El Tiempo* insisted that they were "in a perfect state of conservation."[34] In fact, the Liberal press criticized the Cathedral clerisy at every opportunity. When a priest offered the exhumation commission tattered rags upon which to lay the bones, *El Mundo Semanario Ilustrado* related the comments of an American woman at the scene: "If this were to happen in the United States with the remains of Washington, women would have given their finest cloaks to serve as a bed for those bones."[35]

The most devout custodian of the mortal remains, however, was Hidalgo's own granddaughter, María Guadalupe Hidalgo y Costilla. As part of the official pantheonization process, the Porfirian state recognized Doña Guadalupe as the only surviving direct descendant of Hidalgo and, as such, legitimated her as a daughter of the Patria. As bureaucrats went about their business, she guarded the remains of the insurgents and passed the time recounting stories about her grandfather, "a great silversmith," who forged with his own hands the jewelry she wore and preserved with religious devotion. She circulated the birth certificate that proved her relationship to Hidalgo and reported that President Ignacio Comonfort had granted her a federal pension that she only received when Juárez came to power. But her pension was discontinued in 1871. In September 1895, she consulted with a *junta patriótica* and city elders in her hometown of Xalapa, Veracruz, about restoring her federal pension. They helped her send a notarized letter to the Veracruz mayor and to state governor Teodoro Dehesa. "Since the grito de Dolores," she wrote, "her unforgettable and illustrious grandfather contributed to the increased expenses of the revolution against the oppressive Government and gave back to the sons of México the freedom they had lost." At Governor Dehesa's request, President Díaz directed a recommendation for pecuniary aid to Congress and recognized María Guadalupe Hidalgo y Costilla during the independence holidays.[36]

On Monday, July 29, 1895, Ayuntamiento president Sebastián Camacho, Leopoldo Batres, and other city councilmen acquired the remains of the heroes from the cathedral. The deed was recorded for posterity as the Act of Transfer of the Remains of the Insurgent Caudillos. Authorities placed the urn in the Municipal Palace and regulated the flow of public traffic into the building. The crowd behaved with characteristic disorder, shoving police and provoking armed retaliation. General Luís Carballeda rallied his troops into action; many struck at the unruly mob with their clubs. The Catholic daily *El Tiempo* blamed Carballeda's abusive riot police: "The public guardian has other obligations besides mistreating citizens."[37] The governor, it continued, must teach these policemen to be responsible for their actions. The same might have been said of the crowd. Another reporter witnessed individuals drag a policeman from his mount and beat him while on the ground. Even at midnight, thousands of visitors pushed against authorities trying to get through the small door.[38]

A civic procession and funeral ceremony were planned for July 30, 1895. In the morning, the distant boom of citadel guns mobilized the city, as the army formed a double line extending from the National Palace to the former customs house of Santo Domingo. Federal District governor Pedro Rincón Gallardo led thousands of people in a civic procession from the Municipal Palace to the Alameda and back to the Santo Domingo Plaza. Six coal-black horses pulled a railroad platform car along the streetcar line. Covered with black velvet and roses, the car carried the urn between statues of Hidalgo and Benito Juárez. When the float reached Santo Domingo, General Sóstenes Rocha and hundreds of soldiers presented their swords. With precision timing President Díaz arrived, and bands struck up the National Hymn.[39]

The people who crowded into the plaza heard a speech with the same mythical discourse as government-sponsored historical works and Independence Day orations. General Francisco Ramírez of the Miguel Hidalgo y Costilla Patriotic Society had prepared the funeral ceremony, but society member J. R. Arellano delivered the speech. He called attention to the rapid growth of Hidalgo's reputation over two decades. His patriotic society met in small numbers in the deserted Plazuela del Carmen every July 30 but failed to break the vituperative indifference toward Hidalgo. He admitted that the Hidalgo manifestation flourished only when the supreme government declared the anniversary of Hidalgo's death (July 30) a day of national mourning. Arellano then retraced Mexican history with typical Liberal teleology, emphasizing the connection between the Aztec defenders and the insurgency of Hidalgo and Morelos. He described the horrible conquest of the diverse tribes of Anahuac. With a heroism equal to that of the ancient Greeks, they defended their gods and their laws, their customs and independence. The fertile and vast region of Mexico was subjugated by Hernán Cortés and suffered three hundred years of absolute domination by Spain until Hidalgo "awoke Mexico from its prolonged lethargy." Finally, the eulogist called for "more peace by working hard, respecting authorities, following the shining path of science, and praising the memory of our heroes."[40] Again, the teaching state used the bones of dead men to present its dominant refrain.

After the ceremony, citizens followed President Díaz on foot to the cathedral, where two priests in ecclesiastical robes welcomed the president. The clergy had organized an extravagant reception that included the president passing beneath episcopal pallia to the sound of liturgical hymns. But Romero Rubio felt that this odd return to Baroque extravagance after a century of enlightened moderation would invite criticism from the Liberal press and canceled it.[41] Instead, carpenters pried open the sacrosanct Puerta del Altar del Perdón, an enormous door on the west side of the National Cathedral that was last used for the grand ceremonies of Maximilian and Carlota, to regulate the flow of traffic through the temple. From within the cathedral sounded the National

Hymn. An extraordinary crowd filled the Zócalo to get a glimpse of the urn, and some viewed the event from the great vantage point of the bell towers of the cathedral.

The Independence Heroes funeral ushered in publicity that lasted months. When the ceremony ended, ardent Liberals noted the irony of the heroes' reburial inside the largest Catholic temple in the hemisphere. The insurgents had all been excommunicated and defrocked by the Catholic Church. For Gamboa, this "transcendental detail of the ceremony [was] filled with teachings, and brimming with demands to make amends."[42] Clearly, some of the reasons the cathedral remained the housing place for the Independence Heroes were its central location, awe-inspiring architecture, and accessibility. Even a leading Liberal daily predicted: "From today forward the entire nation will come respectfully and hastily to venerate these relics."[43]

Yet, in the aftermath of the ceremony, Liberals demanded that the government do more for the Independence Heroes. *El Nacional* lamented that Mexico City could not boast a single monument to Hidalgo in 1895.[44] *El Partido Liberal* grumbled that they would have wanted a richer monument in which to place the remains, complaining that sugar barons and obscure industrialists in American cemeteries in Brooklyn had better tombs than Hidalgo and Morelos.[45] The staff opened a national subscription to raise funds for an Independence Heroes palace. The patriotic society La Gratitud Nacional formed exclusively to honor their memory. Officers Manuel Torres, Enrique Pérez Rubio, and Pedro Ordoñez named Díaz the honorary president and established a tradition of having a different public official or prominent citizen place a wreath on the heroes' altar each day of the year. Indeed, they called upon Governor Pedro Rincón Gallardo, Congressman Guillermo Prieto, and Rafael Chousal, the personal secretary of the president, to honor this new tradition. State governors sent telegrams authorizing the society to deposit wreaths at the monument on their behalf. Private delegations such as the women from Villa de Calimaña de Díaz González (Mexico) traveled to the capital to deposit their floral offerings. Wreaths poured in years after the 1895 pantheonization, especially on Hidalgo Day, Independence Day, and the Day of the Dead.[46]

Conscientious civic leaders continued to appeal to Interior Minister Romero Rubio to remove the remains from the cathedral. Emilio García, editor of *El Combate*, argued that Mexico must not allow Hidalgo and Morelos to lie next to Iturbide: "The clergy have no claim to these remains." García preferred to have the remains transferred to the Rotonda de los Hombres Ilustres, where they could lie alongside the true sons of Hidalgo: Lerdo de Tejada, Vallarta, Peña y Peña, and Arista. Within days, García gained the support of the City Council.[47] In the August 9 session, City Councilman José Bandera called for a permanent "temple of civism" at the center of the rotunda. The council planned to ask President Díaz to open a competition for the best monument design. The states and territories were to pay all construction costs. Although the Ayuntamiento voted unanimously in favor of the rotunda project, Councilman Ruíz argued that the rotunda contained persons that contemporary politicians declared illustrious prematurely and that the heroes deserved far better. Díaz nevertheless approved the plan and asked Romero Rubio to lead the project. The city government even displayed the winning design for the Rotunda Monument to the Independence Heroes in the Calpini Eyeglass shop. Artist J. V. Delpiérre envisioned a fifteen-meter-high Gothic structure with six columns, four marble allegorical statues, and a subterranean crypt.[48]

Díaz's endorsement of the project spurred a lively debate in the national press. *El Siglo XIX* joined Ruíz in criticizing the government for glorifying its dead adherents with extravagant sepulchral monuments: "Those fraudulent immortals will rot there in oblivion, and after one generation dies, the following will have forgotten their names, and their tombs will be alone, very alone, destroyed by time, without flowers to adorn it and without a laurel to give it shade."[49] *El Monitor Republicano* clamored for a new temple to be built. Jacobo Barquera renewed his interest in creating a shrine away from all other remains and bones, rotundas and zocalos, cemeteries and churchyards—all those places "where lay thousands of bones that history has not christened." Civic and military ceremonies could take place at a public place accessible to the popular classes, without any thought of the Church. Writers, historians, and composers could draw inspiration from visits to the monument. There, the public orator could raise the national spirit, and the people could wave flags in solemn acts of patriotism. The state could preserve the memory of its leaders and praise their virtues and glories from generation to generation.[50]

The main proponents of another proposal appealed directly to President Díaz. Filomena Mata of the Grupo Reformista y Constitucional asked Díaz to rescind his order to transfer the remains to the Rotonda de los Hombres Ilustres. The *grupo* regarded the rotunda as a poor choice. Moving the remains to a remote and isolated cemetery outside the city center would be substituting plans to abandon the cathedral with a project that abandons the city altogether. The Independence Heroes would likely be forgotten. Mata referred to the tiresome climb and difficulty of finding transportation to the Panteón de Dolores, as well as the shrine's potential vulnerability to vandalism. He asked, Why relegate the nation's architectural and sculptural masterpiece to the solitude of Dolores? Both the memorial and the remains would be in a state of exile. Additionally, Mata believed that the deeds of those buried in the rotunda were incomparable to the achievements of the insurgents. Burying them in the same cemetery would level the heroes and lead foreigners to believe that Mexico was incapable of drawing distinctions between them. Finally, Mexico could not afford an expensive new monument. As evidence, Mata's letter called attention to Mexico City's failure to complete monuments to independence and Juárez. Instead, Mata called for the reburial of the Independence Heroes at the Templo de la Enseñanza, once the state confiscated it from the Church. This plan drew support from major newspapers and Generals Sóstenes Rocha, Jesús Lalanne, Miguel Negrete, and Felipe Berriozábal.[51]

The grupo believed that all of these disadvantages would vanish if the state converted the Templo de la Enseñanza into a mausoleum. By virtue of the law of December 14, 1874, Congress had the authority to expropriate the *templo* for national use. The easily accessible building just off the Zócalo eliminated the cost of a new structure. Citizens could pay tribute to a "cult of patriotism," where the trophies and relics of Hidalgo and Morelos could be exhibited. In the wake of the Independence Heroes' funeral, the Liberal press issued a call for patriotic citizens to donate the relics of outstanding Mexican leaders to the National Museum.[52] Mata's letter to President Díaz was published in the city dailies on the Day of the Dead 1895.[53] The plan drew support but lost momentum and failed for lack of consensus. The editors of *El Siglo XIX* believed that the *templo* was too small to contain both a monument to the heroes and a sizable number of Independence Day visitors.[54]

The search for the remains of other independence heroes nevertheless continued in earnest throughout the Porfiriato. Citizens of Mexico City's fifth ward formed a patriotic society dedicated to finding the bones of Ignacio López Rayón, the insurgent general who died in 1832. Their investigations were wrought with conflicting evidence. López Rayón was buried in either the cemetery adjoining the Church of Santa Veracruz or the Spanish Cemetery. But his grave was never found. On September 24, 1899, the society placed a commemorative tablet at Santa Veracruz and renewed its pledge to find and transfer his remains to the National Cathedral. In April 1900, federal congressmen from Michoacán sponsored legislation to name Rayón a benemérito de la Patria and have his name inscribed in gold in the Chamber of Deputies.[55]

A more successful venture was the exhumation and reburial of independence and early republican leaders Andrés Quintana Roo and his exceptional wife, Leona Vicario. After dying of natural causes, both were honored with elegant private ceremonies; even Santa Anna, president at the time, had attended Vicario's funeral in 1842.[56] City Councilman Pedro Ordoñez consulted with Díaz to transfer them from the closed Panteón de los Angeles to the rotunda.[57] The Yucatecan and Campechen resident colonies of Mexico City attended the civic funeral of May 28, 1900, in respectable numbers. The city government gave the ribbons attached to each dedicated wreath to lawyer, writer, and later *reyista* José Peón del Valle, a descendant of Quintana Roo and Vicario.[58]

When efforts to locate bones proved unsuccessful, life-sized statues were

erected as surrogates. Hermenegildo Galeana and Leonardo Bravo material-
ized as such on the Paseo de la Reforma. The state of Guerrero financed the
two statues, which descendants of Galeana unveiled on May 5, 1898.[59] During diplomatic missions in Spain, Gustavo Baz and General Ramón Corona
searched for the remains of Mariano Abasolo with no success. Investigator
Gabriel Villanueva later announced that he had discovered information that
would reveal Abasolo's grave in Cádiz, Spain. For a while the search was conducted like a sensational treasure hunt, but Villanueva ran out of leads, and
the trail grew cold. The story stimulated enough interest in Mexico City, however, for historian Luis González Obregón to write a pamphlet about Abasolo's
life and speculate on the whereabouts of his precious remains.[60] In 1904, *jéfe
político* of Lagos, Jalisco Margarito González Rubio, enjoined an effort to raise
a monument to Pedro Moreno, one of the thirteen Independence Heroes that
Congress declared beneméritos. President Díaz donated cannon for the base,
and González arranged a garden party to raise funds for the statue. It was inaugurated on the anniversary of Moreno's death (October 27).[61]

The Porfirian government later announced two ambitious projects that
stirred the nation. Contests opened for the best architectural designs for a
Monument to the Heroes of Mexican Independence and a National Pantheon
to house their remains. Contracts were awarded to engineer Guillermo Heredia and Professor Enrico Alciati of the National School of Fine Arts. Díaz laid
the first stone for the Column of Independence in 1902 and broke ground on
the pantheon in 1903. Completed in 1910, the Columna, popularly known as
El Angel, was unveiled during the Centennial of Mexican Independence. The
Mexican Revolution brought an abrupt end to the pantheon project, but El
Angel became permanent home for the remains of the Independence Heroes.[62]
A distinctly Christian symbol of the afterlife crowns this three hundred-
foot-high marble shaft and welcomes the immortals of La Patria into their
paradise.

The Matron and the Magnanimous: The Pantheonizations of Josefa Ortíz de Domínguez and Nicolás Bravo

The Porfirian government requisitioned the mortal remains of heroes from
the exterior states of the republic for ceremonial reburial in the heart of the
nation. The constant repetition of such acts both reflected and contributed
to the regime's centralization of authority. But on one occasion, Mexico City
returned the remains of a beloved historical figure to an exterior state. Josefa
Ortíz de Domínguez, more popularly known as La Corregidora, was exhumed
from her vault in Mexico City and returned triumphantly to her native state of
Querétaro. The funeral ceremony consecrated Querétaro as a national space,

Figure 43. Antonio Rivas Mercado's Column of Independence or El Angel. Hidalgo is featured prominently in the statuary designed and executed by Enrico Alciati. Photo courtesy of the Nettie Lee Benson Latin American Library, University of Texas, Austin.

as demonstrated by one eulogist: "[Querétaro,] the cradle of the revolution; the asylum of the representatives of national power when the footprints of the norteamericanos profaned our territory; the tomb of the unfortunate empire of Napoleon III."[63] Significantly, the government's first official pantheonization was held for a woman outside the dominant power center of Mexico City. With the full blessing of the national government, the state governor of Querétaro presided over religious ceremonies in honor of Doña Josefa. La Corregidora, "the most illustrious of matrons," was the first woman to enter the pantheon of Mexican heroes, an exclusively male reserve until 1894.[64] Nevertheless, the state funeral revealed the patriarchy of the Porfirian state, in this, the first of only two funerals for women.

Mythologizing male national heroes within a patriarchal system that excludes women is common among modern nation-states.[65] Josefa Ortíz de Domínguez, however, was highly regarded in the lore of the original independence movement. As the wife of Miguel Domínguez, the colonial governor of Querétaro, she participated in the Hidalgo and Allende conspiracy. Upon learning that their plot had been compromised, she sent warning to the rebels before colonial authorities could arrest them. Hidalgo had no choice but to launch his fateful revolt from Dolores on September 16. For her indiscretion,

La Corregidora was imprisoned at Mexico City's Convent of Santa Teresa in 1814. Herein lies the problem of her permanent pantheonization in the nation's capital—it was the place of her imprisonment. After three years, Viceroy Apodaca released her but prohibited her from leaving the city.[66] When she died in 1829, the sisters from the Church of Santa Catalina de Sena claimed her body for burial in a church vault. In 1882, the Querétaro state legislature decreed the return of her remains, but the transfer would not take place until 1894.[67]

The pantheonization of La Corregidora was linked with the Independence Heroes' reburial. During a meeting of the Gran Familia Modelo patriotic society early in August 1894, Mariano Soto Domínguez and other descendants of Doña Josefa suggested that her remains join those of the independence martyrs. The family had already secured permission from the Federal District government to exhume the remains. But on August 28, Governor of Querétaro Francisco González Cosío intervened. He wrote to Miguel Iglesias Soto Domínguez, the grandson of La Corregidora, for permission to transfer her remains back to "the theater of her glorious deeds" and, in compliance with the decree of 1882, deposit them with honors in a sacred site. Although a close friend of the Querétaro governor, Soto Domínguez warned that if the state did not fulfill its twelve-year promise before the Gran Familia Modelo concluded its preparations for the Independence Heroes' funeral, the remains of La Corregidora would stay in Mexico City. The family ultimately determined that she would return to "the place where all the preparations for Mexican independence were made and where she was apprehended by the Spanish government."[68]

From the exhumation and departure from Mexico City to the voyage and arrival at Querétaro, each act was preserved for posterity because of an innovation in newspaper reporting: the mobile correspondent. The first of this species of reporter was Manuel Caballero of *El Nacional*, who had reported on the assassination and funeral of Jalisco governor Ramón Corona in Guadalajara in 1889. Caballero listed the names of the public dignitaries and descendants of the heroine who made the round-trip. He described the short departure ceremony of October 21, during which the Federal District governor, General Pedro Rincón Gallardo, kissed the funerary urn and shed tears.[69] On the train ride to Querétaro, Caballero viewed the chapel car. In his spare time, he interviewed General Mariano Escobedo, who deplored the fact that Mexico City did not throw a more decorous farewell for the *patriota*. The locomotive stopped at two stations on its eight-hour journey. In Tula, residents boarded the funeral train to pay homage. At the Cazadero Station in the southernmost limits of Querétaro, residents of San Juan del Río trumpeted her return with patriotic hymns, speeches, and poetry readings. As local *rurales* stood in formation, forty elegantly dressed schoolchildren placed flowers beside the funerary urn.[70] The iron horse eventually powered its way into the city of Querétaro, raising the spirits of three thousand residents who had stood in the rain for hours. A music-filled procession enjoining over fifty carriages followed the urn to its destination of the Municipal Palace.[71] Caballero participated in almost every function, even delivering a eulogy at the funeral ceremony on behalf of all Mexicans.[72]

The place for the official lying-in-state was largely predetermined by history; Josefa Ortíz de Domínguez returned to the palace where she played her crucial role in the independence movement. But the following morning of October 22, the urn was taken to the Iglesia del Carmen for a requiem mass attended by high society. The religious service had been organized by a group of Querétaro's women leaders, among them Guadalupe María González Cosío, wife of the governor (and Doña Josefa's modern counterpart). Following the church ceremony, the urn was conducted back to the palace and publicly displayed.[73] Since the governor had declared October 23 a day of public mourning, twenty thousand citizens witnessed the procession. This was a sizable turnout of both men and women in a city with a population of fifty thousand. Every district in the state sent a delegation to march behind an allegorical float that conveyed the urn. Women textile workers from three different mills constructed the float. Of course, women did not march in the procession, reflecting their status as disenfranchised citizens. At Panteón número 1 (later renamed the Panteón de la Cruz), officials deposited the urn in an elaborate sepulchral monument constructed by engineer Emilio Donde.[74] An evening ceremony held in the Teatro Iturbide completed the pantheonization. Caballero referred to it as the "golden broach of the ceremonies."[75] Querétaro's finest listened to an orchestra perform Chopin and Beethoven; a student choir sang the funeral chorus of Mendelssohn; and the city's leaders eulogized Ortíz de Domínguez on behalf of all who proudly call themselves Mexican.[76]

Although the Federal District surrendered La Corregidora in 1894, it never relinquished its right to induct her into the national pantheon. One month after the reburial, city fathers laid the first stone for a monument erected in her memory in the Plaza of Santo Domingo. The statue project, spearheaded by City Councilman Guillermo Valleto and sponsored by First Lady Carmen Romero Rubio de Díaz, was unveiled on Constitution Day, February 5, 1900. The statue of the seated governess was one of the final ever cast by Jesús F. Contreras. Descendants of Doña Josefa attended the event. Women from the Teacher's College delivered patriotic speeches. One orator deemed her the Mother of Liberty. A six-year-old schoolgirl held aloft the Virgin of Guadalupe banner and shouted, "Behold Mexicans . . . the Mother of God."[77] Solemn demonstrations took place at both the tomb and the statue of the illustrious *matrona* during the *fiestas cívicas* every September.[78] Josefa Ortíz de Domínguez charitable societies formed from Fuente, Coahuila, to Mexico City. *La presidenta* of the all-female society, María de Jésus G. de Treviño, sent Díaz a copy of its charter, which identified its primary objectives as building a Catholic church and cemetery as well as "ameliorating the suffering of the indigent and orphaned."[79] To this day, La Corregidora is one of only four major independence leaders whose giant profiles are illuminated in the Zócalo every September 15–16.

Figure 44. Statue of La Corregidora in the Plaza of Santo Domingo, Mexico City. Carmen Romero Rubio de Díaz unveiled the statue in 1900. Photo by C. B. Waite; courtesy of the Archivo General de la Nación.

In 1902, an earthquake destroyed the Church of Chilpancingo, the historic site where the Continental Congress met in 1813. The quake killed hundreds and damaged property, including the tomb and statue of insurgent hero Nicolás Bravo. An official Bravo cult can be traced to the state of Guerrero's centennial commemoration of Bravo's birth in 1886.[80] To President Díaz, Bravo, his martyred father, Leonardo, and his insurgent brothers were shining examples of southern tenacity during the campaigns of independence. When Leopoldo Batres presented Díaz with a pair of eighteenth-century pistols that had belonged to Nicolás Bravo, the president reportedly "received the precious gift with true pleasure, promising to preserve them in his *sala de armas*."[81] In October 1902, editor of *El Mundo* Constancio Peña Idiáquez, engineer Ignacio de la Barra, and Fidencio Hernández toured the capital city of Guerrero, inspected the condition of Bravo's vault, and recommended that

his remains be transferred to the National Cathedral.[82] The Bravo pantheonization became the project of the Asociación del Colegio Militar and its
honorary president, Porfirio Díaz. Díaz honored a formal request of the association so long as Bravo's descendants consented. Congress authorized federal funds on May 28, 1903. The Interior Ministry asked association members
to carry out the reburial during the annual commemoration of the Chapultepec defense on September 8.[83]

As in other exhumations and reburials, public officials enlisted experts to
authenticate the remains and legalize every official proceeding. Guerrero governor Agustín Mora ordered the construction of a wooden urn and published
the official itinerary of Bravo's posthumous journey from Chilpancingo to
Iguala and on to Mexico City. Mora asked a judge of the Civil Registry, the
Ayuntamiento of Chilpancingo, and a public notary to witness the exhumation. The documents pertaining to Bravo's death and original burial, such as
the *acta de difunción* and *acta de inhumacion*, were sent to the capital with
the bones. To certify the original grave, newspapers published the story of
Bravo's first funeral in 1854. The governor even ordered three of Chilpancingo's oldest residents to confirm the exact site in the parish church where
they had witnessed the burial almost fifty years earlier. Representatives of
the three branches of the state government attended, and two medical doctors stood by.[84] These procedures sanctified the rites that followed, including
a funeral march down Bravo Street and a twenty-four-hour lying-in-state in
the Municipal Palace.[85] On September 5, the remains of the immortal *suriano*
arrived at Iguala. A prominent local family had decorated a funeral car to
bear the remains along Aldama, Negrete, Guerrero, and Constitution streets
to Plaza Juárez. In Cuernavaca, Morelos, Governor Alarcón presided over yet
another ceremony.[86]

In a series of decrees from 1900 to 1903, the municipal administration of the
Federal District was reformed, affecting the Bravo funeral. The former powers of the governor and City Council were redistributed among three officials
appointed by Díaz and dependent on the Interior Ministry: the governor, the
president of the Consejo Superior de Salubridad, and the director general of
public works. Consequently, the governor held less authority, and the Ayuntamiento, while retaining its political functions, surrendered its budgetary
powers and autonomy. *Regidores* (city councilmen) now became officials of
the Consejo Municipal and could not allocate funds for funerals, civic festivals, or public works.[87]

Under this new arrangement, federal and city government moved in
unison with patriotic societies and private citizens to organize the two-day
Bravo event. The Military College Association sent out invitations urging
patriotic citizens to attend the grand civic procession.[88] The secretary of war

ordered a Division of Three Arms to render military honors. The Chamber of Deputies and Senate named delegations to receive the remains at the Buenavista Railroad Station in Mexico City and attend the commemorative ceremony at Chapultepec. Students at the National School of Fine Arts constructed a striking hearse out of a gun carriage, military arms, black velvet, and flags. A second group of young artists decorated the mortuary chamber in the Municipal Palace where Bravo's remains were to lie-in-state overnight. Another committee sent invitations to the Jockey Club, as well as patriotic and working-class societies. City employees and volunteers decorated the processional route.[89] The Consejo Municipal also solicited the capitalino elite to send their finest horse-drawn carriages to the Municipal Palace to take part in the procession. The list of those solicited included Manuel and Pablo Escandón, Tomás Braniff, Julio Limantour, Santiago Méndez, and Porfirio Díaz Jr. Dozens of other wealthy supporters willingly contributed to a luxurious state funeral.[90]

While citizens in Guerrero and Morelos paid tribute to Nicolás Bravo, the Mexico City press busily weighed the merits of the insurgent general. *El Mundo* reported enthusiastic expectations in all parts of the city for the "definitive glorification" and "civic canonization" of one of Mexico's "most conspicuous beneméritos."[91] Articles recalled his distinguished military campaigns under Morelos in the storming of Tenancingo, the defense of Cuautla, the destruction of General Labaqui at Palmar, and his brilliant defense of San Juan Coscomatepec, where he withstood successive Spanish assaults and a siege that lasted several months in 1813. They referred to his role as supreme commander of the south in 1817. Journalists dubbed him the Hero of Palmar and Coscomatepec.[92]

But the story that appeared most often was the rare act of forgiveness that made Bravo a distinctly Christian hero. This parable of September 1812, published in Porfirian newspapers and retold in speeches, began with the evil Spanish viceroy Venegas imprisoning Nicolás's aged father, Leonardo, after the siege of Cuautla. Venegas presented insurgent general Nicolás Bravo with the agonizing choice of surrendering or causing his father's execution. Morelos offered eight hundred Spanish soldiers for Leonardo Bravo's life and relieved Nicolás of his command to make the fateful decision with a clear conscience. Distrustful of royalist promises, however, Bravo decided not to desert the cause and pleaded with the viceroy to accept his life in place of his father's. The viceroy ordered Leonardo Bravo to be executed. Leonardo was garroted to death and became a martyr of independence. An enraged Morelos ordered Nicolás to execute three hundred Spanish prisoners who had been captured at Palmar and Puente del Rey ("Put to the sword all the prisoners you have taken. I command it"). Bravo drew them up for execution but refused to imitate the base conduct of the viceroy and set them free. According to the Porfirian version, the royalist soldiers and other deserters he released immediately offered their services. This famous "Pardon of Medellín" entered the civic catechism of the Porfiriato via the Bravo reburial.[93]

Although Nicolás Bravo entered Mexico City with Iturbide in 1821, he remained a controversial figure for his role on the losing side of at least two subsequent rebellions against constituted Mexican governments. As vice-president under Guadalupe Victoria, he took up arms against his own president only to be defeated by Vicente Guerrero at Otumba and banished to Guatemala and the United States. He returned in 1828 and launched a rebellion against the government of Vicente Guerrero, failing again. Yet his life-long antagonism with Santa Anna, his three brief terms as president, and his defense of Chapultepec against the invading U.S. Army in September 1847 redeemed Bravo. And the mysterious deaths of both him and his wife on the same day (April 22, 1854) inevitably led to conspiracy theories that Santa Anna had them poisoned.[94] These suspicions conveyed possibilities of martyrdom that also reaffirmed Santa Anna's villainy.

Even so, *Diario del Hogar's* editor Filomena Mata believed that placing Bravo's remains with those of the other independence heroes was completely unjustified. In his opinion, the others died *inmaculados*, while Bravo was "one of the creators of that series of difficulties . . . that began in 1824 and did not end until 1867." Moreover, a joint *Niños Héroes–Bravo* ceremony presented a paradox since the former fought for the life of the nation while the latter tried to overthrow the government. Mata worried about diminishing the heroic stature of truly meritorious heroes by incorporating Nicolás Bravo with them.[95]

The Bravo funeral did not come off as planned. Rain and rail imperfections caused a freight train to derail in Mixcoac, delaying the scheduled arrival of Bravo's train by nearly twelve hours. After five hours of waiting, the rain-soaked crowd of Federal District officials, teachers, city employees, workers, and congressional leaders filed out of the Buenavista Station. Everyone returned on the morning of September 7 to see Bravo's urn placed on the modified gun carriage. As the six tall steeds toted the makeshift hearse, a delegation from Iguala held black cords attached to the urn, representing the people's connection to Bravo. As before, the president's coach was incorporated into the procession, but Díaz had likely sent a representative to ride on his behalf. Twenty-five mounted soldiers of the Comandancia Militar also escorted the gun carriage to the Municipal Palace. Officials deposited the urn at the chapel, and City Councilman Pedro Aspe delivered an "electrifying" speech.[96]

The Bravo funeral program lost its civilian and popular-democratic components due to last-minute modifications and rising tensions between two political factions. Bravo's remains were supposed to lie-in-state in two separate

Figure 45. Gun carriage carrying the remains of insurgent general and president Nicolás Bravo. The urn containing Bravo's remains appears just behind the white section of the velvet mourning cloth. Men and women view the scene from buildings in the backdrop. Photo courtesy of Fototeca Instituto Nacional de Antropología e Historia, Pachuca.

locations: the Municipal Palace and the Military College at Chapultepec Castle. After the train's late arrival, organizers had shortened the civil ceremony and canceled the overnight public viewing in favor of retaining the military ceremonies. An incident outside the Municipal Palace confirmed this but also highlighted political divisions in the high Porfiriato. After the brief civil ceremony, the army division that mobilized for the march to Chapultepec was asked to yield the symbolic location directly behind the funeral carriage to Federal District governor Guillermo Landa y Escandón and several city councilmen. This place in the cortege, usually reserved for President Díaz, was always reserved for the highest civilian authority in attendance. General Sebastián Villareal refused Landa the honor, arguing that the Honores de Ordenanza of the secretary of war reserved the position for the head of the army division who marched in the procession. Governor Landa conceded and took a place in front of the gun carriage reserved for mounted *gendarmes* responsible for clearing the crowds. It was not a pleasant experience to join the armed escort, since gendarmes had to carve a path through a compact

Figure 46. The multitude accompanying Nicolás Bravo's remains through congested downtown streets in Mexico City. Mutual societies fly their banners, as delegates from the southern state of Guerrero escort the urn (bottom right corner in white shirts and sombreros). Photo courtesy of Fototeca Instituto Nacional de Antropología e Historia, Pachuca.

multitude. Nevertheless, as *El Imparcial* reported, the conspicuous encounter between the Federal District governor and the general was significant enough to stimulate public opinion all afternoon.[97]

The quarrel points to a well-known rift between two divided camps in 1903, Porfirian *científicos* as represented by the Francophile developmentalist Landa and Porfirian military nationalists as embodied by Villareal. The technocrats had just won a battle when Díaz appointed one of their members, Ramón Corral, as vice-president and legal successor to the seventy-two-year-old president. Bernardo Reyes, a nationalist who had once expressed his ambition to succeed Díaz, had just resigned as secretary of war. Corral's appointment suggested that the future of Mexico was being handed from generals to positivists, which cracked the Porfirian consensus.

Thereafter, the Bravo pantheonization was an homage to the military. The cortege of ten thousand marched on foot along the usual route (Portales of Mercaderes, Plateros, San Francisco, Avenida Juárez, Patoni, Statue of Carlos IV) to the Paseo de la Reforma. The ruling elite rode carriages and electric tramcars from the *paseo* to Chapultepec Park and up the steep climb to the castle. Following a brief military ceremony, the remains lay-in-state overnight in the Military College under the vigilance of officers, cadets, and association members.[98] The following day, September 8, President Díaz and his cabinet attended the dual ceremony honoring Bravo and the martyred cadets of 1847 at the Tribuna Monumental. The program commemorated the Battles of Molino del Rey and Chapultepec. Portraits of the six Niños Héroes hung in the backdrop, while the staff corps and sappers band played the "Mignon Overture" and selections from Meyerbeer's *Huguenots*. Attendees listened to young women from the Escuela Nacional de Artes y Oficios sing "The Hymn to the Martyrs of Chapultepec." Colonel Joaquín Beltrán and Congressman Alfredo Chavero spoke, Amado Nervo recited poetry, and five hundred schoolchildren sang the National Hymn. Cadets read telegrams sent from all parts of the republic by alumni of the Colegio Militar. When the granddaughter of Nicolás Bravo took a seat beside Díaz, the crowd broke out in applause. Together they placed wreaths at the Defenders of Chapultepec and Molino del Rey monuments. One observer encapsulated the aura, performance, and function of the ceremony:

> The scene, taken together, was picturesque and inspiring to patriotism—the tumulous containing the remains of the hero, the sable trappings, the military in their bright gala uniforms, the hemicycle, seeming, in its architecture, object, and surroundings, an evocation of ancient Greece, the crowd of patriotic citizens, the trees, the sky and the sunshine forming a picture that will long live in the memory of those who witnessed it.[99]

Bravo's remains were later taken to the Metropolitan Cathedral and added to the urn containing the skulls of the insurgents.[100]

Mexico is a country with a tragic past. Unfortunately, it is a heartrending history that has been largely controlled by triumphant national governments and ruling classes. States that manipulate the historical record ultimately manipulate people. During the pantheonizations of the Independence Heroes, Josefa Ortíz de Domínguez, and Nicolás Bravo, the Porfirian state deployed time-honored Catholic rituals and discourses on sacrifice, martyrdom, and forgiveness to win the support of the masses. In contrast to the patriarchal and hierarchical character of funerals for the dictator's cronies, pantheonizations generated the largest followings of Mexico's faithful because they most closely resembled Catholic folk tradition. The educated classes also joined President Díaz and the state bureaucracy as "custodians of tradition," showing the expansion of the Porfirian state.[101] Like their U.S. counterparts, they perceived history as a tool to promote a shared sense of the past, national identity, and national community.[102] Mobilizing every means at their disposal—religious, spiritual, scientific, technological, and otherwise—they invoked the past to serve partisan interests. History had few other uses for turn-of-the-century states.

Figure 47. José Guadalupe Posada's *Gran Fandango*. From Roberto Berdecio and Stanley Applebaum, eds., *Posada's Popular Mexican Prints* (New York: Dover Publications, 1972).

Conclusion
Requiem of the Regime

*"Sobre las Olas," the Centenario of 1910, and the
Mexican Revolution*

IN 1892, the young novelist Federico Gamboa strolled through the streets of
downtown Buenos Aires, one of the centers of high culture in Latin America
during the *bella época*. From a store on Florida Street, Gamboa recognized
the sweet-sounding music of one of his countrymen and was delighted to see
copies of "Sobre las Olas" (Over the Waves), the timeless waltz of Juventino
Rosas, for sale in the store window: "Although the incident as such, would not
seem supernatural, nor much less, it seemed so for me. I fastened myself to
the glass mentally humming the harmonies of the piece the chorus of which I
had recognized; in a mad rush the memories of my land assaulted me, echoes
of laughter that I love, the aroma of days in the countryside, in San Angel,
of nights of balls I attended." Gamboa asked the shopkeeper where the pho-
nograph came from. "Germany," he replied. Gamboa then queried, "Do you
know that he is Mexican?" The store owner answered in the affirmative and
then asked if Gamboa hailed from Mexico. Gamboa proudly announced that
indeed he did. He wrote a reminder in his diary to inform Juventino Rosas
that his composition has reached as far as the River Plate: "Something is something!"[1] Both the writings of Gamboa, who began the literary current called
memorialismo, and the waltz "Over the Waves" by Rosas captured the essence
of living in the "beautiful era" of Don Porfirio.

Unbeknownst to Gamboa, the prodigious musician was to die in solitude
and despair two years later in Cuba on July 10, 1894, his life cut short by hepatitis. Rosas was just twenty-eight, and the people of Batabanó buried him in
the local cemetery. There the remains were forgotten until the Mexican consul in Havana arranged for his exhumation in 1909. Porfirio Díaz had shared
Gamboa's appreciation for the waltz and ordered the remains of the brilliant
young composer returned to Mexico. A delegation representing the Sociedad

de Compositores Mexicanos escorted the coffin from Veracruz to the capital. The body lay-in-state at the Conservatorio Nacional de Música, where an orchestra played the immortal "Over the Waves." In a solemn state funeral, Rosas became the final person interred in the Rotunda of Illustrious Men during the Porfiriato.[2] "Sobre las Olas" represented the requiem of the regime.

Scholars have written superb analyses of the Centennial of Mexican Independence in 1910.[3] But the Centenario has never been contextualized as the culmination of thirty-five years of political performances. Ushering in the month of September, the Catholic Church held its Te Deum in the National Cathedral followed by the playing of the National Hymn; or as *El Tiempo Ilustrado* stated it, "God first, the Independence Heroes next."[4] Devout Catholics enjoined a religious procession behind a flag with the image of the Virgin of Guadalupe. One young Indian woman with her hands over her heart tossed flowers on the passing flag in a "sublime gesture of intense spiritual piety."[5] While the English colony still mourned the death of Edward VII, the Italian, American, German, and French colonies, delegates, and diplomatic corps laid first stones of monuments to Garibaldi, Washington, Humboldt, and Pasteur, respectively. None could compete with the precious gifts of Spain. The Spanish delegation decorated President Díaz with the insignia of the Royal and Distinguished Order of Charles III and returned the military uniform of insurgent priest José María Morelos. When Spanish officials presented the garment that once draped the shoulders of the Hero of Cuautla to Mexican officials, the crowd yelled, "Viva la Virgen de Guadalupe!" Genaro García wrote: "The religion of liberty fused all beliefs and amalgamated all consciences; the heroic past reconciled all antagonisms; love of country surged with epic pride over all other loves."[6]

Don Porfirio spent September dedicating public works, while the world panegyrized him as the "old paladin" who won Mexico's "second independence." The president unveiled the Juárez Hemicycle and Column of Independence—Mexico's first truly world-class memorials—and the Grand Canal, National Post Office, Penitentiary, Mental Hospital, and Palace of Fine Arts—all modern landmarks. At the dedication of El Angel, a city official read the Acta de Independencia of Chilpancingo. Officials laid commemorative plaques to Leona Vicario and Andrés Quintana Roo—the inscription to the former marking the day she perished: "The illustrious heroine doña Leona Vicario de Quintana Roo died in the corner bedroom of this house at nine at night on the 21 of August 1842." The baptismal font of Hidalgo, the Virgin of Guadalupe banner, and the military uniform of Morelos were marched through the main thoroughfares. On the night of September 15, the Grito de Dolores, Díaz added to his normal repertoire by bellowing: "Viva la Libertad! Viva la Independencia! Viva los Héroes de la Patria! Viva la República! Viva

Figure 48. Giant commemorative wreath dedicated by the residents of Xochimilco to the insurgent heroes during the Centenario of Mexican Independence in 1910. Photo courtesy of Fototeca Instituto Nacional de Antropología e Historia, Pachuca.

el Pueblo Mexicano!" The state had installed nearly 1.5 million electric light bulbs and expended 168 million watts of energy for the occasion.[7]

During the massive cavalcade of Mexican history to cap the month-long event, hundreds of invited Indians from the Huasteca and dozens of allegorical parade floats represented segments of Mexican history from pre-Columbian times to the U.S.–Mexican War, with the conspicuous absence of anything controversial representing the Reform, Intervention, and Porfirian era.[8] The *desfile histórico* was typical Porfirian stagecraft, as audiences of foreigners and native Mexicans were invited to compare the youthful, exotic, and humble agrarian origins of vanquished Mexico in the cavalcade to the massive stone edifices of victorious Mexico that surrounded them. The remains of the Independence Heroes were mercifully left in place in the National Cathedral during the parade, but Mexicans held numerous civic manifestations there and invited the representatives of foreign nations to place wreaths at the altar. On the night of October 9, 1910, a group of ten thousand public leaders, wealthy barons, and foreign delegates crammed into the central patio of the National Palace for the final apotheosis of the Independence Heroes. Before a stone catafalque representing the Patria, Díaz listened to speeches surrounded by Ramón Corral, Enrique Creel, Ignacio León de la Barra, and, of course, Justo

Sierra. These were the men to guide Mexico into its uncertain future, but for now they were all lost in thoughts of the past.

Like centennials and world's fairs, funerals, festivals, and the cultural politics of memorialization were inventions of the long nineteenth century.[9] They place in relief large-scale historical processes that transformed Mexico from a constellation of disjointed cities, towns, and villages into a unified nation. They show the ebb and flow of everyday life as ordinary people adjusted to the intensive demands of urbanization, industrialization, and internationalization. State ceremonial events proudly showcased symbols of modernity; railroads, trolleys, telegraphs, telephones, and electric lighting all exposed the promise and peril of ties with the United States and Europe. The kaleidoscope of change forced people to weigh their traditions against innovations that altered their lifestyles. The government itself selectively preserved or erased landscapes, memories, traditions, and identities while embarking on the largest national modernization project of the century.[10]

The state captivated citizens through three public innovations that went "national": education, ceremony, and space. In Mexico City, performance traditions required converting an everyday business center into a *centro conmemorativo*, where the state constructed and taught an official history while simultaneously presenting evidence of national progress. Modernization was unachievable without the participation of the masses. Because Liberals and positivists believed that the *pueblo* was incapable of grasping abstract notions and contributing to national life, they abridged history and constructed simple mnemonic devices and moral lessons to render the state project intelligible.[11] The teaching state relied on specific sites, designated institutions, fixed dates, classified monuments, and ritualized ceremonies to tell its story.[12] Hegemonic relations were reinforced through linear, vertical, and spatial representations of political power and social order. But counterhegemonic crowds of working-class people interpreted state funerals and commemorative festivals as seasonal fiestas when social distinctions faded away in horizontal open spaces to connote freedom, unity, and equality. Like the annual Grito de Dolores ceremony in the Zócalo, these events inspired people to transcend their role as passive subjects so common in authoritarian regimes. While attendance figures alone cannot confirm popular support for the regime, crowd behavior was amenable to the state. At times, however, not even the organs of state repression could enforce solemnity and order, reflecting modernization itself as a process shaped by all people.

Funerals and festival events exemplified Mexico's conformity with a foreign-inspired fin-de-siècle ethos and aesthetic. As Mauricio Tenorio-Trillo explains, Porfirian modernizers were of two minds when objectifying the nation for foreign consumption: abroad, they upheld the image of a developing nation in need of foreign investment, technology, and science; at home, they portrayed Mexico as rapidly modernizing along European lines. Whereas Mexican exhibits at international expositions abroad stressed the country's rigid socioracial hierarchy, press illustrations of state funerals effaced *mestizo* and Indian elements in a gross distortion that suited the gente decente.[13] The urbane people depicted in sketches could have passed for citizens of any European capital. In fact, those dubbed the "New Creoles" seldom boasted about the fusion of mestizo and indigenous elements into a national ideal. Their repudiation of the *tipo nacional* and disdain for the *clase del pueblo* recurred in Limantour's order for all uniformed attendants of the Congresses of Americanists to be white skinned, in the government distribution of pants to *pelados* during the visit of U.S. Secretary of State Elihu Root, and in the panoramic group photographs of the Centennial of Mexican Independence in 1910. During the photo-developing process, technicians blotted out the heads of Indian trolley conductors who stood interspersed with Díaz and his foreign guests in a blatant act of effacement.[14] According to one critical observer, what resulted was an illusion that betrayed reality: "Everything in the recent centennial fiestas was official, artificial, diplomatic, and vain; everything resounded like something empty, like dying, bloated stomachs, and the gaiety itself wore a grimace of forced laughter, false and contrived. . . . [like] the cadaver of public liberty."[15] The state had become the exclusive agent of a small ruling class, reaffirming the old adage that bellas épocas for some are always bad times for others.[16]

After 1903, growing disinterest in state events and increasing disgust with state policies suggest an erosion of moral consensus that was typical of the long nineteenth century.[17] What William Beezley described as the "Porfirian Persuasion"—passive cooperation with authoritarian consensus—gradually degenerated into what Ricardo García Granados called "the peace of the tombs."[18] Funerals were so frequent and predictable that they suffered a watering-down effect and lost their potency. Thirteen were held in 1904 alone, culminating with four national burials in "Black October." Even the largest funerals for Blas Escontria (1906), Francisco Z. Mena (1908), Joaquín Baranda (1909), and Ignacio Mariscal (1910) were mere expressions of bureaucratic routine. Period photographs show remarkable displays of state power but small audiences. Scientific politics, state planning, and authoritarianism inspired few onlookers, as more citizens turned out to see the American sailors who repatriated Manuel de Aspíroz in 1905 than to bid farewell to honorable men.[19]

While state funerals hardly caused the Mexican Revolution, they highlight one causal connection: the generation gap. At age seventy-four in 1904, Díaz reached the apogee of his power. When Epitacio Huerta died that year, Díaz became the oldest living division general in Mexico. At age eighty in 1910, he

Figure 49. Porfirio Díaz and General Bernardo Reyes during the state funeral of Mexican Ambassador to the U.S. Manuel Aspíroz (1905). The president welcomes the U.S. Navy sailors who repatriated Aspíroz on the orders of President Theodore Roosevelt. Díaz appears in the uniform of a division general, bearing the many medals bestowed upon him by the nations of Europe. He is surrounded by his vice-president, cabinet ministers, and foreign ambassadors in front of the National Palace. Photo courtesy of Fototeca Instituto Nacional de Antropología e Historia, Pachuca.

held sway over a nation with two state governors over eighty, six past seventy, and seventeen past sixty. Of eight remaining ministers, two were over eighty and the youngest was fifty-five.[20] The passing of an entire political class did not portend well for the personalist regime.[21] At the National Liberal Convention of 1903, conscientious leaders such as Justo Sierra, Pablo Macedo, and Francisco Bulnes transcended banal moralization to express concern for a weak judiciary, the absence of democracy, and the insufficient education of the underclass. Díaz and his oligarchy chose to persecute, jail, and exile members of a new generation who called for political and social reform. Gramsci described the crises that follow historical blocs as a new struggle for hegemony in which "the old intellectual and moral leaders of society feel the ground slipping from under their feet, they perceive that their 'sermons' have become precisely mere 'sermons,' i.e. external to reality, pure form without any content, shades without a spirit."[22] As Gramsci commented a generation later: "The crisis consists precisely in the fact that the old is dying and the new cannot be born; in this interregnum a great variety of morbid symptoms appear."[23]

Historians of Porfirian Mexico continue to diagnose the pathology of a flourishing organism instead of autopsying the dead body of the Porfirian state. Until recently, historical writing took on a medical examiner's approach by evaluating the Porfiriato in the light cast back from the revolution, emphasizing overall the flaws of the defunct regime and denying any continuity between it and the revolutionary state.[24] The Latin phrase that describes this exercise in historical forensics, post hoc ergo propter hoc, is an archaic logical fallacy. References to Díaz as *tlatoani* or Caesar or to his regime as tsarist or absolutist are anachronistic; he and his regime were not. The primary anomaly of the Porfirian government was its survival past the eight-month average life span of its seventy-five predecessors. Nor was Porfirian Mexico frozen in time and space like a museum artifact. As Daniel Cosío Villegas once remarked, the petrified, atemporal image of the eighty-year-old dictator has led to the erroneous perception of a static and monolithic era.[25]

If we employ the same method of choosing a random image to symbolize an era, then the photograph of Díaz at thirty tells a different story. Díaz began his political career as an ambitious radical Liberal teaching natural law at the Oaxaca Institute of Arts and Sciences before serving as military governor of Tehuantepec. By his mid-forties in 1876, he was disabused of all notions of political fairness in an authoritarian Liberal Mexico that had "broken the pact with the people which the Constitution represents."[26] Miguel Tinker Salas observed that the developmental slogans of his era's principal leaders—"the new era," "liberty and regeneration," "progress," and "rebirth"—were the language of change.[27] Ruling elites knew that modernizing the entire nation was a pipe dream, so they followed international trends, subordinating actual democracy to abstract nationalism and modernizing urban areas to gain international acceptance. State funerals and commemorative festivals mirrored this turn-of-the-century philosophy of form and facade serving as the substance of nationhood.[28] As the dictator evolved into the foremost practitioner of the very politics that originally excluded him from office, Mexicans of various social classes redefined the terms for their own belle epoque and imagined a national cultural space greater than the Porfirian state, La Patria.

Coercion and violence were the exceptions, not the rule. Díaz is categorized as a dictator less for exercising excessive and arbitrary power than for his permanence in office.[29] Every gross misapplication of force counteracted Porfirian objectives. The Veracruz executions of 1879 left an enduring and painful memory. In his recent opus, historian Paul Vanderwood uses both telescope and microscope to observe how quickly the Federal Army's incompetence at Tomochic turned into a bloody tragedy retained in popular memory.[30] The ongoing military campaigns against, and enslavement of, the Yaqui, Mayo, and Maya Indians diminished the state's effort to control the nation's frontiers. The

Figure 50. Famous photograph of Díaz, age eighty, that has promoted false assumptions and arguments about a monolithic, unchanging, and decrepit old regime. Photo courtesy of the Nettie Lee Benson Latin American Library, University of Texas, Austin.

Figure 51. The young Díaz, age thirty, appearing here in civilian clothing, opposed Juárez and Lerdo on the grounds that they violated the Constitution of 1857. Photo courtesy of the Nettie Lee Benson Latin American Library, University of Texas, Austin.

forced-labor colonies for recalcitrant Indians and petty thieves and the persecution and imprisonment of opposition journalists and anti-reelectionists prompted protests. Two decades after the fact, "Tomochic" became a battle cry for revolutionaries. The Mexican people never forgot labor strikes that were crushed with an iron hand. "Cananea" and "Rio Blanco"—massacres of citizen-workers to protect foreign capital—were resounding calls to arms. These three loci forever marked the landscapes and mindscapes of the Mexican people. Ruling elites achieve more cost-effective social relations when they get commoners to accept their own tacit inferiority and subjugate themselves.

The narratives of hegemony that appear in Porfirian-era documents have a tendency of seeping into the very production of historical knowledge of the era. By forming a new orthodoxy, revisionists risk aiding and abetting the mystification process so as to promote mythical legacies of either or both the Porfiriato and the revolution. Neither these periods nor their historical actors should be so exalted. Top-down nationalism, enforced patriotism, and ritualized deference ultimately reinforce relations of domination rather than individual freedom, political equality, economic security, and social justice. Manipulating the outcomes of elections and revising constitutions to remain in power do not legitimate political leaders in the judgment of history. It just so happens that authoritarian states rewrite laws and engage in conciliatory behavior as the norm, not the exception. This is how ruling classes accomplish a hegemonic order. Díaz's adoring supporters who constituted "the state" modeled their adulatory and self-congratulatory behavior in hopes of common citizens doing the same.

In recent decades, historians have paid closer attention to the works of anthropologists who have identified patterns of human behavior that transcend revolutionary breaks. Clifford Geertz viewed historical change not as a series of bounded epochs but as developmental phases with formal or structural patterns of cumulative activity.[31] Enrique Semo and Alan Knight have cautioned against conceiving the Mexican Revolution as the haymaker that knocked out the old social order with one mighty blow. Changes in the state and in relations of production occurred over the *longue durée*, as challengers dispatched the heavyweight with a flurry of successive jabs, 1810, 1854, and 1910.[32] The Porfirian period contributed its share of blows to bring about bourgeois reform and revolution in more ways than historians have cared to admit. The revolution politicized the urban working class and peasantry, integrating several million into the political life of the nation. But the transition from indifference to a new political awareness, which developed from new identifications with imagined, national interests, did not happen overnight. Nor was any of it irreversible. Scholars have noted revolutionary nationalism's "tragicomic return to nineteenth century positivism."[33] The postrevolutionary regime rewrote the historical memory of the revolution itself to portray mortal enemies (Obregón versus Villa, Carranza versus Zapata) as members of one great Revolutionary Family.[34] The myths of the revolution were not a far cry from the myths of Juárez and Díaz. The state continued to use death alternately to mystify or clarify power relations.

Rarely did a year pass when the men who toppled Díaz did not use his same methods to legitimate their rule and inculcate values in citizens. Revolutionary- and postrevolutionary-era *caciques* continued practicing *pan o palo* tactics.[35] Added to the festival calendar were Revolution Day on November 20, Labor Day on May 1, and a revitalized Constitution Day, after the promulgation of the new national charter in 1917 (February 5). Alvaro Obregón exhumed and reburied Guadalupe Victoria; Plutarco Elías Calles moved the Independence Heroes (once again) to their final resting place under El Angel. The fratricidal character of the revolution ensured that new martyrs would enter the pantheon of Mexican heroes and be commemorated on their death dates annually.[36] Alongside Porfirian generals at the Rotonda de los Hombres Ilustres lie the remains of muralists Diego Rivera, José Clemente Orozco, and Davíd Alfaro Siqueiros and seventy-three others interred from 1919 to 1994.

With the alleged discovery of the last Aztec emperor's remains at Ichcateopán, the Mexican government designated 1949 as the Year of Cuauhtémoc. And 1952 marked the "Year of Posada," the Porfirian-era printmaker whose art graces the pages of this book. The nation also came to terms with its colonial past, without glorifying the Spanish legacy, when it transferred the remains of the Jesuit priest, *creole* nationalist, and precursor of independence Francisco Javier Clavijero on August 6, 1970. After a century of decay, President Luis Echeverría restored the funerary monuments of the rotunda and installed an eternal flame at the center of the site. The 2006 addition of three great twentieth-century women—María Lavalle, Emma Godoy, and Dolores del Río—prompted the name change to the Rotonda de las Personas Ilustres.[37] Yet even the Monument of the Revolution was grafted onto an old Porfirian structure that now serves as the repository for the remains of the Caudillos of the Revolution.[38]

These developments cast doubt on previous explanations of the Porfiriato as a marked deviation from Mexico's Liberal historical trajectory from the Reform through the revolution. The Porfirian state was no such aberration. It seized control of a revolution in cultural politics that began with the Liberal Reform and withstood a decade of horrendous violence and warfare. Like its immediate predecessor and successor, the Porfirian state generally ruled through hegemony rather than force. Even under Eric Hobsbawm's definition of the state as "the framework of the citizens' collective actions, insofar as these were officially recognized," the Porfirian state survived long after most others but outlived its ability to control the collective actions of its citizens.[39] And among the many ironies in Mexican history, Porfirio Díaz, the man of stone, dedicator of monuments to all of his late comrades, was neither buried by his countrymen nor immortalized in bronze or marble. His remains still lie at Montparnasse Cemetery in Paris, *relegado al olvido*, perhaps for time immemorial.[40]

Appendix A

State Funerals, 1878–1910

Year	Hero Honored	Burial Site
1878	José Vicente Miñon	Dolores
	Calixto Bravo	Rotonda de los Hombres Ilustres
1879	Ignacio Ramírez	Tepeyac/Rotonda de los Hombres Ilustres
1880	Miguel Ruelas	Dolores/Rotonda de los Hombres Ilustres
1881	Gabino Barreda	Rotonda de los Hombres Ilustres
	Jesús González Ortega	Rotonda de los Hombres Ilustres
	Mariano Arista (reburial)	Rotonda de los Hombres Ilustres
1883	Ezequiel Montes	
	José María Castillo Velasco	
1885	Francisco Montes de Oca	Rotonda de los Hombres Ilustres
1886	Juan Manuel Flores	Panteón de Dolores
1887	Juan José Baz	Panteón Frances
1888	Andrés Piñon	Panteón de Dolores
1889	Basilio Pérez Gallardo	Rotonda de los Hombres Ilustres
	Sebastián Lerdo de Tejada	Rotonda de los Hombres Ilustres
	Francisco Díaz Covarrubias	Rotonda de los Hombres Ilustres
	Ramón Corona	Panteón de Belen, Guadalajara
1890	Pedro Ogazón Rubio	Rotonda de los Hombres Ilustres
1891	Manuel Dublán	Panteón Frances
	Luis Mier y Terán	Panteón Frances
	Carlos Pacheco	Rotonda de los Hombres Ilustres
	Vicente Mariscal	Panteón Francés

1892	Mariano Jiménez	
	Carlos Fuero	
1893	José Ceballos	Rotonda de los Hombres Ilustres
	Manuel González	Rotonda de los Hombres Ilustres
	Felipe Villanueva	Rotonda de los Hombres Ilustres
	Ignacio Manuel Altamirano	Rotonda de los Hombres Ilustres
	Juan José de la Garza	Rotonda de los Hombres Ilustres
	Ignacio Luis Vallarta	Rotonda de los Hombres Ilustres
1894	Josefa Ortíz de Domínguez	Cementerio No. 1, Querétaro
	Juan N. Méndez	Rotonda de los Hombres Ilustres
	Jesús Preciado	
1895	Manuel de la Peña y Peña	Rotonda de los Hombres Ilustres
	Nicolas Régules	
	Independence Heroes (reburial)	National Cathedral/Column of Independence
	Juan José Espinosa de los Monteros	Rotonda de los Hombres Ilustres
	Manuel Romero Rubio	Panteón Frances
1896	Donato Guerra (reburial)	Rotonda de los Hombres Ilustres
1897	Miguel Negrete	Rotonda de los Defensores de 1847
	Guillermo Prieto	Rotonda de los Hombres Ilustres
	Sóstenes Rocha	Rotonda de los Hombres Ilustres
	Melchor Ocampo (reburial)	Rotonda de los Hombres Ilustres
1898	José María Aguirre de la Barrera	Tlanepantla
	Carlos Diéz Gutiérrez	Panteón El Saucito, San Luis Potosí
1899	Manuel Santibáñez	
	Ignacio Alatorre	
	Matías Romero	Panteón de Dolores
	Rosendo Márquez	
1900	Felipe Berriozábal	Rotonda de los Hombres Ilustres
	Antonio Mier y Celis	
	José María Couttolene	Private hacienda in Puebla
	Miguel Blanco	Panteón Español
	Justo Benítez	Panteón del Tepeyac
	Ponciano Arriaga (reburial)	Rotonda de los Hombres Ilustres
	Andrés Quintana Roo and Leona Vicario (reburial)	Rotonda de los Hombres Ilustres

	Vidal Alcocer	Dolores
	Vicente Filisola	Dolores
1902	José de Teresa y Miranda	Panteón Francés
	Manuel María Contreras	Panteón del Tepeyac
	Mariano Escobedo	Rotonda de los Hombres Ilustres
1903	Ignacio Echegaray	
	Pedro Hinojosa	Rotonda de los Hombres Ilustres
	Francisco Tolentino	Guadalajara
	Luis Pérez Figueroa	Panteón Francés
	Francisco O. Arce	Private hacienda in Jalisco
	Nicolas Bravo (reburial)	National Cathedral
	Rafael Cravioto	Huauchinango, Puebla
1904	Gustavo Baz	
	Francisco Pérez (added)	Panteón Francés
	Agustín Mora	
	Aureliano Rivera	Panteón de Dolores
	Luis Carballeda	
	José Vicente Villada	Panteón General (Toluca)
	Juan de Dios Irizar	
	Miguel Castellanos Sánchez	
	Manuel María de Zamacona	Panteón Español
	Juan Navarro	Tepeyac
	Jesús S. Jiménez	Dolores
	Ignacio Escudero	Panteón Español
	Epitacio Huerta	Michoacán
1905	Manuel de Aspíroz	Rotonda de los Hombres Ilustres
	Jesús Zeñil	
1906	Blas Escontría	Saucito Cemetery, San Luis Potosí
	Juan Villegas	Dolores
	Antonio Tovar	Dolores
	Sebastián Villareal	Dolores
	Genaro Raigosa	Panteón Francés
	Alfredo Chavero	Panteón Francés
	Manuel José Othon Vargas	San Luís Potosí/Rotonda de los Hombres Ilustres
	Ignacio Mejía	Panteón Francés

1907	Rosalino Martínez	Panteón Francés
	Ricardo Castro	
	Felipe Chacón	
1908	Francisco Z. Mena	Panteón Francés
	José Algara	Panteón Francés
	Martín González	
	Francisco Naranjo	
1909	Jesús Alonso Flores	Dolores
	José María Vigíl	
	Joaquín Baranda	Rotonda de los Hombres Ilustres
	Francisco Cañedo	
	Gaspar Sánchez Ochoa	
	Pedro Rincón Gallardo	
	Juventino Rosas de la Cadena	Rotonda de los Hombres Ilustres
1910	Lauro Carrillo	
	Agustín Pradillo	
	Guillermo Valleto	
	Ignacio Mariscal	

Appendix B

State Reburials, 1881–1909

YEAR	HERO HONORED	BURIAL SITE
1881	Mariano Arista	Rotonda de los Hombres Ilustres
	Miguel Ruelas	Rotonda de los Hombres Ilustres
1895	Manuel de la Peña y Peña	Rotonda de los Hombres Ilustres
	Independence Heroes	National Cathedral
	Juan José Espinosa de los Monteros	Rotonda de los Hombres Ilustres
1896	Donato Guerra	Rotonda de los Hombres Ilustres
1897	Melchor Ocampo	Rotonda de los Hombres Ilustres
1900	Andrés Quintana Roo and Leona Vicario	Rotonda de los Hombres Ilustres
	Ponciano Arriaga	Rotonda de los Hombres Ilustres
	Vidal Alcocer	Dolores
	Vicente Filisola	Dolores
1903	Nicolás Bravo	National Cathedral
1909	Juventino Rosas	Rotonda de los Hombres Ilustres

Appendix C

Heroes Buried in the Rotonda de los Hombres Ilustres

HERO HONORED	OCCUPATION	DATE INTERRED
Pedro Letechipia	Colonel	March 21, 1876
Emiliano Diódoro Corella	General	June 17, 1876
Calixto Bravo	Colonel	April 7, 1878
Jesús González Ortega	General	April 1, 1881
Mariano Arista	President	October 8, 1881
Miguel Ruelas	Diplomat	October 30, 1881
Francisco Montes de Oca	General, Surgeon	May 18, 1885
Basilio Pérez Gallardo	Politician	February 6, 1889
Sebastián Lerdo de Tejada	President	May 14, 1889
Pedro Ogazón	General	May 3, 1890
Carlos Pacheco	General, Politician	November 19, 1891
Eligio Ancona	Novelist, Historian, Politician	April 13, 1893
José Ceballos	General	April 22, 1893
Manuel González	President	May 11, 1893
Juan José de la Garza	Jurist	October 18, 1893
Ignacio Luis Vallarta	Jurist, Politician	January 19, 1894
Juan N. Méndez	General	December 3, 1894
Manuel de la Peña y Peña	President	January 2, 1895
Donato Guerra	General	May 27, 1896
Guillermo Prieto	Poet, Politician	March 4, 1897
Sóstenes Rocha	General	April 1, 1897
Melchor Ocampo	Politician	June 3, 1897
Felipe B. Berriozábal	General	January 12, 1900
José María Mata	Diplomat	March 16, 1900
Ponciano Arriaga	Politician	June 22, 1900

Mariano Escobedo	General	May 24, 1902
Manuel de Aspíroz	Diplomat	April 24, 1905
Amado Nervo	Poet	November 14, 1919
Jesús Urueta	Orator, Artist	March 29, 1921
Francisco Díaz Covarrubias	Engineer	October 29, 1921
Juan Alvarez	General	December 27, 1922
Antonio Rosales	General, Politician	January 15, 1923
Salvador Díaz Mirón	Poet	June 16, 1928
Emilio Carranza	Aviator	July 24, 1928
Carlos Rovirosa Pérez	Aviator	May 24, 1930
Pablo L. Sidar	Aviator	May 24, 1930
Francisco González Bocanegra	Musician, Poet	September 27, 1932
Valentín Gómez Farías	President	July 5, 1933
Ignacio Ramírez	Jurist	October 7, 1934
Ignacio Manuel Altamirano	Poet, Writer	November 14, 1934
Luis G. Urbina	Poet, Journalist	December 13, 1934
Basilio Vadillo	Educator, Diplomat	November 5, 1935
Vicente Riva Palacio	General, Writer, Politician	May 20, 1936
Angela Peralta	Opera Singer	April 22, 1937
Francisco Sarabia	Aviator	June 11,1939
Juventino Rosas	Musician	December 17, 1939
Jaime Nunó	Composer	October 11, 1942
Felipe Villanueva	Composer	August 27, 1945
Ricardo Flores Magón	Journalist, Revolutionary	May 1, 1946
Justo Sierra Méndez	Educator, Politician	November 5, 1946
José Juan Tablada	Poet, Journalist	November 5, 1946
Miguel Negrete	General	May 5, 1948
José Clemente Orozco	Muralist	September 8, 1949
Isaac Ochoterena y Mendieta	Scientist	April 12, 1950
Virginia Fábregas	Actress	November 18, 1950
Enrique González Martínez	Poet, Diplomat	February 20, 1952
Mariano Azuela	Novelist	March 2, 1952
Manuel M. Ponce	Composer	October 4, 1952
Agustín Aragón y León	Scientist, Politician	March 31, 1954
Diego Rivera	Muralist	November 26, 1957
Manuel José Othón	Poet, Writer	June 14,1959
Alfonso Reyes	Writer, Diplomat	December 28, 1959

Santos Degollado	General	June 15, 1963
Ramón López Velarde	Poet	June 15, 1963
José María Luis Mora	Journalist	June 24, 1963
Antonio Caso	Philosopher	December 19, 1963
Gerardo Murillo Coronado	Painter	August 16, 1964
Gabino Barreda	Educator, Philosopher	January 22, 1968
Francisco Xavier Clavijero	Educator	August 6, 1970
Agustín Lara	Musician	November 9, 1970
Rosendo Salazar Alamo	Union Organizer	November 19, 1971
Alfonso Caso	Archaeologist	January 7, 1974
Arturo Rosenblueth	Philosopher	January 7, 1974
Ignacio González Guzmán	Scientist	January 8, 1974
David Alfaro Siquieros	Muralist	January 8, 1974
Rosario Castellanos	Poet, Writer, Diplomat	August 7, 1974
Miguel Ramos Arizpe	Politician	June 29, 1974
Julián Carrillo	Composer	January 28, 1975
Nabor Carrillo Flores	Scientist	January 28, 1975
Juan A. Mateos	Poet, Politician	(cenotaph only, no remains)
Rafael Ramírez Castañeda	Educator	March 23, 1976
Silvestre Revueltas Sánchez	Composer	March 23, 1976
Carlos Pellicer	Poet, Museum Curator	March 31, 1977
Genaro Estrada	Diplomat	October 3, 1977
Carlos Chávez Ramírez	Composer	August 3, 1978
Agustín Yáñez	Politician, Educator	January 18, 1980
Joaquín Baranda	Educator, Politician	June 29, 1981
Moises Saenz	Educator	June 29, 1981
Jaime Torres Bodet	Poet, Writer, Diplomat	June 29, 1981
Carlos Ramírez Ulloa	Engineer	August 14, 1981
José María Pino Suárez	Vice-President	November 6, 1986
Jose María Iglesias	Jurist, Politician	January 29, 1987
Pedro Sainz de Baranda	Naval Captain	March 13, 1987
Leandro Valle	General	June 18, 1987
Manuel Sandoval Vallarta	Scientist	September 5, 1988
Jesús Silva Herzog	Economist	November 14, 1988
Vicente Lombardo Toledano	Labor Leader	July 16, 1994
Guillermo Haro Barraza	Astronomer	August 6, 1994
Francisco Martínez de la Vega	Journalist	August 6, 1994
Francisco L. Urquizo Benavides	General, Historian	August 6, 1994

Ignacio Chavez	Doctor, Administrator	February 26, 1997
Jesús Reyes Heroles .	Historian, Politician	March 5, 2003
Manuel Gómez Morín	Founder of the Party of National Action	February 27, 2004
Herberto Castillo	Educator, Ideologue	April 5, 2004
Bernardo Quintana	Civil Engineer	October 20, 2005
María Lavalle	Magistrate, Senator	November 28, 2006
Emma Godoy	Writer	November 28, 2006
Dolores del Río	Actress	November 28, 2006

Note: The rotunda is now called the Rotonda de las Personas Ilustres.

Appendix D

Statues on the Paseo de la Reforma

Hero Honored	State	Date Inaugurated
Ignacio Ramírez	Distrito Federal	February 5, 1889
Leandro Valle	Distrito Federal	February 5, 1889
Rafael Lucio	Veracruz	September 16, 1889
Miguel Lerdo de Tejada	Veracruz	September 16, 1889
Manuel Cepeda Peraza	Yucatán	May 5, 1890
Andrés Quintana Roo	Yucatán	May 5, 1890
Nicolás García de San Vicente	Hidalgo	September 16, 1890
Julián Villagrán	Hidalgo	September 16, 1890
Ignacio Pesqueira	Sonora	November 5, 1891
Jesús García Morales	Sonora	November 5, 1891
Juan Zuazua	Nuevo León	September 15, 1894
Servando Teresa de Mier	Nuevo León	September 15, 1894
Antonio León	Oaxaca	February 14, 1895
Carlos María de Bustamante	Oaxaca	February 14, 1895
Mariano Jiménez	San Luis Potosí	April 4, 1896
Ponciano Arriaga	San Luis Potosí	April 4, 1896
Donato Guerra	Jalisco	April 4, 1896
Manuel López Cotilla	Jalisco	April 4, 1896
Guadalupe Victoria	Durango	May 5, 1896
Francisco Zarco Materos	Durango	May 5, 1896
Manuel Ojinaga	Chihuahua	September 15, 1896
Esteban Cordonado	Chihuahua	September 15, 1896
Juan Antonio de la Fuente	Coahuila	April 2, 1897
Miguel Ramos Arizpe	Coahuila	April 2, 1897
José Eduardo de Cárdenas	Tabasco	April 2, 1897

Gregorio Méndez	Tabasco	April 2, 1897
Francisco Primo de Verdad	Aguascalientes	May 5, 1898
José María Chávez	Aguascalientes	May 5, 1898
Hermenegildo Galeana	Guerrero	May 5, 1898
Leonardo Bravo	Guerrero	May 5, 1898
Antonio Rosales	Sinaloa	September 15, 1898
Ramón Corona	Sinaloa	September 15, 1898
Ignacio López Rayón	Michoacán	April 2, 1899
Francisco Manuel Sánchez de Tagle	Michoacán	April 2, 1899
Juan José de la Garza	Tamaulipas	After 1900
Pedro José Méndez	Tamaulipas	After 1900

Sources: Francisco Sosa, *Las estatuas de la Reforma* (Mexico City: Colección Metropolitana, 1974); Salvador Novo, *Los paseos de la ciudad de México* (Mexico City: Fondo de la Cultura Económica, 1984).

Notes

❧

INTRODUCTION

1. Justo Sierra, *The Political Evolution of the Mexican People*, trans. Charles Ramsdell (Austin: University of Texas Press, 1969), 365–67. The original three-volume, government-subsidized edition was published from 1900 to 1902. Journalist Carleton Beals called it the great Porfirian Bible. It is generally considered the best work of its time. See Carleton Beals, *Porfirio Díaz: Dictator of Mexico* (Philadelphia: J. B. Lippincott, 1932), 327–28; Ricardo García Granados, *Historia de México desde la restauración de la República en 1867, hasta la caída de Huerta*, 2 vols. (Mexico City: Editorial Jus, 1956), 1:455; Thomas Benjamin and Marcial Ocasio-Melendez, "Organizing the Memory of Modern Mexico: Porfirian Historiography in Perspective, 1880s–1980s," *Hispanic American Historical Review* 64, no. 2 (May 1984): 325–27, 329; Charles Hale, *The Transformation of Liberalism in Late Nineteenth-Century Mexico* (Princeton: Princeton University Press, 1989), 58–59.
2. Historian Daniel Cosío Villegas enumerated some of these deaths in a chapter entitled "Muerte sin Fin" (Endless Death), in *El Porfiriato: La vida política interior, segunda parte*, in *Historia Moderna de México*, 9 vols., ed. Daniel Cosío Villegas (Mexico City: Editorial Hermes, 1955–72), 9:494–524. Cosío Villegas borrows "Muerte sin Fin" from the universal masterpiece of the same name by Mexican poet José Gorostiza. During the 1920s wave of Latin American vanguardism, Gorostiza belonged to a literary circle known as los Contemporáneos for their rejection of nineteenth-century modernism; see his *Death without End*, trans. Laura Villaseñor (Austin: University of Texas Press, 1969).
3. Donald Fithian Stevens, *Origins of Instability in Early Republican Mexico* (Durham: Duke University Press, 1991), 10–11; Stephen H. Haber, *Industry and Underdevelopment: The Industrialization of Mexico* (Stanford: Stanford University Press, 1989), 21.
4. See Pedro Santoni, *Mexicans at Arms: Puro Federalists and the Politics of War, 1845–1848* (Fort Worth: Texas Christian University Press, 1996).
5. Sierra, *The Political Evolution of the Mexican People*, 343.
6. Cosío Villegas's nine-volume edited work *Historia Moderna de México* was published between 1955 and 1972.
7. See, for example, the Mexican textbook controversy of the 1990s. Anthony De Palma, "New Battles Erupt Over Conflicting Interpretations of Mexico's Painful Past," *New York Times*, 29 August 1993.
8. Benedict Anderson, *Imagined Communities: Reflections on the Origins and Spread of Nationalism*, rev. ed. (London: Verso, 1991), 160. Anthropologists are often criticized for anthropomorphizing the State, treating it as a living historical personage, an evolving organism, or an animate object of idolatrous worship (statolatry). See James C. Scott, *Seeing like a State: How Certain Schemes to Improve the Human Condition Have Failed* (New Haven: Yale University Press, 1998).
9. *Selections from the Prison Notebooks of Antonio Gramsci*, ed. and intro. by Quintin Hoare and Geoffrey Nowell Smith (New York: International Publishers, 1971), 146–47. See also Peter Guardino, *The Time of Liberty: Popular Political Culture in Oaxaca, 1750–1850* (Durham: Duke University Press, 2005), 8–9.

10. See, for example, William H. Beezley, *Judas at the Jockey Club and Other Episodes of Porfirian Mexico* (Lincoln: University of Nebraska Press, 1987); Gilbert M. Joseph and Daniel Nugent, eds., *Everyday Forms of State Formation: Revolution and the Negotiation of Rule in Modern Mexico* (Durham: Duke University Press, 1994); François-Xavier Guerra, *México, del antigua régimen a la revolución*, 2 vols., trans. Sergio Fernández Bravo (Mexico City: Fondo de Cultura Económica, 1995); William H. Beezley, Cheryl English Martin, and William E. French, eds., *Rituals of Rule, Rituals of Resistance: Public Celebrations and Popular Culture in Mexico* (Wilmington, Del.: SR Books, 1994); Allen Wells and Gilbert M. Joseph, *Summer of Discontent, Seasons of Upheaval: Elite Politics and Rural Insurgency in Yucatán, 1876–1915* (Stanford: Stanford University Press, 1996); Mauricio Tenorio-Trillo, *Mexico at the World's Fairs: Crafting a Modern Nation* (Berkeley: University of California Press, 1996); and Patrick J. McNamara, *Sons of the Sierra: Juárez, Díaz, and the People of Ixtlán, Oaxaca, 1855–1920* (Chapel Hill: University of North Carolina Press, 2006).

11. José López-Portillo y Rojas, *Elevación y caída de Porfirio Díaz* (Mexico City: Librería Española, 1921), 21–22, 151–52, 254, 351–52; García Granados, *Historia de México*, 1:406, 460; Jorge Fernando Iturribarría, *Porfirio Diaz ante la historia* (Mexico City: Unión Gráfica, 1967), 51; Guerra, *México*, 1:10–11.

12. Eric J. Hobsbawm, *The Age of Capital, 1848–1875* (New York: Scribner's Sons, 1975), chap. 12; Eric J. Hobsbawm, *The Age of Empire, 1875–1914* (London: Weidenfeld and Nicolson, 1987), 13–33; Eric J. Hobsbawm and Terence Ranger, eds., *The Invention of Tradition* (Cambridge: Cambridge University Press, 1983); Robert W. Rydell, *All the World's a Fair: Visions of Empire at American International Expositions, 1876–1916* (Chicago: University of Chicago Press, 1984); Tenorio-Trillo, *Mexico at the World's Fairs*; William H. Beezley, "Introduction to Latin American Popular Culture," in Beezley, Martin, and French, *Rituals of Rule, Rituals of Resistance*; William H. Beezley and Linda Curcio-Nagy, eds., *Latin American Popular Culture: An Introduction* (Wilmington, Del.: SR Books, 2000), especially chapters by Ingrid E. Fey, "Peddling the Pampas: Argentina at the Paris Universal Exposition," 61–86, and Blanca E. Muratorio, "Images of Indians in the Construction of Ecuadorian Identity at the End of the Nineteenth Century," 105–20; Jeffrey D. Needell, *A Tropical Belle Epoque: Elite Culture and Society in Turn-of-the-Century Rio de Janeiro* (New York: Cambridge University Press, 1987); Tristan Platt, "Simón Bolívar, the Sun of Justice and the Amerindian Virgin: Andean Conceptions of the Patria in Nineteenth-Century Potosí," *Journal of Latin American Studies* 25 (1993): 159–85; Arlene J. Díaz, "Women, Order, and Progress in Guzmán Blanco's Venezuela, 1870–1888," in *Crime and Punishment in Latin America: Law and Society since Late Colonial Times*, ed. Ricardo D. Salvatore, Carlos Aguirre, and Gilbert M. Joseph (Durham: Duke University Press, 2001), 57.

13. The years periodized as the "Necesariato" (1884–88) followed years of Liberal reconstruction efforts that produced scarce economic gains. Díaz completed the restoration.

14. Ratified on May 10, 1890, the amendment also permitted indefinite reelection of state governors.

15. Porfirio Díaz, speech, 2 April, *Mexican Herald*, 3 April 1903: 2.

16. Wells and Joseph, *Summer of Discontent, Seasons of Upheaval*, 123.

17. The work of Benedict Anderson has proved useful in conceptualizing the relationship of commemoration to state-building, both in Mexico and elsewhere: see his *Imagined Communities*, 9–11; and his *The Spectre of Comparisons: Nationalism, Southeast Asia and the World* (New York: Verso, 1998), 333.

18. Roger Hansen, *The Politics of Mexican Development* (Baltimore: Johns Hopkins University Press, 1971), 15, 27; Barbara Lee Kantz, "A Social History of the Urban Working Class in Mexico City, 1882–1910" (Ph.D. diss., State University of New York at Stony Brook, 1988), xiv; Michael M. Hall and Hobart A. Spalding Jr., "The Urban Working Class and Early Latin American Labour Movements, 1880–1930," in *Cambridge History of Latin America*, vol. 4, ed. Leslie Bethell (New York: Cambridge University Press, 1986), 326–27.

19. Kantz, "A Social History of the Urban Working Class in Mexico City," 42; Moisés González Navarro, *Sociedad y cultura en el porfiriato* (Mexico City: Consejo Nacional para la Cultura y las Artes, 1994), 19. Scholarship on one of the traditional building blocks of nationality—language—proves that only 2.5 percent of all Italians spoke Italian (in 1861), there was no French national language until the Third Republic (1870s), and even Scots and the Irish

spoke "incoherent babble." See T. de Mauro, *Storia linguistica dell'Italia* (Bari, 1972), and Eugen Weber, *Peasants into Frenchmen: The Modernization of Rural France, 1870–1914* (Stanford: Stanford University Press, 1976), both cited in Geoff Eley and Ronald Grigor Suny, eds., *Becoming National: A Reader* (New York: Oxford University Press, 1996), 7.

20. Tony Morgan, "Proletarians, Politicos, and Patriarchs: The Use and Abuse of Cultural Customs in the Early Industrialization of Mexico City, 1880–1910," in Beezley, Martin, and French, *Rituals of Rule, Rituals of Resistance*, 152.

21. William E. French, *A Peaceful and Working People: Manners, Morals, and Class Formation in Northern Mexico* (Albuquerque: University of New Mexico Press, 1996), 3.

22. Pablo Piccato, *City of Suspects: Crime in Mexico City, 1900–1931* (Durham: Duke University Press, 2001), 23.

23. See Philip Corrigan and Derek Sayer, *The Great Arch: English State Formation as Cultural Revolution* (Oxford: Basil Blackwell, 1985); Doris Sommer, *Foundational Fictions* (Berkeley: University of California Press, 1992).

24. Quintin Hoare and Geoffrey Nowell Smith, "Introduction," in *Selections from the Prison Notebooks of Antonio Gramsci*, 45; *Selections from the Prison Notebooks of Antonio Gramsci*, 57; Joseph V. Femia, *Gramsci's Political Thought: Hegemony, Consciousness, and the Revolutionary Process* (New York: Oxford University Press, 1981), 24.

25. *Selections from the Prison Notebooks of Antonio Gramsci*, 12, 182; T. J. Jackson Lears, "The Concept of Cultural Hegemony: Problems and Possibilities," *American Historical Review* 90 (June 1985): 568.

26. *Selections from the Prison Notebooks of Antonio Gramsci*, 182.

27. *El Imparcial*, 26 May 1903: 1.

28. Justo Sierra to Bernardo Reyes, 26 January 1901, Centro de Estudios de Historia de México Condumex, Archivo Bernardo Reyes, carpeta 33, legajo 6573, documento 1. Sierra wrote Reyes from Naples, Italy, and he was undoubtedly influenced by the same intellectual milieu that informed Gramsci's latter-day works.

29. *Selections from the Prison Notebooks of Antonio Gramsci*, 12, 80; Stuart Hall, "Cultural Studies and the Centre: Some Problematics and Problems," in *Culture, Media, Language*, ed. Stuart Hall, Dorothy Hobson, Andrew Lowe, and Paul Willis (London: Hutchinson and Co., 1980), 36; Lears, "The Concept of Cultural Hegemony," 569; William Roseberry, "Hegemony and the Language of Contention," in Joseph and Nugent, *Everyday Forms of State Formation*, 355–56.

30. Beezley, *Judas at the Jockey Club*. Although not particularly sympathetic to the concept of hegemony, Beezley focuses on the tensions between modernization and tradition, elite and popular culture, and rich and poor, pairings that also captivated Gramsci.

31. Kate Crehan, *Gramsci, Culture and Anthropology* (Berkeley: University of California Press, 2002), 5, 166, 199–200, chap. 5; Claudio Lomnitz-Adler, *Exits from the Labyrinth: Culture and Ideology in the Mexican National Space* (Berkeley: University of California Press, 1992), 20–22.

32. Williams preferred Gramsci's notion of "lived dominance" to the study of ideologies that had to be abstracted from lived social processes and generalized. Ideologies, then, become ruling-class ideologies with no attention paid to alternative modes of thought. See Raymond Williams, *Marxism and Literature* (Oxford: Oxford University Press, 1977), 108–9.

33. Lears, "The Concept of Cultural Hegemony," 569, 574; *Selections from the Prison Notebooks of Antonio Gramsci*, 55–60, 80n, 238–39; Gilbert M. Joseph, "Rethinking Mexican Revolutionary Mobilization: Yucatán's Seasons of Upheaval, 1909–1915," in Joseph and Nugent, *Everyday Forms of State Formation*, 139.

34. *Selections from the Prison Notebooks of Antonio Gramsci*, 272–73. I have chosen deliberately not to use the term *subaltern* to describe nonelite groups of Mexican society. While Gramsci is indeed the original author of the term, Ranajit Guha and other Indian theorists founded subaltern studies as a distinct postcolonial enterprise. The term has since become associated with this school of thought and its commitment to the study of the colonial and postcolonial experiences of rural agrarian subjects rather than with Gramsci. On acts of resistance, see the works of James C. Scott as well as E. P. Thompson, "The Moral Economy of the English Crowd in the Eighteenth Century," *Past and Present* 50 (February 1971): 76–136; and E. P. Thompson, *Customs in Common* (New York: New Press, 1991), 6–7.

35. Williams, *Marxism and Literature*, 113.
36. Roseberry, "Hegemony and the Language of Contention," 355–57; George Rudé, *Ideology and Popular Protest* (New York: Pantheon, 1980), 16–31.
37. Florencia Mallon, "Reflections on the Ruins: Everyday Forms of State Formation in Nineteenth-Century Mexico," in Joseph and Nugent, *Everyday Forms of State Formation*, 71. On this point, see also Williams, *Marxism and Literature*, 113.
38. James C. Scott, *Domination and the Arts of Resistance: Hidden Transcripts* (New Haven: Yale University Press, 1990), xii, 3–4.
39. See Antonio Gramsci, "Notes on Italian History," in *Selections from the Prison Notebooks of Antonio Gramsci*, 44–122; Femia, *Gramsci's Political Thought*, 48; Avner Ben-Amos, *Funerals, Politics, and Memory in Modern France, 1789–1996* (New York: Oxford University Press, 2000). *Passive revolution* is a term coined by Neapolitan conservative Vincenzo Cuoco, who wrote during the early stages of Italy's Risorgimiento. Gramsci significantly alters and advances the concept to have modern applicability.
40. Walter L. Adamson, *Hegemony and Revolution: A Study of Antonio Gramsci's Political and Cultural Theory* (Berkeley: University of California Press, 1980), 178.
41. *Selections from the Prison Notebooks of Antonio Gramsci*, 259–60. See also Vincent C. Peloso, "Liberals, Electoral Reform, and the Popular Vote in Mid-Nineteenth Century Peru," in *Liberals, Politics, and Power: State Formation in Nineteenth-Century Latin America*, ed. Vincent C. Peloso and Barbara Tenenbaum (Athens: University of Georgia Press, 1996), 187.
42. For this process in France, see Mona Ozouf, *Festivals and the French Revolution*, trans. Alan Sheridan (Cambridge: Harvard University Press, 1988), 169.
43. *Selections from the Prison Notebooks of Antonio Gramsci*, 244. For a slightly different translation, see Femia, *Gramsci's Political Thought*, 28.
44. Hall, "Cultural Studies and the Centre," 64.
45. Scott, *Domination and the Arts of Resistance*, 48.
46. Carlos Forment, *Democracy in Latin America, 1760–1900, vol. 1: Civic Selfhood and Public Life in Mexico and Peru* (Chicago: University of Chicago Press, 2003), 356–57.
47. For this process in Europe, see Eley and Suny, *Becoming National*, 7–8; and Geoff Eley, "Nations, Publics, and Political Cultures," in Eley and Suny, *Becoming National*, 321–22. Three influential European scholars from different traditions—Elie Kedourie, Ernest Gellner, and Eric Hobsbawm—all point to nationalism's manufactured character by those who stood to benefit most from a shared national identity. As early as 1960, Kedourie declared nationalism "a doctrine invented in Europe. . . . that pretends to supply the criterion for the determination of the unit of population proper to enjoy a government exclusively its own, for the legitimate exercise of power in the state, and for the right organization of a society of states" (cited in Eley and Suny, *Becoming National*, 6). Anderson claims that nationalism emerged first in the American revolution for independence and not in Europe at all. See "Creole Pioneers" in Anderson, *Imagined Communities*; and Sara Castro-Klarén and John Charles Chasteen, eds., *Beyond Imagined Communities: Reading and Writing the Nation in Nineteenth-Century Latin America* (Baltimore: Johns Hopkins University Press, 2004).
48. For this process in an earlier period, see Peter Guardino, "Peasants, Politics, and State Formation in 19th Century Mexico: Guerrero, 1800–1857" (Ph.D. diss., University of Chicago, 1992), 2–4.
49. Claudio Lomnitz, *Deep Mexico, Silent Mexico: An Anthropology of Nationalism* (Minneapolis: University of Minnesota Press, 2001), xii–xv, 3–7, 35–36. See also Lomnitz-Adler, *Exits from the Labyrinth*; and Guardino, "Peasants, Politics, and State Formation in 19th Century Mexico," 149. Lomnitz is also concerned with how states construct citizens in everyday life.
50. Maurice Halbwachs, *On Collective Memory*, ed. and trans. Lewis A. Coser (Chicago: University of Chicago Press, 1992), esp. 65–84; Anderson, *Imagined Communities*, 11–12; Joseph Roach, *Cities of the Dead: Circum-Atlantic Performance* (New York: Columbia University Press, 1996), 13–17; Sarah Radcliffe and Sallie Westwood, *Remaking the Nation: Place, Identity, and Politics in Latin America* (New York: Routledge, 1996), 16; William H. Beezley, *Mexican National Identity: Memory, Innuendo, and Popular Culture* (Tucson: University of Arizona Press, 2008), viii–ix.

51. Justo Sierra, speech commemorating Vasco da Gama, 20 May 1898, Chamber of Deputies, *Mexican Herald*, 21 May 1898: 8.

52. Octavio Paz, *The Labyrinth of Solitude* (New York: Grove Press, 1985), 127. The quest for origins also underlies Juan Preciado's search for Pedro Páramo in the epic novel of Juan Rulfo. Paz also describes the Mexican past as the history of a solitary man searching for his heritage (see *The Labyrinth of Solitude*, 20).

53. Michael Kammen, *Mystic Chords of Memory: The Transformation of Tradition in American Culture* (New York: Knopf, 1991), 9, 13; Ozouf, *Festivals and the French Revolution*, 169; Pierre Nora, "Between Memory and History: *Les Liéux des Mémoire*," *Representations* 26 (Spring 1989): 7–25; Pierre Nora, *Realms of Memory: Rethinking the French Past*, 3 vols., ed. and foreword by Lawrence D. Kritzman, trans. Arthur Goldhammer (New York: Columbia University Press, 1996–98), 3:634; Halbwachs, *On Collective Memory*, 53; Thomas Benjamin, *La Revolución: Mexico's Great Revolution as Memory, Myth, and History* (Austin: University of Texas Press, 2001), 19–20; David Middleton and Derek Edwards, "Introduction," in *Collective Remembering*, ed. David Middleton and Derek Edwards (London: Sage, 1990), 8; John R. Gillis, "Memory and Identity: The History of a Relationship," in *Commemorations: The Politics of National Identity*, ed. John R. Gillis (Princeton: Princeton University Press, 1994), 8; Roach, *Cities of the Dead*, 2–3; Anderson, *Imagined Communities*, 204.

54. Justo Sierra, funeral oration for Manuel de la Peña y Peña, 2 January 1895, Rotonda de los Hombres Ilustres, in Justo Sierra, *Obras Completas*, 14 vols., ed. Agustín Yáñez (Mexico City: Universidad Nacional Autónoma de México, 1948–49), 5:183–95.

55. See Peloso and Tenenbaum, *Liberals, Politics, and Power*, 11–13.

56. Under Juárez the state buried the martyred patriot Melchor Ocampo (1861), Liberal general Santos Degollado (1861), statesman and presidential hopeful Miguel Lerdo de Tejada (1861), famous general of the Cinco de Mayo battle Ignacio Zaragoza (1862), ex-president Ignacio Comonfort (1862), and Liberal generals Ignacio de la Llave (1869), José María Arteaga (1869), Carlos Salazar (1869), and Manuel Doblado (1869).

57. Archivo Histórico del Ex-Ayuntamiento de la Ciudad de México, *Funerales y ceremonias fúnebres*, legajo 1, expedientes 19–31; *Two Republics*, 20 July 1872: 2, 27 July 1872: 2; *Muerte del presidente Juárez* (Mexico City: Secretaría de Trabajo y Previsión Social, 1972); José Fuentes Mares, *Juárez: El imperio y la república* (Mexico City: Editorial Grijalbo, 1983), 356–57; Charles A. Weeks, *The Juárez Myth in Mexico* (Tuscaloosa: University of Alabama Press, 1987), 24.

58. Claudio Lomnitz, *Death and the Idea of Mexico* (New York: Zone Books, 2005), 41–43.

59. *Arte funerario: Coloquio Internacional de Historia del Arte*, 2 vols., coord. Beatriz de la Fuente (Mexico City: Universidad Nacional Autónoma de México, Instituto de Investigaciones Estéticas, 1987). See especially Beatriz de la Fuente, "Palabras de bienvenida a los participantes del Coloquio Internacional de Historia del Arte sobre Arte Funerario," in *Arte funerario*, 1:8.

60. Lomnitz, *Death and the Idea of Mexico*.

61. Paz, *The Labyrinth of Solitude*, 57–58; see also 23, 47–64, passim.

62. For *relatos costumbristas*, see Antonio García Cubas, *El libro de mis recuerdos; Narraciones históricas, anecdóticas y de costumbres mexicanas anteriores al actual estado social* (Mexico City: Impr. de A. García Cubas, hermanos sucesores, 1904); Guillermo Prieto, *Memorias de mis tiempos, de 1828 a 1840* (Paris: Libr. de la Vda. de C. Bouret, 1906); *Los mexicanos pintados por sí mismos. Tipos y costumbres nacionales* (Mexico City: Mungía Press, 1854); Manuel Payno, *Costumbres mexicanas*, vol. 4 of *Obras completas*, 5 vols. (Mexico City: Consejo Nacional para la Cultura y las Artes, 1996–98). See also the novels of Payno, Ignacio Manuel Altamirano, and Vicente Riva Palacio; the memoirs of Federico Gamboa; and the newspaper columns of *cronistas* Facundo and Juvenal. The prevalence of such customs and beliefs in the ethnographic literature written by nation-builders (Prieto was coauthor of the Constitution of 1857) points to a need to inject the "cultural" back into the concept of "hegemony." Lears, "The Concept of Cultural Hegemony."

63. Ozouf, *Festivals and the French Revolution*, 10; Halbwachs, *On Collective Memory*, 65; Roach, *Cities of the Dead*, 5–6, 13, 27.

64. Lomnitz, *Death and the Idea of Mexico*, 295–98, 306–13.

65. Sierra, *The Political Evolution of the Mexican People*, 368; Anderson, *Imagined Communities*, 4, 9–11; Paz, *The Labyrinth of Solitude*, 20.

66. Ozouf, *Festivals and the French Revolution*, 26–27, 31–32, 262–82; Lynn Hunt, "Foreword," in Ozouf, *Festivals and the French Revolution*, xi–xiii; Émile Durkheim, *The Elementary Forms of the Religious Life*, trans. Joseph Ward Swain (Glencoe, Ill.: Free Press, 1954), 2, 415–28; Mary Kay Vaughan, *The State, Education, and Social Class in Mexico, 1880–1928* (De Kalb: Northern Illinois University Press, 1982), 28; William H. Beezley, Cheryl E. Martin, and William E. French, "Introduction: Constructing Consent, Inciting Conflict," in Beezley, Martin, and French, *Rituals of Rule, Rituals of Resistance*, xix.

67. Isabel Fernández Tejedo and Carmen Nava Nava, "Images of Independence in the Nineteenth Century: The Grito de Dolores, History and Myth," in *Viva México! Viva la Independencia! Celebrations of September 16*, ed. William H. Beezley and David E. Lorey (Wilmington, Del.: SR Books, 2001), 3–4.

68. Stephen Palmer, "Getting to Know the Unknown Soldier: Official Nationalism in Liberal Costa Rica, 1880–1900," *Journal of Latin American Studies* 25, no. 1 (February 1993): 66; Avner Ben-Amos, "Molding the National Memory: The State Funerals of the French Third Republic" (Ph.D. diss., University of California, Berkeley, 1988), 124, 160–61.

69. "Las costumbres avanzan entre regaños," in *Del fistol a la linterna: Homenaje a José Tomás de Cuéllar y Manuel Payno en el centenario de su muerte, 1994*, coord. Margo Glantz (Mexico City: Universidad Nacional Autónoma de México, Coordinación de Humanidades, Dirección General de Publicaciones, 1997), 14.

70. For examples of this during the revolution, see Adrian Bantjes, "Burning Saints, Molding Minds: Iconoclasm, Civic Ritual, and the Failed Cultural Revolution," in Beezley, Martin, and French, *Rituals of Rule, Rituals of Resistance*, 263–64; and Adrian Bantjes, *As if Jesus Walked on Earth: Cardenismo, Sonora, and the Mexican Revolution* (Wilmington, Del.: SR Books, 1998), 15–18. Revolutionaries in Sonora used official iconoclasm, satire, and persecution in a "defanatization campaign" to effect desacralization.

71. Philippe Ariès, *Western Attitudes toward Death: From the Middle Ages to the Present*, trans. Patricia M. Ranum (Baltimore: Johns Hopkins University Press, 1974), 73–75, 78–79. And see Guardino, "Peasants, Politics, and State Formation in 19th Century Mexico," 328: "This . . . model was characterized by regular elections, universal manhood suffrage, the inclusion of provincial elites in decision-making, and the demobilization of popular challenges through co-optation and the selective fulfillment of demands rather than widespread repression."

72. Jose G. Rivera, *Reminiscencias del Ilmo. y Rmo. Sr. Dr. Eulogio Gillow y Zavala*, 2nd ed. (Puebla: Escuela Linotipográfica Salesiana, 1921), 348–49; Robert Conger, "Porfirio Díaz and the Church Hierarchy, 1876–1911" (Ph.D. diss., University of New Mexico, 1985), 35.

73. Conger, "Porfirio Díaz and the Church Hierarchy," 34, 37, 69–70; *Two Republics*, 6 February 1891: 4, 7 February 1891: 4, 8 February 1891: 4, 10 February 1891: 4, 11 February 1891: 4; Jorge Adame Goddard, *El pensamiento político y social de los católicos mexicanos, 1867–1914* (Mexico City: Universidad Nacional Autónoma de Mexico, 1981), 105; Enrique Krauze, *Mexico: Biography of Power, a History of Modern Mexico, 1810–1996*, trans. Hank Heifetz (New York: Harper Collins, 1996), 227.

74. Don M. Coerver, "From Confrontation to Conciliation: Church–State Relations in Mexico, 1867–1884," *Journal of Church and State* 32, no. 1 (Winter 1990): 72. For the best work on the Catholic Church that spans throughout the "Great Arch" of the triumphant Liberal state, see Randall S. Hanson, "The Day of Ideals: Catholic Social Action in the Age of the Mexican Revolution, 1867–1929" (Ph.D. diss., Indiana University, 1994).

75. Vaughan, *The State, Education, and Social Class in Mexico*, 21, 39–40, 51–52. Despite rudimentary beginnings, educational expenditures in the Porfiriato increased at a faster rate than public expenditures as a whole, but the Federal District received the lion's share of federal money. Díaz assiduously attended school inaugurations and graduation ceremonies in the D.F., but comparatively few children from outlying states received adequate education. See also Josefina Vázquez de Knauth, *Nacionalismo y educación en México* (Mexico City: Colegio de México, 1970); and Elsie Rockwell, "Schools of the Revolution: Enacting and Contesting State Forms in Tlaxcala, 1910–1930," in Joseph and Nugent, *Everyday Forms of State Formation*, 170–73.

76. Justo Sierra, *La educación nacional. Artículos, actuaciones y documentos*, in *Obras Completas*, 8:167, cited in Vaughan, *The State, Education, and Social Class in Mexico*, 24.

77. Vaughan, *The State, Education, and Social Class in Mexico*, 25.

78. Eric J. Hobsbawm and Terence Ranger, "Introduction: Inventing Tradition," in Hobsbawm and Ranger, *The Invention of Tradition*, 1–2. On the uses of public rituals in zones of encounter and mediation in Brazil, see Roberto da Matta, *Carnivals, Rogues, and Heroes: An Interpretation of the Brazilian Dilemma*, trans. John Drury (Notre Dame: University of Notre Dame Press, 1991), 3–4. See also French, *A Peaceful and Working People*, 63–64; and Mary Louise Pratt, *Imperial Eyes: Travel Writing and Transculturation* (New York: Routledge, 1992), 4, 6.

79. This is Michael Kammen's term for private sector sponsors of patriotic commemorations (see *Mystic Chords of Memory*, 6–9).

80. Cited in Robert M. Buffington and William E. French, "The Culture of Modernity," in *The Oxford History of Mexico*, ed. Michael C. Meyer and William H. Beezley (New York: Oxford University Press, 2000), 401.

81. Scott, *Domination and the Arts of Resistance*, 4, 12.

82. México, Secretaría de Gobernación, *Memoria que el Secretario de Estado y del despacho de Gobernación presenta al Congreso de la Unión, correspondiente al tiempo transcurrido desde el 15 de Diciembre de 1877 hasta el 31 de Diciembre de 1878* (Mexico City: Imprenta del Gobierno, en Palacio a cargo de Sabás A. y Mungía, 1879), 63.

83. *El Nacional*, 15 August 1884: 1.

84. *Diario del Hogar*, 1 September 1903: 1.

85. Lyman L. Johnson, ed., *Body Politics: Death, Dismemberment, and Memory in Latin America* (Albuquerque: University of New Mexico Press, 2004), 6.

86. Ben-Amos, *Funerals, Politics, and Memory in Modern France*, 25.

87. Katherine Verdery, *The Political Lives of Dead Bodies: Reburial and Postsocialist Change* (New York: Columbia University Press, 1999), 5.

88. Reinhart Koselleck, "War Memorials: Identity Formations of the Survivors," in *The Practice of Conceptual History: Timing History, Spacing Concepts*, trans. Todd Samuel Presner, Kerstin Behnke, and Jobst Welge; foreword by Hayden White (Stanford: Stanford University Press, 2002), 287, 295.

89. Lomnitz, *Deep Mexico, Silent Mexico*, 205.

90. Scott, *Seeing like a State*, 4–5, 77, 80.

91. The annual *Memorias* published by federal, state, and local governments compiled the census, legal records, and other data that proved Mexico's nationhood. See also the letters from Nicolás Islas de Bustamante to the personal secretary of Porfirio Díaz, 16 August 1889, in the Archivo Rafael Chousal, Universidad Nacional Autónoma de México, caja 2, expediente 41, folio 45–46. Chousal and Islas demonstrated census-taking methods for Díaz *before* the Ayuntamiento issued the 1890 census in the Federal District.

92. Pratt, *Imperial Eyes*, xi, 5, 7. This also happened in the classrooms of both Mexico and France. See Vázquez de Knauth, *Nacionalismo y educación en México*, 49; Ozouf, *Festivals and the French Revolution*, 197–98, 205–6; Lynn Hunt, *Politics, Culture, and Class in the French Revolution* (Berkeley: University of California Press, 1984), 70, 72–74.

93. Clifford Geertz, "Thick Description: Toward an Interpretive Theory of Culture," in *The Interpretation of Cultures: Selected Essays* (New York: Basic Books, 1973), 15.

94. *Selections from the Prison Notebooks of Antonio Gramsci*, 242, 268; Corrigan and Sayer, *The Great Arch*, 2–5; Gilbert M. Joseph and Daniel Nugent, "Popular Culture and State Formation in Revolutionary Mexico," in Joseph and Nugent, *Everyday Forms of State Formation*, 13, 19–20; Tenorio-Trillo, *Mexico at the World's Fairs*, 7, 64, 84; Radcliffe and Westwood, *Remaking the Nation*, 19.

95. V. G. Kiernan, "The Covenanters: A Problem of Creed and Class," in *History from Below: Studies in Popular Protest and Popular Ideology*, ed. Frederick Krantz (Oxford: Basil Blackwell, 1988), 53.

96. Rodney O. Anderson, *Outcasts in Their Own Land: Mexican Industrial Workers, 1906–1911* (DeKalb: Northern Illinois University Press, 1976), 127.

97. Thompson, *Customs in Common*, 7; Femia, *Gramsci's Political Thought*, 39.

98. Avner Ben-Amos, "The Sacred Center of Power: Paris and Republican State Funerals," *Journal of Interdisciplinary History* 22, no. 1 (Summer 1991): 31–32. See also Sean Wilentz, ed., *Rites of Power: Symbolism, Ritual, and Politics since the Middle Ages* (Philadelphia: University of Pennsylvania Press, 1985).

99. *El Siglo XIX*, 7 January 1878: 3.

100. Vaughan, *The State, Education, and Social Class in Mexico*, 34.

101. Verdery asserts this in *The Political Lives of Dead Bodies* (41).

102. Andrés Molina Enríquez, *Los grandes problemas nacionales* (Mexico City: Carranza e Hijos, 1909), 67. Paul J. Vanderwood explains: "Often the relationship involved a personal loyalty, seemingly a kind of affection, that cut both ways" (*The Power of God against the Guns of Government: Religious Upheaval in Mexico at the Turn of the Nineteenth Century* [Stanford: Stanford University Press, 1998], 241–42). The theme of Díaz's paternalism also recurs in García Granados, *Historia de México*, 1:287, 402, 406, 460.

103. Molina Enríquez highlighted the common phrase of the era: "Esto nos duele, y lo sufrimos sólo por que somos amigos del Sr. Gral. Díaz" (*Los grandes problemas nacionales*, 68). In his critique of Anderson, Lomnitz argues that belonging to an imagined community does not exclusively depend on a "deep horizontal comradeship" but also "vertical ties of loyalty" to lineage or social class (see *Deep Mexico, Silent Mexico*, 9–12).

104. Francie R. Chassen-López, "A Patron of Progress: Juana Catarina Romero, the Nineteenth-Century Cacica of Tehuantepec," *Hispanic American Historical Review* 88, no. 3 (2008): 393–426.

105. Ben-Amos, *Funerals, Politics, and Memory in Modern France*, 272; Molina Enríquez, *Los grandes problemas nacionales*, 134, 147. Molina Enríquez coined the term, which might be translated as "friendification."

106. Da Matta, *Carnivals, Rogues, and Heroes*, 15; Clifford Geertz, "Centers, Kings, and Charisma: Reflections on the Symbolism of Power," in *Local Knowledge: Further Essays in Interpretive Anthropology* (New York: Basic Books, 1983), 143. On Díaz's irremovability, see Sierra, *The Political Evolution of the Mexican People*, 364–65; López-Portillo y Rojas, *Elevación y caída de Porfirio Díaz*, 322–27; Molina Enríquez, *Los grandes problemas nacionales*, 308, 335–36; Francisco Bulnes, "El orden constitucional contra el orden natural," in *Los grandes problemas de México* (Mexico City: SRA-CEHAM, 1981), 93–98, especially discussions on the "necessary man" and "organic or natural dictatorships" that establish peace but negate institutional development. See also Iturribarría, *Porfirio Díaz ante la historia*, 16.

107. López-Portillo y Rojas, *Elevación y caída de Porfirio Díaz*, 322–23: "To have the signature of Díaz on an act of Civil Registry was equivalent to a triumph, a glory; it inspired pride without equal for those who earned the distinction" (324).

108. Ibid., 200–201. There is some of Díaz in Obregón, Calles, and Cárdenas, but López-Portillo also completed his book when Obregón took power. Alan Knight claims that Díaz was a "*caudillo* with populist leanings [who] went the way of many later populists, shifting to the right, spurning his popular constituency, cutting deals with the Church, oligarchs, and businessmen"; see his "Populism and Neo-populism in Latin America, Especially Mexico," *Journal of Latin American Studies* 30, no. 2 (May 1998): 235n54. Florencia Mallon ("Reflections on the Ruins," 72–73) also found that twentieth-century revolutionary state-makers reached deeply into the reservoir of popular traditions from the Liberal Reform and restored republic, although it remains unclear where she situates the Porfirian state. The "puzzling combination of populism and authoritarianism that underlay PRI rule," about which Mallon wrote, also applies to the Díaz regime ("Reflections on the Ruins," 101).

109. Lomnitz, *Deep Mexico, Silent Mexico*, 104.

110. See petitions and statements in the Colección General Porfirio Díaz, Universidad de las Américas, Cholula, Puebla.

111. Lears, "The Concept of Cultural Hegemony," 573; Hoare and Smith, "Introduction," 116n80; Femia, *Gramsci's Political Thought*, 225. State ceremonies were "socially constituted and socially constitutive." See Williams, *Marxism and Literature*, 110; William Roseberry, *Anthropologies and Histories: Essays in Culture, History, and Political Economy* (New Brunswick: Rutgers University Press, 1989), 42.

112. Scott, *Domination and the Arts of Resistance*, 188.

CHAPTER 1

1. Justo Sierra, *Obras Completas*, 14 vols., ed. Agustín Yáñez (Mexico City: Universidad Nacional Autónoma de México, 1948–49), 5:29–30. Sierra laid the first stone for the pantheon in 1900. A year later, engineer Guillermo de Heredia's project was presented to the secretary of communications and public works. The "Heroes of Independence Monument" would have been constructed at the entrance of Calle Humboldt. See *El Imparcial*, 27 May 1901: 1.

2. Sierra, *Obras Completas*, 5:29–30; Luís González y González, Emma Cosío Villegas, and Guadalupe Monroy, *La república restaurada: La vida social*, in *Historia Moderna de México*, 9 vols., ed. Daniel Cosío Villegas (Mexico City: Editorial Hermes, 1955–72), 3:481 (hereafter cited as *HMM* followed by volume and page numbers); México, Congreso, Cámara De Diputados, *Diario de los Debates de la Cámara de Diputados, Año de 1880* (Mexico City: Tipografía Literaria de F. Mata, 1880), 1:561.

3. Juan Pedro Viqueira Albán, *Propriety and Permissiveness in Bourbon Mexico*, trans. Sonya Lipsett-Rivera and Sergio Rivera Ayala (Wilmington, Del.: SR Books, 1999), 31. Besides daily funeral processions, Viqueira notes that "it was not unusual to see some poor soul—clearly intoxicated—standing next to the corpse of a family member, asking for donations to pay for the funeral" (*Propriety and Permissiveness in Bourbon Mexico*, 100). John McManners referred to the eighteenth-century French landscape as "Death's Arbitrary Empire"; see his *Death and the Enlightenment: Changing Attitudes to Death among Christians and Unbelievers in Eighteenth-Century France* (New York: Oxford University Press, 1981), 5–23.

4. Moisés González Navarro, *Sociedad y cultura en el porfiriato* (Mexico City: Consejo Nacional para la Cultura y las Artes, 1994), 30.

5. Claudia Agostoni, *Monuments of Progress: Modernization and Public Health in Mexico City, 1876–1910* (Boulder: University of Colorado Press, 2003), xii–xiv, 21–22, 26–27, 66.

6. Despatch No. 75, David Hunter Strother to William Hunter, Second Assistant Secretary of State, 1 September 1880, *Despatches from United States Consuls in Mexico City, 1822–1906*, M296, roll 9, General Records of Department of State, RG 59, NACP, in *Porte Crayon's Mexico: David Hunter Strother's Diaries in the Early Porfirian Era, 1879–1885*, ed. John E. Stealey III (Kent: Kent State University Press, 2006), 1004; Agostoni, *Monuments of Progress*, 26.

7. Despatch No. 75, Strother to Hunter, 1 September 1880.

8. González Navarro, *Sociedad y cultura en el porfiriato*, 31–32.

9. Moisés González Navarro, *El Porfiriato: La vida social*, in *HMM* 4:xviii, 52; González Navarro, *Sociedad y cultura en el porfiriato*, 35; Fanny Chambers Gooch [Iglehart], *Face to Face with the Mexicans* (New York: Fords, Howard, and Hulbert, 1887), 191.

10. Ayuntamiento de la Ciudad de México, *Discurso del Sr. Lic. Miguel S. Macedo, Presidente del Ayuntamiento en 1899. Discurso del Sr. D. Guillermo de Landa y Escandon Presidente del Ayuntamiento en 1900. Contestación del Gobernador del Distrito Federal Sr. Lic. Rafael Rebollar y Memoria Documentada de los trabajos municipales de 1899* (Mexico City: Tip. y Lit. "La Europea," 1900), 300. See also Robert Buffington and Pablo Piccato, "Tales of Two Women: The Narrative Construal of Porfirian Reality," *The Americas* 55, no. 3 (January 1999): 391–424; Pablo Piccato, *City of Suspects: Crime in Mexico City, 1900–1931* (Durham: Duke University Press, 2001); and James Alex Garza, *The Imagined Underworld: Sex, Crime, and Vice in Porfirian Mexico City* (Lincoln: University of Nebraska Press, 2007).

11. Michel Vovelle, "On Death," in *Ideologies and Mentalities*, trans. Eamon O'Flaherty (Chicago: University of Chicago Press, 1990), 72.

12. Claudio Lomnitz, *Death and the Idea of Mexico* (New York: Zone Books, 2005).

13. See William H. Beezley, *Judas at the Jockey Club and Other Episodes of Porfirian Mexico* (Lincoln: University of Nebraska Press, 1987). Beezley's pioneering study uses foreign traveler accounts and English-language newspapers to reconstruct cultural aspects of Mexican life that are not accessible in other period documents.

14. The best bibliographies of such sources are Drewey Wayne Gunn, *American and British Writers in Mexico, 1556–1973* (Austin: University of Texas Press, 1974); Drewey Wayne Gunn, *Mexico in American and British Letters: A Bibliography of Travel Books, Citing Original Editions* (Metuchen, N.J.: Scarecrow Press, 1974); Garold L. Cole, *American Travelers to Mexico, 1821–1972: A Descriptive Bibliography* (Troy, N.Y.: Whitston Pub. Co., 1978); and José

Iturriaga de la Fuente, *Anecdotario de viajeros extranjeros en México: Siglos XVI–XX*, 3 vols. (Mexico City: Fondo de Cultura Económica, 1988–92). See also Clinton Harvey Gardiner, "Foreign Travelers' Accounts of Mexico, 1810–1910," *The Americas* 8 (1952): 321–51.

15. *El Mundo Semanario Ilustrado*, 3 November 1895: 5. In this issue the editors speculated that "some of their readers might consider our descriptions of well known popular customs unnecessary to everyone in this country" and then admitted that such overzealous reports appealed to their foreign readership.

16. Philippe Ariès, *Western Attitudes toward Death: From the Middle Ages to the Present*, trans. Patricia M. Ranum (Baltimore: Johns Hopkins University Press, 1974), 1–12, 104. On the ritual act of dying in the eighteenth century, see "Preparation for Death" and "Deathbeds" in McManners, *Death and the Enlightenment*, 191–269.

17. Ariès, *Western Attitudes toward Death*, 66; Vovelle, "On Death," 79–80; McManners, *Death and the Enlightenment*, 234–39.

18. McManners, *Death and the Enlightenment*, 239–43; Ariès, *Western Attitudes toward Death*, 66.

19. Ariès, *Western Attitudes toward Death*, 55–56, 63–66, 68.

20. Lomnitz, *Death and the Idea of Mexico*, 199.

21. Wallace Gillpatrick, *Wanderings in Mexico: The Spirited Chronicle of Adventure in Mexican Highways and Byways* (London: Eveleigh Nash, 1912), 76–81. This book was also published in the United States as *The Man Who Likes Mexico* (New York: Century Co., 1911). As a correspondent for the *Mexican Herald*, Gillpatrick had a keen eye for detail. His column appeared under the title "The Man Who Likes Mexico."

22. Gillpatrick, *Wanderings in Mexico*, 80–81. Excellent photographs of the funeral procession and church altar by professional photographer C. B. Waite appear on page 78 of the 1912 edition.

23. Peter Burke, *Popular Culture in Early Modern Europe* (New York: New York University Press, 1978).

24. Maturin M. Ballou, *Aztec Land* (New York: Houghton, Mifflin, and Co., 1890), 204.

25. Henry McElwin, *New Orleans Exposition, Texas and Old Mexico, a Series of Letters* (St. Louis: n.p., 1885), [49]. McElwin was a newspaper correspondent with the *St. Louis Dispatch*.

26. Gooch, *Face to Face with the Mexicans*, 191–92.

27. Stanton Davis Kirkham, *Mexican Trails: A Record of Travel in Mexico, 1904–1907, and a Glimpse at the Life of the Mexican Indian* (New York: G. P. Putnam's Sons, 1909), 93–94; E. H. Blichfeldt, *A Mexican Journey* (New York: Thomas Y. Crowell Co., 1912), 217–18.

28. Col. Albert S. Evans, *Our Sister Republic: A Gala Trip Through Mexico in 1869–1870* (Hartford, Conn.: Columbian Book Co., 1870), 96. For further reports on memorial crosses, see Gooch, *Face to Face with the Mexicans*, 149; A. Gringo, *Through the Land of the Aztecs* (London: Sampson Low, Marston and Co., 1892), 192; Dillon Wallace, *Beyond the Mexican Sierras* (Chicago: A. C. McClurg and Co., 1910), 131, 233.

29. Ballou, *Aztec Land*, 54, 60–61.

30. William Seymour Edwards, *On the Mexican Highlands, With a Passing Glimpse of Cuba* (Cincinnati: Press of Jennings and Graham, 1906), 158.

31. W. E. Carson, *Mexico: The Wonderland of the South* (1909; New York: Macmillan Co., 1914), 97–98. See also Ethel Brilliana Harley (Mrs. Alec) Tweedie, *Mexico as I Saw It* (London: Hurst and Blackett, 1901; New York: Macmillan Co., 1902), 214.

32. William Henry Bishop, *Old Mexico and Her Lost Provinces: A Journey in Mexico, Southern California, and Arizona by Way of Cuba* (New York: Harper and Brothers, 1883), 49–50; Gooch, *Face to Face with the Mexicans*, 191–92; Hugh Bertie Campbell Pollard, *A Busy Time in Mexico: An Unconventional Record of Mexican Incident* (New York: Duffield and Co., 1913), 76–77; Nevin O. Winter, *Mexico and Her People of Today* (1907; rev. ed., Boston: L. C. Page and Co., 1923), 62–63. Prices rose slightly by 1901. See Adolfo Prantl, *La ciudad de México, novísima guía universal de la capital de la República Mexicana* (Mexico City: Librería Madrileña, 1901), 923–26.

33. Carson, *Mexico*, 97–98; Thomas L. Rogers, *Mexico? Sí, Señor* (Boston: Collins Press, 1893), 148.

34. Ireneo Paz, *Nueva Guía de México* (Mexico City: Imprenta de Ireneo Paz, 1882), 719–25; Solomon Bulkey Griffin, *Mexico of To-day* (New York: Harper and Brothers, 1886), 113;

Nellie Bly, *Six Months in Mexico* (New York: Munro/American Publishers Corp., 1888), 180–81; *Diario Oficial*, 15 August 1895: 2; Jaspar T. Moses, *Today in the Land of Tomorrow: Sketches of Life in Mexico*, 2nd ed. (Indianapolis: Christian Women's Board of Missions, 1909), 67–70.

35. *El Siglo XIX*, 7 March 1878: 1; *Mexican Herald*, 3 November 1895: 8.

36. Jesús Galindo y Villa, *Historia sumaria de la ciudad de México* (Mexico City: Editorial Cultura, 1925), 227–29; Percy Falcke Martin, *Mexico of the Twentieth Century* (London: Edward Arnold, 1907), 232; Ballou, *Aztec Land*, 129–30; M. H. Pastor, *Impresiones y recuerdos de mis viajes a México* (San Sebastián, Spain: La Voz de Guipúzcoa, 1900), 57; Mary Wright Plummer, *Roy and Ray in Mexico* (New York: Henry Holt and Co., 1907), 90–91; Gringo, *Through the Land of the Aztecs*, 123; Thomas U. Brocklehurst, *Mexico To-Day: A Country with a Great Future* (London: John Murray, 1883), 50; Charlotte Cameron, *Mexico in Revolution: An Account of an English Woman's Experiences and Adventures in the Land of Revolution* (London: Seeley, Service and Co. Ltd., 1925), 53–54; Pollard, *A Busy Time in Mexico*, 76–77.

37. Galindo y Villa, *Historia sumaria de la ciudad de México*, 229; *El Imparcial*, 16 January 1900: 1; Hira de Gortari Rabiela and Regina Hernández Franyuti, eds., *Memoria y encuentros: La ciudad de México y el Distrito Federal (1824–1928)*, 3 vols. (Mexico City: Departamento del Distrito Federal, Instituto de Investigaciones Dr. José María Luís Mora, 1988), 2:260–61; Tony Morgan, "Proletarians, Politicos, and Patriarchs: The Use and Abuse of Cultural Customs in the Early Industrialization of Mexico City, 1880–1910," in *Rituals of Rule, Rituals of Resistance: Public Celebrations and Popular Culture in Mexico*, ed. William H. Beezley, Cheryl English Martin, and William E. French (Wilmington, Del.: SR Books, 1994), 153; Martin, *Mexico of the Twentieth Century*, 232–33.

38. Blichfeldt, *A Mexican Journey*, 217–18; Pollard, *A Busy Time in Mexico*, 76–77. The Philadelphia company of J. G. Brill exported the electric streetcars to Mexico. General Electric produced the generators.

39. Martin, *Mexico of the Twentieth Century*, 233–35.

40. Ariel Rodríguez Kuri, *La experiencia olvidada. El Ayuntamiento de México: Política y gobierno, 1876–1912* (Mexico City: El Colegio de México, Centro de Estudios Históricos, Universidad Autónoma Metropolitana, Atzcapotzalco, 1996), 172.

41. Moisés González Navarro, *El Porfiriato: La vida social*, in *HMM* 9:695.

42. Piccato, *City of Suspects*, 24–25.

43. Robert Buffington and William E. French, "The Culture of Modernity," in *The Oxford History of Mexico*, ed. Michael C. Meyer and William H. Beezley (New York: Oxford University Press, 2000), 400.

44. *Mexican Herald*, 19 January 1900: 5.

45. Mary Barton, *Impressions of Mexico with Brush and Pen* (New York: Macmillan, 1911), 45–46; Michael C. Meyer, William L. Sherman, and Susan M. Deeds, *The Course of Mexican History*, 4th ed. (New York: Oxford University Press, 1991), 468; Mary Elizabeth Blake and Margaret Francis Buchanan Sullivan, *Mexico: Picturesque, Political, and Progressive* (Boston: Lee and Shepard Publishers, 1888), 90–91; *El Imparcial*, 9 November 1899: 2.

46. *Mexican Herald*, 3 April 1910: 6.

47. González Navarro, *El Porfiriato*, in *HMM* 9:695; Morgan, "Proletarians, Politicos, and Patriarchs," 153; Patrick Frank, *Posada's Broadsheets: Mexican Popular Imagery, 1890–1910* (Albuquerque: University of New Mexico Press, 1998), 190–91.

48. *Don Gregorito*, 29 March 1877: 4; *El Universal*, 5 September 1893: 2; *El Mundo Semanario Ilustrado*, 1 January 1899: 4; *El Imparcial*, 25 June 1908: 6; *El Tiempo Ilustrado*, 25 April 1909: 295; Adolfo Dollero, *México al día (impresiones y notas de viaje)* (Paris: Librería de la Vda. de C. Bouret, 1911), 879.

49. Bly, *Six Months in Mexico*, 72.

50. Ballou, *Aztec Land*, 203–4.

51. James A. Wilson, *Bits of Old Mexico* (San Francisco: n.p., 1910), 10; Alfred Oscar Coffin, *Land Without Chimneys; or The Byways of Mexico* (Cincinnati: Editor Publishing Co., 1898), 168; Galindo y Villa, *Historia sumaria de la ciudad de México*, 30.

52. Cora Hayward Crawford, *The Land of the Montezumas* (Cincinnati: Robert Clarke Co., 1889), 71–72. See also Ballou, *Aztec Land*, 203; Alden Buell Case, *Thirty Years with the*

Mexicans in Peace and Revolution (New York: Fleming H. Revell Co., 1917), 43; Winter, *Mexico and Her People of Today*, 62.

53. Wallace, *Beyond the Mexican Sierras*, 174; Joseph Hendrickson McCarty, *Two Thousand Miles Through the Heart of Mexico* (New York: Phillips and Hunt, 1886), 184. The scarcity and high cost of wood perpetuated an infinite number of traditions in Mexico. See William H. Beezley, "Rocks and Rawhide in Rural Society: Tools and Technology in Porfirian Mexico," in *Judas at the Jockey Club*, 67–88.

54. Bly, *Six Months in Mexico*, 181.

55. Crawford, *The Land of the Montezumas*, 71–72.

56. Charles Macomb Flandrau, *Viva Mexico!* ed. and intro. by C. Harvey Gardiner (Urbana: University of Illinois Press, 1964), 30.

57. Tweedie, *Mexico as I Saw It*, 213.

58. Even the watchman at the Dolores Cemetery was arrested for pilfering a $150 monument and trying to sell it to the Quintana Brothers' shop. *Two Republics*, 14 January 1885: 4. See also *Mexican Herald*, 19 March 1900: 2.

59. Bishop, *Old Mexico and Her Lost Provinces*, 50.

60. A. A. Graham, *Mexico with Comparisons and Conclusions* (Topeka: Crane and Co., 1907), 239.

61. *El Siglo XIX*, 27 June 1879: 3; *El Monitor Republicano*, 4 February 1894: 3; Ballou, *Aztec Land*, 203–4; Pollard, *A Busy Time in Mexico*, 77; Herbert Cerwin, *These Are the Mexicans* (New York: Reynal and Hitchcock, 1947), 140. Many postmortem photographs from turn-of-the-century Mexico show lifelike images of *angelitos*, who were photographed with their eyes open to uphold the belief in life after death and perpetuate visual memory of the deceased. The practice of photographing the deceased prevailed throughout Europe, Latin America, and the United States. See Dan Meinwald, "*Memento Mori*: Death in Nineteenth Century Photography," *California Museum of Photography Bulletin* 9, no. 4 (1990): 1–7.

62. Pollard, *A Busy Time in Mexico*, 77.

63. Flandrau, *Viva Mexico!* 32. See also the observations of the U.S. consul-general, in Stealey, *Porte Crayon's Mexico*, 248.

64. William E. French, "Prostitutes and Guardian Angels: Women, Work, and the Family in Porfirian Mexico," *Hispanic American Historical Review* 72, no. 4 (1992): 529–33; Manuel Carreño, *Manual de urbanidad y buenas maneras* (New York: Appleton, 1857), 182, 242–44; Gooch, *Face to Face with the Mexicans*, 277; Gringo, *Through the Land of the Aztecs*, 123. I am indebted to Victor Macías for pointing out this information.

65. Rogers, *Mexico?* 65–66, 237–38; Wallace, *Beyond the Mexican Sierras*, 174; Evans, *Our Sister Republic*, 132–34; Carson, *Mexico*, 360–62; Case, *Thirty Years with the Mexicans in Peace and Revolution*, 43; Harry A. Franck, *Tramping Through Mexico, Guatemala and Honduras; Being the Random Notes of an Incurable Vagabond* (New York: Century Co., 1916), 51–54; Thomas W. Knox, *The Boy Travellers in Mexico* (New York: Harper and Brothers, 1902), 206; Frederick A. Ober, *Travels in Mexico and Life Among the Mexicans* (Boston: Estes and Lauriat; and San Francisco: J. Dewing, 1884), 263.

66. Evans, *Our Sister Republic*, 132–34.

67. *El Correo de las Doce*, 24 May 1883: 3.

68. *Mexican Herald*, 23 July 1898: 4.

69. Franck, *Tramping Through Mexico*, 52–53; Reau Campbell, *Campbell's Complete Guide and Descriptive Book of Mexico* (Chicago: Poole Bros., 1895), 191. See also Henry C. R. Becher, *A Trip to Mexico; Being Notes of a Journey from Lake Erie to Lake Tezcuco and Back* (Toronto: Willing and Williamson, 1880), 76.

70. *Mexican Herald*, 23 July 1898: 4. The reporter was referring to the church cemetery of Campo Florido.

71. Ballou, *Aztec Land*, 79.

72. *Two Republics*, 17 July 1889: 4.

73. *El Imparcial*, 21 August 1900: 3.

74. Franck, *Tramping Through Mexico*, 54.

75. Bly, *Six Months in Mexico*, 181.

76. See Enrique Florescano, *Memory, Myth, and Time: From the Aztecs to Independence*, trans. Albert G. Bork (Austin: University of Texas Press, 1994).

77. For a brief history of the Day of the Dead during colonial times, see Pamela Voekel, *Alone before God: The Religious Origins of Modernity in Mexico* (Durham: Duke University Press, 2002), 212–16.

78. González Navarro, *El porfiriato*, in *HMM* 4:464; González y González et al., *La república restaurada*, in *HMM* 3:517; Marie Robinson Wright, *Picturesque Mexico* (Philadelphia: J. B. Lippincott Co., 1897), 49–50; *Mexican Herald*, 1 November 1900: 4.

79. *El Mundo Semanario Ilustrado*, 3 November 1895: 5.

80. *Two Republics*, 1 November 1895: 1; *Mexican Herald*, 3 November 1895: 8; *El Monitor Republicano*, 3 November 1895: 1; Robert Wesley Habenstein, *Funeral Customs the World Over*, rev. ed. (Milwaukee: Bulfin Printer, 1974), 583–85; Rosa María Sánchez Lara, "Vida y muerte en el arte popular mexicano," in *Arte funerario: Coloquio Internacional de Historia del Arte*, 2 vols., coord. Beatriz de la Fuente (Mexico City: Universidad Nacional Autónoma de México, Instituto de Investigaciones Estéticas, 1987), 1:281; *Diccionario Porrúa de Historia, Biografía y Geografía de México*, 3 vols., 3rd ed. (Mexico City: Editorial Porrúa, 1967), 1:419–20, 2:1569–70; Albert Louis Deverdun, *The True Mexico: Mexico-Tenochtitlan* (Menasha, Wisc.: George Banta Publishing Co., 1938), 177–78; Wallace, *Beyond the Mexican Sierras*, 109–10; Mary Rhodes Carbutt (Mrs. E. H.), *Five Months' Fine Weather in Canada, Western U.S., and Mexico* (London: Sampson, Low, Marston, Searle and Rivington, 1889), 228; Gooch, *Face to Face with the Mexicans*, 248–49; Gringo, *Through the Land of the Aztecs*, 129; Pollard, *A Busy Time in Mexico*, 75–77.

81. There were exceptions. On March 15, 1879, in the municipality of Allende, soldiers and police enforced the Reform Laws on townspeople praying at a churchyard cemetery, beating several and severely wounding two. See Robert Conger, "Porfirio Díaz and the Church Hierarchy, 1876–1911" (Ph.D. diss., University of New Mexico, 1985), 88–89.

82. On Holy Week, see Beezley, *Judas at the Jockey Club*. On the Day of the Dead, see Lomnitz, *Death and the Idea of Mexico*, chaps. 5–8.

83. Wright, *Picturesque Mexico*, 50. The quote also appears in the *Mexican Herald*, 1 November 1900: 4.

84. John Greenleigh, *The Days of the Dead: Mexico's Festival of Communion with the Departed* (San Francisco: Collins, 1991), 21; Gringo, *Through the Land of the Aztecs*, 129; Carbutt, *Five Months' Fine Weather in Canada, Western U.S., and Mexico*, 207–8; Evans, *Our Sister Republic*, 175; Gooch, *Face to Face with the Mexicans*, 248–49; Wright, *Picturesque Mexico*, 50; *Two Republics*, 3 November 1885: 4, 27 October 1889: 4, 1 November 1889: 4, 1 November 1895: 1; *El Partido Liberal*, 1 November 1891: 1; *El Universal*, 5 October 1895: 1; *El Mundo Semanario Ilustrado*, 3 November 1895: 5, 12 November 1899: 280; *El Imparcial*, 3 November 1899: 1, 3 November 1900: 1–2, 1 November 1905: 1; *Mexican Herald*, 3 November 1897: 8, 1 November 1900: 4, 3 November 1901: 8, 2 November 1904: 2; Stealey, *Porte Crayon's Mexico*, 143, 307–8, 498.

85. Current-day calaca (also calavera) tableaux—miniaturized skeleton figures performing duties in modern settings, such as factories (seamstresses), business offices (typists), and public streets (trolley drivers)—originated with the rise of industrial, commercial, and transportation sectors in Porfirian Mexico. For a wonderful photographic collection of these figurines and other Day of the Dead handicrafts, see Greenleigh, *The Days of the Dead*, 30–33; Antonio García Cubas, *El libro de mis recuerdos; Narraciones historicas, anecdóticas y de costumbres mexicanas anteriores al actual estado social* (Mexico City: Impr. de A. García Cubas, hermanos sucesores, 1904); Frank, *Posada's Broadsheets*.

86. *La Patria Ilustrada*, 2 November 1891: 528.

87. Beezley, *Judas at the Jockey Club*, 98, 111–12; Edward Larocque Tinker, *Corridos and Calaveras* (Austin: University of Texas Press, 1961), 21, 25–26; *El Hijo del Ahuizote*, 9 September 1885: 4, 1 November 1885: 1, 8 April 1886: 8.

88. *Mexican Herald*, 3 November 1897: 8, 14 September 1898: 2. As one elderly Mexican woman said to a *Herald* reporter, "Nearly everybody over this way who buys a tombstone nowadays has the photograph of the dead person put over the date. It's the fashion." On death and photography, see Meinwald, "*Memento Mori*," 3, 5–7, 18.

89. Wright, *Picturesque Mexico*, 50.

90. *Mexican Herald*, 3 November 1896: 8; *El Imparcial*, 3 November 1902: 1, 4 November 1902: 1.

91. *Mexican Herald*, 3 November 1896: 8, 3 November 1901: 8. The *zempasúchil* (marigold), *aliento de niño* (baby's breath), and *creste de gallo* (purple cockscomb) were the flowers of choice among all social classes. One Bostonian tourist with Raymond's Excursions marveled over the work and care that went into each holiday floral arrangement sold at the flower market. After paying 50 centavos for an enormous bouquet, he took it apart and counted 30 red roses, 50 white roses, 28 violets, 30 heliotropes, and 20 white and 30 pink rosebuds, concluding that there were 192 flowers in all. Perhaps because of his bewildered state, his math does not add up. See Arthut L. Spring, *Beyond the Rio Grande* (Boston: J. S. Adams, 1886), 37.

92. Beezley, *Judas at the Jockey Club*, 90, 108.

93. Ayuntamiento de la Ciudad de México, *Discurso del Sr. Lic. Miguel S. Macedo, Presidente del Ayuntamiento en 1899*, 300; Ayuntamiento de la Ciudad de México, *Discursos del Sr. D. Fernando Pimentel y Fagoaga, Presidente interino del Ayuntamiento en 1902; del Sr. D. Ramón Corral, Gobernador del Distrito Federal y del Sr. D. Guillermo de Landa y Escandon, Presidente del Ayuntamiento en 1903 y Memoria Documentada de los trabajos municipales de 1902*, 2 vols. (Mexico City: Tip. y Lit. "La Europea," 1903), 2:433–43.

94. *El Imparcial*, 2 November 1900: 2; *Mexican Herald*, 3 November 1903: 3, 3 November 1904: 2.

95. William E. French, *A Peaceful and Working People: Manners, Morals, and Class Formation in Northern Mexico* (Albuquerque: University of New Mexico Press, 1996), 6.

96. *El Imparcial*, 3 November 2001: 1.

97. See Voekel, *Alone before God*, 209.

98. Ayuntamiento de la Ciudad de México, *Discurso del Sr. Lic. Miguel S. Macedo, Presidente del Ayuntamiento en 1899*, 300.

99. Wright, *Picturesque Mexico*, 52; *Mexican Herald*, 3 November 1897: 8, 1 November 1900: 4, 1 November 1902: 5.

100. Scenes include part 1: act 1. Libertinism and Scandal, act 2. Dexterity, act 3. Profanation, and act 4. The Devil at the Gates of Heaven; and part 2: act 1. The Ghost of Doña Inés, act 2. The Statue of Don Gonzalo, and act 3. The Mercy of God and Final Apotheosis. *Mexican Herald*, 2 November 1902: 8; Oscar Mandel, ed., *The Theatre of Don Juan: A Collection of Plays and Views, 1630–1963* (Lincoln: University of Nebraska Press, 1963), 470–538.

101. *Mexican Herald*, 3 November 1897: 8, 1 November 1900: 4; Wright, *Picturesque Mexico*, 52.

102. Wright, *Picturesque Mexico*, 52–53.

103. Ibid., 53; Mandel, *The Theatre of Don Juan*, 537–38.

104. *Mexican Herald*, 3 November 1897: 8. For his part, Zorrilla was crowned in Granada before the royal court and fourteen thousand spectators in 1889 and buried in a royal funeral in 1893. Mandel, *The Theatre of Don Juan*, 465.

105. Wright, *Picturesque Mexico*, 52–53.

106. Rosendo Pineda to Rafael Chousal, 24 May 1892, Archivo Rafael Chousal, Universidad Nacional Autónoma de México, caja 5, expediente 75, folio 93. Pineda was the personal secretary of Interior Minister Manuel Romero Rubio. I thank Dr. Eduardo Garcia Villada for translation assistance.

107. Wright, *Picturesque Mexico*, 52.

108. *Mexican Herald*, 2 November 1902: 8.

109. Ibid., 9 November 1902: 11; italics mine.

110. Joseph Roach, *Cities of the Dead: Circum-Atlantic Performance* (New York: Columbia University Press, 1996), 35; McManners, *Death and the Enlightenment*, 303–4; Thomas A. Kselman, *Death and the Afterlife in Modern France* (Princeton: Princeton University Press, 1993), 170–71; James Stevens Curl, *The Victorian Celebration of Death* (London: David and Charles, 1972), 42; Lawrence J. Taylor, "Introduction: The Uses of Death in Europe," *Anthropological Quarterly* 62, no. 4 (October 1989): 151; Clare Gittings, *Death, Burial and the Individual in Early Modern England* (London: Croom Helm, 1984), 166–70; Eugen Weber, *Peasants into Frenchmen: The Modernization of Rural France, 1870–1914* (Stanford: Stanford University Press, 1976), 372–73.

111. Voekel, *Alone before God*, 5–6, 39–42.

112. The Conde de Revillagigedo founded the General, Canelo, San Lázaro, and Santa María la Redonda cemeteries. For a well-documented summary of Spanish colonial burial practices

and attitudes toward the cemetery reforms of Charles III, see Ramón Gutiérrez, "Notas sobre los cementerios españoles y americanos, 1787–1850," in *Arte funerario*, 2:311–29; *Diccionario Porrúa de Historia, Biografía y Geografía de México*, 3 vols., 2nd ed. (Mexico City: Editorial Porrúa, 1964), 1:301. For similar changes in Brazil, see João José Reis, *Death Is a Festival: Funeral Rites and Rebellion in Nineteenth-Century Brazil*, trans. H. Sabrina Gledhill (Chapel Hill: University of North Carolina Press, 2003).

113. Voekel, *Alone before God*, 204.

114. Charles A. Hale, *Mexican Liberalism in the Age of Mora, 1821–1853* (New Haven: Yale University Press, 1968), 133; Arturo Casado Navarro, "Cinco monumentos funerarios de la época porfirista en la ciudad de México," in *Arte funerario*, 2:253; *Diccionario Porrúa*, 2nd ed., 1:301; Anne Staples, "La lucha por los muertos," *Diálogos* 13, no. 5 (1977): 15–20; Fausto Ramírez, "Tipología de la escultura tumbal en México, 1860–1920," in *Arte funerario*, 1:183. A reform law of December 4, 1860, also made the ringing of church bells subject to civil ordinance. See Hale, *Mexican Liberalism in the Age of Mora*, 108n; and Anne Staples, "Policía y Buen Gobierno: Municipal Efforts to Regulate Public Behavior, 1821–1857," in Beezley, Martin, and French, *Rituals of Rule, Rituals of Resistance*, 118.

115. Amanda López, "In Search of a 'Dignified Necropolis': Liberalism, Public Welfare, and the Panteón de Dolores, 1875–1879," paper presented at the annual meeting of the Rocky Mountain Council for Latin American Studies, Flagstaff, Ariz., April 9–12, 2008; México, Secretaría de Gobernación, *Memoria que el Secretario de Estado y del despacho de Gobernación presenta al Congreso de la Unión, correspondiente el periodo trascurrido del 1° de Enero de 1879 al 20 de Noviembre de 1880* (Mexico City: Tip. de Gonzalo A. Esteva, 1881), 714–15 (hereafter cited as *Memoria de Gobernación* [1879–80]); Arturo Sotomayor, *La Rotonda de los Hombres Ilustres* (Mexico City: Colección Metropolitana, 1976), 11–13; Alfredo Desentis M., *Rotonda de los Hombres Ilustres* (Mexico City: Departamento del Distrito Federal, 1985), 13–14. Other major cities founded public municipal cemeteries during the restored republic and Porfiriato. The cemetery of Mezquitán in Guadalajara dates from the former period.

116. The Federal District government ordered the closure of these cemeteries on July 27, 1871, but it was a dead letter. Authorities did not permanently shut them down until the end of Díaz's first term. See México, Secretaría de Gobernación, *Memoria que el Secretario de Estado y del despacho de Gobernación presentó al Congreso de la Unión el día 14 de Diciembre de 1877* (Mexico City: Imprenta del Gobierno, 1878), 25 (hereafter cited as *Memoria de Gobernación* [1877]).

117. *La Voz de México*, 20 May 1896: 3; *Memoria de Gobernación* (1879–80), 714–18; Archivo Histórico del Ex-Ayuntamiento de la Ciudad de México, *Panteones en general* (1898–1900), legajo 7, numeros 824–25, 834; Galindo y Villa, *Historia sumaria de la ciudad de México*, 210; Sotomayor, *La Rotonda de los Hombres Ilustres*, 13; Manuel Rivera Cambas, *México pintoresco, artístico y monumental*, 3 vols. (Mexico City: Editorial del Valle de México, 1972), 1:377, 2:70, 251; *Diccionario Porrúa*, 3rd ed., 2:1079, 1569–70, 1691, 1809; Desentis M., *La Rotonda de los Hombres Ilustres*, 12–16; González Navarro, *El porfiriato*, in *HMM* 4:102; Charles William Drees, *Thirteen Years in Mexico (From Letters of Charles W. Drees)*, ed. Ada M. C. Drees (New York: Abingdon Press, 1915), 236; *Actas de Cabildo del Ayuntamiento Constitucional de México, Años de 1886–1896*, Edición de "El Municipio Libre" (Mexico City: Imp. de la Escuela Correccional de Artes y Oficios, 1886–1900), 49–212; *El Siglo XIX*, 26 June 1879: 3, 14 August 1879: 3; *Mexican Herald*, 23 July 1898: 4, 4 September 1898: 8; *Two Republics*, 21 November 1886: 4, 13 March 1888: 4, 16 October 1888: 4.

118. Casado Navarro, "Cinco monumentos funerarios de la época porfirista en la ciudad de México," 254. Lerdo may have been inspired by the German Pantheon of Valhalla, located on the banks of the Danube.

119. Ayuntamiento de la Ciudad de México, *Discurso del C. Ingeniero Sebastián Camacho Presidente del Ayuntamiento de 1895. Al instalarse el de 1896. Contestación del C. Gobernador del Distrito Federal Gral. Pedro Rincon Gallardo y Memoria Documentada de los trabajos municipales de 1895* (Mexico City: Imp. y Lit. "La Europea," 1896), 147; Sotomayor, *La Rotonda de los Hombres Ilustres*, 12; *Diccionario Porrúa*, 3rd ed., 2:1239; *Two Republics*, 20 October 1885: 4; *El Imparcial*, 3 November 2001: 1.

120. Archbishop Labastida inaugurated the Spanish Cemetery on December 5, 1886. *Two Republics*, 5 December 1886: 5; Rivera Cambas, *México pintoresco, artístico y monumental*,

1:329–30; *Memoria de Gobernación* (1877), 25; México, Secretaría de Gobernación, *Memoria que el Secretario de Estado y del despacho de Gobernación presentó al Congreso de la Unión el día 14 de diciembre de 1877* (Mexico City: Imprenta de Gobierno, 1878), 83 (hereafter cited as *Memoria de Gobernación* [1878]); *El Universal*, 2 November 1895: 1–6; *El Monitor Republicano*, 3 November 1895: 1.

121. Ballou, *Aztec Land*, 201–2; Rogers, *Mexico?* 159–60.

122. Bishop, *Old Mexico and Her Lost Provinces*, 126–27; James Hale Bates, *Notes of a Tour in Mexico and California* (New York: Burr Printing House, 1887), 69; Campbell, *Campbell's Complete Guide and Descriptive Book of Mexico*, 96; Crawford, *The Land of the Montezumas*, 270. Gilbert Haven, *Our Next-Door Neighbor: A Winter in Mexico* (New York: Harper and Brothers, 1875), 257–61.

123. Griffin, *Mexico of To-day*, 175.

124. *Memoria de Gobernación* (1878), 81–83; *Two Republics*, 25 July 1880: 3; Rivera Cambas, *México pintoresco, artístico y monumental*, 1:376–78; Casado Navarro, "Cinco monumentos funerarios de la época porfirista en la ciudad de México," 254; *El Universal*, 2 November 1895: 1–6.

125. *Two Republics*, 2 May 1886: 4. The government did not furnish funds for all the funerary monuments at the rotunda. The monument of Melchor Ocampo, produced by Alciati, was paid for by Ocampo's survivors after the government transferred his remains from Morelia in 1897. See Casado Navarro, "Cinco monumentos funerarios de la época porfirista en la ciudad de México," 257.

126. Nigel Llewellyn, "English Renaissance Tombs: Commemoration in Society," in *Arte funerario*, 2:144; Casado Navarro, "Cinco monumentos funerarios de la época porfirista en la ciudad de México," 254–55.

127. Llewellyn, "English Renaissance Tombs," 144–54.

128. *El Tiempo Ilustrado*, 1 November 1908: 704–8.

129. Keith McElroy, "Death and Photography in Nineteenth-Century Peru," in *Arte funerario*, 2:279–85.

130. Jan Bialostocki, "The Image of Death and Funerary Art in European Tradition," in *Arte funerario*, 1:14; Ramírez, "Tipología de la escultura tumbal en México," 184–85; *El Tiempo Ilustrado*, 1 November 1908: 704–8.

131. Ramírez, "Tipología de la escultura tumbal en México," 184–208; Emilio Zafra, "La elegancia del arte funerario en la ciudad de México, 1850–1930," *México Desconocido* 15, no. 182 (April 1992): 46–50; Jesús Franco Carrasco, "El inicio de la loza funeraria en Puebla," in *Arte funerario*, 1:307–8; Desentis M., *La Rotonda de los Hombres Ilustres*, 96–97.

132. Benedict Anderson, "Replica, Aura, and Late Nationalist Imaginings," in *The Spectre of Comparisons: Nationalism, Southeast Asia and the World* (New York: Verso, 1998), 46–57.

133. *Two Republics*, 25 September 1885: 4; *Mexican Herald*, 7 September 1899: 5.

134. *El Tiempo Ilustrado*, 25 May 1903: 229–31; *El Imparcial*, 12 April 1905: 1, 19 December 1905: 1.

135. Nina Tumarkin comments about the "relaxed fatalism" and "acceptance of the inevitability of death" in modern Russia; see her *The Living and the Dead: The Rise and Fall of the Cult of World War II in Russia* (New York: Basic Books, 1994), 7.

136. Avner Ben-Amos, "The Other World of Memory: State Funerals of the French Third Republic as Rites of Commemoration," *History and Memory* 1 (1989): 85–108; Florescano, *Memory, Myth, and Time*, 184, 221–27.

CHAPTER 2

1. Próspero Cahuantzi, governor in perpetuity of Tlaxcala, later declared November 16 a state holiday. In 1896, he erected a commemorative monument at the hacienda of Tecoac near Huamantla to mark the twentieth anniversary of Porfirio's victory. See Ricardo Rendón Garcini, *El prosperato: Tlaxcala de 1885 a 1911* (Mexico City: Universidad Iberoamericana/Siglo Veintiuno Editores, 1993), 43. Tecoac was a bloody but decisive battle. Each army numbered around four thousand men. The Federal Army sustained 1,900 dead, 800 wounded, and 1,563 captured. The *porfirista* rebel army lost 859 men, with 575 wounded. *Two Republics*, 25 November 1876: 3. Enrique Chávarri (Juvenal), cited in Diego Arenas Guzmán,

Cincuenta retablos de la vida porfiriana (Mexico City: B. Costa-Amic, 1966), 9–10; *Two Republics*, 8 November 1876: 3.

2. *Two Republics*, 15 November 1876: 3.
3. Daniel Cosío Villegas, *The United States versus Porfirio Díaz*, trans. Nettie Lee Benson (Lincoln: University of Nebraska Press, 1963), 13–16.
4. *El Monitor Republicano*, 14 September 1877: 1.
5. *Two Republics*, 21 September 1878: 2.
6. *El Monitor Republicano*, 9 July 1879: 3.
7. Ibid., 9 October 1881: 1; italics added.
8. Robert Darnton, *The Great Cat Massacre and Other Episodes in French Cultural History* (New York: Basic Books, 1984), 4.
9. *El Monitor Republicano*, 8 October 1881: 3.
10. For this in France, see Mona Ozouf, *Festivals and the French Revolution*, trans. Alan Sheridan (Cambridge: Harvard University Press, 1988), 16–19, 127–30.
11. Juan Pedro Viqueira Albán, *Propriety and Permissiveness in Bourbon Mexico*, trans. Sonya Lipsett-Rivera and Sergio Rivera Ayala (Wilmington, Del.: SR Books, 1999), 27–29, 35, 39, 75, 93, 106. See also David Cahill's remarks on mechanisms of social leveling in his article "Popular Religion and Appropriation: The Example of Corpus Christi in Eighteenth-Century Cuzco," *Latin American Research Review* 31, no. 2 (1996): 79–81.
12. E. P. Thompson, "The Moral Economy of the English Crowd in the Eighteenth Century," *Past and Present* 50 (February 1971): 78. See also Suzanne Desan, "Crowds, Community, and Ritual in the Work of E. P. Thompson and Natalie Davis," in *The New Cultural History*, ed. Lynn Hunt (Berkeley: University of California Press, 1989), 47–71. For the argument that Carnival and other raucous street entertainments restore a "customary equilibrium" among various social classes, see Viqueira Albán, *Propriety and Permissiveness in Bourbon Mexico*, 106–7.
13. Ozouf, *Festivals and the French Revolution*, 83–92. See examples of passive resistance in William H. Beezley, Cheryl English Martin, and William E. French, eds., *Rituals of Rule, Rituals of Resistance: Public Celebrations and Popular Culture in Mexico* (Wilmington, Del.: SR Books, 1994); and William H. Beezley and Linda Curcio-Nagy, eds., *Latin American Popular Culture: An Introduction* (Wilmington, Del.: SR Books, 2000).
14. Thomas U. Brocklehurst, *Mexico To-Day: A Country with a Great Future* (London: John Murray, 1883), 50. Brocklehurst spent seven months in Mexico and witnessed the Arista funeral.
15. *El Monitor Republicano*, 9 October 1881: 1.
16. Ibid.
17. Pablo Piccato, "*Cuidado con los Rateros*: The Making of Criminals in Modern Mexico City," in *Crime and Punishment in Latin America: Law and Society since Late Colonial Times*, ed. Ricardo D. Salvatore, Carlos Aguirre, and Gilbert M. Joseph (Durham: Duke University Press, 2001), 235.
18. Ozouf, *Festivals and the French Revolution*, 2–3.
19. This was a major theme in Abraham Lincoln's funeral. In 1885, former Confederate soldiers marched in the funeral procession for Union general Ulysses S. Grant. See Barry Schwartz, "Mourning and the Making of a Sacred Symbol: Durkheim and the Lincoln Assassination," *Social Forces* 70, no. 2 (December 1991): 343–64. For the Soviet experience, see Nina Tumarkin, *The Living and the Dead: The Rise and Fall of the Cult of World War II in Russia* (New York: Basic Books, 1994), 2, 8.
20. Katherine Verdery, *The Political Lives of Dead Bodies: Reburial and Postsocialist Change* (New York: Columbia University Press, 1999), 4–6.
21. *La Patria*, 5 January 1878: 3; *El Siglo XIX*, 7 January 1878: 3, 8 April 1878: 3; *Two Republics*, 21 September 1878: 2; *El Monitor Republicano*, 6 January 1878, 9 April 1878: 3; *El Combate*, 6 January 1878: 3; *La Libertad*, 9 April 1878: 3.
22. A. Lozano [Oficial Mayor Tesorería], certified document, 17 July 1877, Colección General Porfirio Díaz, Universidad Iberoamericana, legajo 2, caja 3, documento 1103 (hereafter cited as CPD followed by legajo, caja, and documento numbers). General Juan N. Méndez [General Jefe de la Línea de Oriente] to Tte. Corl. Manuel Barrón, 11 August 1877, CPD 2:3:1107; General Feliciano Chavarría to General Vicente Riva Palacio, 16 December 1876, CPD 2:3:1108.

23. Juan A. Mateos to Vicente García Torres [Director of *El Monitor Republicano*], n.d., *El Monitor Republicano*, 18 June 1879: 3; *El Combate*, 19 June 1879: 1.

24. *La Patria*, 17 June 1879: 1; *El Combate*, 19 June 1879: 1; *Two Republics*, 21 June 1879: 3, 26 September 1880: 3; *El Republicano*, 17 June 1879: 2; David R. Maciel, *Ignacio Ramírez, ideólogo del liberalismo social en México* (Mexico City: Universidad Nacional Autónoma de México, 1980), 159; Ramón Eduardo Ruiz, *Triumphs and Tragedy: A History of the Mexican People* (New York: W. W. Norton and Co., 1992), 223, 264; México, Congreso, Cámara de Diputados, *Diario de los Debates de la Cámara de Diputados, Años de 1887–1910* (Mexico City: Imprenta de "El Partido Liberal," 1890–1910), *Año de 1887*, 223–24 (hereafter cited as *Diario de los Debates, Año de 1887*); *El Porfiriato, la vida política interior, primera parte*, in *Historia Moderna de México*, 9 vols., ed. Daniel Cosío Villegas (Mexico City: Editorial Hermes, 1970), 8:277–79 (hereafter cited as *HMM* followed by volume and page numbers).

25. Juan A. Mateos to Vicente García Torres, *El Monitor Republicano*, 18 June 1879: 3. Mateos, who was at Ramírez's side, stated: "Neither clerics nor notaries appeared at his deathbed; he did not believe in the first and had no need for the second since he died in poverty."

26. "Acta del acuerdo extraordinario del dia 15 de Junio de 1879," *Diario Oficial*, 17 June 1879: 3; *El Siglo XIX*, 17 June 1879: 2; *El Monitor Republicano*, 17 June 1879: 3; *La Libertad*, 17 June 1879: 2, 18 June 1879: 3. Ramírez's sisters later asked Díaz to reserve a second-class gravesite in the Panteón de Dolores for their mother. See Clara and María Ramírez to Díaz, 26 September 1895, Archivo Rafael Chousal, Universidad Nacional Autónoma de México, caja 11, expediente 151, folio 24.

27. Porfirio Díaz to Marcos Carrillo, 2 November 1885, CPD 41:3:57; Porfirio Díaz to Luis E. Torres, 2 November 1885, CPD 41:3:58; Luís G. Carbó to Porfirio Díaz, 5 November 1885, CPD 10:21:10023.

28. *Esquela de defunción*, *El Siglo XIX*, 17 June 1879: 3.

29. *La Patria*, 20 June 1879: 3.

30. *El Combate*, 19 June 1879: 1; *Diario Oficial*, 20 June 1879: 3.

31. *La Voz de México*, 22 June 1879: 1.

32. On these republican principles, see Richard Warren, "Elections and Popular Political Participation in Mexico, 1808–1836," in *Liberals, Politics, and Power: State Formation in Nineteenth-Century Latin America*, ed. Vincent C. Peloso and Barbara A. Tenenbaum (Athens: University of Georgia Press, 1996), 30–58. Radical federalists in the York rites Masonic lodges launched campaigns to politicize the masses from 1823 to 1830.

33. *El Monitor Republicano*, 17 June 1879: 3, 18 June 1879: 1; *El Siglo XIX*, 17 June 1879: 3.

34. *El Siglo XIX*, 19 June 1879: 3.

35. *La Patria*, 20 June 1879: 3.

36. Ignacio M. Altamirano, funeral oration for Ignacio Ramírez, 18 June 1879, Chamber of Deputies, in *La Libertad*, 19 June 1879: 1; and *El Hijo del Trabajo*, 29 June 1879: 2.

37. Jorge Hammeken Mejía, funeral oration for Ignacio Ramírez, 18 June 1879, Chamber of Deputies, in *La Libertad*, 19 June 1881: 2; and *El Hijo del Trabajo*, 29 June 1879: 2–3. Juan A. Mateos to Vicente García Torres, n.d., *El Monitor Republicano*, 18 June 1879: 3.

38. Porfirio Parra, funeral oration for Ignacio Ramírez, 18 June 1879, Chamber of Deputies, in *La Libertad*, 19 June 1879: 2; and *El Hijo del Trabajo*, 29 June 1879: 3.

39. *Diario Oficial*, 16 June 1879: 3.

40. Ozouf, *Festivals and the French Revolution*, 5; Nicole Loraux, *The Invention of Athens: The Funeral Oration in the Classical City* (Cambridge: Harvard University Press, 1986), 17–19.

41. From 1877 to 1878, thirteen veteran officers of the Liberation Wars died. Of this number, five had earned promotion to general, but only two received state burials. In addition, early military funerals were merely "lucid burials" compared to the often extravagant affairs for civilian leaders. See *La Patria*, 5 January 1878: 3.

42. The 1885 funeral for Brigadier General Francisco Montes de Oca was staged at the Hospital of Medicine to highlight his achievements as a surgeon. Decorators surrounded his casket with modern surgical instruments instead of war trophies.

43. Charles A. Hale, *The Transformation of Liberalism in Late Nineteenth-Century Mexico* (Princeton: Princeton University Press, 1989), 62. Ramírez's funeral also served as a model for other diplomats and legal minds, such as Secretary of Foreign Affairs Miguel Ruelas, Minister of Justice Ezequiel Montes, and *Constituyente* Juan José Baz.

44. CPD 5:3:1001–1115.
45. *La Libertad*, 9 April 1880: 3.
46. Jorge Fernando Iturribarría, "La política de la conciliación del general Díaz y el arzobispo Gillow," *Historia Mexicana* 14, no. 53 (July–September 1974), 92; Enrique Krauze, *Mexico: Biography of Power, a History of Modern Mexico, 1810–1996*, trans. Hank Heifetz (New York: Harper Collins, 1996), 227.
47. Ozouf, *Festivals and the French Revolution*, 95; Eric J. Hobsbawm and Terence Ranger, "Introduction: Inventing Tradition," in *The Invention of Tradition*, ed. Eric J. Hobsbawm and Terence Ranger (Cambridge: Cambridge University Press, 1983), 6.
48. *El Siglo XIX*, 8 April 1880: 1; *La Libertad*, 9 April 1880: 3, 10 April 1880: 2–3, 11 April 1880: 3; *Two Republics*, 11 April 1880: 3; Tomas de Rojas to Díaz, CPD 6:1:225. A memorial book that collected poems and eulogies for Delfina was published as *Corona fúnebre a la memoria de la estimable Sra. Delfina Ortega de Díaz*, Edición de El Libre Sufragio (Mexico City: Imprenta de Ignacio Cumplido, 1880).
49. François-Xavier Guerra, *México, del antigua régimen a la revolución*, 2 vols., trans. Sergio Fernández Bravo (Mexico City: Fondo de Cultura Económica, 1995), 1:52.
50. "Gen. Díaz's Report of the Battle of Tecoac to the Governor of the State of Oaxaca," *Two Republics*, 25 November 1876: 3.
51. Don M. Coerver, *The Porfirian Interregnum: The Presidency of Manuel González of Mexico, 1880–1884* (Fort Worth: Texas Christian University Press, 1979), 8–9.
52. Alberto María Carreño, ed., *Archivo del General Porfirio Díaz, Memorias y Documentos*, 30 vols. (Mexico City: Editorial Elede, 1949–61), 2:7–8.
53. Alluding to the contrived "election" of the former Conservative González, a cynical *El Monitor Republicano* claimed "We Have a Pope" and sarcastically concluded: "May God save the nation." See Coerver, *The Porfirian Interregnum*, 28.
54. Hale, *The Transformation of Liberalism in Late Nineteenth-Century Mexico*, 23–24 and chaps. 5–6; Karl M. Schmitt, "The Mexican Positivists and the Church–State Question, 1876–1911," *Journal of Church and State* 8, no. 2 (Spring 1966): 203.
55. *Diario Oficial*, 12 March 1881: 1; *La Libertad*, 12 March 1881: 2; *El Monitor Republicano*, 15 March 1881: 1; *Two Republics*, 20 March 1881: 4.
56. The funeral program was published in *La República*, 15 March 1881: 2; *Oración fúnebre pronunciada en la Biblioteca de la Escuela Nacional Preparatoria, ante el cadáver del doctor don Gabino Barreda, en la velada que organizó el profesorado de dicha Escuela, el 11 de marzo de 1881*, in Justo Sierra, *Obras Completa*, 14 vols., ed. Agustín Yáñez (Mexico City: Universidad Nacional Autónoma de México, 1948–49), 5:52–54; *El Monitor Republicano*, 15 March 1881: 3, 16 March 1881: 2; *La Libertad*, 17 March 1881: 3. Barreda's remains were transferred to the Rotonda de los Hombres Ilustres in 1968.
57. Ivie E. Cadenhead Jr., *Jesús González Ortega and Mexican National Politics* (Fort Worth: Texas Christian University Press, 1972), 136.
58. *El Nacional*, 3 March 1881: 2–3, 31 March 1881: 1; *Two Republics*, 6 March 1881: 5; Justo Sierra, *Juárez: Su obra y su tiempo*, intro. by Agustín Yáñez (Mexico City: Editorial Porrúa, 1989), 173–74, 183–85, 193; Cadenhead, *González Ortega*, 34–37, 44. Juárez replaced Santos Degollado with González Ortega as commander in chief after the Battle of Silao.
59. Sierra, *Juárez*, 229–30, 321–24, 332–33. The defense of Puebla won González Ortega international renown. European observers compared it to the sieges of Strasburg and Metz. See Cadenhead, *González Ortega*, 74–75.
60. Sierra, *Juárez*, 167, 246–47, 350–58, 408.
61. *El Defensor de la Constitución* (Zacatecas), 1 March 1881: 1, 5 March 1881: 4, 31 March,1881: 2; *La Libertad*, 3 March 1881: 3; *El Monitor Republicano*, 6 March 1881: 3, 18 March 1881: 3; *La República*, 19 March 1881: 3; *El Siglo XIX*, 17 March 1881: 3; *El Nacional*, 3 March 1881: 2–3, 8 March 1881: 3, 17 March 1881: 3.
62. Manuel González to Jesús Aréchiga, telegram, 3 March 1881, in *Diario Oficial*, 4 March 1881: 1; and *El Defensor de la Constitución* (Zacatecas), 5 March 1881: 4. J. Aréchiga to Minister of War Gerónimo Treviño, telegram, 4 March 1881, *El Defensor de la Constitución* (Zacatecas), 5 March 1881: 4; Minister of War Gerónimo Treviño to Sr. Gobernador [Evaristo Madero], telegram, 3 March 1881, Jesús González Ortega Collection, Folder 14: "Correspondence and literary productions relating to his death," Nettie Lee Benson Latin American Library,

University of Texas at Austin. Aréchiga later gained notoriety for ordering the assassination of Díaz's rival Trinidad García de la Cadena. See Carleton Beals, *Porfirio Díaz: Dictator of Mexico* (Philadelphia: J. B. Lippincott, 1932), 287–97.

63. J. Montesinos to M. O. Nogueras, 9 March 1881; J. Montesinos to Gral. M. O. Nogueras, 16 March 1881; and J. Montesinos to Coronel F. Calderón, 21 March 1881, all in *Libro de actas del Gral. Manuel González, correspondiente a los años 1880-1881*, Archívo Histórico de la Biblioteca Nacional de Antropología y Historia, cartas 153, 155, 158 (hereafter cited as AHBNAH followed by carta number). *El Defensor de la Constitución* (Zacatecas), 10 March 1881: 4, 29 March 1881: 4; *El Diario Oficial*, 25 March 1881: 1; mortuary announcement of Jesús González Ortega, 24 March 1881, Archivo Histórico del Ex-Ayuntamiento de la Ciudad de México, *Funerales y ceremonias fúnebres (1779-1915)*, legajo 1, expediente 35 (hereafter cited as AHEACM, *Funerales*, followed by legajo and expediente numbers); *El Nacional*, 17 March 1881: 1; J. Aréchiga to General Manuel González, telegram, 4 March 1881, *El Defensor de la Constitución* (Zacatecas), 5 March 1881: 4; *El Monitor Republicano*, 10 March 1881: 3; *El Siglo XIX*, 15 March 1881: 2; J. Aréchiga to Minister of Gobernación Diez Gutiérrez, telegram, 4 March 1881, *El Defensor de la Constitución* (Zacatecas), 4 March 1881: 4; Aréchiga to President of the Republic, telegram, 11 March 1881, *El Monitor Republicano*, March 16, 1881: 1; González to Aréchiga, telegram, 14 March 1881, *El Monitor Republicano*, March 16, 1881: 3; E. Madero to Treviño, telegram, 4 March 1881, *Periódico Oficial del Gobierno del Estado de Coahuila de Zaragoza*, 7 March 1881: 1; E. Madero to Sr. Gobernador Jesús Aréchiga, telegram, 4 March 1881, *Periódico Oficial del Gobierno del Estado de Coahuila de Zaragoza*, 7 March 1881: 1.

64. James C. Scott, *Domination and the Arts of Resistance: Hidden Transcripts* (New Haven: Yale University Press, 1990), xii.

65. *El Monitor Republicano*, 22 March 1881: 3, 23 March 1881: 3; *El Defensor de la Constitución* (Zacatecas), 10 March 1881: 4; Eusebio Carrillo, funeral oration for Jesús González Ortega, Palacio del Ejecutivo (Zacatecas), in *El Monitor Republicano*, 22 March 1881: 3; *El Nacional*, 22 March 1881: 2–3; *El Payaso* (León), 27 March 1881, reprinted in *El Monitor Republicano*, 2 April 1881: 3; *Periódico Oficial* (Querétaro), 27 March 1881, reprinted in *El Monitor Republicano*, 1 April 1881: 3; Arenas Guzmán, *Cincuenta retablos de la vida porfiriana*, 99–100; Eliseo Rangel Gaspar, *Jesús González Ortega (Caudillo de la Reforma)*, prologue by Agustín Cue Canovas (Mexico City: Gráficos Galeza, 1960), 137–38; Manuel F. Loera [Junta President] to Dario Balandario [Director of *El Diario Oficial*], n.d., AHEACM, *Funerales*, 1:35.

66. *El Monitor Republicano*, 27 March 1881: 4; *El Siglo XIX*, 28 March 1881: 2, 29 March 1881: 3, 2 April 1881: 1; *La Libertad*, 29 March 1881: 2, 2 April 1881: 1; *El Nacional*, 2 April 1881: 1; *El Socialista*, 31 March 1881: 2–3; *La Patria*, 2 April 1881: 1; Arenas Guzmán, *Cincuenta retablos de la vida porfiriana*, 100–101; Ozouf, *Festivals and the French Revolution*, 9, 133–34; Barbara A. Tenenbaum, "Streetwise History: The Paseo de la Reforma and the Porfirian State, 1876–1910," in Beezley, Martin, and French, *Rituals of Rule, Rituals of Resistance*, 127–50.

67. *El Nacional*, 2 April 1881: 1.

68. Ibid.; *La Patria*, 2 April 1881: 1.

69. *El Monitor Republicano*, 24 March 1881: 3, 25 March 1881: 3, 27 March 1881: 3–4, 2 April 1881: 3; *El Siglo XIX*, 28 March 1881: 2, 1 April 1881: 3; *Diario Oficial*, 26 March 1881: 1; *La Libertad*, 29 March 1881: 2, 2 April 1881: 1; *La Patria*, 2 April 1881: 1; *Two Republics*, 3 April 1881: 5; *La Voz de México*, 3 April 1881: 1; *La República*, 2 April 1881: 1; Arenas Guzmán, *Cincuenta retablos de la vida porfiriana*, 101.

70. *El Siglo XIX*, 2 April 1881: 1.

71. González's alleged sickness had nothing to do with his absence, since programs published in advance on March 29 indicated that Minister of War Treviño would represent the president. See *La Libertad*, 29 March 1881: 2. *Diario Oficial*, 1 April 1881: 3; *El Monitor Republicano*, 2 April 1881: 3; *El Siglo XIX*, 1 April 1881: 3; *La Patria*, 2 April 1881: 1; *Two Republics*, 3 April 1881: 5; *La Voz de México*, 3 April 1881: 1; *La República*, 2 April 1881: 1; Arenas Guzmán, *Cincuenta retablos de la vida porfiriana*, 102.

72. *La Voz de México*, 3 April 1881: 1. See also *El Nacional*, 2 April 1881: 1.

73. González Ortega to Pedro Ogazón, 30 October 1859, and *Diario de Avisos*, 26 August 1859,

both cited in Cadenhead, *González Ortega*, 24–26. The nickname "Devil Preacher" owed something to the late-colonial play *El diablo predicador*, which was banned by the censor and Inquisition. See Viqueira Albán, *Propriety and Permissiveness in Bourbon Mexico*, 64. Even Justo Sierra labeled him "an enraged anti-clerical," "the persecutor of priests," and "the terror of the bishops; see Sierra, *Juárez*, 173.

74. General José Montesinos, funeral oration for Jesús González Ortega, 1 April 1881, Mining College, *Diario Oficial*, 4 April 1881: 1.

75. Reprinted in *El Monitor Republicano*, 22 March 1881: 3; and *El Hijo de Trabajo*, 3 April 1881: 1.

76. *El Monitor Republicano*, 22 March 1881: 3

77. Ibid. See also Juvenal's editorial in *El Monitor Republicano*, 29 March 1881: 1.

78. *La Libertad*, 1 April 1881: 2. Other clerical organs heavily criticized González Ortega. *El Semanario Religioso* of Monterrey attacked him as a vulgar bandit, sparking *La Revista* of the same city to respond: "Reactionaries and traitors have always called the chiefs of the liberal army this. From the mouths of such men the word bandit, applied to patriots, is a title of glory. The executioners of Tacubaya, the assassins of Ocampo and Comonfort, the lackeys of Napoleon III, the traitors to their country in Miramar and traitors to Maximilian in México, they cannot insult the republicans without praising them" (reprinted in *El Monitor Republicano*, 30 March 1881: 3). *El Socialista* of Mexico City also returned fire: "Our esteemed colleague *Semanario Religioso* needs more than libel to slander truly historic and glorious reputations such as that of General González Ortega" (31 March 1881: 1).

79. *El Partido Liberal*, 1 March 1895: 3; *Mexican Herald*, 31 May 1895: 5.

80. Montesinos, funeral oration for Jesús González Ortega, 1 April 1881.

81. Ibid.; Arnulfo M. García, funeral oration for Jesús González Ortega, 2 March 1881, Saltillo, *El Defensor de la Constitucion* (Zacatecas), 7 April 1881: 3. Poet-nationalist Manuel Gutiérrez Nájera recounted González Ortega's triumphal entry into Mexico City on December 25, 1860, in *El Nacional*, 31 March 1881: 1.

82. See Charles A. Weeks, *The Juárez Myth in Mexico* (Tuscaloosa: University of Alabama Press, 1987).

83. *La Libertad*, 1 April 1881: 2.

84. Ibid., 27 September 1881: 2.

85. Ibid., 30 October 1880: 1, 6 October 1881: 1; *El Siglo XIX*, 8 October 1881: 2; *Two Republics*, 9 October 1881: 5; *Semanario Literario Ilustrado de El Tiempo*, 4 March 1901: 117; Pedro Santoni, *Mexicans at Arms: Puro Federalists and the Politics of War, 1845–1848* (Fort Worth: Texas Christian University Press, 1996), 30, 37; Nereo Rodríguez Barragán, *El General Dn. Mariano Arista (en el centenario de su muerte)* (San Luís Potosí: Universitaria, 1955), 6–9, 15–21.

86. On his deathbed, Arista asked that his heart be removed and sent to his former secretary, Manuel Gutiérrez, for burial in San Luís Potosí. Consul Batalha complied and gave the organ to Fernando Ramírez, who happened to be returning to Mexico after travels in Belgium. Ramírez turned it over to a partisan of Arista who then gave it to ex-governor of San Luís Potosí Juan Bustamante. Bustamante deposited it in a crystal vase, but the heart was passed from bureaucrat to bureaucrat for over a decade. See Manuel Gutiérrez Nájera's article in *El Siglo XIX*, 11 October 1881: 3; and Rodríguez Barragán, *El General Dn. Mariano Arista*, 9–10. As macabre as this story sounds, it is likely true since Gutiérrez Nájera, the extraordinary poet-nationalist of the Porfirian era, was the son of Arista's personal secretary and had read the correspondence between his father and Batalha.

87. Félix Romero, congressional speech, 22 September 1881, Chamber of Deputies, *El Siglo XIX*, 23 September 1881: 1; Guillermo Prieto, funeral oration for Mariano Arista, 8 October 1881, Rotonda de los Hombres Ilustres, *El Siglo XIX*, 17 October 1881: 1; Guillermo Prieto, congressional speech, 24 September 1881, in México, Congreso, Cámara de Diputados, *Diario de los Debates de la Cámara de Diputados, 10a Legislatura Constitucional de la Unión, Año de 1881*, 3 vols. (Mexico City: Tip. Literaria de Filomena Mata, 1881), 3:104 (hereafter cited as *Diario de los Debates, Año de 1881*).

88. José Ceballos, funeral oration for Mariano Arista, 8 October 1881, Mining Palace, in *Diario de los Debates, Año de 1881*, October 10, 1881, 3:1; and *El Monitor Republicano*, 9 October 1881: 4.

89. Joaquín Alcalde, speech, 12 October 1880, Chamber of Deputies, in México, Congreso, Cámara de Diputados, *Diario de los Debates de la Cámara de Diputados, Décima Legislatura Constitucional de la Union, Año de 1880,* 3 vols. (Mexico City: Tipografía de F. Mata, 1880), 1:390 (hereafter cited as *Diario de los Debates, Año de 1880*). See also Couttolenne, speech, 22 October 1880, Chamber of Deputies, in ibid., 1:487–88; and the article in *La Libertad,* 30 October 1880: 1.

90. *La Libertad,* 30 October 1880: 1.

91. *Diario de los Debates, Año de 1880,* 1:388–89.

92. Ibid., 1:390–91; italics added.

93. Ibid., 1:391, 486–88; *Diario de los Debates, Año de 1881,* 3:73–74, 99–100, 105, 921; AHEACM, *Funerales,* 1:34; *Diario Oficial,* 23 September 1881: 1; *El Siglo XIX,* 23 September 1881: 1, 1 October 1881: 1.

94. *Diario de los Debates, Año de 1881,* 3:82, 98–104; *Diario Oficial,* 26 September 1881: 1, 29 September 1881: 1, 1 October 1881: 2, 6 October 1881: 1; *La Libertad,* 28 September 1881: 3, 30 September 1881: 2; *El Siglo XIX,* 3 October 1881: 2–3, 5 October 1881: 1; *El Monitor Republicano,* 4 October 1881: 2; *El Nacional,* 4 October 1881: 2; *El Socialista,* 27 September 1881: 3.

95. *Diario de la Marina* (Havana), reprinted in *El Siglo XIX,* 29 September 1881: 1; *La Libertad,* 30 September 1881: 2; *Diario Oficial,* 30 September 1881: 1; *El Siglo XIX,* 3 October 1881: 2–3, 15 October 1881: 1; *El Nacional,* 1 October 1881: 1, 8 October 1881: 2; *El Monitor Republicano,* 6 October 1881: 3, 7 October 1881: 3.

96. *El Siglo XIX,* 5 October 1881: 1, 6 October 1881: 2, 8 October 1881: 1–2; *El Nacional,* 8 October 1881: 2; *El Hijo del Trabajo,* 9 October 1881: 1.

97. Ignacio Revueltas [Gral. Comandante Militar] to Secretario de Guerra [Gerónimo Treviño], 4 October 1881, AHBNAH, 262; Treviño to Revueltas, 3 October 1881, AHBNAH , 261.

98. Revueltas to Secretario de Guerra, 11 October 1881, AHBNAH, 265.

99. Brocklehurst, *Mexico To-Day,* 50. See also John E. Stealey III, ed., *Porte Crayon's Mexico: David Hunter Strother's Diaries in the Early Porfirian Era, 1879–1885* (Kent: Kent State University Press, 2006), 380.

100. José Ceballos, funeral oration for Mariano Arista, 8 October 1881, Mining Palace, *El Siglo XIX,* 10 October 1881: 1.

101. *El Siglo XIX,* 26 September 1881: 2, 6 October 1881: 2, 10 October 1881: 2; *El Nacional,* 27 September 1881: 3, 1 October 1881: 2, 4 October 1881: 2; *Two Republics,* 2 October 1881: 5, 9 October 1881: 5; *Diario Oficial,* 6 October 1881: 1; *El Monitor Republicano,* 7 October 1881: 2; *El Hijo del Trabajo,* 9 October 1881: 1; Rodríguez Barragán, *El General Dn. Mariano Arista,* 14.

102. *Diario de los Debates, Año de 1881,* 3:100; AHEACM, *Funerales,* 1:34; *El Siglo XIX,* 26 September 1881: 2, 7 October 1881: 2, 10 October 1881: 1; *Diario Oficial,* 7 October 1881: 1; *La República,* 8 October 1881: 3.

103. *Diario de los Debates, Año de 1881,* 3:177.

104. See the participating organizations in Manuel Dublán's funeral in *México Gráfico,* 7 June 1891: 3–6.

105. Mary Ryan, "The American Parade: Representations of the Nineteenth-Century Social Order," in Hunt, *The New Cultural History,* 134.

106. William E. French and Katherine Elaine Bliss, eds., *Gender, Sexuality, and Power in Latin America since Independence* (Wilmington, Del.: Rowman and Littlefield, 2007), 2.

107. *El Siglo XIX,* 11 October 1881: 3; *El Nacional,* 13 October 1881: 2. The Spanish sailors were praised by everyone who delivered a speech that week. Guillermo Prieto's words were exemplary: "Noble Spain, obeying your maternal instincts, Spain which is known for its glory and chivalry, you were given custody of a hero whose veins carry Mexican blood and who has given us fame. A thousand thanks, you generous warriors who have come to identify with the veneration of our hero and our sorrow over his loss" (funeral oration for Mariano Arista, 2).

108. *El Nacional,* 8 October 1881: 3; *El Siglo XIX,* 8 October 1881: 2, 12 October 1881: 2; *Two Republics,* 9 September 1887: 2; *El Imparcial,* 7 September 1900: 1, 23 February 1901: 1, 26 February 1901: 2; *El Mundo Ilustrado,* 17 February 1901: [8]; *Mexican Herald,* 26 February 1901: 2; Rodríguez Barragán, *El General Dn. Mariano Arista,* 13.

109. Coerver, *Porfirian Interregnum,* 63–65, 100–101, 192–93, 247–303.

110. Manuel Romero Rubio to Bernardo Reyes, telegram (n.d., 1885), Archivo General Bernardo Reyes, Archivo Condumex, Mexico City, carpeta 3, legajo 538, documento 1.

111. *Letters by J. A. Zabriskie to the Tucson "Star": Mexico in 1889* (San Francisco: n.p., 1889), 34.

112. Frank A. Knapp Jr., *The Life of Sebastián Lerdo de Tejada, 1823–1889: A Study of Influence and Obscurity* (Austin: University of Texas Press, 1951), vii, 265.

113. *El Siglo XIX,* 22 April 1889: 1; *Diario del Hogar,* 23 April 1889: 1; *Two Republics,* 23 April 1889: 1; Máximo Silva, *Sebastián Lerdo de Tejada, 1823–1889: In Memoriam* (Mexico City: Tip. de "El Partido Liberal," 1889), 27–31, 45–48; Knapp, *The Life of Lerdo de Tejada,* 251–54; Friedrich Katz, "Mexico: Restored Republic and Porfiriato," in *Cambridge History of Latin America,* ed. Leslie Bethell (New York: Cambridge University Press, 1986), 5:16–20; *El Porfiriato,* in *HMM* 8:106, 250–52.

114. See Knapp, *The Life of Lerdo de Tejada,* 255–63.

115. The telegram from Romero Rubio to Lerdo de Tejada was published in *Diario Oficial,* 23 April 1889: 1; *El Siglo XIX,* 23 April 1889: 1; *El Partido Liberal,* 24 April 1889: 2; *Diario del Hogar,* 24 April 1889: 1; and *La Patria,* 24 April 1889: 3, 25 April 1889: 1.

116. *Diario del Hogar,* 24 April 1889: 2, 26 April 1889: 3, 30 April 1889: 3; *Diario Oficial,* 27 April 1889: 2; *El Partido Liberal,* 30 April 1889: 2.

117. *Diario del Hogar,* 24 April 1889: 1, 1 May 1889: 1. See similar comments in *Two Republics,* 24 April 1889: 1.

118. *Diario del Hogar,* 30 April 1889: 3, 4 May 1889: 3; *Two Republics,* 30 April 1889: 4, 4 May 1889: 14, 12 May 1889: 4; *El Siglo XIX,* 10 May 1889: 3, 11 May 1889: 1, 14 May 1889: 3; Silva, *Sebastián Lerdo de Tejada,* 55–60.

119. Benedict Anderson, *Imagined Communities: Reflections on the Origin and Spread of Nationalism,* rev. ed. (London: Verso, 1991), 11–12.

120. *El Monitor Republicano,* 14 May 1889: 2; *Two Republics,* 9 May 1889: 2, 14 May 1889: 4; *El Siglo XIX,* 10 May 1889: 1, 11 May 1889: 1, 13 May 1889: 2, 14 May 1889: 3; *El Tiempo,* 14 May 1889: 2.

121. Cosío Villegas remarked that Escobedo finally accomplished what he failed to do in 1878. See *El Porfiriato,* in *HMM* 8:251, 289; *Two Republics,* 14 May 1889: 4; *El Monitor Republicano,* 14 May 1889: 2.

122. *El Monitor Republicano,* 15 May 1889: 2; *El Siglo XIX,* 14 May 1889: 2; *Two Republics,* 9 May 1889: 2, 14 May 1889: 2.

123. *Two Republics,* 9 May 1889: 2, 14 May 1889: 4; *El Siglo XIX,* 10 May 1889: 2, 11 May 1889: 1, 13 May 1889: 2; *El Monitor Republicano,* 12 May 1889: 3.

124. *El Tiempo,* 15 May 1889: 2. Quotes from *El Siglo XIX,* 14 May 1889: 2.

125. Scott, *Domination and the Arts of Resistance,* xiii, 15: "It is particularly in the latter realm of relative discursive freedom, outside the earshot of powerholders, where the hidden transcript is to be sought. The disparity between what we find here and what is said in the presence of power is a rough measure of what has been suppressed from power-laden political communication" (25).

126. William Roseberry, "Hegemony and the Language of Contention," in *Everyday Forms of State Formation: Revolution and the Negotiation of Rule in Modern Mexico,* ed. Gilbert M. Joseph and Daniel Nugent (Durham: Duke University Press, 1994), 364.

127. E. P. Thompson, *Customs in Common* (New York: New Press, 1991), 8; Scott, *Domination and the Arts of Resistance,* 160–61. Scott's assertion that oral cultures are more resistant to domination creates a false dichotomy between literate and oral cultures. If anything, workers formed their ideas from a fluid mix of oral traditions, public experiences, and unrestricted access to newspapers that were passed around and sometimes read aloud in the workplace and in homes. The fact that this journalist recorded and reported their testimony in *El Siglo XIX* suggests a working-class readership. I wish to acknowledge the anonymous reviewer for this critique.

128. For Scott's notion of a "public transcript" in hegemonic societies, see the introduction of this study; and Scott, *Domination and the Arts of Resistance,* 4, 18.

129. *El Partido Liberal,* 23 April 1889: 1–2, 24 April 1889: 1; *El Siglo XIX,* 23 April 1889: 2; *Diario Oficial,* 25 April 1889: 2, 9 May 1889: 2; *Two Republics,* 9 May 1889: 2, 12 May 1889: 4, 14 May 1889: 4; *Diario del Hogar,* 24 April 1889: 2, 11 May 1889: 1; *La Patria,* 12 May 1889:

3; *El Monitor Republicano,* 12 May 1889: 3. Prieto's speech was reprinted in *El Siglo XIX,* 24 April 1889: 1.

130. José López-Portillo y Rojas asserts that Mexican constitutional history ended in 1888; see his *Elevación y caída de Porfirio Díaz* (Mexico City: Librería Española, 1921), 209.

131. *Two Republics,* 10 May 1889: 4, 15 May 1889: 4; *El Siglo XIX,* 9 May 1889: 1, 14 May 1889: 2, 20 May 1889: 1, 21 May 1889: 1, 22 May 1889: 1. Lerdo was extolled as a "man of law" even in the memorial book dedicated to him. See Silva, *Sebastián Lerdo de Tejada,* 15–19.

132. The full text appeared in *El Siglo XIX,* 15 May 1889: 1; and Silva, *Sebastián Lerdo de Tejada,* 73–75.

133. *El Monitor Republicano,* 15 May 1889: 2; *El Porfiriato,* in *HMM* 8:252. *El Tiempo* regarded Bulnes's speech as "allusive." Historian Daniel Cosío Villegas, who cared little for Bulnes, described his speech as "inconsequential"; see *HMM* 8:290.

134. *Two Republics,* 15 May 1889: 4.

135. *El Siglo XIX,* 14 May 1889: 2; *Letters by J. A. Zabriskie to the Tucson "Star,"* 33–34; *Two Republics,* 4 May 1889: 4, 14 May 1889: 2, 15 May 1889: 4; *El Monitor Republicano,* 15 May 1889: 2.

136. *El Porfiriato,* in *HMM* 8:290–92.

137. Roseberry, "Hegemony and the Language of Contention," 364.

138. *El Porfiriato,* in *HMM* 8:xiv.

139. Ibid., xv.

140. On the funeral as spontaneous uprising, see Avner Ben-Amos, "The Sacred Center of Power: Paris and Republican State Funerals," *Journal of Interdisciplinary History* 22, no. 1 (Summer 1991): 27–48.

141. Ozouf, *Festivals and the French Revolution,* 11.

CHAPTER 3

1. Federico Gamboa, *Mi diario: Mucho de mi vida y algo de la de otros,* 5 vols. (Mexico City: Consejo Nacional de la Cultura y las Artes, 1994), 1:139–40.

2. Benedict Anderson, *The Spectre of Comparisons: Nationalism, Southeast Asia and the World* (New York: Verso, 1998), 26.

3. *La Libertad,* 5 May 1879: 3; *Two Republics,* 21 September 1878: 2, 6 May 1885: 4, 6 May 1886: 4, 5 May 1891: 4, 6 May 1891: 4; Aurelio de los Reyes, *Cine y sociedad en México, 1896–1930* (Mexico City: Universidad Nacional Autónoma de México, Cineteca Nacional, 1981), 21–23.

4. See Rebecca Earle, "'Padres de la Patria' and the Ancestral Past: Commemorations of Independence in Nineteenth-Century Spanish America," *Journal of Latin American Studies* 34, no. 4 (November 2002): 775–805.

5. Even after September 16 was assigned to the calendar, Conservative regimes chose to celebrate Mexican independence on September 27. In 1849, *El Universal* attacked the tradition of celebrating independence on the anniversary of Hidalgo's cry for independence. Edited by Conservative polemicist, historian, and statesman Lucas Alamán, the newspaper put forth September 27 as the "Great Day of the Nation," and an Iturbide cult flourished in the Conservative writings of 1846–53. See Charles A. Hale, *Mexican Liberalism in the Age of Mora, 1821–1853* (New Haven: Yale University Press, 1968), 12–18, 21–22. For the first Independence Day celebrated on September 16, see Luis González Obregón, *México viejo y anecdótico,* 3rd ed. (Mexico City: Espasa-Calpe Mexicana, 1966), 154–56.

6. William H. Beezley, "Amending Memories: The Nimble Mnemonics of Nineteenth-Century Celebrations of Independence," in *Viva Mexico! Viva la Independencia! Celebrations of September 16,* ed. William H. Beezley and David E. Lorey (Wilmington, Del.: SR Books, 2001), 5–6, 12–18. In the same collection, see Carmen Nava Nava and Isabel Fernández Tejeda, "Images of Independence in the Nineteenth Century. The Grito de Dolores: History and Myth," 1–42.

7. Bastille Day was not incorporated permanently into the French national calendar until 1880. See John R. Gillis, "Memory and Identity: The History of a Relationship," in *Commemorations: The Politics of National Identity,* ed. John R. Gillis (Princeton: Princeton

University Press, 1994), 3–24; Michael Kammen, *Mystic Chords of Memory: The Transformation of Tradition in American Culture* (New York: Knopf, 1991).

8. Hubert Howe Bancroft, *History of Mexico*, 6 vols. (San Francisco: History Co., 1888), 6:447, 621; Carleton Beals, *Porfirio Díaz: Dictator of Mexico* (Philadelphia: J. B. Lippincott, 1932), 239; Ethel Brilliana Harley (Mrs. Alec) Tweedie, *The Maker of Modern Mexico: Porfirio Díaz* (New York: John Lane Co., 1906), 284.

9. For this trend in France, see Mona Ozouf, *Festivals and the French Revolution*, trans. Alan Sheridan (Cambridge: Harvard University Press, 1988), 33–34.

10. Don M. Coerver, *The Porfirian Interregnum: The Presidency of Manuel González of Mexico, 1880–1884* (Fort Worth: Texas Christian University Press, 1979), 6; Bancroft, *History of Mexico*, 6:447.

11. Baz to Porfirio Díaz, 17 October 1890, Colección General Porfirio Díaz, legajo 15, caja 24, documento 11821 (hereafter cited as CPD followed by legajo, caja, and documento numbers).

12. Garcia Martínez to Rafael Chousal, 7 September 1893, Archivo Rafael Chousal, Universidad Nacional Autónoma de México, caja 8, expediente 101, folio 60–63 (hereafter cited as ACH followed by caja, expediente, and folio numbers); Garcia Martínez to Chousal, 12 September 1893, ACH 8:101:65–67; Garcia Martínez to Chousal, 18 September 1893, ACH 8:101:69–70.

13. Supreme Court Justice Félix Romero, toast to Díaz, *Mexican Herald*, 15 September 1899: 8. Romero congratulated Díaz annually on behalf of the Oaxacan colony in Mexico City.

14. *El Imparcial*, 8 September 1899: 1.

15. C. Ventimilla to Rafael Chousal, 11 July 1892, ACH 6:77:20; Ventimilla to Chousal, [n.d.] July 1892, ACH 6:77:24; Círculo de Amigos [Pedro Rincón Gallardo, Guillermo Landa y Escandón et al.], [September 1893], ACH 8:101:34.

16. *El Imparcial*, 15 September 1904: 1, 16 September 1904: 1.

17. Juan A. Hernández to Díaz, 17 September 1895, ACH 10:139:20–21.

18. Hernández to Díaz, 31 August 1895, ACH 10:139:71–72; Díaz to Hernández, 5 September 1895, ACH 10:139:73; Hernández to Díaz, 2 September 1895, ACH 10:139:65–66; Díaz to Hernández, 7 September 1895, ACH 10:139:58; Hernández to Díaz, 7 September 1895, ACH 10:139:56–57. Quotes from Hernández to Díaz, 21 September 1895, ACH 10:139:9–10; Díaz to Hernández, [September 1895], ACH 10:139:11; Hernández to Díaz, 26 September 1895, ACH 10:139:1–2.

19. *El Imparcial*, 16 September 1902: 1.

20. Ibid., 13 September 1899: 1, 16 September 1899: 1–2.

21. Eric J. Hobsbawm and Terence Ranger, "Introduction: Inventing Traditions," in *The Invention of Tradition*, ed. Eric J. Hobsbawm and Terence Ranger (Cambridge: Cambridge University Press, 1983), 1–2; Eric J. Hobsbawm, "Mass-Producing Traditions: Europe 1870–1914," in Hobsbawm and Ranger, *The Invention of Tradition*, 263–65.

22. Lucas Alamán, *Historia de Méjico desde los primeros movimientos que prepararon su independencia en el año de 1808 hasta la época presente*, 5 vols. (Mexico City: Instituto Cultural Hélenico, Fondo de Cultura Económica, 1985), 1:375–76; Nava and Fernández, "Images of Independence in the Nineteenth Century," 8–19.

23. William H. Beezley, Cheryl English Martin, and William E. French, "Introduction: Constructing Consent, Inciting Conflict," in *Rituals of Rule, Rituals of Resistance: Public Celebrations and Popular Culture in Mexico*, ed. William H. Beezley, Cheryl English Martin, and William E. French (Wilmington, Del.: SR Books, 1994), xviii; Colin M. MacLachlan and William H. Beezley, *El Gran Pueblo: A History of Greater Mexico* (New York: Prentice Hall, 1994), 83. Maximilian issued a public *grito* on Independence Day 1864, but from Dolores Hidalgo. See Robert H. Duncan, "Political Legitimation and Maximilian's Second Empire in Mexico, 1864–1867," *Mexican Studies/Estudios Mexicanos* 12, no. 1 (Winter 1996): 54–57; Fernando Serrano Migallon, *El Grito de Independencia: Historia de una pasión nacional*, prologue by Andrés Henestrosa (Mexico City: Miguel Angel Porrúa, 1988), 117–21. *Two Republics*, 19 September 1868: 2; 16 September 1870: 3; 21 September 1873: 3; 20 September 1874: 3; 25 August 1875: 3; 20 September 1876: 3; 15 September 1877: 3; 22 September 1877: 2–3; 21 September 1878: 3; 20 September 1879: 3; 19 September 1880: 3; 18 September 1881: 5; 17 September 1882: 3; 15 September 1883: 4; 16 September 1883: 4; 18 September

1883: 2, 4; 15 September 1885: 4. *El Siglo XIX*, 14 September 1878: 1, 4; *El Nacional*, 16 September 1884: 2; *Actas de Cabildo del Ayuntamiento Constitucional de México*, Edición de "El Municipio Libre" (Mexico City: Imprenta de Dublan y Companía, 1885), January 2, 1884, 15; Moisés González Navarro, *El Porfiriato: La vida social*, in *Historia Moderna de México*, 9 vols., ed. Daniel Cosío Villegas (Mexico City: Editorial Hermes, 1955–72), 4:702 (hereafter cited as *HMM* followed by volume and page numbers); *Mexican Herald*, 15 June 1896: 1.

24. Serrano Migallon, *El Grito de Independencia*, 151–55; *El Nacional*, 18 September 1887: 2; *Two Republics*, 1 October 1887: 4. Guillermo Valleto headed the festivities committee of the City Council in 1887. From 1887 to 1903, the federal and city governments jointly spent 10,000–13,050 pesos a year on Independence Day decorations. México, Secretaría de Gobernación, *Memoria que el Secretario de Estado y del despacho de Gobernación presentada al Congreso de la Unión, correspondiente al período transcurrido del 1° de Enero de 1879 al 20 de Noviembre de 1880* (Mexico City: Tip. de Gonzalo A. Esteva, 1881), 89–90 (hereafter cited as *Memoria de Gobernación* [1879–80]). August and September budgets are in *Actas de Cabildo del Ayuntamiento Constitucional de México, Años 1886–1896*, Edición de "El Municipio Libre" (Mexico City: Imp. de la Escuela Correccional de Artes y Oficios, 1886–1900); *Actas de Cabildo del Ayuntamiento Constitucional de México, Años de 1897–1898* (Mexico City: Imprenta "Central," 1900–1902); *Actas de Cabildo del Ayuntamiento de la Ciudad de México, Años de 1898–1899* (Mexico City: A. Carranza y Comp., 1904); *Actas de Cabildo del Ayuntamiento Constitucional de México, Años de 1900–1901* (Mexico City: Imp. de "El Correo Español," 1905–7); *Actas de Cabildo del Ayuntamiento de la Ciudad de México, Años de 1901–1902* (Mexico City: A. Carranza e Hijos, 1909–10); *Actas Modernas de Cabildo, 1903* (Mexico City: Imp. particular G. Oropeza Velasco, 1911). All editions hereafter cited as *Actas de Cabildo* followed by year and page numbers. The Mexican national emblem is an eagle perched upon a nopal cactus and devouring a serpent.

25. *El Nacional*, 18 September 1887: 2.

26. Alfred Oscar Coffin, *Land Without Chimneys; or The Byways of Mexico* (Cincinnati: Editor Publishing Co., 1898), 211–12; Thomas U. Brocklehurst, *Mexico To-Day: A Country with a Great Future* (London: John Murray, 1883), 46; Nevin O. Winter, *Mexico and Her People of Today* (1907; rev. ed., Boston: L. C. Page and Co., 1923), 37; Salvador Novo, *Los paseos de la ciudad de México* (Mexico City: Fondo de la Cultura Económica, 1984), 10; González Navarro, *El Porfiriato*, in *HMM* 4:702; *Two Republics*, 15 September 1892: 1, 16 September 1892: 1. *Mexican Herald*, 15 September 1900: 8; 16 September 1900: 10, 16; 16 September 1901: 8; 16 September 1902: 5; 16 September 1903: 1. *Diario del Hogar*, 20 September 1891: 1; *El Popular*, 16 September 1907: 1. Writers in *Diario del Hogar* scolded the "false patriots who use the pretext of honoring the fatherland to shout 'mueras'": "It is not necessary for anyone to die, in order for Mexicans to live."

27. *Mexican Herald*, 16 September 1901: 8.

28. Claudio Lomnitz-Adler, *Exits from the Labyrinth: Culture and Ideology in the Mexican National Space* (Berkeley: University of California Press, 1992), 9.

29. Pierre Bourdieu, *Outline of a Theory of Practice*, trans. Richard Nice (New York: Cambridge University Press, 1977), 72, 76.

30. *El Imparcial*, 17 September 1904: 2.

31. *Actas de Cabildo* (1887), 372, 379, 383, 398, 451, 533, 537; Guillermo Valleto to Chousal, 7 July 1896, ACH 13:163:157–158; Ayuntamiento de la Ciudad de México, *Discurso del C. Ingeniero Sebastián Camacho Presidente del Ayuntamiento de 1896 al instalarse el de 1897. Contestación del C. Gobernador del Distrito Federal C. Lic. Rafael Rebollar y Memoria Documentada de los trabajos municipales de 1896* (Mexico City: Imp. y Lit. "La Europea," 1897), 170; Alfonso Alcocer, *La Campana de Dolores* (Mexico City: Departamento del Distrito Federal, 1985), 25–62; *Mexican Herald*, 18 June 1896: 2, 23 June 1896: 8, 29 June 1896: 8.

32. *Mexican Herald*, 29 June 1896: 8.

33. Alcocer, *La Campana de Dolores*, 63–85; *Actas de Cabildo* (1896), 180–81, 446, 461; Guillermo Valleto to Chousal, 7 July 1896, ACH 13:163:157–158; A. E. Hernández to Chousal, 25 August 1896, ACH 13:164:20; Thomas H. Russell, *Mexico in Peace and War* (Chicago: Reilly and Britton Syndicate, 1914), 161–63; González Navarro, *El Porfiriato*, in *HMM* 4:702; *El Mundo Semanario Ilustrado*, 12 July 1896: 23–24; *La Voz de México*, 29 July 1896: 2, 31 July 1896: 3. *Mexican Herald*, 17 August 1896: 2, 8; 25 August 1896: 8;

3 September 1896: 8; 4 September 1896: 8; 5 September 1896: 8; 13 September 1896: 2; 16 September 1896: 8.

34. Díaz's speech appears in the *Mexican Herald*, 15 September 1896: 1.

35. *Mexican Herald*, 7 September 1899: 5, 18 September 1899: 5; *El Imparcial*, 8 September 1900: 1, 11 September 1900: 1, 13 September 1900: 1.

36. Ayuntamiento de la Ciudad de México, *Discurso del Sr. Lic. Miguel S. Macedo, Presidente del Ayuntamiento en 1899. Discurso del Sr. D. Guillermo de Landa y Escandon Presidente del Ayuntamiento en 1900. Contestación del Gobernador del Distrito Federal Sr. Lic. Rafael Reballar y Memoria Documentada de los trabajos municipales de 1899* (Mexico City: Tip. y Lit. "La Europea," 1900), 275.

37. *El Tiempo Ilustrado*, 20 September 1908: 606, 27 September 1908: 622.

38. Ibid. Dozens of Catholic workers' associations joined the archbishop of Mexico to commemorate Iturbide on September 27. See *El Tiempo*, 27 September 1904: 2–3, 28 September 1904: 2–3.

39. *Mexican Herald*, 16 September 1901: 8.

40. For examples in other locales, see Ozouf, *Festivals and the French Revolution*, 126–28; Lynn Hunt, "Foreword," in Ozouf, *Festivals and the French Revolution*, x–xi; and Hobsbawm and Ranger, *The Invention of Tradition*, 9.

41. Secretaría del Gran Maestro de Ceremonias, "Ceremonial. Disposiciones Generales para la Fiesta Nacional del 16 de Setiembre de 1865," Archivo Histórico de la Biblioteca Nacional de Antropología e Historia (hereafter cited as AHBNAH), 1a Serie de papeles sueltos, caja 7, legajo 10, no. 26; Secretaría del Gran Maestro de Ceremonias, "Ceremonial que se observara para la inauguración de la Estatua de Morelos el día 30 de Setiembre de 1865, en la plazuela de Guardiola que tomará el nombre de Plazuela de Morelos," AHBNAH, 1a Serie de papeles sueltos, caja 7, legajo 10, no. 27. On this occasion four veterans unveiled the statue. In his own quest for legitimacy, Maximilian encouraged both Mexican nationalism and neo-Aztecism. See Duncan, "Political Legitimation and Maximilian's Second Empire in Mexico."

42. *Two Republics*, 23 September 1871: 2. Memorial services and military award ceremonies never took place on Independence Day under Lerdo de Tejada or during Díaz's first term or the González interregnum. See holiday programs in *Two Republics*, 21 September 1873: 3, 20 September 1874: 3, 25 August 1875: 3, 20 September 1876: 3, 15 September 1877: 3, 22 September 1877: 2–3, 21 September 1878: 3, 20 September 1879: 3, 19 September 1880: 3, 18 September 1881: 5.

43. *El Siglo XIX*, 14 September 1878: 1, 4; *El Correo de las Doce*, 15 September 1882: 3, 26 September 1882: 1; *El Nacional*, 15 September 1883: 4; *Two Republics*, 16 September 1886: 4, 17 September 1886; Duncan, "Political Legitimation and Maximilian's Second Empire in Mexico," 43. In 1885, there were only thirty surviving veterans of the Independence Wars, most of whom lived in other states and did not attend the ceremony. See *Two Republics*, 15 September 1885: 4. Independence Day memorial publications were expensive at 1 peso per copy, but since renowned poets and prose writers contributed to them they were often literary gems. See *Two Republics*, 17 September 1884: 4.

44. *El Tiempo Ilustrado*, 27 September 1908: 622.

45. *Mexican Herald*, 9 September 1895: 4; 16 September 1895: 4; 17 September 1895: 1; 17 September 1896: 1, 8; 11 September 1897: 1; 16 September 1897: 1; 2 September 1898: 1; 6 September 1898: 1; 8 September 1898: 1; 10 September 1898: 2; 12 September 1898: 3; 7 September 1899: 5; 10 September 1899: 5, 8; 12 September 1899: 8; 15 September 1899: 8; 16 September 1899: 1; 17 September 1899: 8; 17 September 1900: 1, 8; 11 September 1903: 5; 16 September 1903: 1; 17 September 1903: 1. *El Mundo Semanario Ilustrado*, 15 September 1895: 6; *El Imparcial*, 12 September 1899: 1, 17 September 1899: 1, 17 September 1900: 1–2, 17 September 1901: 1, 15 September 1905: 1, 16 September 1905: 1; *El Nacional*, 14 September 1900: 2; *El Popular*, 15 September 1907: 1, 17 September 1907: 3; Gustavo Casasola, *Efemérides Ilustrados del México de ayer*, 5 vols. (Mexico City: Ediciones Archivo Casasola, n.d.), 1:83, 269–70. Sosa and Casasús spoke in 1886.

46. *El Imparcial*, 17 September 1908: 1, 6–7.

47. Shortly after his visit, Congress authorized a payment of 2,000 pesos to Nunó for composing the music for the National Hymn. The decree, dated November 11, 1901, appears in Manuel Dublán and José María Lozano, eds., *Legislación mexicana, o colección completa*

de las disposiciones legislativas expedidas desde la independencia de la República, 34 vols. (Mexico City: Imprenta y Litografía de Eduardo Dublán y Comp., 1876–1904), 33 (1901): 367. *Mexican Herald*, 11 September 1901: 8; 13 September 1901: 2, 8; 16 September 1901: 8; 17 September 1901: 1–2; 18 September 1901: 8. *El Imparcial*, 18 September 1901: 2, 20 November 1901: 1, 21 November 1901: 1, 24 November 1901: 1; *Semanario Literario Ilustrado de El Tiempo*, 23 September 1901: 463; *Actas de Cabildo* (1901), 1172, 1175, 1184; Casasola, *Efemérides Ilustrados del México de ayer*, 1:169; *El Tiempo Ilustrado*, 14 October 1904: 2, 26 July 1908: 478; México, Secretaría de Gobernación, "Rotonda de los Hombres Ilustres" (pamphlet); Alfredo Desentis M., *Rotonda de los Hombes Ilustres* (Mexico City: Departamento del Distrito Federal, 1985), 85.

48. The full text of the speech appears in the *Mexican Herald*, 17 September 1896: 8; and *El Imparcial*, 17 September 1899: 1.
49. John E. Stealey III, ed., *Porte Crayon's Mexico: David Hunter Strother's Diaries in the Early Porfirian Era, 1879–1885* (Kent: Kent State University Press, 2006), 628.
50. On this problem of representation, see James C. Scott, *Domination and the Arts of Resistance: Hidden Transcripts* (New Haven: Yale University Press, 1990), 45–46.
51. "Informe que rinde la Comisión de Antiguedades al Señor Presidente de la República," 7 September 1895, ACH 11:147:182–187; Cahuantzi to Díaz, 7 September 1895, ACH 11:147:178–181; Díaz to Cahuantzi, 9 September 1895, ACH 11:147:188.
52. *Mexican Herald*, 11 November 1895: 4, 18 February 1896: 4. Subsecretary of War Escudero authorized Reyes to preserve the historic rifles in Nuevo León. See Reyes to Ignacio M. Escudero, 1 May 1895, Archivo General Bernardo Reyes, Archivo Condumex, Mexico City, carpeta 23, legajo 4449, documento 1 (hereafter cited as ABR followed by carpeta, legajo, and documento numbers); Escudero to Reyes, 4 May 1895, ABR 23:4455:1.
53. Reyes to Bernardo W. Gutiérrez, 22 June 1895, ABR Copiadores 18:11336; Reyes to Francisco Flores Saldaña, 22 June 1895, ABR Copiadores 18:11337; Reyes to Flores Saldaña, 25 June 1895, ABR Copiadores 18:11348; Reyes to Gutiérrez, 25 June 1895, ABR Copiadores 18:11349; Porfirio Díaz to Reyes, 9 July 1895, ABR 23:4530:1; Díaz to Reyes, 17 September 1895, ABR 23:4583:1; Escudero to Reyes, 28 September 1895, ABR 24:4603:1; [Reyes to Escudero], [n.d.] September 1895, ABR 24:4603:2; Díaz to Berriozábal, 17 September 1895, ACH 10:138:74; Reyes to Díaz, 26 September 1895, ACH 11:151:4.
54. Felipe Berriozábal to Porfirio Díaz, 19 September 1895, ACH 10:138:43.
55. *Mexican Herald*, 23 January 1898: 8; *El Mundo Semanario Ilustrado*, 1 July 1900: [6–7]. On the relationship between the public museum and the state, see Eric Davis, "The Museum and the Politics of Social Control in Modern Iraq," in Gillis, *Commemorations*, 90–104. In 1880, Congress debated whether to permit the French archaeologist Desiré Charnay to export objects he excavated in Yucatán to Europe where they would be placed on public display. Nationalists in Congress passed legislation against it, but Justo Sierra delivered an unpopular but reasoned speech in favor of exportation. See México, Congreso, Cámara de Diputados, *Diario de los Debates de la Cámara de Diputados, Décima Legislatura Constitucional de la Union, Año de 1880*, 3 vols. (Mexico City: Tipografía de F. Mata, 1880), 1:540, 542.
56. *Mexican Herald*, 11 November 1895: 4. For his role in rescuing the precious relic, Velásquez was hailed as a patriot. He went on to earn notoriety during the assassination attempt on Díaz in 1897. As police chief, Velásquez secretly orchestrated the execution of Díaz's would-be assassin Arnulfo Arroyo. When his conspiracy was exposed, he committed suicide while in police custody.
57. *El Imparcial*, 6 May 1903: 1.
58. *Mexican Herald*, 11 November 1895: 5, 3 December 1895: 5, 18 February 1896: 5, 22 September 1896: 2, 12 February 1898: 8, 16 September 1899: 1, 5 September 1898: 2, 1 September 1898: 8, 14 September 1898: 8; *El Imparcial*, 16 September 1899: 1–2, 13 September 1900: 1, 14 September 1900: 1, 16 September 1908: 1, 17 September 1908: 1; *Two Republics*, 21 August 1885: 4, 18 September 1887: 2, 12 September 1888: 4. For Independence Day 1898, passenger fares on the *Gran Pacifico* line that ran from Cuernavaca to Mexico City were 5 pesos for first class and 2.50 for second class. On the cult of the Virgin of Guadalupe, see Jacques Lafaye, *Quetzalcoatl and Guadalupe: The Formation of Mexican National Consciousness, 1531–1813*, trans. Benjamin Keen (Chicago: University of Chicago Press, 1976),

99–136, 288–300; Juan Gómez-Quiñones, "Social Change and Intellectual Discontent: The Growth of Mexican Nationalism, 1890–1911" (Ph.D. diss., University of California, Los Angeles, 1972), 21; Nava and Fernández, "Images of Independence in the Nineteenth Century," 20. The Mexican passion to recover antiquities was well illustrated when one nationalistic citizen stole a pre-Columbian codex from the Louvre. The act was lauded as patriotic. Beezley, Martin, and French, "Introduction," xviii; Beezley, "Amending Memories," 18–19; *Crónica oficial de las fiestas del primer Centenario de la Independencia de México, publicada bajo la dirección de Genaro García, por acuerdo de la Secretaría de Gobernación* (Mexico City: Talleres del Museo Nacional, 1911). Clementina Díaz de Ovando, *Las fiestas pátrias en el México hace un siglo, 1883* (Mexico City: Centro de Estudios de Historia de México Condumex, 1984); González Navarro, El Porfiriato, in *HMM* 4:702–3.

59. Guillermo Colín Sánchez, *Ignacio Zaragoza: Evocación de un héroe* (Mexico City: Editorial Porrúa, 1963), 249, 252.

60. Ibid., 246–51; Archivo Histórico del Ex-Ayuntamiento de la Ciudad de México, *Funerales y ceremonias fúnebres, 1779–1915,* legajo 1, expediente 22 (hereafter cited as AHEACM, *Funerales,* followed by legajo and expediente numbers). Extraordinary state funeral rites elevate the political and symbolic status of the deceased. For this argument as applied to Abraham Lincoln's assassination and sacred burial, see Barry Schwartz, "Mourning and the Making of a Sacred Symbol: Durkheim and the Lincoln Assassination," *Social Forces* 70, no. 2 (December 1991): 343–64.

61. AHEACM, *Funerales,* 1:22; Colín Sánchez, *Ignacio Zaragoza,* 262. The Colín Sánchez commemorative history, published in honor of the centennial of Cinco de Mayo and Zaragoza's death (the state of Coahuila declared 1962 the "Year of Zaragoza"), enumerates the hundreds of memorial acts performed over the century. The exhaustive study even lists every city and primary school named after Zaragoza. See Colín Sánchez, *Ignacio Zaragoza,* 254–76; Ignacio Manuel Altamirano, in Hira de Gortari Rabiela and Regina Hernández Franyuti, eds., *Memoria y encuentros: La ciudad de México y el Distrito Federal (1824–1928),* 3 vols. (Mexico City: Departamento del Distrito Federal, Instituto de Investigaciones Dr. José María Luís Mora, 1988), 2:260–61; *Two Republics,* 5 May 1868: 2, 9 May 1868: 1–2, 1 May 1869: 2, 5 May 1869: 2, 8 May 1869: 2, 7 May 1870: 3, 11 May 1872: 3, 10 May 1873: 2, 10 May 1874: 2–3, 5 May 1875: 3, 10 May 1876: 3.

62. Patrick J. McNamara, *Sons of the Sierra: Juárez, Díaz, and the People of Ixtlán, Oaxaca, 1855–1920* (Chapel Hill: University of North Carolina Press, 2006), 135.

63. Col. Cresencio González to Porfirio Díaz, 5 May 1877, CPD 2:2:2862; Manuel J. de Lizaola to Díaz, 25 May 1877, CPD 2:2:775.

64. *Two Republics,* 5 May 1877: 3; Díaz circular, 6 May 1877, CPD 2:3:1109.

65. Alberto María Carreño, ed., *Archivo del General Porfirio Díaz, Memorias y Documentos,* 30 vols. (Mexico City: Editorial Elede, 1949–61), 29:61–62; *Periódico Oficial del Gobierno del Distrito Federal,* 5 May 1878: 1; *Two Republics,* 4 May 1878: 2–3, 11 May 1878: 3, 5 February 1887: 2, 6 May 1887: 4, 24 June 1887: 4; *La Libertad,* 4 May 1879: 3. To recognize Miguel Negrete's role at Cinco de Mayo, the revolutionary state added a ceremony to him at his tomb at the Dolores Cemetery every May 5. For the civic calendar of 1940, see Manuel de J. Solís, *Historia de la Bandera, Himno, Escudo y Calendario Civico Nacionales* (Mexico City: n.p., 1940), 131–220.

66. *Memoria de Gobernación* (1879–80), 89–90; México, Secretaría de Gobernación, *Memoria que presenta al Congreso el Lic. Manuel Romero Rubio Secretario de Estado y del Despacho de Gobernación. Corresponde al período transcurrido del 1° de Diciembre de 1884 al 30 de Junio de 1886* (Mexico City: Imprenta del Gobierno, 1887), "Sección Tercera," 19–20. *Actas de Cabildo* (1886), 220, 222; (1887), 199, 215, 219, 222, 233; (1888) 211, 214, 223, 226; (1889) 136, 154, 166; (1890) 145, 157, 161.

67. *Two Republics,* 8 May 1881: 5, 7 May 1882: 3, 6 May 1883: 3, 5 May 1885: 4, 6 May 1885: 4, 5 May 1893: 4; *El Imparcial,* 3 May 1900: 1, 5 May 1900, 1. For photographs showing the militaristic character of Cinco de Mayo, see May issues of *El Mundo Semanario Ilustrado,* especially 9 May 1897 and 15 May 1898. Photographs also appear in Casasola, *Efemérides Ilustrados del México de ayer,* 1:46, 226, 316.

68. Editor J. Mastella Clarke, in *Two Republics,* 6 May 1887: 2. If patriotic ritual failed, Díaz could fall back on force. Clarke continued: "With a regularly paid, well-fed and disciplined

army at his command and railway facilities for the rapid movement of troops, the stability of President Díaz's administration would be assured even if it did not possess, as it does, the loyal and patriotic support of the great majority of the Mexican people."

69. *El Imparcial*, 2 May 1901: 1, 6 May 1901: 1, 6 May 1902: 1.

70. *Two Republics*, 3 May 1879: 3, 10 May 1879: 2, 9 May 1880: 3, 8 May 1881: 5, 6 May 1883: 3, 5 May 1885: 4, 6 May 1885: 4, 4 May 1886: 4, 5 May 1886: 4, 5 May 1887: 4, 6 May 1887: 2, 6 May 1888: 4, 3 May 1890: 4, 4 May 1890: 4, 6 May 1890: 4, 5 May 1891: 4, 6 May 1891: 4, 4 May 1892: 1, 6 May 1892: 1, 5 May 1893: 4, 6 May 1893: 4, 6 May 1894: 4; *El Correo de las Doce*, 5 May 1882: 1, 7 May 1882: 1, 5 May 1883: 2, 9 May 1883: 3. *Mexican Herald*, 5 May 1896: 8; 6 May 1896: 8; 5 May 1897: 1; 6 May 1897: 5; 2 May 1898: 8; 5 May 1898: 8; 6 May 1898: 4, 8; 3 May 1899: 8; 5 May 1899: 2, 5; 6 May 1899: 8; 6 May 1900: 9, 16; 5 May 1901: 16; 6 May 1901: 1–2; 6 May 1902: 2; 6 May 1903: 1; 6 May 1904: 1. *El Nacional*, 7 May 1887: 2. *El Imparcial*, 6 May 1899: 1; 6 May 1900: 1; 5 May 1906: 1; 6 May 1906: 1; 5 May 1909: 1; 6 May 1909: 1; 7 May 1909: 1, 8. *El Tiempo*, 6 May 1903: 1, 6 May 1904: 1, 5 May 1905: 1, 6 May 1905: 1. For photographs of this annual commemoration, see *El Mundo Semanario Ilustrado*, 7 May 1899: 323, 12 May 1901: [6–7]; *El Tiempo Ilustrado*, 7 May 1905: 278, 14 May 1905: 305; and *El Mundo Ilustrado*, 8 May 1910: [6–7].

71. *Two Republics*, 6 May 1891: 4.

72. Emeterio de la Garza, public oration, 5 May 1898, Alameda, *Mexican Herald*, 6 May 1898: 4.

73. *El Imparcial*, 7 January 1901: 1–2, 8 January 1901: 1. Díaz had laid the first stone for the monument in 1896. The French Colony of Puebla organized the inauguration ceremony in 1901.

74. Benedict Anderson, *Imagined Communities: Reflections on the Origin and Spread of Nationalism*, rev. ed. (London: Verso, 1991), 9. Plans to bury common citizen-soldiers who were killed in battle actually existed since the French Revolution, but they were never enacted. In 1792, for example, republican revolutionaries proposed to bury fallen soldiers in a place of burial in the heart of Paris, but nothing ever came of this. Ordinary soldiers were consigned to oblivion until after World War I. See Gillis, "Memory and Identity," 9.

75. de la Garza, public oration, 5 May 1898, 4.

76. Manuel Flores, Cinco de Mayo speech, *El Imparcial*, 6 May 1899: 1.

77. *La Libertad*, 5 May 1879: 3. *Two Republics*, 5 May 1885: 4; 6 May 1885: 4; 5 May 1886: 4; 6 May 1886: 4; 6 May 1887: 4; 3 May 1888: 4; 6 May 1888: 2, 4; 4 May 1889: 4; 5 May 1889: 4; 7 May 1889: 2, 4; 6 May 1890: 4; 5 May 1891: 4; 6 May 1891: 4. *La Voz de México*, 3 May 1896: 2; *Mexican Herald*, 5 May 1897: 8; Ayuntamiento de la Ciudad de México, *Discurso del C. Ingeniero Sebastián Camacho, Presidente del Ayuntamiento de 1896 al instalarse el de 1897*, 171; *El Imparcial*, 3 May 1899: 1, 5 May 1899: 1, 6 May 1899: 1. See Appendix D for a list of the monuments on the Paseo de la Reforma.

78. Jesús F. Contreras to Díaz, 24 November 1890, CPD 15:27:13200.

79. General Díaz, address to his victorious troops, 2 April 1862, Puebla, *Mexican Herald*, 23 November 1902: 10.

80. Francisco P. Mendoza to Mena, 29 September 1903, ACH 26:235:1–4; Mendoza to Mena, 17 August 1903, ACH 26:235:5–12; *El Imparcial*, 2 April 1906: 1, 3 April 1906: 1.

81. A coterie of military officers who fought on April 2 sent their well-wishes to Díaz annually. See Simón Arlat and Cátulo A. Vera to Díaz, 2 April 1878, CPD 3:1:306; Amado Santa Cruz to Díaz, 2 April 1878, CPD 3:1:324; Felipe Serra to Díaz, 2 April 1878, CPD 3:1:327; Francisco Palencia to Díaz, 2 April 1879, CPD 4:1:53.

82. Juan Mateos, oration, 2 April 1906, *El Imparcial*, 3 April 1906: 1.

83. Tony Morgan, "Proletarians, Politicos, and Patriarchs: The Use and Abuse of Cultural Customs in the Early Industrialization of Mexico City, 1880–1910," in Beezley, Martin, and French, *Rituals of Rule, Rituals of Resistance*, 153; *El Imparcial*, 3 April 1906: 1.

84. *El Imparcial*, 2 April 1903: 1.

85. *Two Republics*, 6 April 1878: 2–3, 3 April 1879: 3, 3 April 1881: 5, 28 February 1888: 2, 3 April 1888: 2, 2 April 1892: 4, 3 April 1894: 4; Francisco Ramírez Castañeda to Chousal, 25 March 1892, ACH 5:73:44–45; *Mexican Herald*, 3 April 1899: 8.

86. *Two Republics*, 2 April 1886: 4, 2 April 1887: 4, 3 April 1887: 4, 28 February 1888: 2, 3 April 1888: 2, 2 April 1889: 4, 3 April 1890: 4, 3 April 1891: 4; *Mexican Herald*, 2 April 1895: 1,

3 April 1896: 2, 3 April 1897: 1, 2 April 1898: 5, 3 April 1898: 4, 3 April 1899: 8, 4 April 1899: 2; *El Imparcial*, 12 March 1900: 1, 18 March 1900: 1, 2 April 1900: 1, 3 April 1900: 1, 3 April 1901: 1, 3 April 1902: 1, 2 April 1903: 1, 3 April 1903: 1, 3 April 1909: 1; *El Tiempo Ilustrado*, 9 April 1905: 230; Casasola, *Efemérides Ilustrados del México de ayer*, 1:37, 308, 409.

87. *Mexican Herald*, 3 April 1897: 1.

88. Porfirio Díaz, speech, 2 April 1903, *Mexican Herald*, 3 April 1903: 2.

89. *Mexican Herald*, 3 April 1900: 2.

90. Entrenching tools were used by infantrymen to dig trenches and build defensive fortifications. As multipurpose tools, the spade and pick could be deadly in hand-to-hand combat. When folded flat, they went into a cover and were carried in the haversack (pack) with the handle facing down along the back. Most modern twentieth-century armies were equipped with them. I thank U.S. Marine Sgt. Major Jerry S. Nicolas for this information.

91. *El Imparcial*, 2 April 1901: 1, 17 September 1901: 1, 2 April 1902: 1, 31 March 1904: 1; *El Tiempo Ilustrado*, 7 May 2005: 135.

92. *El Imparcial*, 2 April 1905: 1, 3 April 1905: 1, 3 April 1906: 1; J. M. Flores to Chousal, 2 April 1890, ACH 3:49:22.

93. William H. Beezley, *Judas at the Jockey Club and Other Episodes of Porfirian Mexico* (Lincoln: University of Nebraska Press, 1987)

94. *Two Republics*, 2 April 1885: 4, 4 April 1885: 4; *Mexican Herald*, 3 April 1896: 2, 4 April 1896: 7. In 1885, for example, April 2 fell on Holy Thursday. The Federal District government was busily preparing for the grand Paseo de las Flores (Flower Parade) along the Viga Canal. The city always contributed to the popular celebration of Holy Week by setting up *enramadas*, long pavilions with chairs, and providing military bands to play music.

95. *Mexican Herald*, 2 April 1901: 5; Casasola, *Efemérides Ilustrados del México de ayer*, 1:112–13.

96. François-Xavier Guerra, *México, del antigua régimen a la revolución*, 2 vols., trans. Sergio Fernández Bravo (Mexico City: Fondo de Cultura Económica, 1995), 1:10–11, 29–38.

97. William E. French, *A Peaceful and Working People: Manners, Morals, and Class Formation in Northern Mexico* (Albuquerque: University of New Mexico Press, 1996), 6–7; Guerra, *México, del antigua régimen a la revolución*, 1:29.

98. *Two Republics*, 8 February 1868: 2, 12 February 1870: 3, 10 February 1872: 3, 8 February 1873: 3, 10 February 1875: 3, 10 February 1877: 3, 8 February 1879: 3, 8 February 1880: 3, 9 February 1882: 3, 5 February 1884: 4, 5 February 1885: 4, 5 August 1886: 4. The Templo de San Felipe de Jesús was originally the chapel of Our Lady of Aranzazu. Candlemas was also observed privately in homes by burning candles before altars that featured pictures of the Virgin Mary. San Felipe, a Franciscan missionary and native of Mexico, was crucified in Japan on February 5, 1537. On the religious origins and celebrations of San Felipe de Jesús during the colonial period, see Antonio García Cubas, *El libro de mis recuerdos; Narraciones historicas, anecdoticas y de costumbres mexicanas anteriores al actual estado social* (Mexico City: Impr. de A. García Cubas, hermanos sucesores, 1904), 305–7; and Pamela Voekel, *Alone before God: The Religious Origins of Modernity in Mexico* (Durham: Duke University Press, 2002), 20–21.

99. Thirty-one of the ninety-three original signers were still alive in February 1885. In addition to the eight mentioned, they were Pedro Baranda, Ignacio Sánchez Ochoa, León Guzmán, José Eligio Muñoz, Francisco de P. Lendejas, Blas Balcárcel, Manuel Fernández Soto, Félix Romero, Rafael González Paez, Miguel Auza, Basilio Pérez Gallardo, Ramón I. Alcaráz, Juan de D. Arias, Manuel Buenrostro, J. Antonio Gamboa, Benito Gómez Farías, Manuel E. Goytia, Pedro I. Irigoyen, Agustín López de Nava, Gregorio Payro, Benito Quintana, José Luis Revilla, and Mariano Vega. Only twenty-six of the Constituyentes were still living in 1891. *El Siglo XIX*, 12 February 1878: 3; *Two Republics*, 1 February 1885: 1, 4 February 1886: 1, 5 February 1886: 4, 5 February 1889: 4, 5 February 1891: 4. For political biographies of the prominent living Constituyentes, see *El Mundo Semanario Ilustrado*, 10 February 1895: 1–5.

100. *Two Republics*, 5 February 1887: 4; 6 February 1887: 4; 1 February 1888: 1; 4 February 1888: 4; 5 February 1888: 2, 4; 7 February 1888: 2, 4; 7 February 1886: 4. The rural constabulary hosted an annual dinner for Romero Rubio on Constitution Day.

101. Ibid., 3 February 1885: 4; 5 February 1885: 4; 5 February 1887: 4; 6 February 1887: 4;

1 February 1888: 1; 4 February 1888: 4; 5 February 1888: 2, 4; 7 February 1888: 2, 4; 3 February 1889: 4; 5 February 1890: 4; 3 February 1891: 4; 7 February 1891: 4; 5 February 1892: 1; 6 February 1892: 4; 6 February 1894: 4; 5 February 1890: 4; 3 February 1891: 4; 7 February 1891: 4; 5 February 1892: 1.

102. Ibid., 6 February 1886: 4.

103. Ibid., 3 February 1889: 4; 5 February 1889: 2, 4; 6 February 1889: 4. *Mexican Herald*, 6 February 1896: 7, 6 February 1900: 8.

104. Prior to 1889, the festivities committee commonly spent 200–300 pesos for the civic festival. This dropped to 138–150 pesos from 1889 to 1898, even though the overall annual festivities budget grew. Prior to 1888, the Gran Congreso Obrero and Asociación Patriótica Mexicana helped the City Council organize the Constitution Day program; after 1889 they merely sent delegations. For budgetary allotments, see *Actas de Cabildo* (1886), 52, 67, 72; (1887), 55, 64, 70; (1888), 48, 53, 64–65, 71, 79; (1889), 62, 68, 75; (1890), 20, 24, 31, 42; (1891), 26, 30, 33, 49; (1892), 35, 41, 43, 58; (1893), 37, 44, 46–47, 57; (1894), 66, 78, 83; (1895), 64, 67; (1896), 67–68; (1897), 146, 151–52, 170–71; (1898), 50, 58–59, 63, 79. *Two Republics*, 6 February 1890: 4, 3 February 1891: 4, 4 February 1891: 2; *Mexican Herald*, 5 February 1896: 8, 6 February 1896: 7, 2 February 1898: 8.

105. Bernardo Reyes to Chousal, 13 February 1904, ACH 27:241:90–91, including translation of press clipping from the *Laredo Times*, 6 February 1904.

106. *Two Republics*, 29 April 1885: 4; James C. Scott, *Weapons of the Weak: Everyday Forms of Peasant Resistance* (New Haven: Yale University Press, 1985), 28–47.

107. Jesús Aréchiga [Governor of Zacatecas] to Díaz, 18 October 1895, CPD 20:3963:13987.

108. Francisco Tolentino to Díaz, 4 November 1885, CPD 10:22:10784; Díaz to Tolentino, 10 November 1885, CPD 10:22:10785. The governor of Jalisco asked for 150 men during the *feria de San Juan de los Lagos*. José Vicente Villada to Díaz, 4 September 1889, CPD 14:20:9897; Díaz to Villada, 6 September 1889, CPD 14:20:9898.

109. Mariano Ruíz to Díaz, 25 September 1889, CPD 14:20:9747; Luis Bringas G. to Eulalio Vela, 28 August 1889, CPD 14:20:9885–9888; Alejandro Prieto to Díaz, 30 August 1895, ACH 11:152:111–113; Prieto to Díaz, 3 September 1895, ACH 11:152:105–106; Prieto to Díaz, 4 September 1895, ACH 11:152:95–97; Díaz to Prieto, 10 September 1895, ACH 11:152:98; Díaz to Prieto, 13 September 1895, ACH 11:152:114.

110. Quote from Epifanio Reyes [Interim Governor of Michoacán] to Díaz, 30 October 1890, CPD 15:28:13882. Mariano Jiménez to Díaz, 9 November 1886, CPD 11:25:12244; Díaz to Jiménez, 12 November 1886, CPD 11:25:12245; Aristeo Mercado to Chousal, 8 October 1893, ACH 8:103:76. See the train ticket and invitation to Pátzcuaro sent to Chousal in ACH 8:103:73–75. The remains of the martyrs of Uruapan were interred at the Panteón de San Fernando.

111. de la Garza, public oration, 5 May 1898, 4.

CHAPTER 4

1. The theme of progress rose to the surface in the national burials of Finance Minister Manuel Dublán (1891), Development Minister Carlos Pacheco (1891), ex-president Manuel González (1893), General Juan N. Mendez (1894), Interior Minister Manuel Romero Rubio (1895), poet-nationalist Guillermo Prieto (1897), Mexican Ambassador to the U.S. Matías Romero (1899), War Minister Felipe Berriozábal (1900), General Mariano Escobedo (1902), and Mexican Ambassador to the U.S. Manuel Aspíroz (1905).

2. State funeral legislation is found in Manuel Dublán and José María Lozano, eds., *Legislación mexicana, o colección completa de las disposiciones legislativas expedidas desde la independencia de la República*, 34 vols. (Mexico City: Imprenta y Litografía de Eduardo Dublán y Comp., 1876–1904). Military protocol for the army and navy during state funeral honors appears in México, Secretaría de Guerra y Marina, *Memoria que el Secretaría de Estado y del Despacho de Guerra y Marina Gral. de División Felipe Berriozábal presenta al Congreso de la Unión y comprende de 19 de Marzo de 1896 á 30 de Junio de 1899. Parte Expositiva* (Mexico City: Tipografía de "El Partido Liberal," 1899), 112–15, 174–79 (hereafter cited as *Memoria de la Secretaria de Guerra* [1896–99]). See also the War Minister Felipe Berriozábal's circular letter, 24 July 1899, Archivo General Bernardo Reyes, Archivo Condumex, Mexico City,

carpeta 28, legajo 5581, documento 1 (hereafter cited as ABR followed by carpeta, legajo, and documento numbers). Of course, any funeral regulation or law could be modified by executive decree. See, for example, "Orden General Extraordinaria de la Plaza de Mexico," in *El País*, 23 May 1902: 2; and *Diario del Hogar*, 24 May 1902: 2.

3. Avner Ben-Amos, "Molding the National Memory: The State Funerals of the French Third Republic" (Ph.D. diss., University of California, Berkeley, 1988), 210; Avner Ben-Amos, "The Sacred Center of Power: Paris and Republican State Funerals," *Journal of Interdisciplinary History* 22, no. 1 (Summer 1991): 27–48. Ben-Amos constructs his model from the writings of anthropologists Victor Turner, Arnold Van Gennep, and Clifford Geertz.

4. Quote is from Philip Corrigan and Derek Sayer, *The Great Arch: English State Formation as Cultural Revolution* (Oxford: Basil Blackwell, 1985), 5. See Ben-Amos, "Molding the National Memory," 10.

5. John H. Coatsworth, "Obstacles to Economic Growth in Nineteenth Century Mexico," *American Historical Review* 83, no. 1 (February 1978): 98; Stephen H. Haber, "Assessing the Obstacles to Industrialization: The Mexican Economy, 1830–1940," *Journal of Latin American Studies* 24, no. 1 (February 1992): 10–26; Robert H. Holden, *Mexico and the Survey of Public Lands: The Management of Modernization, 1876–1911* (DeKalb: Northern Illinois University Press, 1994), 7; José López-Portillo y Rojas, *Elevación y caída de Porfirio Díaz* (Mexico City: Libreria Española, 1921), 155, 192–93, 196–99, 333–35; Jorge Fernando Iturribarría, *Porfirio Diaz ante la historia* (Mexico City: Unión Gráfica, 1967), 94–95, 124–29; Don M. Coerver, *The Porfirian Interregnum: The Presidency of Manuel González of Mexico, 1880–1884* (Fort Worth: Texas Christian University Press, 1979), 42–43, 216–19; Michael C. Meyer, William L. Sherman, and Susan M. Deeds, *The Course of Mexican History*, 8th ed. (New York: Oxford University Press, 2007), 382–84, 387.

6. John H. Coatsworth, *Growth against Development: The Economic Impact of Railroads in Porfirian Mexico* (DeKalb: Northern Illinois University Press, 1981), 36–37; Francisco Bulnes, *The Whole Truth about Mexico: President Wilson's Responsibility*, trans. Dora Scott (New York: M. Bulnes, 1916), 109; Colin M. MacLachlan and William H. Beezley, *El Gran Pueblo: A History of Greater Mexico* (New York: Prentice Hall, 1994), 85–91, 97–100; Meyer, Sherman, and Deeds, *The Course of Mexican History*, 8th ed., 384–86.

7. Quoted in Michael Johns, *The City of Mexico in the Age of Díaz* (Austin: University of Texas Press, 1997), 17.

8. Ricardo García Granados, *Historia de México desde la restauración de la República en 1867, hasta la caída de Huerta*, 2 vols. (Mexico City: Editorial Jus, 1956), 1:355–62, 366–67; Iturribarría, *Porfirio Díaz ante la historia*, 135–36, 171, 192–97, 200, 214, 247; Bulnes, *The Whole Truth about Mexico*, 23; López-Portillo y Rojas, *Elevación y caída de Porfirio Díaz*, 263, 268, 279; Meyer, Sherman, and Deeds, *The Course of Mexican History*, 8th ed., 392.

9. Quoted in Bulnes, *The Whole Truth about Mexico*, 194.

10. Moisés González Navarro, *Estadísticas sociales del Porfiriato, 1877–1910* (Mexico City: Dirección General de Estadística, 1956), 9; Moisés González Navarro, *Sociedad y cultura en el porfiriato* (Mexico City: Consejo Nacional para la Cultura y las Artes, 1994), 89; Moisés González Navarro, *El Porfiriato: La vida social*, in *Historia Moderna de México*, 9 vols., ed. Daniel Cosío Villegas (Mexico City: Editorial Hermes, 1955–72), 4:85, 102–3, 126 (hereafter cited as HMM followed by volume and page numbers); Jesús Galindo y Villa, *Historia sumaria de la ciudad de México* (Mexico City: Editorial Cultura, 1925), 223–25, 231–35, 237–41, 243–49; Allen Wells and Gilbert M. Joseph, *Summer of Discontent, Seasons of Upheaval: Elite Politics and Rural Insurgency in Yucatán, 1876–1915* (Stanford: Stanford University Press, 1996), 123–25; Robert John Lear, "Workers, *Vecinos*, and Citizens: The Revolution in Mexico City, 1909–1917" (Ph.D. diss., University of California, Berkeley, 1993), 50–51.

11. *El Mundo Ilustrado*, 19 May 1901: [9]; Barbara A. Tenenbaum, "Streetwise History: The Paseo de la Reforma and the Porfirian State, 1876–1910," in *Rituals of Rule, Rituals of Resistance: Public Celebrations and Popular Culture in Mexico*, ed. William H. Beezley, Cheryl English Martin, and William E. French (Wilmington, Del.: SR Books, 1994), 127–50; Galindo y Villa, *Historia sumaria de la ciudad de México*, 210–14; *Two Republics*, 21 May 1886: 1; *Mexican Herald*, 2 April 1896: 7; Lear, "Workers, *Vecinos*, and Citizens," chap. 3; Tony Morgan, "Proletarians, Politicos, and Patriarchs: The Use and Abuse of Cultural Customs

in the Early Industrialization of Mexico City, 1880–1910," in Beezley, Martin, and French, *Rituals of Rule, Rituals of Resistance*, 152; Johns, *The City of Mexico in the Age of Díaz*, 7–9.

12. Mona Ozouf, *Festivals and the French Revolution*, trans. Alan Sheridan (Cambridge: Harvard University Press, 1988), 126–27; *El Siglo XIX*, 16 April 1878: 3; *La Libertad*, 1 April 1881: 3; *La Voz de México*, 1 April 1881: 2–3; Tenenbaum, "Streetwise History," 130, 135–36, 141; Francisco Sosa, *Las estatuas de la Reforma* (Mexico City: Colección Metropolitana, 1974); Thomas Benjamin, *La Revolución: Mexico's Great Revolution as Memory, Myth, and History* (Austin: University of Texas Press, 2001), 121. I wish to thank Tom Benjamin for this information.

13. Bulnes, *The Whole Truth about Mexico*, 23–24; and Francisco Bulnes, *El verdadero Díaz y la Revolución* (Mexico City: Editora Nacional, 1960), 42. Bulnes claimed that the federal government's payroll grew from 7.7 million pesos in 1868 to 70 million in 1910. See also Andrés Molina Enríquez, *Los grandes problemas nacionales* (Mexico City: Carranza e Hijos, 1909), 216–17; Iturribarría, *Porfirio Díaz ante la historia*, 135–36, 240; Carleton Beals, *Porfirio Díaz: Dictator of Mexico* (Philadelphia: J. B. Lippincott, 1932), 302; and García Granados, *Historia de México*, 1:287, 2:20–22. Gramsci considered the bureaucracy as an element of stability within the state, until oversaturation turns it into a narrow clique that jealously guards its selfish privileges. See *Selections from the Prison Notebooks of Antonio Gramsci*, ed. and intro. by Quintin Hoare and Geoffrey Nowell-Smith (New York: International Publishers, 1971), 189. Justo Sierra stressed that the Mexican middle class was patriotic out of necessity: "The whole class formed a single party, taking a name and a personality for common denominator: Porfirio Díaz. . . . General Díaz, in turn, is the creation of the middle class" (*The Political Evolution of the Mexican People*, trans. Charles Ramsdell [Austin: University of Texas Press, 1969], 360–61). González Navarro expanded this to all urban classes: "The worker was converted into a soldier; the man of science into a subsidized *sabio* [learned one]; merchants and property owners into associates of the government, and the people of 'medio pelo' into government bureaucrats" (*El Porfiriato*, in *HMM* 4:388–89). Friedrich Katz called this process "The Taming of the Middle Class"; see his "Mexico: Restored Republic and Porfiriato," in *Cambridge History of Latin America*, ed. Leslie Bethell (New York: Cambridge University Press, 1986), 5:61–62. Molina Enríquez described middle-class *mestizos* as the most patriotic class in Mexico (*Los grandes problemas nacionales*, 270–71). François-Xavier Guerra found that 82 percent of the Porfirian elite were professionals, the majority of them lawyers (57 percent); see his *México, del antigua régimen a la revolución*, 2 vols., trans. Sergio Fernández Bravo (Mexico City: Fondo de Cultura Económica, 1995), 1:65.

14. Quote is from Eric J. Hobsbawm, "Mass-Producing Traditions: Europe, 1870–1914," in *The Invention of Tradition*, ed. Eric J. Hobsbawm and Terence Ranger (Cambridge: Cambridge University Press, 1983), 263–64. English-born Mexicanist Alan Knight might relate to Hobsbawm's humorous quip. Knight told me that as a child he was conscripted into the royal funeral of Winston Churchill. On other captive participants, see Corrigan and Sayer, *The Great Arch*, 5–6; Gilbert M. Joseph and Daniel Nugent, "Popular Culture and State Formation," in *Everyday Forms of State Formation: Revolution and the Negotiation of Rule in Modern Mexico*, ed. Gilbert M. Joseph and Daniel Nugent (Durham: Duke University Press, 1994), 13, 19–20; James C. Scott, "Foreword," in Joseph and Nugent, *Everyday Forms of State Formation*, xi–xii; William H. Beezley, Cheryl English Martin, William E. French, "Introduction," in Beezley, Martin, and French, *Rituals of Rule, Rituals of Resistance*, xiii; William H. Beezley and Linda Curcio-Nagy, "Introduction," in *Latin American Popular Culture: An Introduction*, ed. William H. Beezley and Linda Curcio-Nagy (Wilmington, Del.: SR Books, 2000), xviii.

15. Juárez reestablished republican funerals and allocated more funds for them than for Independence Day celebrations. When he died unexpectedly of a heart attack on July 18, 1872, his funeral was a major national event that set the standard to which all others were compared. See Archivo Histórico del Ex-Ayuntamiento de la Ciudad de México, *Funerales y ceremonias fúnebres, 1779–1915*, legajo 1, expedientes 19–31 (hereafter AHEACM, *Funerales*, followed by legajo and expediente numbers); *Two Republics*, 20 July 1872: 2, 27 July 1872: 2; *Muerte del presidente Juárez* (Mexico City: Secretaría de Trabajo y Previsión Social, 1972); Charles A. Weeks, *The Juárez Myth in Mexico* (Tuscaloosa: University of Alabama Press, 1987), 24.

16. AHEACM, *Funerales*, 1:34; *El Hijo del Trabajo*, 9 October 1881: 1; *El Nacional*, 23 August 1894: 2; *Actas de Cabildo del Ayuntamiento Constitucional de México, Julio a Diciembre, 1894*, edición "El Municipio Libre" (Mexico City: Imprenta de la Escuela Correccional, 1896), 114, 140, 148, 367, 373 (hereafter all editions of *Actas de Cabildo del Ayuntamiento Constitucional de México* are cited as *Actas de Cabildo* followed by months, years, and page numbers—see the bibliography for publishing details); *Actas de Cabildo* (Enero a Junio 1895), 8–9; *Acta de la Junta provisional organizada para la errección de un monumento en esta Ciudad que perpetúa la memoria del Sr. General de División D. Manuel González*, 5 February 1893, Archivo Rafael Chousal, Universidad Nacional Autonoma de México, caja 7, expediente 87, folio 62 (hereafter cited as ACH followed by caja, expediente, and folio numbers).

17. Ramón Prida, *De la dictadura al la anarquia. Apuntes para la historia política de México durante la última cuarenta y tres años*, 2 vols. (El Paso: Imprenta de "El Paso del Norte," 1914), 1:79.

18. This is according to the English-language business daily *Two Republics* (2 June 1891: 2). Historians recognize the critical contributions of Dublán. See García Granados, *Historia de México*, 1:304–5; Iturribarría, *Porfirio Díaz ante la historia*, 171–73; and MacLachlan and Beezley, *El Gran Pueblo*, 87–91.

19. *El Partido Liberal*, 3 June 1891: 2; *El Tiempo*, 2 June 1891: 2; *El Siglo XIX*, 3 June 1891: 2–3; AHEACM, *Funerales*, 1:39 and accompanying mortuary announcement; *Diario Oficial*, 1 June 1891: 1.

20. *El Monitor Republicano*, 2 June 1891: 3. Crowd estimates were not calculated with mathematical precision. A reporter from *El Tiempo* (3 June 1891: 2) stood at the main entrance of the National Palace and counted one hundred people pass per minute, extrapolating that ninety-six thousand had passed after sixteen hours of continuous visitation.

21. Eric Hobsbawm and Terence Ranger describe how modern states often borrow from the archbishop's storeroom when inventing traditions; see their "Introduction: Inventing Traditions," in Hobsbawm and Ranger, *The Invention of Tradition*, 6. *El Tiempo*, 3 June 1891: 2. While fewer in number, funerals for high Church officials such as Archbishops Labastida and Próspero María Alarcón drew as many people as state funerals. See Jorge Adame Goddard, *El pensamiento político y social de los católicos mexicanos, 1867–1914* (Mexico City: Universidad Nacional Autónoma de México, 1981), 105.

22. *El Monitor Republicano*, 3 June 1891: 3; *El Siglo XIX*, 3 June 1891: 2–3; *El Partido Liberal*, 3 June 1891: 2; *Diario del Hogar*, 3 June 1891: 1; *Two Republics*, 3 June 1891: 4; *El Tiempo*, 3 June 1891, 2; AHEACM, *Funerales*, 1:39. For illustrations, see *México Gráfico*, 7 June 1891: 3–6; and *La Patria Ilustrada*, 8 June 1891: 270–71.

23. Luis Labastida, funeral oration for Manuel Dublán, 2 June 1891, French Cemetery, in *El Monitor Republicano*, 3 June 1891: 3; *El Partido Liberal*, 4 June 1891: 1–2; and *Diario Oficial*, 1 June 1891: 1.

24. *La Patria Ilustrada*, 8 June 1891: 270–71.

25. On saving the treasury, see Manuel Andrade to Porfirio Díaz, 8 June 1891, Colección General Porfirio Díaz, Universidad Iberoamericana, legajo 16, caja 12, documento 5938 (hereafter cited as CPD followed by legajo, caja, and documento numbers); Crispin Jiménez to Díaz, 5 June 1891, CPD 16:14:6514. The letters on improving the nation's credit are found in CPD, legajo 16, cajas 12–15: Agustin Arroyo de Anda to Díaz, 5 June 1891, 5900; A. B. Cervantes to Díaz, 1 June 1891, 6086; Manuel Dondé to Díaz, 8 June 1891, 6242; Francisco González to Díaz, 1 June 1891, 6465; Jesús Rábago to Díaz, 2 June 1891, 7019. The letters on joining Diaz are found in CPD, legajo 16, cajas 12–14: Miguel Ahumada to Díaz, 4 June 1891, 5913; Abraham Bandala to Díaz, 3 June 1891, 5968; Pedro Baranda to Díaz, 4 June 1891, 5989; A. K. Coney [Consulate General of Mexico in San Francisco] to Díaz, 12 June 1891, 6127; José Castelló to Díaz, 9 June 1891, 6148; R. B. Cueto to Díaz, 1 June 1891, 6165; Carlos Diez Gutiérrez to Díaz, 2 June 1891, 6236; Daniel Traconis to Díaz, 7 June 1891, 6312; Jesús F. López to Díaz, 7 June 1891, 6532; Pedro Martínez to Díaz, 4 June 1891, 6696; Agustín Mora to Díaz, 6 June 1891, 6732.

　　For combinations, see Simón Parra to Díaz, 4 June 1891, CPD 16:14:6815; Rosendo Pineda to Bernardo Reyes, 3 October 1895, and Bernardo Reyes to Díaz, 1 June 1891, ABR 2:1127:1. As these groupings suggest, the business elite hailed Dublán for financial accomplishments, while state governors and military zone commanders expressed greater appreciation for his political loyalty to Díaz.

26. Ahumada to Díaz, 4 June 1891, CPD 16:17:8237; Parra to Díaz, 29 June 1891, CPD 16:17:8237; Traconis to Díaz, 25 June 1891, CPD 16:18:8553.

27. "La muerte del Sr. D. Manuel Dublán en Tacubaya y su entierro en la Capital en el panteón francés," *Gaceta Callejera*, n.d.; *El Partido Liberal*, 2 June 1891: 1.

28. López-Portillo y Rojas, *Elevación y caída de Porfirio Díaz*, 212–13; García Granados, *Historia de México*, 1:306; *El Siglo XIX*, 17 September 1891: 2; *Diario del Hogar*, 18 September 1891: 3. Paz quoted in *La Patria*, 17 September 1891: 3; and *La Patria Ilustrada*, 21 September 1891: 446. Díaz quoted in *Two Republics*, 18 September 1891: 4.

29. García Granados, *Historia de México*, 1:183; *Two Republics*, 17 September 1891: 2; *El Tiempo*, 19 September 1891: 2; *La Patria Ilustrada*, 21 September 1891: 446; Iturribarría, *Porfirio Díaz ante la historia*, 120–21.

30. Pacheco to Díaz, 2 April 1891, CPD 16:9:4065–4066; Díaz to Pacheco, 7 April 1891, CPD 16:9:4067.

31. See Leslie Byrd Simpson, *Many Mexicos*, 4th ed. (Berkeley: University of California Press, 1966), 244–49.

32. President Manuel González was also an amputee, suffering the dismemberment of an arm at the defense of Puebla in 1863 and reinjuring the stump at the Battle of Tecoac. And despite his role in the Veracruz executions of 1879, General Luis Mier y Terán, who suffered from psychotic episodes and a persecution complex, appeared to be forgiven during his state funeral. See *El Partido Liberal*, 22 August 1891: 1–2, 23 August 1891: 2; John E. Seward, "The Veracruz Massacre of 1879," *The Americas* 32, no. 4 (April 1976): 585–96.

33. Daniel Cosío Villegas, *El Porfiriato: La vida política interior, segunda parte*, in *HMM* 9:306.

34. *El Siglo XIX*, 16 September 1891: 1. See also *México Gráfico*, 20 September 1891: 6. On the use and abuse of dismemberment as political capital, see Lyman L. Johnson, ed., *Body Politics: Death, Dismemberment, and Memory in Latin America* (Albuquerque: University of New Mexico Press, 2004).

35. Quoted in *Diario del Hogar*, 18 September 1891: 1; *El Siglo XIX*, 17 September 1891: 2; and *El Partido Liberal*, 18 September 1891: 1.

36. The article in *El Hijo del Ahuizote* was reproduced in *El Monitor Republicano*, 24 September 1891: 3.

37. García Granados, *Historia de México*, 1:202; Iturribarría, *Porfirio Díaz ante la historia*, 87; Beals, *Porfirio Díaz*, 286. Bulnes claimed that one government code existed—the code of theft—composed of the following articles: (1) graft, (2) usury, (3) illegal gambling houses, (4) sale of judicial decisions, (5) sale of national goods at an inflated price, and (6) virulent contracts. Bulnes epitomized the "transformed Liberals" of Charles Hale's outstanding work but missed his calling as an independent Liberal polemicist like Cabrera, Filomena Mata, García Granados, and other "indomitable champions of liberty." These troublesome detractors are the protagonists of García Granados's *Historia de México* (see 1:320–36). Like Ricardo, they all suffered multiple imprisonments during the repressive stages of the dictatorship and were intellectual precursors of the Mexican Revolution. See Charles A. Hale, *The Transformation of Liberalism in Late-Nineteenth Century Mexico* (Princeton: Princeton University Press, 1989); and James D. Cockcroft, *Intellectual Precursors of the Mexican Revolution, 1900–1913* (Austin: Institute of Latin American Studies, University of Texas Press, 1968).

38. *Diario Oficial*, 17 September 1891: 1, 18 September 1891: 1; *El Siglo XIX*, 17 September 1891: 2, 18 September 1891: 2; *El Monitor Republicano*, 18 September 1891: 2, 19 September 1891: 3; *Two Republics*, 18 September 1891: 4; *Diario del Hogar*, 18 September 1891: 3; *La Patria*, 19 September 1891: 2; *El Tiempo*, 19 September 1891: 2. In his second edition, Benedict Anderson referred to "the census's abstract quantification/serialization of persons, the map's logoization of political space, and the museum's 'ecumenical,' profane genealogizing" as the grammar of nationalism; see his *Imagined Communities: Reflections on the Origin and Spread of Nationalism*, rev. ed. (London: Verso, 1991), xiv, 160, 163–64, 183–84. See also Mauricio Tenorio-Trillo's chapter "Statistics, Maps, Patents, and Governance," in *Mexico at the World's Fairs: Crafting a Modern Nation* (Berkeley: University of California Press, 1996), 125–41.

39. *La Patria*, 20 September 1891: 3; *Two Republics*, 19 September 1891: 4, 20 September 1891: 4; *El Siglo XIX*, 19 September 1891: 2; *El Partido Liberal*, 20 September 1891: 3; *El Tiempo*, 22 September 1891: 2.

40. Jesús Preciado, *Corona fúnebre dedicada a la memoria del general de división Carlos Pacheco por y el gobernador constitutional del estado de Morelos general Jesus H. Preciado* (Cuernavaca: Gobierno de Morelos, 1891), 1–4; *Primer Almanaque Mexicano de Artes y Letras* 2 (1895): 12; *El Monitor Republicano*, 20 September 1891: 3; Ayuntamiento de la Ciudad de México, *Discurso del C. Lic. Miguel S. Macedo, Presidente del Ayuntamiento, Contestación del Gobernador del Distrito Federal C. Lic. Rafael Rebollar y Memoria Documentada de los trabajos municipales de 1898. Formada por el Secretario C. Lic. Juan Bribiesca* (Mexico City: Tip. y Lit. "La Europea," de J. Aguilar Vera y Cª, 1899), 136; *Mexican Herald*, 12 September 1895: 4, 12 September 1896: 4, 10 December 1895: 4; *El Siglo XIX*, 31 October 1895: 2, 5 November 1895: 2; *El Nacional*, 4 November 1895: 2, 3 November 1896: 2; *El Mundo*, 10 November 1895: 7; *El Mundo Semanario Ilustrado*, 8 November 1896: 287.

41. González Navarro, *El Porfiriato*, in *HMM* 4:532. The literacy rate in Mexico City grew from 38 percent in 1895 to 50 percent in 1910. There were 250,000 readers in the Federal District alone.

42. *El Combate*, 6 April 1897: 2; *El Imparcial*, 1 April 1897: 1; *El Mundo*, 1 April 1897: 1.

43. José López Portillo y Rojas to Bernardo Reyes, 12 November 1889, ABR 3:599:1; *El Mercurio Occidental* (Guadalajara), 11 November 1889: 1; *Homenaje a Ramón Corona en el primer centenario de su muerte* (Guadalajara: Secretaría de Educación y Cultura, Programa de Estudias Jaliscienses, 1989), 197; González Navarro, *El Porfiriato*, in *HMM* 4:677.

44. *Gaceta Callejera*, no. 26, 3 October 1895.

45. On the reburial of Ocampo, see *Decreto autorizado al ejecutivo para que erogue los gastos que sean necesarios al trasladarse a la rotonda de los hombres ilustres, los restos del gran Melchor Ocampo*, Archivo General de la Nación, Ramo Gobernación, Decretos y Circulares, caja 704, expediente 6; *Actas de Cabildo* (1897), 481, 946, 983; Dublán and Lozano, *Legislación mexicana*, 26 (1896): 173; *Two Republics*, 20 May 1896: 8; *El Siglo XIX*, 20 May 1896: 2; *El Imparcial*, 1, 2 June 1897: 1, 3 June 1897: 2, 4 June 1897: 1, 5 June 1897: 2. Mateos's quote is found in *El Universal*, 27 May 1893: 1.

46. Quoted in *Two Republics*, 1 April 1897: 8; *El Combate*, 6 April 1897: 1; and *El Imparcial*, 1 April 1897: 1–2. Rocha was editor in chief of the anticlerical newspaper *El Combate*.

47. *El Imparcial*, 23 May 1902: 1. Only the reporter of *El Imparcial* gained access to the death chamber. Since no other newspaper published Escobedo's last words, his statement may well have been fabricated for its political utility. In 1902, increased circulation brought Escobedo's last words to fifty-nine hundred literate citizens, perhaps even more since single copies of newspapers were often passed around in working-class circles. See González Navarro, *El Porfiriato*, in *HMM* 4:679–80; Iturribarría, *Porfirio Díaz ante la historia*, 112–13.

48. In an attempt to restore Lerdo de Tejada, Escobedo rose against Díaz in the summer of 1877. After a year of unsuccessful rebellion in Coahuila and Veracruz, he was captured at Cuatro Ciénegas. Following a long interview, Díaz spared his life. His rebellion suggests the irony of his advice, but other prominent Lerdo supporters abdicated the principles of *Lerdismo* in favor of *servilismo* and material progress. Three former Lerdists, Escobedo, Rocha, and Manuel María de Zamacona, directed the Junta Central Porfirista of 1892. See López-Portillo y Rojas, *Elevación y caída de Porfirio Díaz*, 214; and García Granados, *Historia de México*, 1:307.

49. Avner Ben-Amos, *Funerals, Politics, and Memory in Modern France, 1789–1996* (New York: Oxford University Press, 2000), 283.

50. Juan A. Mateos to Vicente García Torres, *El Monitor Republicano*, 18 June 1879: 3. Mateos, who was at Ramírez's side, stated: "Neither clerics nor notaries appeared at his deathbed; he did not believe in the first and had no need for the second since he died in poverty."

51. *La Voz de México*, 2 June 1891: 2.

52. For Mier y Terán, see *El Tiempo*, 22 August 1891: 2. Matthew D. Esposito, "Death and Disorder in Mexico City: The State Funeral of Manuel Romero Rubio," in Beezley and Curcio-Nagy, *Latin American Popular Culture*, 87–103. On Guillermo Prieto, see *La Voz de México*, 6 March 1897: 2–3; *Mexican Herald*, 4 March 1897: 1, 5 March 1897: 8; *El Mundo*, 4 March 1897: 2. *El Mundo* clarified that Prieto allowed a priest to speak to him and place a crucifix

in his hand just before death, which does not substantiate conversion. But *La Voz* asserted that Prieto reached out and accepted the crucifix, and listed the names of all witnesses to prove that the conversion occurred. On Escobedo, see *El País*, 23 May 1902: 2; *Diario del Hogar*, 24 May 1902: 2.

53. Artist Manuel Islas used this death mask in his grand memorial of Juárez at the Panteón de San Fernando. For a photograph of Juárez's mascarilla, see *El Imparcial*, 24 March 1906: 1. Admittedly, some likenesses of Juárez are not as likable. See Helen Escobedo's catalog of Juárez statues in *Mexican Monuments: Strange Encounters*, photographs by Paolo Gori, essays by Nestor García Canclini et al. (New York: Abbeville Press, 1989).

54. *Diario del Hogar*, 30 April 1889: 3.

55. Porfirio Díaz to Bernardo Reyes, 18 November 1891, ABR 15:2851:1; *El Nacional*, 4 October 1895: 2; *El Tiempo*, 4 October 1895: 2, 5 October 1895: 2; *Two Republics*, 5 October 1895: 1.

56. Manuel Diaz Mimiaga, letter of introduction for Contreras, 13 December 1888, Archivo Jesús Contreras, caja 4, documento 41 (hereafter cited as AJC followed by caja and documento numbers); Secretary of Justice and Public Instruction Joaquín Baranda, letter of introduction for Contreras, 22 October 1887, AJC 4:42; Baranda to Contreras, 21 April 1888, AJC 4:43; Porfirio Díaz to Archbishop Próspero María Alarcón, letter of introduction for Contreras, AJC 4:61.

57. *Acta Constitutiva de la Fundición Artística Mexicana*, 1899, AJC 4. For examples of the foundry's sculptures, see *El Mundo*, 2 April 1897: 1; *Diario del Hogar*, 2 April 1897: 2; *Two Republics*, 2 April 1897: 5; *El Imparcial*, 1 April 1897: 1, 2 April 1897: 1; *El Combate*, 6 April 1897: 1–2; *El Monitor Republicano*, 2 December 1894: 3; *El Universal*, 17 January 1899: 2.

58. *Manuel Romero Rubio, su expediente personal*, Archivo Histórico "Genaro Estrada," Secretaría de Relaciones Exteriores, I/131/2863, documentos 111–17. Letters and telegrams from foreign legations are also in this folder, docs. 119–214. Rosendo Pineda to Bernardo Reyes, 3 October 1895, ABR 24:4610:1–2; [Reyes] to [Ignacio M. Escudero], October 1895, ABR 24:4608:1. On the communicative effects of mass transit, see Hobsbawm, "Mass-Producing Traditions," 274; and Patricia O'Brien, "Michel Foucault's History of Culture," in *The New Cultural History*, ed. Lynn Hunt (Berkeley: University of California Press, 1989), 27–34.

59. Luís González y González, *San José de Gracia: Mexican Village in Transition*, trans. John Upton (Austin: University of Texas Press, 1974), 96, 99–101. See also Miguel Tinker Salas, *In the Shadow of the Eagles: Sonora and the Transformation of the Border during the Porfiriato* (Berkeley: University of California Press, 1997), 145–48.

60. See letters from municipal presidents to Díaz in CPD and published in *El Nacional*, 10 January 1900: 3. Anderson, *Imagined Communities*, 35–36, 145.

61. Corrigan and Sayer, *The Great Arch*, 5. To take this further, Gramsci argues that the State "operates according to a plan, urges, incites, solicits, and punishes" (see *Selections from the Prison Notebooks of Antonio Gramsci*, 247).

62. José Tomás de Cuéllar's novel *Having a Ball* demonstrates how efficient the grapevine was among capitalinos.

63. *El Imparcial*, 23 May 1902: 1; *Diario del Hogar*, 4 October 1895: 3; *Mexican Herald*, 4 October 1895: 1; *La Voz de México*, 5 October 1895: 2, 6 October 1895: 2; *Two Republics*, 4 October 1895: 1; *El Siglo XIX*, 4 October 1895: 2; *El Partido Liberal*, 5 October 1895: 3; *El Tiempo*, 3 October 1895: 3, 5 October 1895: 2.

64. State funeral legislation was published in México, Congreso, Cámara de Diputados, *Diario de los Debates de la Cámara de Diputados, 8a legislatura constitucional de la Nácion, Años de 1877–1911* (Mexico City: Tip. Literaria, 1877–1911); in Dublán and Lozano, *Legislación mexicana*; and in period newspapers. López-Portillo y Rojas, *Elevación y caída de Porfirio Díaz*, 154; *El Siglo XIX*, 17 June 1879: 3.

65. Spíndola to Chousal, 24 March 1892, ACH 5:73:63. Jimenez was governor of Michoacán at the time of his death.

66. For example, see Antonio Leon Trasloheros to Chousal, 6 October 1893, ACH 8:103:62–63; Traslosheros to Chousal, 23 October 1893, ACH 8:103:66.

67. *El Siglo XIX*, 19 May 1893: 2; *Two Republics*, 6 June 1893: 4.

68. *Memoria de la Secretaria de Guerra* (1896–99), "Decretos," 57; *Diario del Hogar*, 26 July 1895: 3; *El Mundo Semanario Ilustrado*, 4 August 1895: 9–10. See the interior secretary's

request to bury the mother of General Leandro Valle at Dolores in *Actas de Cabildo* (Julio a Diciembre 1895), 120, 146.

69. Josefa Fernández de Jimenez to Carmen Romero Rubio, 26 March 1893, ACH 7:88:8–9; Romero Rubio to Fernández de Jiménez, [March 1893], ACH 7:88:10. See other solicitations to Carmen in ACH 7:88–90, 92, 97; 9:108–29; 10:130–33.

70. *El Monitor Republicano*, 19 December 1891: 1. Only fifty guests attended the private ceremony for Iglesias. Editors complained about the public's response for the *inmaculado olvidado*: "There are no civic processions, no organized demonstrations, no corporations that marched behind the funeral convoy."

71. Ben-Amos, "The Sacred Center of Power," 34; *El Siglo XIX*, 30 November 1894: 1, 1 December 1894: 2, 4 December 1894: 2; *Diario del Hogar*, 1 December 1894: 1; *Two Republics*, 1 December 1894: 4, 4 December 1894: 4; *El Monitor Republicano*, 1 December 1894: 3, 2 December 1894: 3, 4 December 1894: 2; *El Mundo Semanario Ilustrado*, 2 December 1894: 3; *El Nacional*, 2 December 1894: 2–3, 4 December 1894: 2; *Actas de Cabildo* (Julio a Diciembre 1894), 321.

72. AHEACM, *Funerales*, 1:19; Sierra, *The Political Evolution of the Mexican People*, 255; *Decreto autorizado al ejecutivo para que erogue los gastos que sean necesarios al trasladarse a la rotonda de los hombres ilustres, los restos del gran Melchor Ocampo*, Archivo General de la Nación, Ramo Gobernación, Decretos y Circulares, caja 704, expediente 6; *Two Republics*, 20 May 1896: 8; *El Siglo XIX*, 20 May 1896: 2; *El Imparcial*, 1 June 1897: 1, 2 June 1897: 1, 3 June 1897: 2, 4 June 1897: 1, 5 June 1897: 2; *El Universal*, 3 June 1893: 1.

73. *El Monitor Republicano*, 27 February 1895: 1; *El Siglo XIX*, 27 February 1895: 2, 1 March 1895: 1–2; *Diario Oficial*, 27 February 1895: 1; *El Partido Liberal*, 28 February 1895: 1; *Diario del Hogar*, 17 March 1900: 3; *El Imparcial*, 11 March 1900: 2, 12 March 1900: 1, 13 March 1900: 1, 14 March 1900: 1, 15 March 1900: 1, 17 March 1900: 1–2.

74. *Decreto autorizado al ejecutivo para que ordene la exhumación de los restos de Ponciano Arriaga*, Archivo General de la Nación, Ramo Gobernación, Decretos y Circulares, caja 745, expediente 10; *Actas de Cabildo* (1900), 564 65; *El Imparcial*, 5 May 1900: 1, 19 June 1900: 1, 21 June 1900: 1, 23 June 1900: 1; *Diario Oficial*, 8 May 1900: 2; *Diario del Hogar*, 10 May 1900: 2, 23 June 1900: 3; *El Nacional*, 20 June 1900: 2–3, 21 June 1900: 2, 23 June 1900: 2; *El Pais*, 23 June 1900: 1; *El Universal*, 24 June 1900: 2; Francisco Martínez Calleja, funeral oration for Ponciano Arriaga, 22 June 1900, Chamber of Deputies, *Diario del Hogar*, 24 June 1900: 1; Félix Romero, funeral oration for Ponciano Arriaga, 22 June 1900, Chamber of Deputies, *Diario del Hogar*, 23 June 1900: 1.

75. *El Diario del Hogar*, 25 July 1895: 2; Enrique Fernández Castelló to Señor Bribiesca [Secretary of the Ayuntamiento], n.d., AHEACM, *Funerales*, 1:42. Agreeing to send carriages "with pleasure" were Francisco Suinaga, J. Diego Liberes, Telesforo García, Luis G. Lavie, A. Alvarez Rul, Luis Escalante, Miguel Alonzo Peón, and José Solórzano y Mata. *Two Republics*, 5 October 1895: 1; *Mexican Herald*, 5 October 1895: 1; *El Tiempo*, 5 October 1895: 2; *El Siglo XIX*, 5 October 1895: 1; *El Gil Blas*, 6 October 1895: 2.

76. Ramón Fernández to Secretario de Relaciones, 19 January 1893, Secretaria de Relaciones Exteriores, "Lic. Ignacio M. Altamirano. Su expediente personal," expediente 1/131/71, vol. 2, documento 34 (hereafter cited as SRE followed by volume and documento numbers); Fernández to Minister Develle, 15 February 1893, SRE 2:42; Fernández to Secretario de Relaciones, 17 February 1893, SRE 2:49; F. de P. Pasalagua to Secretario de Relaciones Exteriores, 27 February 1893, SRE 2: d. 70.

77. *Mexican Herald*, 2 January 1899: 1, 16 January 1899: 8; *El Imparcial*, 2 January 1899: 1; *El Nacional*, 2 January 1899: 3, 11 January 1899: 2, 16 January 1899: 3; *El Tiempo Ilustrado*, 30 April 1905: 268; *El Mundo*, 24 April 1905: 1, 26 April 1905: 1; *Diario del Hogar*, 26 April 1905: 2, 27 April 1905: 2. Mata's commentary appears in the latter.

78. *Actas de Cabildo* (1893), 226, 241; *Two Republics*, 10 May 1893: 2; *El Universal*, 10 May 1893: 1; *El Siglo XIX*, 11 May 1893: 4. Posada captured the soldierly essence of the mortuary chamber. *El Mundo*, 4 March 1897: 1, 5 March 1897: 1; *El Nacional*, 10 January 1900: 3; *El Imparcial*, 11 January 1900: 1. For the Independence Heroes' reburial, see *El Diario del Hogar*, 25 July 1895: 2; *El Gil Blas*, 28 July 1895: 3, 1 August 1895: 1; *El Nacional*, 29 July 1895: 2; *El Tiempo*, 31 July 1895: 2; *El Noticioso*, 31 July 1895: 3; *El Mundo Semanario Ilustrado*, 4 August 1895: 9; *El Municipio Libre*, 9 August 1895: 1, 14 August 1895: 1.

79. *Mexican Herald*, 15 October 1896: 4, 23 June 1900: 2; *La Voz de México*, 6 October 1895: 2; *Two Republics*, 5 October 1895: 1; *El Mundo Semanario Ilustrado*, Suplemento, 6 October 1895: 4. Liberals demanded that the government replace Pacheco's coffin, which was topped with a silver cross. See *La Patria*, 20 September 1891: 3; *Two Republics*, 19 September 1891: 4, 20 September 1891: 4; *El Siglo XIX*, 19 September 1891: 2; *El Monitor Republicano*, 20 September 1891: 3; and *El Partido Liberal*, 20 September 1891: 3. Complaints against the Masons are found in *La Voz de México*, 2 June 1891: 2; and *El Tiempo*, 2 June 1891: 2.

80. *El Tiempo*, 28 May 1896: 2. *El Siglo XIX*, *Two Republics*, and *El Monitor Republicano* also noted the scant number of visitors to the National Palace. See *El Siglo XIX*, 27 May 1896: 2, 28 May 1896: 2; *Two Republics*, 28 May 1896: 8; *El Monitor Republicano*, 28 May 1896: 2.

81. Benedict Anderson, *The Spectre of Comparisons: Nationalism, Southeast Asia and the World* (New York: Verso, 1998), 56.

82. *Actas de Cabildo* (1893), 290–92; *El Universal*, 12 May 1893: 1. Sierra, Chavero, and Prieto organized the funeral ceremony. AHEACM, *Funerales*, 1:40; *El Nacional*, 10 January 1900: 3; *Two Republics*, 11 May 1893: 4.

83. *El Universal*, 12 May 1893: 1, 13 May 1893: 1.

84. *El Mundo Semanario Ilustrado*, 4 August 1895: 9.

85. *El Tiempo*, 31 July 1895: 2; *El Municipio Libre*, 30 July 1895: 3, 31 July 1895: 1, 13 August 1895: 1; *La Voz de México*, 1 August 1895: 2, 4 August 1895: 2, 5 October 1895: 2; *El Gil Blas*, 31 July 1895: 3, 1 August 1895: 1; *Two Republics*, 31 July 1895: 1; *El Partido Liberal*, 1 August 1895: 2; *La Federación*, 3 August 1895: 1; *El Mundo Semanario Ilustrado*, 4 August 1895: 9, 14 January 1900: 4–5; Federico Gamboa, *Mi diario: Mucho de mi vida y algo de la de otros*, 5 vols. (Mexico City: Consejo Nacional de la Cultura y las Artes, 1994), 1:171; *El Nacional*, 11 January 1900: 3; *El Imparcial*, 11 January 1900: 1, 12 January 1900: 1.

86. A month after Díaz took power, Development Minister Vicente Riva Palacio ordered horse-drawn trams to move at a velocity no faster than a horse's trot and that drivers behave courteously, that they make complete stops at every corner, and that they not allow too many passengers to cram into the vehicles. His decrees were dead letters. Streetcar drivers continued to operate their vehicles with reckless abandon, producing hundreds of casualties a year, and people continued to fill trams "like cigarettes in a cigarette pack." Romero Rubio's reforms of May 3, 1894, requiring animals to be tame, reined, and not ill, injured, or mistreated and drivers to wear uniforms, lay off the whips, and drive safely were hardly enforced either. Instead, horses keeled over in the streets, and drivers "distinguished themselves with their filthy vocabulary. Particularly in times of rain there was nobody as insolent as a coach driver." See González Navarro, *El Porfiriato*, in *HMM* 4:694–95.

87. *El Nacional*, 13 January 1900: 3; *El Imparcial*, 11 January 1900: 1, 13 January 1900: 1–2.

88. *La Voz de México*, 6 October 1895: 2; *Two Republics*, 5 October 1895: 1; *El Mundo Semanario Ilustrado*, Suplemento, 6 October 1895: 4.

89. *El Nacional*, 18 October 1894: 2, 25 October 1894: 2; *La Sombra de Arteaga* (Querétaro), 21 October 1894: 377–78, 28 October 1894: 393. *Actas de Cabildo* (Enero a Junio 1894), 90, 360; (Julio a Diciembre 1894), 65; (Julio a Diciembre 1895), 27–28, 51, 55, 66, 96, 100; (1899), 896–97, 900, 986; (1900), 68–69, 80, 109. *Two Republics*, 31 July 1895: 1; *El Tiempo*, 27 July 1895: 2, 31 July 1895: 2; *El Mundo Semanario Ilustrado*, 4 August 1895: 7–10; AHEACM, *Funerales*, 1:42; *El Imparcial*, 13 August 1903: 1, 30 August 1903: 1, 8 September 1903: 1; *Mexican Herald*, 8 September 1903: 2; *El Pais*, 8 September 1903: 1; *El Mundo Ilustrado*, 13 September 1903: [3–6]; México, Secretaría de Gobernación, *Memoria de la Secretaria de Gobernación correspondiente al cuatrienio de 1° de Diciembre de 1900 a 30 de Noviembre de 1904* (Mexico City: Imprenta del Gobierno Federal, 1906), 16.

90. *Two Republics*, 12 May 1893: 4; *El Universal*, 12 May 1893: 1; *El Nacional*, 13 January 1900: 3.

91. Johns, *The City of Mexico in the Age of Díaz*, 23, 27–28; Michael C. Meyer, William L. Sherman, and Susan M. Deeds, *The Course of Mexican History*, 6th ed. (New York: Oxford University Press, 1999), 434.

92. *Selections from the Prison Notebooks of Antonio Gramsci*, 123–207: Gramsci states: "The fact of hegemony presupposes that account be taken of the interests of the groups over which hegemony is to be exercised, and that a certain compromise equilibrium should be formed—in other words, that the leading group should make sacrifices of an

economic-corporate kind" (161). James C. Scott refers to this as the "symbolic alignment of elite and subordinate class values" (see *Weapons of the Weak: Everyday Forms of Peasant Resistance* [New Haven: Yale University Press, 1985], 39–40).

93. See Pamela Voekel, *Alone before God: The Religious Origins of Modernity in Mexico* (Durham: Duke University Press, 2002), 56.

94. *El Tiempo*, 3 June 1891: 2.

95. *Two Republics*, 5 October 1895: 1; *El Noticioso*, 5 October 1895: 1–2; *Mexican Herald*, 5 October 1895: 1; *El Siglo XIX*, 5 October 1895: 1; *El Mundo Semanario Ilustrado*, Suplemento, 6 October 1895: 3–4, 13 October 1895: 13. Catholics attributed crimes against high-profile Church figures during *fiestas cívicas* on the laicization of society. In response, the Liberal daily *El Monitor Republicano* begged for statistics on thefts, public drunkenness, and homicides during Holy Week to prove that the Catholic faith hardly deterred crime on religious feast days. For this polemic, see González Navarro, *El Porfiriato*, in *HMM* 4:425. On bourgeois notions of the moral turpitude of the working class, see William E. French, *A Peaceful and Working People: Manners, Morals, and Class Formation in Northern Mexico* (Albuquerque: University of New Mexico Press, 1996), 60–85.

96. *Mexican Herald*, 5 October 1895: 1; *Two Republics*, 5 October 1895: 1; *El Noticioso*, 5 October 1895: 1–2. William H. Beezley, *Judas at the Jockey Club and Other Episodes of Porfirian Mexico* (Lincoln: University of Nebraska Press, 1987), 5–6.

97. See Tenorio-Trillo, *Mexico at the World's Fairs*.

98. Patrick Frank, *Posada's Broadsheets: Mexican Popular Imagery, 1890–1910* (Albuquerque: University of New Mexico Press, 1998), 9.

99. *El Noticioso*, 4 December 1894: 1; *El Nacional*, 5 December 1894: 2; *El Monitor Republicano*, 5 December 1894: 2.

100. Jeffrey Pilcher, *Que Vivan los Tamales! Food and the Making of Mexican Identity* (Albuquerque: University of New Mexico Press, 1998), 83–84. Pilcher cites a 1902 study by Demetrio Sodi that correlated increased pulque consumption with a rise in crime levels.

101. *El Imparcial*, 12 January 1900: 1; *El Nacional*, 12 January 1900: 3; *Diario del Hogar*, 17 January 1900: 1. Comments like these landed Mata in jail over thirty times. See López-Portillo y Rojas, *Elevación y caída de Porfirio Díaz*, 220.

102. *El Imparcial*, 25 May 1902: 3; *Diario del Hogar*, 25 May 1902: 2; *Mexican Herald*, 25 May 1902: 2.

103. Nicole Loraux, *The Invention of Athens: The Funeral Oration in the Classical City* (Cambridge: Harvard University Press, 1986), 2–3; Ben-Amos, "The Sacred Center of Power," 33; Ben-Amos, "Molding the National Memory," 190.

104. Morgan, "Proletarians, Politicos, and Patriarchs," 152; Daniel Cosío Villegas, "Cuarta llamada particular," in *HMM* 4:xxi; Josefina Vázquez de Knauth, *Nacionalismo y educación en México* (Mexico City: Colegio de México, 1970), 49.

105. *Mexican Herald*, 4 October 1896: 1, 4; *El Mundo Semanario Ilustrado*, 4 October 1896: 208; *Discursos y poesias pronunciados en honor del Señor Licenciado Manuel Romero Rubio en el Panteón Francés el dia de Octubre de 1896, y en el Teatro Nacional el 14 del mismo mes y año* (Mexico City: Imp. y Lit. de F. Díaz de Leon, 1896), 2–3, 8–9.

106. Emeterio de la Garza, Cinco de Mayo speech, 5 May 1898, Alameda, *Mexican Herald*, 6 May 1898: 4.

107. *Mexican Herald*, 15 October 1896: 4; *Discursos y poesias pronunciados en honor del Señor Licenciado Manuel Romero Rubio*, 35–36, 51. The speech also appears in Joaquín D. Casasús, *En honor de los muertos*, 2nd ed. (Mexico City: Consejo Editorial del Gobierno del Estado de Tabasco, 1981), 9–25.

108. Bernardo Reyes, funeral oration for Mariano Escobedo, 24 May 1902, Chamber of Deputies, in *El Imparcial*, 25 May 1902: 1; *Diario del Hogar*, 27 May 1902: 1; and *Mexican Herald*, 25 May 1902: 2.

109. Escobedo hailed from Galeana, Nuevo León, a state that Bernardo Reyes had governed prior to his cabinet appointment. Born in Guadalajara, Reyes opposed the Plan de Tuxtepec but was co-opted by Díaz and appointed provisional governor of Nuevo León from 1885 to 1887 and from 1889 to 1900.

110. *Diario del Hogar*, 17 January 1900: 1. Mariscal uttered other shamelessly servile and nationally embarrassing comments to flatter his U.S. hosts in Chicago in 1898. See García

Granados, *Historia de México*, 1:393–94. From 1846 to 1848, the nation failed to mobilize in common defense against a foreign invader. See Pedro Santoni, *Mexicans at Arms: Puro Federalists and the Politics of War, 1845–1848* (Fort Worth: Texas Christian University Press, 1996); and Pedro Santoni, "The Failure of Mobilization: The Civic Militia of Mexico in 1846," *Mexican Studies/Estudios Mexicanos* 12, no. 2 (Summer 1996): 169–94. The heroic defense of Chapultepec Castle has become an enduring myth of republican Mexico, but at what cost? See Pedro Santoni, "'Where Did the Other Heroes Go?' Exalting the 'Polko' National Guard Battalions in Nineteenth-Century Mexico," *Journal of Latin American Studies* 34, no. 4 (November 2002): 807–44.

111. *El Universal*, 10 May 1893: 1. This may have been an excerpt from Joaquín Baranda's unfavorably received apologia, which motivated adverse comments. See García Granados, *Historia de México*, 1:332.

112. CPD 20:3963–3979:13931–14839.

113. Ayuntamiento de la Ciudad de México, *Discurso del C. Ingeniero Sebastián Camacho Presidente del Ayuntamiento de 1895. Al instalarse el de 1896. Contestación del C. Gobernador del Distrito Federal Gral. Pedro Rincon Gallardo y Memoria Documentada de los trabajos municipales de 1895* (Mexico City: Imp. y Lit. "La Europea," 1896), 34.

114. *Siglo XIX*, 5 October 1895: 2; *Corona fúnebre dedicada a la memoria del señor Ministro de Gobernación Licenciado Manuel Romero Rubio por el Gobierno del Estado y la Sociedad Científica literaria "Tamaulipas"* (Victoria, Tamaulipas: Imprenta del Gobierno del Estado, 1895), 9, 59–60. For his role during the Revolution of Ayutla, the state of Tamaulipas declared Romero Rubio a citizen. He also married a *tampiqueña*.

115. *El Monitor Republicano*, 15 October 1895: 2.

116. *El Nacional*, 4 November 1895: 2. Díaz and family visited his tomb on Todos Santos (All Saint's Day), November 1. *El Tiempo*, 3 November 1895: 2.

117. *El Nacional*, 5 November 1895: 2.

118. *El Monitor Republicano*, 15 October 1895: 2, 7 November 1895: 3; *El Siglo XIX*, 4 November 1895: 3, 6 November 1895: 1–2; *El Mundo Semanario Ilustrado*, 10 November 1895: 7.

119. Sóstenes Rocha et al. to Chousal, 9 September 1896, ACH 13:165:99; Thomas Braniff to Díaz, 28 September 1896, ACH 13:165:24.

120. Andrés Arroyo to Bernardo Reyes, 25 November 1889, ABR 11:2033:1–2; Reyes to Arroyo, 1 December 1889, ABR 11:2033:2; Reyes to General B. Dávalos, 13 September 1890, ABR Copiadores 4:2101; Díaz to Reyes, 27 February 1891, ABR 14:2634, 1; Díaz to Reyes, 27 February 1891, CPD 16:3:1398; Reyes to Díaz, 3 March 1891, ABR Copiadores 2:1095.

121. Reyes to F. Gutiérrez Cortina and Juan Dublán, 25 May 1893, ABR Copiadores 11:6999.

122. Reyes to Felipe Berriozábal, 17 June 1893, ABR Copiadores 9:5540.

123. Reyes to Juan E. Guerra, 21 August 1893, ABR Copiadores 11:7311; Reyes to Ma. Antonia de la Garza Vda. de Zuazua, 26 November 1898, ABR Copiadores 28:15187.

124. Manuel Romero Rubio to Bernardo Reyes, 17 March 1891, ABR 30:5868:1.

125. *El Nacional*, 9 May 1894, 2; *El Universal*, 30 May 1893: 2; *El Siglo XIX*, 30 May 1893: 3; *Actas de Cabildo* (1893), 290–92; AHEACM, *Funerales*, 1:34. *El Imparcial*, 26 May 1901: 1, 3; 31 May 1902: 1; 3 June 1902: 1; 7 June 1902: 1. *El Mundo Ilustrado*, 22 February 1903: [8], 30 January 1910: 22–23. *Actas de Cabildo* (Julio a Diciembre 1903), 384–85, 436, 463, 486, 644, 673–74, 743, 787; López-Portillo y Rojas, *Elevación y caída de Porfirio Díaz*, 199; Preciado, *Corona fúnebre dedicada a la memoria del general de división Carlos Pacheco*, 1–4.

126. Guerra, *México, del antigua régimen a la revolución*, 1:74, 2: "Anexo II," 384–92.

CHAPTER 5

1. Sóstenes Rocha, Guillermo Prieto, José Vicente Villada, et al. to Porfirio Díaz, 15 September 1886, Colección General Porfirio Díaz, Universidad Iberoamericana, legajo 11, caja 21, documento 10275 (hereafter cited as CPD followed by legajo, caja, and documento numbers); Díaz to Rocha et al., 22 September 1886, CPD 11:21:10276; Rocha to Díaz, 16 November 1886, CPD 11:25:12367–12368.

2. Manuel Sánchez Marmol, public oration to Benito Juárez, 18 July 1899, San Fernando Cemetery, *Mexican Herald*, 19 July 1899: 7.

3. *El Imparcial*, 16 February 1899: 1.

4. Díaz rarely attended the annual commemorations of the Battle of Churubusco and the execution of the Tacubaya martyrs, both held in Mexico City suburbs. On Miramón's orders, Leonardo Márquez executed fifty-three Liberal sympathizers, including doctors, nurses, and the young poet Juan Díaz Covarrubias on April 11, 1859. The victims were buried in the churchyard of San Pedro, and the city erected a small obelisk to mark the spot. During his first term, Díaz placed a wreath at the monument every April 11 but discontinued this in the 1880s. For more on the martyrs of Tacubaya, see *El Combate*, 11 April 1878: 3; *El Mundo Ilustrado*, 14 April 1901: [4]; *El Imparcial*, 12 April 1901: 1, 27 March 1904: 1.

5. See Manuel de J. Solís, *Historia de la Bandera, Himno, Escudo y Calendario Civico Nacionales* (Mexico City: n.p., 1940), 131–220.

6. Barbara Lee Kantz, "A Social History of the Urban Working Class in Mexico City, 1882–1910" (Ph.D. diss., State University of New York at Stony Brook, 1988), 77n28.

7. William Roseberry, *Anthropologies and Histories: Essays in Culture, History, and Political Economy* (New Brunswick: Rutgers University Press, 1989), 45; Raymond Williams, *Marxism and Literature* (Oxford: Oxford University Press, 1977), 110; see also Raymond Williams's definition of *consensus* and *hegemony* in *Keywords* (New York: Oxford University Press, 1976), 67–68, 118; Pierre Bourdieu, *Outline of a Theory of Practice*, trans. Richard Nice (New York: Cambridge University Press, 1977), 72, 76, 78–80, 118; James C. Scott, *Domination and the Arts of Resistance: Hidden Transcripts* (New Haven: Yale University Press, 1990), 74; Kate Crehan, *Gramsci, Culture and Anthropology* (Berkeley: University of California Press, 2002), 5, chap. 5; Claudio Lomnitz-Adler, *Exits from the Labyrinth: Culture and Ideology in the Mexican National Space* (Berkeley: University of California Press, 1992), 20–22.

8. *Two Republics*, 1 October 1885: 1. Most states of the republic had already declared that date a public holiday, and the national decree of 1873 also specified that national flags were to be raised on public buildings on the anniversaries of Juárez's birth and death. The resolution also empowered Congress to arrange pensions for Juárez's family members and appoint a commission to award a cash prize for the best biography of the benemérito. See Charles A. Weeks, *The Juárez Myth in Mexico* (Tuscaloosa: University of Alabama Press, 1987), 27.

9. *Two Republics*, 19 July 1873: 3, 21 July 1875: 3, 25 July 1880: 2–3; *El Siglo XIX*, 19 July 1879: 2; Weeks, *The Juárez Myth in Mexico*, 1–2, 26–33; Claudia Agostoni, *Monuments of Progress: Modernization and Public Health in Mexico City, 1876–1910* (Boulder: University of Colorado Press, 2003), 105.

10. Laurens Ballard Perry, *Juárez and Díaz: Machine Politics in Mexico* (DeKalb: Northern Illinois University Press, 1978), 44.

11. Working-class organizations such as the Convención Radical and the Gran Círculo de Obreros had adopted Juárez as their favorite son during the Lerdo administration.

12. Sóstenes Rocha et al. to Díaz, 15 September 1886, CPD 11:21:10275; Díaz to Rocha et al., 22 September 1886, CPD 11:21:10276; Pedro Hinojosa to Bernardo Reyes, 2 November 1886, Centro de Estudios de Historia de México Condumex, Archivo Bernardo Reyes, carpeta 5, legajo 989, documento 1 (hereafter cited as ABR followed by carpeta, legajo, and documento numbers); Reyes to Hinojosa, ABR 5:989:2.

13. *Two Republics*, 17 April 1885: 4, 5 December 1886: 4, 16 April 1886: 4, 27 April 1887: 4; *El Combate*, 6 March 1887: 1, cited in Weeks, *The Juárez Myth in Mexico*, 8, 142n13. See Enrique Torres Torija's Cinco de Mayo speech for a reference to the "Apostles" of Juárez in *El Imparcial*, 6 May 1902: 1.

14. *Two Republics*, 3 February 1885: 4, 5 February 1885: 4; México, Congreso, Cámara de Diputados, *Diario de los Debates de la Cámara de Diputados, Años de 1887–1910* (Mexico City: Imprenta de "El Partido Liberal," 1890–1910), *Año de 1887*, 372–77 (hereafter cited as *Diario de los Debates* followed by year and page numbers); *Two Republics*, 18 July 1886: 4, 20 March 1887: 4, 6 November 1887: 4, 27 November 1887: 4.

15. *Diario de los Debates, Año de 1887*, 372–73.

16. Ayuntamiento de la Ciudad de México, *Discurso del Señor Don Guillermo de Landa y Escandon, Presidente del Ayuntamiento en 1900. Discurso del Señor Don Ramón Corral, Gobernador del Distrito Federal y Memoria Documentada de los trabajos municipales de 1900*, 2 vols. (Mexico City: Tip. y Lit. "La Europea," 1901), 1:388.

17. *Diario de los Debates, Año de 1887*, 372.

18. Ibid., 373.
19. Ibid., 373–77.
20. Manuel Dublán, transcript of speech, [18] July 1887, CPD 12:13:6260–6262.
21. Díaz to Tomaso Gagliari, 6 October 1888, CPD 13:20:9772; Gagliardi to Díaz, 4 October 1888, CPD 13:20:9773; Gagliardi to Díaz, 9 March 1889, CPD 14:5:2265; Díaz to Gagliardi, 6 March 1889, CPD 14:5:2266; Giuseppe Trabacechi et al. to Díaz, 19 February 1889, CPD 14:8:3903; [Díaz] to Trabacechi, 3 April 1889, CPD 14:8:3904.
22. Weeks, *The Juárez Myth in Mexico*, 45.
23. *El Partido Liberal*, 19 July 1891: 2–3; Ayuntamiento de la Ciudad de México, *Discurso del C. Ingeniero Sebastián Camacho Presidente del Ayuntamiento de 1895. Al instalarse el de 1896. Contestación del C. Gobernador del Distrito Federal Gral. Pedro Rincon Gallardo y Memoria Documentada de los trabajos municipales de 1895* (Mexico City: Imp. y Lit. "La Europea," 1896), 134; Weeks, *The Juárez Myth in Mexico*, 35; *El Imparcial*, 10 July 1902: 1, 18 July 1902: 2–3, 22 August 1902: 1, 17 July 1903: 1, 18 July 1903: 1.
24. Lomnitz-Adler, *Exits from the Labyrinth*, 26.
25. See Mary Louise Pratt, *Imperial Eyes: Travel Writing and Transculturation* (New York: Routledge, 1992).
26. *Two Republics*, 19 July 1895: 1.
27. *Mexican Herald*, 18 July 1901: 8; *El Imparcial*, 18 July 2001: 1, 19 July 2001: 1–3.
28. *El Imparcial*, 19 July 1902: 2.
29. The City Council allotted $500 for the first official Juárez commemoration. See *Actas de Cabildo del Ayuntamiento Constitucional de México, Años de 1886–1896*, Edición de "El Municipio Libre" (Mexico City: Imp. de la Escuela Correcional de Artes y Oficios, 1886–1900), *Año de 1887*, 364–65. *Two Republics*, 8 July 1888: 2; 17 July 1888: 2, 4; 18 July 1888: 2, 4; 19 July 1888: 2, 4; 20 July 1888: 4; 18 July 1889: 2, 4; 19 July 1889: 4; 18 July 1890: 4; 19 July 1890: 2, 4; 18 July 1891: 2, 4; 19 July 1891: 4; 19 July 1892: 4; 19 July 1893: 4; 19 July 1894: 1. *El Partido Liberal*, 19 July 1891: 3; *La Patria*, 19 July 1891: 2; *El Mundo Semanario Ilustrado*, 19 July 1896: 35–37; *El Paladin*, 20 July 1902: 1. *Mexican Herald*, 18 July 1900: 8; 19 July 1900: 5, 8; 18 July 1901: 1; 19 July 1904: 1.
30. *El Siglo XIX*, 18 July 1894: 1–2, 19 July 1894: 2; *El Mundo Semanario Ilustrado*, 14 July 1895: 10, 21 July 1895: 8–9; *El Imparcial*, 18 July 1899: 1, 19 July 1899: 1, 19 July 1902: 1–2; *Mexican Herald*, 18 July 1899: 8, 19 July 1899: 1, 2, 5, 7–8.
31. Rodolfo Reyes, public oration to Benito Juárez, 18 July 1899, San Fernando Cemetery, *El Imparcial*, 19 July 1899: 1. Civic marchers on Juárez Day doubled from ten thousand in 1888 to twenty thousand in 1899.
32. Rosendo Pineda, oration, 18 July 1902, San Fernando Cemetery, *El Imparcial*, 19 July 1902: 1.
33. The Santacilia, de la Barra, Corona, and Arteaga families all had blood ties to Juárez. *El Partido Liberal*, 19 July 1891: 3; *Mexican Herald*, 19 July 1898: 8; *El Imparcial*, 19 July 1901: 1–3.
34. Sánchez Marmol, public oration, 18 July 1899, 7.
35. *Mexican Herald*, 19 July 1899: 7.
36. *El Siglo XIX*, 19 July 1894: 2; Reyes to Rafael Chousal, 27 June 1892, ABR Copiadores 8:5010; Chousal to Reyes, 30 June 1892, ABR 16:3194:1; Reyes to Chousal, 5 July 1892, ABR Copiadores 8:5021; Reyes to Chousal, 27 June 1892, Archivo Rafael Chousal, Universidad Nacional Autonoma de México, caja 6, expediente 77, folio 47 (hereafter cited as ACH followed by caja, expediente, and folio numbers); Chousal to Reyes, 30 June 1892, ACH 5:76:54; Chousal to Bernabé Bravo, 30 June 1892, ACH 5:76:55; Bravo to Chousal, 1 July 1892, ACH 6:77:47; Reyes to Chousal, 4 July 1892, ACH 6:77:81; Chousal to Reyes, 8 July 1892, ACH 6:77:82. Reyes spent 30–60 pesos a year on such wreaths and believed that the money could be better spent. See Reyes to Francisco M. Ramírez, 23 July 1894, ABR Copiadores 16:10248; Reyes to José del Valle, 16 July 1895, ABR Copiadores 18:11422.
37. *El Imparcial*, 19 July 1902: 2–3; 18 July 1905: 1; 19 July 1905: 1; 17 July 1906: 1; 19 July 1906: 1, 3; 19 July 1908: 1.
38. *Two Republics*, 3 March 1888: 4; 20 March 1888: 4; 22 March 1888: 2, 4; 22 March 1891: 4; 22 March 1898: 5. Comité Directivo de la Gran Liga Liberal "Benito Juárez" to Díaz, 30 August 1895, ACH 11:147:14–15; *El Mundo Semanario Ilustrado*, 15 July 1900: [5]; *Mexican Herald*, 19 July 1904: 1.

39. *Mexican Herald*, 20 July 1897: 3. The former emperor Iturbide was shot at Padilla on July 19, 1824. In 1838, his remains were conveyed to the National Cathedral and buried with official pomp beneath the Chapel of San Felipe de Jesús. See Charles A. Hale, *Mexican Liberalism in the Age of Mora, 1821–1853* (New Haven: Yale University Press, 1968), 26.

40. For information on the treatment of Maximilian's corpse, see *Two Republics*, 21 September 1867: 2, 28 September 1867: 1, 6 November 1867: 2. For the controversy surrounding Cantu's *History of the Last Thirty Years*, see *Two Republics*, 1 November 1885: 4.

41. Francisco Bulnes, *El verdadero Juárez y la verdad sobre la Intervention y el Imperio* (Mexico City: La viuda de C. Bouret, 1904). On the Bulnes polemic, see Weeks, *The Juárez Myth in Mexico*, chap. 5, 54–70; *El Imparcial*, 29 August 1904: 1, 30 August 1904: 1, 31 August 1904: 1, 1 September 1904: 1, 2 September 1904: 1, 5 September 1904: 1, 7 September 1904: 1, 9 September 1904: 1, 17 September 1904: 4; Francisco Cosmes, *El verdadero Bulnes y su falso Juárez* (Mexico City: Talleres de Tipografía, 1904).

42. Bulnes, *El verdadero Juárez y la verdad sobre la Intervention y el Imperio*; Francisco Bulnes to Chousal, 10 March 1904, ACH 27:242:148; Chousal to "My dear philosoph," 11 March 1904, ACH 27:242:149.

43. *Two Republics*, 8 July 1888: 2, 17 July 1888: 2, 17 July 1888: 4.

44. *Mexican Herald*, 11 March 1890: 8. This was the latest of a number of clubs named with pan-American solidarity in mind, including the Mexico–Cuba Club and the Morelos and Maceo Club.

45. Ibid., 1 February 1899: 8.

46. *El Imparcial*, 26 April 1905: 1, 8 May 1905: 1, 12 May 1905: 1, 9 October 1905: 1, 10 January 1906: 1, 11 January 1906: 1, 14 January 1906: 1, 21 January 1906: 1, 11 February 1906: 1–2, 18 February 1906: 1, 4 March 1906: 1, 11 March 1906: 1, 15 March 1906: 1, 20 March 1906: 1, 21 March 1906: 1, 22 March 1906: 1, 23 March 1906: 1, 24 March 1906: 1–2, 25 March 1906: 1.

47. Reyes to Ramón Corral, 16 January 1906, ABR 36:7171:1; Reyes to Corral, 11 February 1906, ABR 36:7175:1; Corral to Reyes, 20 February 1906, ABR 36:7179:1; Reyes to Porfirio Díaz, 31 March 1906, ABR 36:7185:1; Díaz to Reyes, 6 April 1906, ABR 36:7188:1.

48. Weeks, *The Juárez Myth in Mexico*, 48.

49. Juárez became a kind of euphemism for Díaz. See Scott, *Domination and the Arts of Resistance*, 52–53; Weeks, *The Juárez Myth in Mexico*, chap. 4, 43–53; Paul Garner, *Porfirio Díaz* (New York: Longman, 2001), 12. Charles Weeks deconstructs the Centenario de Juárez in his pioneering book *The Juárez Myth in Mexico*. Weeks contends that reconstructing Juárez as a comrade-in-arms and precursor of Díaz provoked a backlash from opponents on the Left and Right. Juárez maintained his status as the savior of the Patria and the paramount symbol of liberalism, republicanism, civil liberties, civilian rule, anticlericism, and democracy. But to the enemies of Díaz, the dictator became Juárez's antithesis as the sellout of the Patria and reviled symbol of repression, military rule, pro-clericalism, and authoritarianism. Weeks emphasizes the contentious intellectual debates that surfaced within the bourgeois literary culture of Mexico City. The attacks, however, were directed not against Díaz so much as those perceived to be running his government. Bulnes and the *científicos* were odd targets in the public debate that led Mexican critics to blame them for lies about Juárez. Díaz, as he was so apt to do, steered clear of such debates.

50. Lucas Alamán, *Historia de Méjico desde los primeros movimientos que prepararon su independencia en el año de 1808 hasta la época presente*, 5 vols. (Mexico City: Instituto Cultural Hélenico, Fondo de Cultura Económica, 1985), 1:374–75, 422–36.

51. Governor Rafael Rebollar uncovered a statue of Hidalgo in the suburb of Guadalupe Hidalgo in 1899, but in 1910 the editors of *El Mundo Semanario Ilustrado* still complained that although many "obscure warriors" were represented in bronze on the Paseo de la Reforma, the Federal District had yet to boast of a statue to Hidalgo (14 May 1899: 336, 27 February 1910: [8]). In a letter to Enrique Creel, Nuevo León governor Bernardo Reyes declined to donate to Chihuahua's fund to erect a Hidalgo monument. Creel was the president of the Junta Patriótica de Chihuahua. Reyes to Creel, 8 November 1889, ABR Copiadores 4:1924.

52. Thomas Benjamin and Marcial Ocasio-Melendez, "Organizing the Memory of Modern Mexico: Porfirian Historiography in Perspective, 1880s–1980s," *Hispanic American Historical Review* 64, no. 2 (May 1984): 332.

53. Vicente Riva Palacio, Alfredo Chavero, Julio Zárate, Enrique Olavarría y Ferrari, and José María Vigil, *México a través de los siglos*, 5 vols. (Barcelona: Espasa y companía, 1886–89); and Justo Sierra, *The Political Evolution of the Mexican People*, trans. Charles Ramsdell (Austin: University of Texas Press, 1969).
54. Emeterio de la Garza, public oration, 5 May 1898, Alameda, *Mexican Herald*, 6 May 1898: 4.
55. *Catálogo del Museo Nacional de Artilleria* (Mexico City: Talleres del Departamento de Estado Mayor, 1910).
56. California sculptor W. H. Mullins sent Governor Bernardo Reyes a copper-sheet bust of Hidalgo for presentation to Díaz. Reyes to W. H. Mullins, 7 May 1896, ABR Copiadores 19:12158; Reyes to Mullins, 22 June 1896, ABR Copiadores 19:12272.
57. *Two Republics*, 13 August 1887: 4, 2 December 1885: 4.
58. Francisco Cravioto to Díaz, 28 November 1885, CPD 10:23:11463; Díaz to Cravioto, 5 December 1885, CPD 10:23:11464; Cravioto to Díaz, 5 July 1886, CPD 11:17:8065.
59. [Díaz] to Ramón Corona, 30 November 1888, CPD 13:21:10487; [Díaz to Corona,] [n.d.], CPD 14:1:119; Ramón Corona to Díaz, 2 January 1889, CPD 14:1:120; Luis Curiel to Díaz, 29 December 1890, CPD 15:29:14179; Díaz to Curiel, 3 January 1891, CPD 15:29:14181. See also the letters from the dilatory governors of San Luís Potosí, Puebla, Zacatecas, México, Sinaloa, and Aguascalientes: Carlos Díaz Gutiérrez to Díaz, 20 May 1886, CPD 11:11:5039; Rosendo Márquez to Díaz, 25 January 1888, CPD 13:2:535; Márquez to Díaz, 2 August 1889, CPD 14:17:8284; Chávez M. Morfín to Díaz, 23 January 1888, CPD 13:2:597; José Zubieta to Díaz, 20 January 1888, CPD 13:2:998; Francisco Cañedo to Díaz, 4 February 1888, CPD 13:4:1706; Alejandro Vázquez del Mercado to Díaz, 1 August 1889, CPD 14:18:8801.
60. *Two Republics*, 9 September 1885: 4, 19 December 1889: 4; Carlos Pacheco to Reyes, January 1886, ABR 3:599:1; Reyes to Pacheco, 7 May 1886, ABR 3:599:2; Porfirio Díaz to Reyes, 14 May 1886, ABR 4:681:1; Reyes to Díaz, 28 May 1886, ABR 4:681:2; Reyes to Pacheco, 31 May 1886, ABR 4:705:1; M. Fernández to Reyes, 16 June 1886, ABR 4:727:1; Reyes to Fernández, 24 June 1886, ABR 4:727:2.
61. *Two Republics*, January 26, 1886, 4; Barbara A. Tenenbaum, "Streetwise History: The Paseo de la Reforma and the Porfirian State, 1876–1910," in *Rituals of Rule, Rituals of Resistance: Public Celebrations and Popular Culture in Mexico*, ed. William H. Beezley, Cheryl English Martin, and William E. French (Wilmington, Del.: SR Books, 1994), 145–47.
62. Lauro Carrillo to Díaz, 16 August 1888, CPD 13:16:7555–7556; Carrillo to Díaz, 21 November 1888, CPD 13:22:10531–10534; Carrillo to Díaz, 27 August 1889, CPD 14:19:9049; Carillo to Díaz, 30 August 1889, CPD 14:19:9051–9052; Díaz to Carrillo, 6 September 1889, CPD 14:19:9053.
63. Reyes to Díaz, 24 November 1891, ABR Copiadores 2:1282. See also Reyes to Creel, 8 November 1889, ABR Copiadores 4:1924.
64. *Two Republics*, 1 August 1880: 3, 31 July 1886: 2, 17 April 1888: 4, 29 July 1888: 4, 31 July 1888: 4, 30 July 1889: 4, 28 July 1889: 4, 31 July 1889: 4, 31 July 1889: 4, 29 July 1890: 4, 31 July 1890: 4, 30 July 1891: 4, 31 July 1892: 4; *El Partido Liberal*, 30 July 1891: 2; *El Monitor Republicano*, 28 July 1893: 3; *El Siglo XIX*, 30 July 1894: 2; J. P. Gallardo y Rincón et al. to Díaz, 1889, CPD 14:17:8228; Gallardo y Rincón to Díaz, 9 September 1889, CPD 14:19:9351; Díaz to Gallardo y Rincón, 10 September 1889, CPD 14:19:9352; Félix Luna et al. [Sociedad Mutua "Miguel Hidalgo y Costilla"] to Presidente de la Cámara de Diputados, 5 May 1891, CPD 16:9:4435. See *Actas de Cabildo* for the years 1887–1903 for Hidalgo Day expenditures.
65. Agustín Avendaño, public oration, 30 July 1897, Orrin's Theater, *Mexican Herald*, 31 July 1897: 8.
66. *La Voz de México*, 29 July 1896: 3, 31 July 1896: 2; *Mexican Herald*, 31 July 1896: 8, 31 July 1897: 8, 26 July 1898: 1, 27 July 1898: 8, 29 July 1898: 8, 31 July 1898: 8, 27 July 1900: 1; *El Imparcial*, 28 May 1897: 1, 31 July 1901: 1, 29 July 1902: 1, 30 July 1902: 1, 31 July 1902: 1, 29 July 1902: 1, 31 July 1904: 1, 31 July 1906: 1, 31 July 1908: 1, 8.
67. Porfirio Díaz, in *El Mundo Semanario Ilustrado*, 22 September 1895: 4.
68. William E. French, "Progreso Forzado: Workers and the Inculcation of the Capitalist Work Ethic in the Parral Mining District," in Beezley, Martin, and French, *Rituals of Rule, Rituals of Resistance*, 191–92, 201–2.

69. *El Popular*, 31 July 1903: 1–2, 1 August 1903: 2; *El Imparcial*, 30 July 1903: 1, 31 July 1903: 1; *El Mundo*, 31 July 1903: 1; *El Pais*, 31 July 1903: 1.

70. *El Imparcial*, 8 April 1901: 1, 9 May 1902: 1.

71. Alfred Oscar Coffin, *Land Without Chimneys; or The Byways of Mexico* (Cincinnati: Editor Publishing Co., 1898), 116.

72. Tenenbaum, "Streetwise History," 133–34; Ramón Eduardo Ruiz, *Triumphs and Tragedy: A History of the Mexican People* (New York: W. W. Norton and Co., 1992), 100, 157, 159.

73. *Two Republics*, 14 August 1869: 3; Manuel Rivera Cambas, *México pintoresco, artístico y monumental*, 3 vols. (Mexico City: Editorial del Valle de México, 1972), 2:185–86.

74. "Discurso pronunciado por el C. Presidente de la República," *El Nacional*, 19 September 1884: 2.

75. Cited in Garner, *Porfirio Díaz*, 18.

76. Federico Gamboa, *Mi diario: Mucho de mi vida y algo de la de otros*, 5 vols. (Mexico City: Consejo Nacional de la Cultura y las Artes, 1994), 2:45–52, 173. Gamboa delivered the speech at a literary event commemorating the founding of the Escuela Nacional Preparatoria. The speech was also attacked by Manuel Sánchez Marmól in *Diario del Hogar*. Gamboa, the nephew of José María Iglesias, regained Díaz's favor the following year and served the government as ambassador to Central America.

77. Jeffrey Pilcher, *Que Vivan los Tamales! Food and the Making of Mexican Identity* (Albuquerque: University of New Mexico Press, 1998), 78–80.

78. *El Nacional*, 20 August 1887: 3.

79. "Discurso pronunciado por el C. Presidente de la República," *El Nacional*, 18 September 1887: 1.

80. *El Nacional*, 20 August 1887: 3.

81. *Two Republics*, 23 August 1892: 4; *Mexican Herald*, 5 August 1898: 4, 22 August 1898: 2, 22 August 1900: 2, 20 August 1904: 3, 21 August 1904: 3, 22 August 1904: 8; *El Imparcial*, 22 August 1900: 1–2, 22 August 1903: 1, 22 August 1904: 1, 22 August 1905: 1, 22 August 1906: 1.

82. *El Siglo XIX*, 9 September 1878: 3; *Two Republics*, 13 September 1879: 3, 12 September 1880: 3, 10 September 1882: 3, 8 September 1885: 4, 8 September 1886: 4, 9 September 1886: 4, 1 September 1887: 4, 9 September 1890: 4, 8 September 1892: 4. *Mexican Herald*, 4 September 1897: 1; 8 September 1897: 5; 9 September 1897: 5; 8 September 1898: 8; 9 September 1898: 8; 9 September 1899: 1; 8 September 1900: 2; 9 September 1900: 1, 8, 10; 9 September 1901: 8; 7 September 1902: 8; 9 September 1902: 8. *El Imparcial*, 8 September 1899: 1, 9 September 1899: 2, 9 September 1902: 1, 9 September 1904: 1; *El Tiempo Ilustrado*, 10 September 1905: 574, 578; Gustavo Casasola, *Efemérides Ilustradas del México de ayer*, 5 vols. (Mexico City: Ediciones Archivo Casasola, n.d.), 1:166, 262, 356. One of the Niños Héroes, either Fernando Montes de Oca or Juan Escutia, reportedly wrapped himself in the Mexican flag and plunged from the heights of the castle to his death. The revolutionary state fastened onto these six heroes and built an enormous monument to them at Chapultepec. Six tall columns (one for each cadet) reach into the sky and are crowned with stones in the shape of a flaming torch. It is a most impressive structure, but one that owes its historical genealogy to the Porfirian state.

83. Under Manuel González a contract was signed with Pottier & Stymus of New York to carry out the interior renovation and decoration of the living quarters at Chapultepec. The government spent 200,000 pesos to restore the castle to serve as Díaz's presidential palace and summer home after November 1885. *Two Republics*, 15 August 1885: 4, 27 April 1886: 4, 7 May 1886: 4; *Mexican Herald*, 8 September 1900: 2, 9 September 1900: 8–10; *Semanario Literario Ilustrado de "El Tiempo,"* 15 September 1902: 607; *El Imparcial*, 9 September 1902: 1. Limantour was official director of public works at Chapultepec.

84. A description and photograph of the stirring allegorical scene appear in *El Tiempo Ilustrado*, 10 September 1905: 574, 578; Casasola, *Efemérides Ilustrados del México de ayer*, 1:356.

85. Pedro Santoni, "'Where Did the Other Heroes Go?' Exalting the 'Polko' National Guard Battalions in Nineteenth-Century Mexico," *Journal of Latin American Studies* 34, no. 4 (November 2002): 844.

86. *Mexican Herald*, 8 September 1901: 11.

87. *El Imparcial*, 9 September 1901: 1, 9 September 1908: 1.

88. Antonio Ramos Pedrueza, speech, *Mexican Herald*, 9 September 1901: 8.
89. See J. M. Tornel to Mariano Riva Palacio, 1 December 1842, Mariano Riva Palacio Papers, Benson Latin American Library, University of Texas, cited in William Forrest Sprague, *Vicente Guerrero, Mexican Liberator: A Study in Patriotism* (Chicago: R. R. Donnelley and Sons, 1939), 123. Mariano Riva Palacio was Guerrero's son-in-law.
90. See *El Tiempo Ilustrado*, 27 September 1908: 625.
91. *Two Republics*, 15 September 1886: 4; *Mexican Herald*, 12 February 1898: 4, 15 February 1898: 4, 14 February 1904: 1, 15 February 1904: 1; *El Imparcial*, 15 February 1901: 1, 15 February 1902: 1, 2 February 1905: 1, 12 February 1905: 1, 15 February 1905: 1, 11 January 1906: 1, 30 January 1906: 1, 11 February 1906: 1, 15 February 1906: 1, 15 February 1909: 1, 8.
92. *El Tiempo Ilustrado*, 10 April 1908: 638.
93. Wilbert H. Timmons, *Morelos: Priest, Soldier, Statesman of Mexico* (El Paso: Texas Western College Press, 1963), 167–68.
94. *Two Republics*, 22 December 1887: 4, 23 December 1888: 4, 20 December 1889: 2, 23 December 1891: 4; *El Siglo XIX*, 21 December 1894: 2; *El Imparcial*, 14 December 1901: 1, 23 December 1908: 1; *Mexican Herald*, 23 December 1904: 1, 20 December 1905: 1, 23 December 1905: 1–2.
95. *Mexican Herald*, 23 December 1897: 4.
96. Porfirio Díaz, inscription in a testimonial album in honor of Morelos, 30 September 1891, Casa de Morelos in Morelia, cited in Timmons, *Morelos*, 167.
97. Gamboa, *Mi diario*, 1:160.
98. *Mexican Herald*, 18 June 1896, 21 June 1896.
99. Colin M. MacLachlan and William H. Beezley, *El Gran Pueblo: A History of Greater Mexico* (New York: Prentice Hall, 1994), 157; *Mexican Herald*, 15 September 1895, 16 September 1895, 17 September 1895, 14 June 1898: 5, 14 June 1898: 5.
100. *El Imparcial*, 26 May 1903: 1.
101. Aristeo Mercado to Chousal, 26 December 1896, ACH 14:168:21–22.
102. *El Imparcial*, 8 September 1904: 1, 9 October 1904: 1, 20 October 1904: 1, 16 November 1904: 1, 20 November 1904: 1, 23 November 1904: 1, 24 November 1904: 1, 25 November 1904: 1, 26 November 1904: 1, 29 November 1904: 1, 30 November 1904: 1, 2 December 1904: 1–2, 3 December 1904: 1, 4 December 1904: 1, 5 December 1904: 1.
103. Agustín del Río to Chousal, October 1896, ACH 14:166:66.
104. *El Imparcial*, 7 February 1906: 1.
105. Elite alignment with popular values and appropriation of popular traditions continued into the twentieth century. A recent example was found in Tepoztlán, Morelos, where local elites who wanted to build a golf course near the traditional town tried to cull popular support by claiming ideological descent from Zapata. See Lomnitz-Adler, *Exits from the Labyrinth*, 27.

CHAPTER 6

1. For a similar process in France, see Avner Ben-Amos, "The Sacred Center of Power: Paris and Republican State Funerals," *Journal of Interdisciplinary History* 22, no. 1 (Summer 1991): 27. See Appendix B for the reburials of the Porfirian era.
2. González Obregón to Díaz, 23 September 1895, Archivo Rafael Chousal, Universidad Nacional Autonóma de México, caja 10, expediente 145, folio 45–53 (hereafter cited as ACH followed by caja, expediente, and folio numbers); Díaz to González Obregón, 26 September 1895, ACH 10:145:54.
3. Lyman L. Johnson, ed., *Body Politics: Death, Dismemberment, and Memory in Latin America* (Albuquerque: University of New Mexico Press, 2004), 5.
4. *El Universal*, 27 May 1893: 1.
5. *Mexican Herald*, 17 September 1901: 2.
6. For example, the rebels committed heinous decapitations and mutilations as frequently as the royalists. The abominable massacres and massive pillage of Guanajuato and Guadalajara in October and November 1810 set a hideous pattern of brutality during the Mexican Wars of Independence. See Lucas Alamán, *Historia de Méjico desde los primeros movimientos que*

prepararon su independencia en el año de 1808 hasta la época presente, 5 vols. (Mexico City: Instituto Cultural Hélenico, Fondo de Cultura Económica, 1985), 1:403–4.

7. Félix Romero, congressional speech, 22 September 1881, Chamber of Deputies, *El Siglo XIX*, 23 September 1881: 1.

8. Vicente Riva Palacio, Alfredo Chavero, Julio Zárate, Enrique Olavarría y Ferrari, and José María Vigil, *México a través de los siglos*, 5 vols. (Barcelona: Espasa y companía, 1886–89), 3: *La Guerra de Independencia*, 222.

9. Justo Sierra, *The Political Evolution of the Mexican People*, trans. Charles Ramsdell (Austin: University of Texas Press, 1969), 155.

10. Carlos María de Bustamante, *Cuadro histórico de la revolución mexicana*, 3 vols., reprint ed. (Mexico City: Ediciones de la Comisión Nacional para la Celebración del Sesquicentenario de la Proclamación de la Independencia Nacional y del Cinquentenario de la Revolución Mexicana, 1961), 1:198; José María Luís Mora, *México y sus revoluciones*, 2nd ed. (Mexico City: Editorial Porrua, 1950), 4:147–48; Alamán, *Historia de Méjico*, 1:190; Riva Palacio et al., *México a través de los siglos*, 3:211–13, 217–18; Hugh M. Hamill Jr., *The Hidalgo Revolt: Prelude to Mexican Independence* (Gainesville: University of Florida Press, 1966), 210–16; John Anthony Caruso, *The Liberators of Mexico* (Glouchester, Mass.: Peter Smith, 1967), 78.

11. Alamán, *Historia de Méjico*, 2:194–95, 203–4; Bustamante, *Cuadro histórico de la revolución mexicana*, 1:198–202; Riva Palacio et al., *México a través de los siglos*, 3:222; Hamill, *The Hidalgo Revolt*, 210–16, 249n; Caruso, *The Liberators of Mexico*, 75–80.

12. Alamán, *Historia de Méjico*, 2:204; Hamill, *The Hidalgo Revolt*, 216; Riva Palacio et al., *México a través de los siglos*, 3:222; *El Tiempo*, 30 July 1895: 2; *El Universal*, 27 May 1893: 1; Carmen Nava Nava and Isabel Fernández Tejeda, "Images of Independence in the Nineteenth Century. The Grito de Dolores: History and Myth," in *Viva Mexico! Viva la Independencia! Celebrations of September 16*, ed. William H. Beezley and David E. Lorey (Wilmington, Del.: SR Books, 2001), 24.

13. Alamán, *Historia de Méjico*, 3:259–60, 4:14, 74–75; Bustamante, *Cuadro histórico de la revolución mexicana*, 1:453–54, 646–47, 2:60–61; Riva Palacio et al., *México a través de los siglos*, 3:322, 417, 425, 430; Wilbert H. Timmons, *Morelos: Priest, Soldier, Statesman of Mexico* (El Paso: Texas Western College Press, 1963), 128, 131; Ernesto Lemoine Villicaña, *Morelos, su vida revolucionaria a través de sus escritos y de otros testimonios de la época* (Mexico City: Universidad Nacional Autónoma de México, 1965), 138–39, 456, 475–78; Caruso, *The Liberators of Mexico*, 118–20, 141–42, 148; Agustín Rivera, "Viaje á las Ruinas del Fuerte del Sombrero," *El Gil Blas*, 28 July 1895: 3. In 1860, a patriotic society marked the spot of Matamoros's public humiliation by placing an inscribed marble plaque in the Plaza of the Martyrs in Morelia.

14. Lemoine Villicaña, *Morelos*, 144.

15. Alamán, *Historia de Méjico*, 4:316, 325–26; Lemoine Villicaña, *Morelos*, 632–38, 656–57. A commemorative history, Lemoine's work was published on the bicentennial of Morelos's birth and the 150th anniversary of his execution. On Morelos's degradation ceremony, see the reports entitled "Autillo y degradación del cura Morelos" written by eyewitness Ramón Roca and published in the royalist government newspaper *Noticioso General* from November 25–29, 1815, and "Acta oficial, no destinada al público de la ceremonia de degradación de las órdenes sacerdotales de Morelos, efectuada en el salón principal del Santo Oficio," reprinted in Lemoine Villicaña, *Morelos*, 632–39. Lemoine described the ritual of degradation as a "black ceremony" and Rocha's report as "perverse" and one of the "most embarrassing infamies" committed by the Old Regime. In this he follows a Liberal legacy established by Bustamante, who considered the degradation ceremony of Hidalgo "an ecclesiastical farse" executed by "incompetent judges, and trampling all legal procedures, not listening to the prisoner, and acting it out in a harebrained, ridiculous, and capricious way" (*Cuadro histórico de la revolución mexicana*, 2:198).

16. Bustamante, *Cuadro histórico de la revolución mexicana*, 2:146, 650–53.

17. Alamán, *Historia de Méjico*, 4:331, 333–34; Bustamante, *Cuadro histórico de la revolución mexicana*, 2:171–79; Hubert Howe Bancroft, *History of Mexico*, 6 vols. (San Francisco: History Co., 1888), 4:679–80; Riva Palacio et al., *México a través de los siglos*, 3:487–88, 495–98; Timmons, *Morelos*, 156–67; Caruso, *The Liberators of Mexico*, 157–58. Bustamante,

a deputy at the Congress of Chilpancingo, glorified Morelos like no other; see Christon I. Archer, "Deaths Patriots—Celebration, Denunciation, and Memories of Mexico's Independence Heroes: Miguel Hidalgo, José María Morelos, and Agustín de Iturbide," in Johnson, *Body Politics*, 80.

18. Bustamante, *Cuadro histórico de la revolución mexicana*, 2:649, 655–58, 662; Alamán, *Historia de Méjico*, 4:626–27. We might add to the list of martyrs Vicente Guerrero, who survived long enough to serve as Mexico's second president but was executed in 1831 by Conservatives loyal to Anastasio Bustamante. The Oaxacan state legislature decreed that the body of the insurgent be removed from Cuilapa on April 30, 1833, and transferred to the Church of Santo Domingo in Oaxaca, where it was deposited. The National Congress passed a resolution declaring him a benemérito de la Patria on November 16, 1833. The name of Cuilapa was changed to Ciudad Guerrero, and the region where he fought was renamed the state of Guerrero. On December 2, 1842, Guerrero's remains were brought to Mexico City and reburied in the Santa Paula Cemetery during the interim presidency of Nicolás Bravo, Guerrero's close friend and later bitter rival. See J. M. Tornel to Mariano Riva Palacio, 1 December 1842, Mariano Riva Palacio Collection, Benson Latin American Library, University of Texas, cited in William Forrest Sprague, *Vicente Guerrero, Mexican Liberator: A Study in Patriotism* (Chicago: R. R. Donnelley and Sons, 1939), 123. Riva Palacio was Guerrero's son-in-law.

19. Bustamante, *Cuadro histórico de la revolución mexicana*, 2:662; *El Hijo del Ahuizote*, 4 August 1895: 5; *El Mundo Semanario Ilustrado*, 4 August 1895: 8; Timmons, *Morelos*, 166.

20. Bustamante, *Cuadro histórico de la revolución mexicana*, 2:663.

21. *El Universal*, 14 May 1893: 1, 27 May 1893: 1; *El Mundo Semanario Ilustrado*, 4 August 1895: 8; *El Hijo del Ahuizote*, 4 August 1895: 5; Riva Palacio et al., *México a través de los siglos*, 3:425.

22. Francisco de la Maza, "Los restos de Hernán Cortés," *Cuadernos Americanos* 32 (1947): 153–74; Charles A. Hale, *Mexican Liberalism in the Age of Mora, 1821–1853* (New Haven: Yale University Press, 1968), 99; Nava and Fernández, "Images of Independence in the Nineteenth Century," 49–50.

23. Bustamante, *Cuadro histórico de la revolución mexicana*, 2:665–66.

24. For a full description of the costly pyre, see ibid., 666–71.

25. City Councilman Jesús Galindo y Villa recounted the story of the first burial of the Independence Heroes as it was told to him by an eyewitness of the event. His account was published in *El Municipio Libre*, 7 August 1895: 1–2. For similar versions of the original burial, see also *El Universal*, 14 May 1893: 1; *La Voz de México*, 2 August 1895: 2; *El Mundo Semanario Ilustrado*, 4 August 1895: 8; *El Gil Blas*, 31 July 1895: 1; and *El Hijo del Ahuizote*, 4 August 1895: 5. Compare these versions to Bustamante, *Cuadro Histórico de la revolución mexicana*, 2:663–72.

26. Bustamante, *Cuadro histórico de la revolución mexicana*, 2:672.

27. *La Libertad*, 9 September 1881: 3.

28. See Pola's account of the crypt visit in *El Universal*, 14 May 1893: 1.

29. *El Universal*, 27 May 1893: 1.

30. *El Nacional*, 21 August 1894: 3; *El Mundo Semanario Ilustrado*, 4 August 1895: 7–10; *El Tiempo*, 27 July 1895: 2.

31. Ayuntamiento de la Ciudad de México, *Discurso del C. Ingeniero Sebastián Camacho Presidente del Ayuntamiento de 1895. Al instalarse el de 1896. Contestación del C. Gobernador del Distrito Federal Gral. Pedro Rincon Gallardo y Memoria Documentada de los trabajos municipales de 1895* (Mexico City: Imp. y Lit. "La Europea," 1896), 135; *El Tiempo*, 27 July 1895: 2; *Two Republics*, 28 July 1895: 2; *El Mundo Semanario Ilustrado*, 4 August 1895: 8. Newspapers reported the expenditure of 3,500 pesos for the purchase and installation of both the monument and urn. *El Tiempo* reported that 8,000 pesos had been spent on the importation of wood from Havana, but this figure cannot be corroborated.

32. The city approved an additional 350 pesos to cover expenses. *Diario del Hogar*, 25 July 1895: 2; *El Gil Blas*, 28 July 1895: 3, 1 August 1895: 1; *El Nacional*, 29 July 1895: 2; *El Tiempo*, 31 July 1895: 2; *El Noticioso*, 31 July 1895: 3; *El Mundo Semanario Ilustrado*, 4 August 1895: 9; *El Municipio Libre*, 9 August 1895: 1, 14 August 1895: 1.

33. *Two Republics*, 28 July 1895: 2; *El Gil Blas*, 28 July 1895: 3; *El Municipio Libre*, 30 July 1895: 3. The editors of *El Gil Blas* later corrected themselves and agreed that the large bones belonged to Pedro Moreno (see 31 July 1895: 1). Mexican historian Alfonso Teja Zabre has suggested that Morelos's remains were not among those of the other Independence Heroes in 1895. Morelos's illegitimate son, General Juan Nepumuceno Almonte, may have moved them to a secret grave, the whereabouts of which are still unknown. See Alfonso Teja Zabre, *Vida de Morelos* (Mexico City: Universidad Nacional Autonóma de México, 1959), 298.

34. *Diario del Hogar*, 26 July 1895: 3; *El Tiempo*, 27 July 1895: 2.

35. *El Mundo Semanario Ilustrado*, 4 August 1895: 9.

36. *Diario del Hogar*, 26 July 1895: 3; *El Mundo Semanario Ilustrado*, 4 August 1895: 9–10; Dehesa to Díaz, 25 September 1895, ACH 10:140:5; Díaz to Dehesa, 30 September 1895, ACH 10:140:6; María Guadalupe Hidalgo y Costilla to Jefatura Política del Canton de Veracruz," 7 September 1895, ACH 10:140:7–11.

37. *El Mundo Semanario Ilustrado*, 4 August 1895: 9; *El Tiempo*, 31 July 1895: 2.

38. *El Municipio Libre*, 30 July 1895: 3, 13 August 1895: 1; *La Voz de México*, 4 August 1895: 2; *El Gil Blas*, 31 July 1895: 3; Federico Gamboa, *Mi diario: Mucho de mi vida y algo de la de otros*, 5 vols. (Mexico City: Consejo Nacional de la Cultura y las Artes, 1994), 1:171.

39. *Two Republics*, 31 July 1895: 1; *El Tiempo*, 31 July 1895: 2; *El Municipio Libre*, 28 July 1895: 3, 30 July 1895: 1, 31 July 1895: 1, 10 August 1895: 1; *El Gil Blas*, 1 August 1895: 1; *El Mundo Semanario Ilustrado*, 4 August 1895: 9.

40. J. R. Arellano, funeral oration for the Independence Heroes, 30 July 1895, Municipal Palace, *El Municipio Libre*, 2 August 1895: 2.

41. Gamboa, *Mi diario*, 1:171–72.

42. Ibid., 172.

43. *El Monitor Republicano*, 3 October 1895: 1

44. *El Nacional*, 30 July 1895: 1.

45. *El Partido Liberal*, 6 August 1895: 1.

46. *El Gil Blas*, 8 August 1895: 3; Bernardo Reyes to Joaquín Trejo, 30 August 1895, Centro de Estudios de Historia de México Condumex, Archivo Bernardo Reyes, Copiadores, carpeta 18, legajo 11524; Manuel Torres to Rafael Chousal, 25 March 1896, ACH 12:159:47; Chousal to Torres, 25 March 1896, ACH 12:159:48; *El Monitor Republicano*, 3 October 1895: 3, 1 November 1895: 3, 6 November 1895: 2; *El Tiempo*, 5 November 1895: 3; *Mexican Herald*, 9 April 1898: 1; *El Imparcial*, 12 September 1899: 1.

47. *El Combate*, in *Diario del Hogar*, 1 August 1895: 1; *El Siglo XIX*, 20 August 1895: 1. In his diary, Gamboa also pondered why the remains were not buried at the rotunda (*Mi diario*, 1:172).

48. *El Mundo Semanario Ilustrado*, 4 August 1895: 10; *El Siglo XIX*, 20 August 1895: 1; *El Municipio Libre*, 13 August 1895: 1; *El Universal*, 2 November 1895: 3; *El Tiempo*, 5 November 1895: 2; Ayuntamiento de la Ciudad de México, *Discurso del C. Ingeniero Sebastián Camacho Presidente del Ayuntamiento de 1895*, 146.

49. *El Siglo XIX*, 20 August 1895: 1.

50. *El Monitor Republicano*, 3 October 1895: 1–2.

51. *El Mundo Semanario Ilustrado*, 4 August 1895: 10; *Diario del Hogar*, 7 August 1895: 1; *El Partido Liberal*, 8 August 1895: 3.

52. *El Partido Liberal*, 10 August 1895: 1.

53. The group's proposal was signed and dated on October 26, 1895, but not published until days later in *El Monitor Republicano*, 2 November 1895: 1. The signers included Mata, Vice President Enrique M. de los Rios, First Secretary José P. Rivera, Second Secretary Daniel Cabrera, and Treasurer Antonio de J. Lozano. Luis Toro summarized the group's arguments in *El Monitor Republicano* (6 November 1895: 1) and supported the proposal of the Grupo Reformista because it had numerous signatures whereas Bandera only had "his own personal feelings."

54. *El Siglo XIX*, 20 August 1895: 1.

55. *Mexican Herald*, 7 September 1899: 5; *El Imparcial*, 9 September 1899: 1, 13 September 1899: 1, 1 October 1899: 1, 9 November 1899: 1, 10 April 1900: 1, 11 May 1902: 1.

56. Genaro García, *Leona Vicario, heroína insurgente* (Mexico City: Secretaría de Educación

Pública, 1945), 88–89. Vicario died on August 21, 1842, in Mexico City. Her private funeral was held in the Santo Domingo temple, after which Santa Anna and others processed to the Panteón de los Angeles. Quintana Roo passed away in 1851.

57. *Actas de Cabildo del Ayuntamiento Constitucional de Mexico, Años de 1900–1901* (Mexico City: Imp. de "El Correro Español," 1905–7), *De 10 de Enero a 3 de Julio, Año de 1900*, 173 (hereafter cited as *Actas de Cabildo* [1900]). Ordoñez also wanted to transfer the remains of *illustrious* philanthrope Vidal Alcocer and General Vicente Filisola, both buried in the Panteón de los Angeles, to the rotunda. Instead, they were reburied in the first-class section of the Dolores Cemetery at the request of the secretary of justice. Díaz ordered the federal treasury to cover the expenses. See *Actas de Cabildo* (1900), 416; *Diario del Hogar*, 22 March 1900: 3, 14 April 1900: 2, 28 April 1900: 3, 1 May 1900: 3.

58. *Actas de Cabildo* (1900), 229, 319, 377, 388, 412, 478–79, 524, 533, 555, 562, 586; *El Nacional*, 28 May 1900: 2; *El Pais*, 28 May 1900: 1; *Diario del Hogar*, 29 May 1900: 3; *Two Republics*, 29 May 1900: 4; *El Universal*, 29 May 1900: 2. For photographs of this civic event, see *El Mundo Semanario Ilustrado*, 3 June 1900: [10]. Leona Vicario was the first woman buried in a necropolis reserved for "illustrious men," a fact discussed in *El Imparcial*, February 28 1901: 1.

59. *Mexican Herald*, 5 May 1898: 8, 6 May 1898: 8.

60. *Two Republics*, 12 December 1884: 4; *El Municipio Libre*, 1 August 1895: 3; *El Tiempo*, 4 August 1895: 2; *Diario del Hogar*, 6 August 1895: 2; *El Gil Blas*, 6 August 1895: 2; *El Siglo XIX*, 9 August 1895: 2.

61. *El Imparcial*, 20 March 1904: 1.

62. Timmons, *Morelos*, 166; *El Imparcial*, 4 June 1897: 1; Barbara A. Tenenbaum, "Streetwise History: The Paseo de la Reforma and the Porfirian State, 1876–1910," in *Rituals of Rule, Rituals of Resistance: Public Celebrations and Popular Culture in Mexico*, ed. William H. Beezley, Cheryl English Martin, and William E. French (Wilmington, Del.: SR Books, 1994), 145–48; *Crónica oficial de las fiestas del primer Centenario de la Independencia de México, publicada bajo la dirección de Genaro García, por acuerdo de la Secretaría de Gobernación* (Mexico City: Talleres del Museo Nacional, 1911).

63. José María Carrillo, funeral oration for Josefa Ortíz de Domínguez, 23 October 1894, Panteón Número 1, *La Sombra de Arteaga, Periódico Oficial del Gobierno del Estado* (Querétaro), 4 November 1894: 406–7.

64. Manuel Caballero, funeral oration for Josefa Ortíz de Domínguez, 23 October 1894, Teatro de Iturbide, *La Sombra de Arteaga*, 4 November 1894: 406.

65. Eric Zolov, *Refried Elvis: The Rise of the Mexican Counterculture* (Berkeley: University of California Press, 1999), 5, 9.

66. Alamán, *Historia de Méjico*, 1:368–69; Riva Palacio et al., *México a través de los siglos*, 3:395.

67. *El Nacional*, 18 October 1894: 2; *La Sombra de Arteaga*, 21 October 1894: 379–81, 28 October 1894: 386.

68. *El Nacional*, 21 August 1894: 3, 25 August 1894: 2, 18 October 1894: 2. The letter from Governor González Cosío to Mariano Soto Domínguez appeared in *La Sombra de Arteaga*, 28 October 1894: 387.

69. *La Sombra de Arteaga*, 14 October 1894: 371–72, 28 October 1894: 387–89; *El Nacional*, 18 October 1894: 2, 23 October 1894: 2.

70. *La Sombra de Arteaga*, 14 October 1894: 371–72; *El Nacional*, 18 October 1894: 2, 23 October 1894: 2; *El Siglo XIX*, 24 October 1894: 2.

71. *El Nacional*, 18 October 1894: 2, 23 October 1894: 2.

72. The government of Querétaro thought so highly of Caballero's reporting that it reprinted his articles from *El Nacional* in the state newspaper. See *La Sombra de Arteaga*, 28 October 1894: 387–92.

73. Ibid., 14 October 1894: 371–72, 28 October 1894: 389–90; *El Nacional*, 18 October 1894: 2, 24 October 1894: 2; 25 October 1894: 3; *El Monitor Republicano*, 24 October 1894: 2, 25 October 1894: 2; *El Siglo XIX*, 24 October 1894: 1–2.

74. *El Nacional*, 18 October 1894: 2, 25 October 1894: 2; *La Sombra de Arteaga*, 21 October 1894: 377–78, 28 October 1894: 393.

75. *El Nacional*, 26 October 1894: 2.

76. *El Monitor Republicano*, 24 October 1894: 2, 26 October 1894: 2; *El Nacional*, 26 October 1894: 2; *La Sombra de Arteaga*, 28 October 1894: 390–92; Manuel Caballero, funeral oration for Josefa Ortíz de Domínguez, 23 October 1894, Teatro de Iturbide, in *El Nacional*, 27 October 1894: 1; and *La Sombra de Arteaga*, 4 November 1894: 404–6.

77. *Actas de Cabildo del Ayuntamiento Constitucional de México, Años de 1886–1896*, Edición de "El Municipio Libre" (Mexico City: Imp. de la Escuela Correcional de Artes y Oficios, 1886–1900), 90. The Ayuntamiento allocated 1,200 pesos in its session of February 9, 1894. *El Monitor Republicano*, 1 December 1894: 3; *Actas de Cabildo* (1900), 68–69, 80, 109; *El Imparcial*, 9 November 1899: 1, 7 February 1900: 1. Quote is from *Mexican Herald*, 6 February 1900: 8.

78. *El Imparcial*, 7 September 1899: 1.

79. Sociedad de Señoras "Josefa Ortíz de Domínguez" to Rafael Chousal, [n.d.], ACH 13:161:93–103; Sociedad de Señoras to Chousal, 5 May 1896, ACH 13:161:98.

80. See Francisco O. Arce, *Album literario dedicado al eminente patricio general Nicolás Bravo en el centenario de su nacimiento, septiembre 10 de 1886* (Mexico City: Oficina tip. de la Secretaría de Fomento, 1886); Francisco O. Arce to Díaz, 27 March 1886, Colección General Porfirio Díaz, Universidad Iberoamericana, legajo 11, caja 7, documento 3361 (hereafter cited as CPD followed by legajo, caja, and documento numbers); Arce to Díaz, 9 April 1886, CPD 11:7:3404. Congress allocated $5,000 for the *centenario* of Bravo, but Arce had difficulty financing the construction of a new Bravo statue. See Flavio Maldonado to Díaz, 3 July 1886, CPD 11:16:7841; Díaz to Maldonado, CPD 11:16:7842; Arce to Díaz, 30 June 1886, CPD 11:17:8128; Díaz to Arce, CPD 11:17:8129. Díaz authorized the governor to collect them from the customs house of Acapulco. See Arce to Díaz, 14 July 1886, CPD 11:17:8176.

81. Batres to Chousal, 21 May 1890, ACH 3:50:10; Chousal to Batres, 23 May 1890, ACH 3:50:11.

82. *El Mundo Ilustrado*, 26 January 1902: 1; *El Imparcial*, 17 January 1902: 1, 18 January 1902: 1, 19 January 1902: 1, 21 January 1902: 1, 22 January 1902: 1–2, 6 September 1903: 4; *Mexican Herald*, 9 September 1903: 2.

83. México, Secretaría de Gobernación, *Memoria de la Secretaría de Gobernación correspondiente al cuatrienio de 1° de Diciembre de 1900 a 30 de Noviembre de 1904* (Mexico City: Imprenta del Gobierno Federal, 1906), 16, 193 (hereafter cited as *Memoria de Gobernación* [1900–1904]); "Programa para la translación de Chilpancingo a la Ciudad de México é inhumación de los restos del Benemérito General Don Nicolas Bravo," Archivo Histórico del Ex-Ayuntamiento de la Ciudad de México, *Funerales y ceremonias fúnebres, 1779–1915*, legato 1, expediente 42 (hereafter cited as AHEACM, *Funerales*, followed by legato and expediente numbers); *El Imparcial*, 21 March 1903: 1, 3 August 1903: 2, 29 August 1903: 1; *La Voz de México*, 29 August 1903: 1.

84. See the "Acta de exhumación en Chilpancingo" published in *El Imparcial*, 19 August 1903: 1, 9 September 1903: 3; *La Voz de México*, 4 September 1903: 1; *El Mundo Ilustrado*, 13 September 1903: [3–6].

85. *El Imparcial*, 31 August 1903: 1, 1 September 1903: 1, 2 September 1903: 1, 9 September 1903: 3.

86. Ibid., 5 September 1903: 1, 9 September 1903: 3; *El Mundo*, 29 August 1903: 1; *El Mundo*, 7 September 1903: 1.

87. *Memoria de Gobernación* (1900–1904), 40, 392–409.

88. Constancio Peña Idiáquez, F. Hernández, and Ignacio L. de la Barra to President of the Ayuntamiento, 22 August 1903, AHEACM, *Funerales*, 1:42; Constancio Peña Idiáquez, Fidencio Hernández, and Ignacio de la Barra to Presidente del Consejo Municipal, 27 August 1903, ibid.

89. *El Pais*, 1 September 1903: 2; *El Imparcial*, 3 August 1903: 2, 26 August 1903: 1, 3 September 1903: 1, 4 September 1903: 1, 8 September 1903: 2; *El Tiempo*, 27 August 1903: 2; *El Mundo*, 29 August 1903: 1, 7 September 1903: 1; *Diario Oficial*, 12 September 1903: 178.

90. Enrique Fernández Castelló to Señor Bribiesca [Secretary of the Ayuntamiento], n.d., AHEACM, *Funerales*, 1:42. Reply letters to the city government agreeing to send carriages "with pleasure" include Francisco Suinaga to Enrique Fernández Castelló, Agustín Alfredo Nuñez, and Nicolas Mariscal, 4 September 1903; J. Diego Liberes to Enrique Fernández

Castelló, Agustín Alfredo Nuñez, and Nicolas Mariscal, 4 September 1903; Telesforo García to Enrique Fernández Castelló, Agustín Alfredo Nuñez, and Nicolas Mariscal, 4 September 1903; Luis G. Lavie to Enrique Fernández Castelló, Agustín Alfredo Nuñez, and Nicolas Mariscal, 4 September 1903; A. Alvarez Rul to Juan Bribiesca, 4 September 1903; Luis Escalante to [Ayuntamiento], 5 September 1903; Miguel Alonzo Peón to Enrique Fernández Castelló, Agustín Alfredo Nuñez, and Nicolas Mariscal, 5 September 1903; and José Solórzano y Mata to Enrique Fernández Castelló, Agustín Alfredo Nuñez, and Nicolas Mariscal, 5 September 1903—all in ibid.

91. *El Mundo*, 3 September 1903: 1.
92. *El Mundo Ilustrado*, 6 September 1903: [3].
93. When Bravo was finally captured in December 1817, Viceroy Apodaca repaid Bravo's gesture at Medellin by sparing his life. For renditions of the Pardon of Medellin, see *Mexican Herald*, 1 September 1903: 1, 7 September 1903: 2; *El Mundo Ilustrado*, 6 September 1903: [3]; *La Tribuna*, 8 September 1903. Pedro Aspe's speech is reprinted in *Mexican Herald*, 8 September 1903: 2. Alfredo Chavero's funeral oration is in *El Mundo*, 10 September 1903: 2–3; and *Mexican Herald*, 9 September 1903: 2. Bravo's own testimony, originally published by Lucas Alamán, was reprinted. Historians have generally upheld the historical veracity of the Pardon of Medellin. See Alamán, *Historia de Méjico*, 1:260–61; Leslie Byrd Simpson, "Santa Anna's Leg," in *Many Mexicos*, 4th ed. (Berkeley: University of California Press, 1966), 230–55; Caruso, *The Liberators of Mexico*.
94. See *La Patria*, 4 September 1903: 1; *El Imparcial*, 6 September 1903: 4; and *Mexican Herald*, 6 September 1903: 1.
95. *Mexican Herald*, 7 September 1903: 2, 8 September 1903: 2–3; *Diario del Hogar*, 1 September 1903: 1, 9 September 1903: 1.
96. *El Imparcial*, 13 August 1903: 1, 30 August 1903: 1, 7 September 1903: 1, 8 September 1903: 1; *Mexican Herald*, 1 September 1903: 1, 7 September 1903: 1, 8 September 1903: 2; *El Mundo*, 7 September 1903: 1; *El Tiempo*, 7 September 1903: 2; *El Pais*, 6 September 1903: 1, 8 September 1903: 1; *El Mundo Ilustrado*, 13 September 1903: [3–6]; *Memoria de Gobernación* (1900–1904), 16.
97. *El Imparcial*, 8 September 1903: 1–2.
98. Ibid., 3; *Mexican Herald*, 8 September 1903: 2; *El Pais*, 1 September 1903: 2, 8 September 1903: 1. See *El Mundo Ilustrado*, September 1903; *Semanario Literario Ilustrado de El Tiempo*, September 1903; and Gustavo Casasola, *Efemérides Ilustradas del México de ayer*, 5 vols. (Mexico City: Ediciones Archivo Casasola, n.d.), 1:355–56, for photographs of the celebration.
99. *Mexican Herald*, 9 September 1903: 2.
100. "Programa especial," AHEACM, *Funerales*, 1:42; *El Imparcial*, 21 August 1903: 1, 28 August 1903: 1, 9 September 1903: 1; *Mexican Herald*, 1 September 1903: 1, 9 September 1903: 2; *El Pais*, 9 September 1903: 1, 10 September 1903: 1; *La Patria*, 10 September 1903: 1; *La Voz de México*, 11 September 1903: 2; *Memoria de Gobernación* (1900–1904), 16; *El Mundo Ilustrado*, 13 September 1903: [3–6]; Casasola, *Efemérides Ilustradas del Mexico de ayer*, 1:355–56; *Semanario Literario Ilustrado de El Tiempo*, 14 September 1903: 463–73.
101. The term is from Michael Kammen, *Mystic Chords of Memory: The Transformation of Tradition in American Culture* (New York: Knopf, 1991), 10–11.
102. Benedict Anderson, *Imagined Communities: Reflections on the Origin and Spread of Nationalism*, rev. ed. (London: Verso, 1991).

CONCLUSION

1. Federico Gamboa, *Mi diario: Mucho de mi vida y algo de la de otros*, 5 vols. (Mexico City: Consejo Nacional de la Cultura y las Artes, 1994), 1:13–14.
2. *El Imparcial*, 6 October 1908: 8, 19 November 1908: 8, 5 March 1909: 1, 8. Arturo Palomino to Sr. Alcalde Municipal de Batabanó, 20 April 1909; Alcalde Municipal P.S. to Sr. Celador del Cementerio, 23 April 1909; Arturo Palomino to Sr. Alcalde Municipal de Batabanó, 29 April 1909; and Acta de exhumación, 23 June 1909—all in *Expediente relativa á las diligencias que hay que practicar para la exhumación de los restos del ciudadano Mexicano Juventino Rosas*, Instituto Nacional de Antropología e Historia, Biblioteca Manuel Orozco

y Berra, Departamento de Investigaciones Históricas. Diego Arenas Guzmán, *Cincuenta retablos de la vida porfiriana* (Mexico City: B. Costa-Amic, 1966), 152-58.

3. Thomas F. Reese and Carol McMichael Reese, "Revolutionary Urban Legacies: Porfirio Díaz's Celebrations of the Centennial of Mexican Independence in 1910," in *Arte, historia e identidad en América: Visiones comparativas*, ed. Gustavo Curiel, Renato González Mello, and Juana Gutiérrez Haces (Mexico City: Universidad Nacional Autónoma de México Instituto de Investigaciones Estéticas, 1994), 361-73; Mauricio Tenorio-Trillo, "1910 Mexico City: Space and Nation in the City of the Centenario," *Journal of Latin American Studies* 21, no. 1 (1996): 75-104. The starting point for any study of the Centenario is *Crónica oficial de las fiestas del primer Centenario de la Independencia de México, publicada bajo la dirección de Genaro García, por acuerdo de la Secretaría de Gobernación* (Mexico City: Talleres del Museo Nacional, 1911).

4. See *El Tiempo Ilustrado*, 25 September 1910: 642-43.

5. Ibid., 642.

6. *Crónica oficial de las fiestas del primer Centenario de la Independencia de México*, 72.

7. Ibid., 147-62.

8. William H. Beezley, *Mexican National Identity: Memory, Innuendo, and Popular Culture* (Tucson: University of Arizona Press, 2008), 95-97.

9. See Eric J. Hobsbawm, *The Age of Capital, 1848-1875* (New York: Scribner's Sons, 1975), chap. 12; Eric J. Hobsbawm, *The Age of Empire, 1875-1914* (London: Weidenfeld and Nicolson, 1987), 13-33; Eric J. Hobsbawm and Terence Ranger, eds., *The Invention of Tradition* (Cambridge: Cambridge University Press, 1983); Robert W. Rydell, *All the World's a Fair: Visions of Empire at American International Expositions, 1876-1916* (Chicago: University of Chicago Press, 1984); Mauricio Tenorio-Trillo, *Mexico at the World's Fairs: Crafting a Modern Nation* (Berkeley: University of California Press, 1996).

10. See Eugen Weber, *France, Fin de Siècle* (Cambridge: Harvard University Press, 1986), 4; Eugen Weber, *Peasants into Frenchmen: The Modernization of Rural France, 1870-1914* (Stanford: Stanford University Press, 1976), 261; Tenorio-Trillo, *Mexico at the World's Fairs*, 9; Miguel Tinker Salas, *In the Shadow of the Eagles: Sonora and the Transformation of the Border during the Porfiriato* (Berkeley: University of California Press, 1997), 2, 16; Paul Vanderwood, *The Power of God against the Guns of Government: Religious Upheaval in Mexico at the Turn of the Nineteenth Century* (Stanford: Stanford University Press, 1998), 15; Vincent C. Peloso and Barbara A. Tenenbaum, "Introduction," in *Liberals, Politics, and Power: State Formation in Nineteenth-Century Latin America*, ed. Vincent C. Peloso and Barbara A. Tenenbaum (Athens: University of Georgia Press, 1996), 11, 13. Few have captured the stark extremes of Mexican modernity and tradition like turn-of-the-century American photographer C. B. Waite. A recently published collection also reflects the schism between *la vida citadina y la vida campesina*. See Francisco Montellano, comp., *C. B. Waite, Fotógrafo: Una mirada diversa sobre el México de principios del siglo XX*, presented by Aurelio de los Reyes (Mexico City: Grijalbo, 1994).

11. For examples in Europe, see Eric J. Hobsbawm, "Mass-Producing Traditions: Europe, 1870-1914," in Hobsbawm and Ranger, *The Invention of Tradition*, 271. In Gramsci's thought the State "educates" consent through the private organisms and initiatives of the ruling class. See *Selections from the Prison Notebooks of Antonio Gramsci*, ed. and intro. by Quintin Hoare and Geoffrey Nowell-Smith (New York: International Publishers, 1971), 259-60.

12. Mexico appears to have adopted French trends. See Pierre Nora, *Realms of Memory: Rethinking the French Past*, 3 vols., ed. and foreword by Lawrence D. Kritzman, trans. Arthur Goldhammer (New York: Columbia University Press, 1996-98), 3:636.

13. Tenorio-Trillo, *Mexico at the World's Fairs*, 19; Jeffrey Pilcher, *Que Vivan los Tamales! Food and the Making of Mexican Identity* (Albuquerque: University of New Mexico Press, 1998), 84.

14. Andrés Molina Enríquez, *Los grandes problemas nacionales* (Mexico City: Carranza e Hijos, 1909), 310; Carleton Beals, *Porfirio Díaz: Dictator of Mexico* (Philadelphia: J. B. Lippincott, 1932), 323; Jorge Fernando Iturribarría, *Porfirio Diaz ante la historia* (Mexico City: Unión Gráfica, 1967), 59. Thanks go to Russ Thomas, Carmen Sacomani, and Michael Hironymous for showing me photos housed at the Nettie Lee Benson Latin American Library, University of Texas at Austin.

15. Heriberto Frias, in *El Constitucional*, 5 October 1910: 1.
16. Avner Ben-Amos, "The Sacred Center of Power: Paris and Republican State Funerals," *Journal of Interdisciplinary History* 22, no. 1 (Summer 1991): 42; Weber, *France, Fin de Siècle*, 2, 15.
17. Hobsbawm, *The Age of Empire*, 9; Weber, *France, Fin de Siècle*, 20. Émile Durkheim discussed the erosion of moral consensus in the nineteenth century. By challenging and modifying Comte's assumptions and concepts, Durkheim's sociology actually reinvigorated and renewed interest in positivism.
18. Ricardo García Granados, *Historia de México desde la restauración de la República en 1867, hasta la caída de Huerta*, 2 vols. (Mexico City: Editorial Jus, 1956), 1:270–71.
19. *El Tiempo Ilustrado*, 7 May 1905: 260–70. With the *hombres destacados* gone by 1905, the only notable leaders rewarded with national funerals were Mexican Ambassador Aspíroz, Communications Minister Escontría, Division General Mena, former justice and education minister Baranda, and Foreign Relations Minister Mariscal. For the Aspíroz obsequies, see the month-long coverage from March 25 to April 26, 1905, in *El Imparcial*.
20. Francisco Bulnes, *The Whole Truth about Mexico: President Wilson's Responsibility*, trans. Dora Scott (New York: M. Bulnes, 1916), 116–17; Beals, *Porfirio Díaz*, 373.
21. François-Xavier Guerra, *México, del antigua régimen a la revolución*, 2 vols., trans. Sergio Fernández Bravo (Mexico City: Fondo de Cultura Económica, 1995), 1:74, 2: "Anexo II," 384–92.
22. *Selections from the Prison Notebooks of Antonio Gramsci*, 242n.
23. Ibid., 276. Acknowledgment goes to Allen Wells and Gilbert M. Joseph, who cited this as their epigraph in *Summer of Discontent, Seasons of Upheaval: Elite Politics and Rural Insurgency in Yucatán, 1876–1915* (Stanford: Stanford University Press, 1996). Bulnes, who pointed to "bureaucratic cannibalism" as a principal flaw of the regime, described the generational problem with a different metaphor: "[The Porfirian administration] was a home for the aged with a standing account at the druggists. The younger generation was justified in wanting to expel the hordes of fossils which had fastened upon the public posts as the trilobites of old upon rocks." The Revolution of 1910 was intended "to rebuild the shattered ambitions of the younger generation and those of the older generation, anxious to pose as belonging to the former" (see Bulnes, *The Whole Truth about Mexico*, 117, 99).
24. Revisionist scholarship has continued Cosío Villegas's trend to evaluate the restored republic and Porfiriato on their own terms instead of in the retrospective shadow of the Mexican Revolution. See Allen Wells, "Out from the Shadows: Recent Scholarship on Late-Nineteenth-Century Mexico," *Latin American Research Review* 35, no. 1 (2000): 172–73; and Paul Garner, *Porfirio Díaz* (New York: Longman, 2001), chap. 1.
25. *El Porfiriato: La vida política interior, primera parte*, in *Historia moderna de México*, 9 vols., ed. Daniel Cosío Villegas (Mexico City: Editorial Hermes, 1955–72), 8:xiv.
26. Díaz, cited in Garner, *Porfirio Díaz*, 48.
27. Tinker Salas, *In the Shadows of the Eagles*, 128.
28. Tenorio-Trillo, *Mexico at the World's Fairs*, xii–xiii, 4–5, 33. On this point, see also William E. French, "Imagining and the Cultural History of Nineteenth-Century Mexico," *Hispanic American Historical Review* 79, no. 2 (1999): 251–52; and Luis González y González, *San José de Gracia: Mexican Village in Transition*, trans. John Upton (Austin: University of Texas Press, 1974), 106.
29. Guerra, *México, del antigua régimen a la revolución*, 1:57.
30. Vanderwood, *The Power of God against the Guns of Government*.
31. For examples elsewhere, see Clifford Geertz, *Negara: The Theatre State in Nineteenth-Century Bali* (Princeton: Princeton University Press, 1980), 5; William Roseberry, *Anthropologies and Histories: Essays in Culture, History, and Political Economy* (New Brunswick: Rutgers University Press, 1989), 7.
32. Alan Knight, "The Mexican Revolution: Bourgeois? Nationalist? Or Just a 'Great Rebellion'?" *Bulletin of Latin American Research* 4, no. 2 (1985): 3; Enrique Semo, *Historia Méxicana: Economía y lucha de clases* (Mexico City: Ediciones Era, 1979), 299.
33. Roger Bartra, *The Cage of Melancholy: Identity and Metamorphosis in the Mexican Character*, trans. Christopher J. Hall (New Brunswick: Rutgers University Press, 1992), 114.
34. See Ilene V. O'Malley, *The Myth of the Revolution: Hero Cults and the Institutionalization*

of the Mexican State, 1920–1940 (New York: Greenwood Press, 1986); Eric Zolov, *Refried Elvis: The Rise of the Mexican Counterculture* (Berkeley: University of California Press, 1999), 3–4.

35. Alan Knight, "*Caciquisimo* in Twentieth-Century Mexico," in *Caciquismo in Twentieth-Century Mexico*, ed. Alan Knight and Wil Pansters (London: Institute for the Study of the Americas, 2005), 16.

36. Manuel de J. Solís, *Historia de la Bandera, Himno, Escudo y Calendario Civico Nacionales* (Mexico City: n.p., 1940).

37. Arturo Sotomayor, *La Rotonda de los Hombres Ilustres* (Mexico City: Colección Metropolitana, 1976), 12. In 1976, the secretaria de obras y servicios of the Federal District published Sotomayor's *La Rotonda de los Hombres Ilustres* as part of its low-priced Metropolitan collection that sold in bookstores and in the streets for 5 pesos. The purpose of the collection, the cost of which was subsidized by the government, was to revive interest in national culture by providing citizens with inexpensive books in commemoration of the 650th anniversary of the founding of Tenochtitlán and the 150th anniversary of the creation of the Federal District. The Metropolitan edition of Sotomayor's book marked the centennial of the *rotonda*.

38. Thomas Benjamin, *La Revolución: Mexico's Great Revolution as Memory, Myth, and History* (Austin: University of Texas Press, 2001); and Elaine C. Lacy, "The 1921 Centennial Celebration of Mexican Independence: State Building and Popular Negotiation," in *Viva Mexico! Viva la Independencia! Celebrations of September 16*, ed. William H. Beezley and David E. Lorey (Wilmington, Del.: SR Books, 2001), 199–232. See also the essays in Lyman L. Johnson, ed., *Body Politics: Death, Dismemberment, and Memory in Latin America* (Albuquerque: University of New Mexico Press, 2004).

39. Hobsbawm, "Mass-Producing Traditions," 264; Avner Ben-Amos, "The Other World of Memory: State Funerals of the French Third Republic as Rites of Commemoration," *History and Memory* 1 (1989): 97.

40. For a full description of Díaz's death and funeral, see Martín Luis Guzmán, *Muertes históricas* (Mexico City: Consejo Nacional para la Cultura y las Artes, Dirección General de Publicaciones, 1990), 9–17; and Carlos Tello Díaz, *El exilio: Un relato de familia* (Mexico City: Cal y Arena, 1993). A unique pilgrimage to the tomb of Porfirio Díaz in Paris can be seen in the film *Paris, Je t'aime*. This study concludes not with a critical reading of Don Porfirio's funeral but with the same ambivalence that Mexicans demonstrated during Díaz's exile in 1911 and death in 1915. Nonetheless, while the remains of the eight-term dictator are consigned to oblivion, the Porfirian legacy did not end in Paris.

Bibliography

PRIMARY SOURCES

Newspapers and Periodicals

El Combate (1876–80, 1887, 1897–98)
El Correo de las Doce (1883–88)
Diario del Hogar (1882–1911)
El Diario Oficial (1877–1911)
El Gil Blas (1892–95)
El Hijo de Ahuizote (1885–1902)
El Hijo del Trabajo (1877–84)
El Imparcial (1896–1914)
La Libertad (1878–84)
Mexican Herald (1895–1911)
México Gráfico (1888–93)
Modern Mexico (1910)
El Monitor Republicano (1876–96)
El Mundo (1889–91, 1896–1906)
El Mundo Semanario Ilustrado (1894–99)
El Municipio Libre (1877–96)
El Nacional (1880–84, 1894–1900, 1902, 1911)
New York Times (1876–1911)
El Noticioso (1894–95)
El País (1899–1911)
El Partido Liberal (1885–96)
La Patria (1877–1911)
La Patria Ilustrada (1883–96)
El Popular (1897–1908)
Semanario Literario de "El Tiempo" (1901)
Semanario Literario Ilustrado (1902–4)
El Siglo XIX (1876–96)
El Socialista (1876–88)
El Tiempo (1883–1911)
El Tiempo Ilustrado (1891–1912)
La Tribuna (1879–80, 1901–3)
Two Republics (1876–1900)
El Universal (1888–91, 1893, 1895–1901)
La Voz de México (1876–1911)

Archival Sources

Archivo General Bernardo Reyes, Archivo Condumex, Mexico City.

Archivo General de la Nación, Mexico City: Ramo Gobernación.

Archivo General Porfirio Díaz, Universidad Ibéroamericana, Mexico City: Archivo Jesús F. Contreras, Colección General Manuel González, Colección General Porfirio Díaz.

Archívo Histórico de la Biblioteca Nacional de Antropología e Historia, Mexico City.

Archivo Histórico del Ex-Ayuntamiento de la Ciudad de México, Mexico City: *Funerales y ceremonias fúnebres, Panteones en general.*

Archivo Histórico "Genaro Estrada" de la Secretaría del Estado y Despacho de Relaciones Exteriores, Mexico City.

Archivo Histórico, Universidad Nacional Autónoma de México, Mexico City: Archivo Rafael Chousal, Archivo Jesús Díaz de León, Centro de Estudios Sobre la Universidad, Fondo Justo Sierra.

Carreño, Alberto María, ed. *Archivo del General Porfirio Díaz, Memorias y Documentos*, 30 vols. Mexico City: Editorial Elede, 1949–61.

Colección General Porfirio Díaz, Universidad de las Américas, Cholula, Puebla.

Instituto Nacional de Antropología e Historia, Biblioteca Manuel Orozco y Berra, Departamento de Investigaciones Históricas: *Expediente relativa á las diligencias que hay que practicar para la exhumación de los restos del ciudadano Mexicano Juventino Rosas.*

Nettie Lee Benson Latin American Library, University of Texas, Austin: Jesús González Ortega Collection, Genaro García Collection.

Government Publications

Actas de Cabildo del Ayuntamiento Constitucional de México. Edición de "El Municipio Libre." Mexico City: Imprenta de Dublan y Compañía, 1885.

Actas de Cabildo del Ayuntamiento Constitucional de México, Años de 1886–1896. Edición de "El Municipio Libre." Mexico City: Imp. de la Escuela Correcional de Artes y Oficios, 1886–1900.

Actas de Cabildo del Ayuntamiento Constitucional de México, Años de 1897–1898. Mexico City: Imprenta "Central," 1900–1902.

Actas de Cabildo del Ayuntamiento Constitucional de México, Años de 1898–1899. Mexico City: A. Carranza y Comp., 1904.

Actas de Cabildo del Ayuntamiento Constitucional de México, Años de 1900–1901. Mexico City: Imp. de "El Correo Español," 1905–7.

Actas de Cabildo del Ayuntamiento Constitucional de México, Julio a Diciembre, 1894. Edición "El Municipio Libre." Mexico City: Imprenta de la Escuela Correccional, 1896.

Actas de Cabildo del Ayuntamiento de la Ciudad de México, Años de 1901–1902. Mexico City: A. Carranza e Hijos, 1909–10.

Actas Modernas de Cabildo, 1903. Primer Semestre. Enero a Junio. Mexico City: Imp. particular, G. Oropeza Velasco, 1911.

Ayuntamiento de la Ciudad de México. *Discurso del C. Ingeniero Sebastián Camacho Presidente del Ayuntamiento de 1894. Al instalarse el de 1895. Contestación del C. Gobernador del Distrito Federal Gral. Pedro Rincon Gallardo y Memoria Documentada de los trabajos municipales de 1894.* Mexico City: Imp. y Lit. "La Europea," 1895.

———. *Discurso del C. Ingeniero Sebastián Camacho Presidente del Ayuntamiento de 1895. Al instalarse el de 1896. Contestación del C. Gobernador del Distrito Federal Gral. Pedro Rincon Gallardo y Memoria Documentada de los trabajos municipales de 1895.* Mexico City: Imp. y Lit. "La Europea," 1896.

———. *Discurso del C. Ingeniero Sebastián Camacho Presidente del Ayuntamiento de 1896 al instalarse el de 1897. Contestación del C. Gobernador del Distrito Federal C. Lic. Rafael Rebollar y Memoria Documentada de los trabajos municipales de 1896.* Mexico City: Imp. y Lit. "La Europea," 1897.

———. *Discurso del C. Ingeniero Sebastián Camacho Presidente del Ayuntamiento de 1897 al instalarse el de 1898. Discurso del C. Lic. Miguel S. Macedo Presidente del Ayuntamiento de 1898. Contestación del C. Gobernador del Distrito Federal C. Lic. Rafael Rebollar y Memoria Documentada de los trabajos municipales de 1897.* Mexico City: Imp. y Lit. "La Europea," 1898.

———. *Discurso del C. Lic. Miguel S. Macedo, Presidente del Ayuntamiento, Contestación del Gobernador del Distrito Federal C. Lic. Rafael Rebollar y Memoria Documentada de los trabajos municipales de 1898. Formada por el Secretario C. Lic. Juan Bribiesca.* Mexico City: Tip. y Lit. "La Europea," de J. Aguilar Vera y C^a, 1899.

———. *Discurso del Señor Don Guillermo de Landa y Escandon, Presidente del Ayuntamiento en 1900. Discurso del Señor Don Ramón Corral, Gobernador del Distrito Federal y Memoria Documentada de los trabajos municipales de 1900,* 2 vols. Mexico City: Tip. y Lit. "La Europea," 1901.

———. *Discurso del Sr. D. Guillermo de Landa y Escandon Presidente del Ayuntamiento en 1901. Discurso del Sr. D. Ramón Corral, Gobernador del Distrito Federal y Memoria Documentada de los trabajos municipales de 1901,* 2 vols. Mexico City: Tip. y Lit. "La Europea," 1902.

———. *Discurso del Sr. D. Fernando Pimentel y Fagoaga, Presidente del Ayuntamiento en 1903 y Memoria Documentada de los trabajos municipales en el primer semestre de 1903.* Mexico City: Tip. y Lit. "La Europea," 1903.

———. *Discurso del Sr. Lic. Miguel S. Macedo, Presidente del Ayuntamiento en 1899. Discurso del Sr. D. Guillermo de Landa y Escandon Presidente del Ayuntamiento en 1900. Contestación del Gobernador del Distrito Federal Sr. Lic. Rafael Rebollar y Memoria Documentada de los trabajos municipales de 1899.* Mexico City: Tip. y Lit. "La Europea," 1900.

———. *Discurso leido el 1° de Enero de 1889 por el C. Gral. Manuel González Cosío como Presidente del Ayuntamiento de 1888 dando cuenta de su administración. Discurso del C. Gobernador del Distrito Federal al instalar la nueva corporación.* Mexico City: Impresa por Francisco Díaz de Leon, 1889.

———. *Discurso leido el 1° de Enero de 1890 por el C. Gral. Manuel González Cosío como Presidente del Ayuntamiento de 1889 dando cuenta de su administración. Discurso del C. Gobernador del Distrito Federal al instalar la nueva corporación.* Mexico City: Impresa por Francisco Díaz de Leon, 1890.

———. *Discurso leido el 1° de Enero de 1892 por el C. Gral. Manuel González Cosío como Presidente del Ayuntamiento de 1891 dando cuenta de su administración. Discurso del C. Gobernador del Distrito Federal al instalarse la nueva corporación.* Mexico City: Impresa por Francisco Díaz de Leon, 1892.

———. *Discurso leido el 1° de 1893 por el C. Manuel Ma. Contreras como Presidente del Ayuntamiento de 1892 dando cuenta de su administración. Discurso de contestación del C. Dr. Manuel Domínguez Presidente del Ayuntamiento de 1893. Discurso del C. Gobernador del Distrito Federal al instalarse la nueva corporacion.* Mexico City: Imp. de F. Díaz de Leon, 1893.

———. *Discurso pronunciado por el Sr. Pedro Rincón Gallardo, Regidor primero del ayuntamiento Constitucional de Mexico, Memoria del Ayuntamiento.* Mexico City: n.p., 1882.

———. *Discursos del Sr. D. Fernando Pimentel y Fagoaga, Presidente interino del Ayuntamiento en 1902; del Sr. D. Ramón Corral, Gobernador del Distrito Federal y del Sr. D. Guillermo de Landa y Escandon, Presidente del Ayuntamiento en 1903 y Memoria Documentada de los trabajos municipales de 1902,* 2 vols. Mexico City: Tip. y Lit. "La Europea," 1903.

———. *Memoria del H. Ayuntamiento de Mexico en 1904.* Mexico City: Imprenta de Ignacio Escalante, 1908.

Catálogo del Museo Nacional de Artilleria. Mexico City: Talleres del Departamento de Estado Mayor, 1910.

Crónica oficial de las fiestas del primer Centenario de la Independencia de México, publicada bajo la dirección de Genaro García, por acuerdo de la Secretaría de Gobernación. Mexico City: Talleres del Museo Nacional, 1911.

Dublán, Manuel, and José María Lozano, eds. *Legislación mexicana, o colección completa de las disposiciones legislativas expedidas desde la independencia de la República,* 34 vols. Mexico City: Imprenta y Litografía de Eduardo Dublán y Comp., 1876–1904.

México, Congreso, Cámara de Diputados. *Diario de los Debates de la Cámara de Diputados, Año de 1880.* Mexico City: Tipografía Literaria de F. Mata, 1880.

——. *Diario de los Debates de la Cámara de Diputados, Años de 1887–1910*. Mexico City: Imprenta de "El Partido Liberal," 1890–1910.

——. *Diario de los Debates de la Cámara de Diputados, Décima Legislatura Constitucional de la Union, Año de 1880*, 3 vols. Mexico City: Tipografía de F. Mata, 1880.

——. *Diario de los Debates de la Cámara de diputados, 8a legislatura constitucional de la Nación, Años de 1877–1911*. Mexico City: Tip. Literaria, 1877–1911.

——. *Diario de los Debates de la Cámara de Diputados, 10a Legislatura Constitucional de la Unión, Año de 1881*, 3 vols. Mexico City: Tip. Literaria de Filomena Mata, 1881.

México, Secretaría de Gobernación. *Memoria de la Secretaria de Gobernación correspondiente al cuatrienio de 1° de Diciembre de 1900 a 30 de Noviembre de 1904*. Mexico City: Imprenta del Gobierno Federal, 1906.

——. *Memoria de la Secretaría de Gobernación Correspondiente al período transcurrido del 1° de Diciembre de 1880 al 30 de Noviembre de 1884. Presentada al Congreso de la Unión por el Secretario del Ramo C. General Carlos Díez Gutiérrez*. Mexico City: Imprenta del Gobierno Federal, en Palacio, 1884.

——. *Memoria presentada al Congreso de la Unión por el Secretario de Estado y del Despacho de Fomento, Colonización, Industria y Comercio de la República mexicana General Carlos Pacheco, corresponde a los años trascurridos de diciembre de 1877 a diciembre de 1882*, 3 vols. Mexico City: Oficina de la Secretaria de Fomento, 1885.

——. *Memoria que el Secretario de Estado y del despacho de Gobernación presenta al Congreso de la Unión, correpondiente al tiempo trascurrido desde el 15 de Diciembre de 1877 hasta el 31 de Diciembre de 1878*. Mexico City: Imprenta del Gobierno, en Palacio a cargo de Sabás A. y Mungía, 1879.

——. *Memoria que el Secretario de Estado y del despacho de Gobernación presenta al Congreso de la Unión, correspondiente el periodo trascurrido del 1° de Enero de 1879 al 20 de Noviembre de 1880*. Mexico City: Tip. de Gonzalo A. Esteva, 1881.

——. *Memoria que el Secretario de Estado y del despacho de Gobernación presentó al Congreso de la Unión el día 14 de diciembre de 1877*. Mexico City: Imprenta de Gobierno, 1878.

——. *Memoria que presenta al Congreso el Lic. Manuel Romero Rubio Secretario de Estado y del Despacho de Gobernación. Corresponde al período transcurrido del 1° de Diciembre de 1884 al 30 de Junio de 1886*. Mexico City: Imprenta del Gobierno, 1887.

México, Secretaría de Guerra y Marina. *Memoria que el Secretario de Estado y del Despacho de Guerra y Marina Gral. de Division Felipe B. Berriozábal presenta al Congreso de la Unión y comprende de 19 de Marzo de 1896 a 30 de Junio de 1899. Parte Expositiva*. Mexico City: Tipografía de "El Partido Liberal," 1899.

——. *Memoria que el Secretario de Estado y del Despacho de Guerra y Marina presenta al Congreso de la Union en 30 de Junio de 1883 y comprende del 1° de Enero de 1882 al 30 de Junio de 1883, con un apéndice de varios documentos*, 3 vols. Mexico City: Tipografía y Litografía de "La Epoca," 1884.

Coronas Fúnebres, Homenajes, *Memoirs, and Published Funeral Orations*

Arce, Francisco O. *Album literario dedicado al eminente patricio general Nicolás Bravo en el centenario de su nacimiento, septiembre 10 de 1886*. Mexico City: Oficina tip. de la Secretaría de Fomento, 1886.

Capdevielle, Enrique, comp. *Corona Fúnebre* [Juan N. Mirafuentes]. Toluca: Impr. Del Instituto Literario, 1881.

Casasús, Joaquín D. *En honor de los muertos*. 2nd ed. Mexico City: Consejo Editorial del Gobierno del Estado de Tabasco, 1981.

Corona fúnebre a la memoria de la estimable Sra. Delfina Ortega de Díaz. Edición de El Libre Sufragio. Mexico City: Imprenta de Ignacio Cumplido, 1880.

Corona fúnebre conteniendo las piezas literarias leídas en la velada que los amigos del Sr. General D. Pedro Baranda, consagraron a su memoria, en la capital del estado de Tabasco. Tabasco: Juan S. Trujillo, 1891.

Corona fúnebre dedicada a la memoria del señor Ministro de Gobernación Licenciado Manuel Romero Rubio por el Gobierno del Estado y la Sociedad Científica literaria "Tamaulipas." Victoria, Tamaulipas: Imprenta del Gobierno del Estado, 1895.

Corona fúnebre dedicada al señor general de division Juan N. Méndez por algunos ciudadanos de Tetela de Ocampo, amigos y admiradores del ilustre soldado del progreso y la democracia. Mexico City: Impr. de D. Cabrera, 1895.

Corona fúnebre del Señor Gral. D. José Vicente Villada, gobernador del Estado de México, Mayo 6 de 1904. Toluca: Escuela de artes y oficios, 1905.

Corona fúnebre que la gratitud publica coloca sobre la tumba del General Juan Crisóstomo Bonilla. Mexico City: Francisco Díaz de Leon, 1884.

Discursos y poesias pronunciados en honor del Señor Licenciado Manuel Romero Rubio en el Panteón Francés el día de Octubre de 1896, y en el Teatro Nacional el 14 del mismo mes y año. Mexico City: Imp. y Lit. de F. Díaz de Leon, 1896.

Gamboa, Federico. *Mi diario: Mucho de mi vida y algo de la de otros,* 5 vols. Mexico City: Consejo Nacional de la Cultura y las Artes, 1994.

Gaxiola, Francisco Javier, comp. *Corona fúnebre del señor Gral. d. José Vicente Villada.* Toluca: Of. tip. del gob. en la Escuela de artes y oficios, 1905.

Gutiérrez Zamora, Juan Manuel. *Corona fúnebre dedicada a la memoria del Sr. General de división Luís Mier y Terán y obsequiada en el primer aniversario de su muerte a su distinguida dama la Sra. Adela Cuesta de Mier y Terán.* Mexico City: Impr. de El Nacional, 1892.

Hernández, Juan A. *Reseña de los trabajos emprendidos: Por el Señor Gral. Juan A. Hernández, jefe de la 2a. zona militar para llevar a cabo la traslación de los restos del Señor Gral. de División Donato Guerra a la rotunda de los hombres ilustres.* Chihuahua: Tip. del Gobierno en Palacio, 1901.

Homenaje a Ramón Corona en el primer centenario de su muerte. Guadalajara: Secretaria de Educación y Cultura, Programa de Estudias Jaliscienses, 1989.

Mejía, Francisco. *Memorías de Francisco Mejía.* Mexico City: Ediciones del Boletín Bibliográfico de la Secretaria de Hacienda y Crédito Público, 1958.

Muerte del presidente Juárez. Mexico City: Secretaría de Trabajo y Previsión Social, 1972.

Preciado, Jesús. *Corona fúnebre dedicada a la memoria del general de división Carlos Pacheco por el gobernador constitucional del estado de Morelos general Jesus H. Preciado.* Cuernavaca: Gobierno de Morelos, 1891.

Prieto, Guillermo. *Memorias de mis tiempos, de 1828 a 1840.* Paris: Libr. de la Vda. de C. Bouret, 1906.

Rivera, Jose G. *Reminiscencias del Ilmo. y Rmo. Sr. Dr. Eulogio Gillow y Zavala.* 2nd ed. Puebla: Escuela Linotipográfica Salesiana, 1921.

Sierra, Justo. *Discurso pronunciado por el Sr. lic. d. Justo Sierra, la noche del 2 de enero de 1895 en el acto conmemorativo ordenado por el ayuntamiento de la ciudad de México, en honor del exmo. sr. d. Manuel de la Peña y Peña con ocasión de la traslación de sus restos efectuados el mismo dia, del clausurado Panteón de San Diego a la Rotonda de Hombres Ilustres en el de Dolores.* Mexico City: Talleres de la Librería Religiosa, 1895.

Silva, Máximo. *Sebastián Lerdo de Tejada, 1823–1889: In Memoriam.* Mexico City: Tip. de "El Partido Liberal," 1889.

Vázquez, Andrés Clemente. *Reminiscencias americanas, el ilustre mexicano Manuel Romero Rubio.* Havana: Imprenta "El Figaro," 1896.

Travel Narratives, Diaries, and Descriptive Guides

Aguilar, Federico C. *Ultimo año de residencia en México.* Bogotá: Imprenta de Ignacio Borda, 1885.

Arnold, Channing, and Frederick J. Tabor Frost. *The American Egypt: A Record of Travel in Yucatán.* New York: Doubleday, Page and Co., 1909.

Baedeker, Karl, ed. *The United States, with an excursion into Mexico. Handbook for Travellers.* 2nd rev. ed. New York: C. Scribner's Sons, 1899.

Baker, Frank Collins. *A Naturalist in Mexico: Being a Visit to Cuba, Northern Yucatan, and Mexico.* Chicago: D. Oliphant, 1895.

Ballou, Maturin M. *Aztec Land.* New York: Houghton, Mifflin, and Co., 1890.

Bandelier, Adolph Francis Alphonse. *A Scientist on the Trail; Travel Letters of A. F. Bandelier; 1880–1881.* Ed. George Peter and Edgar F. Goad. Berkeley: Quivira Society, 1949.

Barrett, Robert S. *The Standard Guide to the City of Mexico and Vicinity.* Mexico City: Modern Mexico Publishing Co., 1901.

Barton, Mary. *Impressions of Mexico with Brush and Pen*. New York: Macmillan, 1911.

Bates, James Hale. *Notes of a Tour in Mexico and California*. New York: Burr Printing House, 1887.

Becher, Henry C. R. *A Trip to Mexico; Being Notes of a Journey from Lake Erie to Lake Tezcuco and Back*. Toronto: Willing and Williamson, 1880.

Birkinbine, John. *Industrial Progress of Mexico*. Philadelphia: n.p., 1909.

Bishop, William Henry. *Mexico, California, and Arizona; Being a New and Revised Edition of Old Mexico and Her Lost Provinces*. New York: Harper and Bros, 1883.

———. *Old Mexico and Her Lost Provinces: A Journey in Mexico, Southern California, and Arizona by Way of Cuba*. New York: Harper and Brothers, 1883.

Blake, Mary Elizabeth, and Margaret Francis Buchanan Sullivan. *Mexico: Picturesque, Political, and Progressive*. Boston: Lee and Shepard Publishers, 1888.

Blichfeldt, E. H. *A Mexican Journey*. New York: Thomas Y. Crowell Co., 1912.

Bly, Nellie. *Six Months in Mexico*. New York: Munro/American Publishers Corp., 1888.

Brocklehurst, Thomas Unett. *Mexico To-Day: A Country with a Great Future*. London: John Murray, 1883.

Butler, John W. *Sketches of Mexico in Prehistoric, Primitive, Colonial, and Modern Times*. New York: Hunt and Eaton, 1894.

Caballero, Manuel. *Primer Almanaque Histórico, Artístico y Monumental de la República Mexicana*. Mexico City: Green Printing, 1883.

Cameron, Charlotte. *Mexico in Revolution: An Account of an English Woman's Experiences and Adventures in the Land of Revolution*. London: Seeley, Service and Co. Ltd., 1925.

Campbell, Reau. *Campbell's Complete Guide and Descriptive Book of Mexico*. Chicago: Poole Bros., 1895.

———. *Mexico; Tours through the Egypt of the New World*. New York: C. G. Crawford, 1890.

Carbutt, Mary Rhodes (Mrs. E. H.). *Five Months' Fine Weather in Canada, Western U.S., and Mexico*. London: Sampson Low, Marston, Searle, and Rivington, 1889.

Cardona, S. Adalberto de. *Mexico y sus capitales; reseña histórica del pais desde los tiempos mas remotos hasta el presente*. Mexico City: Tip. de J. Aguilar Vera, 1900.

Carpenter, Frank George. *Mexico*. Garden City, N.Y.: Doubleday, 1924.

Carson, W. E. *Mexico: The Wonderland of the South*. 1909; rev. ed., New York: Macmillan Co., 1914.

Case, Alden Buell. *Thirty Years with the Mexicans in Peace and Revolution*. New York: Fleming H. Revell Co., 1917.

Castro, Lorenzo. *The Republic of Mexico in 1882*. New York: Thomson and Moreau Printers, 1882.

Cerwin, Herbert. *These Are the Mexicans*. New York: Reynal and Hitchcock, 1947.

Cockrell, Thos. J. *Mexican Typical View Album*. New York: Albertype Co., 1889.

Coffin, Alfred Oscar. *Land Without Chimneys; or The Byways of Mexico*. Cincinnati: Editor Publishing Co., 1898.

Collins, Michael D. *Cultured Mexico: An Unknown Land to North Americans*. Chicago: M. H. Wiltzius Co., 1921.

Conkling, Alfred R. *Appleton's Guide to Mexico*. New York: D. Appleton and Co., 1884.

Conkling, Howard. *Mexico and the Mexicans; or Notes of Travel in the Winter and Spring of 1883*. New York: Taintor Brothers, Merrill and Co., 1883.

Conrotte, Manuel. *Notas mejicanas*. Madrid: Romo y Fussel, 1899.

Cossio, Jose L. *Guia retrospectiva de la ciudad de Mexico*. Mexico City: Segumex, 1990.

Crawford, Cora Hayward. *The Land of the Montezumas*. Cincinnati: Robert Clarke Co., 1898.

Croffut, William Augustus. *Folks Next Door; The Log Book of a Rambler*. 3rd ed. Washington, D.C.: Eastside Publishing Co., 1904.

Deverdun, Alfred Louis. *The True Mexico: Mexico-Tenochtitlan*. Menasha, Wisc.: George Banta Publishing Co., 1938.

Dollero, Adolfo. *México al dia (impresiones y notas de viaje)*. Paris: Librería de la Vda. de C. Bouret, 1911.

Drees, Charles William. *Thirteen Years in Mexico (From Letters of Charles W. Drees)*. Ed. Ada M. C. Drees. New York: Abingdon Press, 1915.

Edwards, William Seymour. *On the Mexican Highlands, With a Passing Glimpse of Cuba*. Cincinnati: Press of Jennings and Graham, 1906.

Esteva, Adalberto A. *Mexico pintoresco; antologia de articulos descriptivos del pais*. Mexico City: Tip. y lit. "La Europea" de J. Aguilara Vera y Compania, 1905.

Evans, Albert S. *Our Sister Republic: A Gala Trip Through Mexico in 1869–1870*. Hartford, Conn.: Columbian Book Co., 1870.

Evans, T. B. *From Geneva to Mexico: A Record of a Tour Through the Western Part of the United States and the Greater Part of Old Mexico*. Geneva, Ill.: Geneva Republican, 1893.

Ferguson, A. *Mexico*. Washington, D.C.: Bureau of the American Republics, 1891.

Figueroa Domenech, J. *Guía general descriptiva de la República Mexicana*. Mexico City: R. de S. N. Araluce, [1899].

Flandrau, Charles Macomb. *Viva Mexico!* Ed. and intro. by C. Harvey Gardiner. Urbana: University of Illinois Press, 1964.

Flippin, J. R. *Sketches from the Mountains of Mexico*. Cincinnati: Standard Publishing Co., 1889.

Franck, Harry A. *Tramping Through Mexico, Guatemala and Honduras; Being the Random Notes of an Incurable Vagabond*. New York: Century Co., 1916.

García Cubas, Antonio. *Cuadro geográfico, estadístico, descriptivo e histórico de los Estados Unidos Mexicanos*. Mexico City: Oficina Tip. de la Secretaria de Fomento, 1885.

Gillpatrick, Wallace. *The Man Who Likes Mexico*. New York: Century Co., 1911.

———. *Wanderings in Mexico: The Spirited Chronicle of Adventure in Mexican Highways and Byways*. London: Eveleigh Nash, 1912.

Gooch, Fanny Chambers [Iglehart]. *Face to Face with the Mexicans*. New York: Fords, Howard, and Hulbert, 1887.

Goodhue, Bertram Grosvenor. *Mexican Memories: The Record of a Slight Sojourn below the Yellow Rio Grande*. New York: George M. Allen Co., 1892.

Graham, A. A. *Mexico with Comparisons and Conclusions*. Topeka: Crane and Co., 1907.

Griffin, Solomon Bulkey. *Mexico of To-day*. New York: Harper and Brothers, 1886.

Gringo, A. *Through the Land of the Aztecs*. London: Sampson Low, Marston and Co., 1892.

Guthrie, Patty. *Eliza and Etheldreda in Mexico: Notes of Travel*. New York: Broadway Publishing Co., 1911.

Haven, Gilbert. *Our Next-Door Neighbor: A Winter in Mexico*. New York: Harper and Brothers, 1875.

Jackson, Julia Newell. *A Winter Holiday in Summer Lands*. Chicago: A. C. McClurg and Co., 1890.

Janvier, Thomas A. *Legends of the City of Mexico*. New York: Harper and Brothers, 1910.

———. *The Mexican Guide*. New York: Scribner's, 1888.

Jebb, Bertha (Mrs. John Beveridge Gladwyn). *A Strange Career: Life and Adventure of John Gladwyn Jebb, by his widow*. London: W. Blackwood and Sons, 1894.

Kirkham, Stanton Davis. *Mexican Trails: A Record of Travel in Mexico, 1904–1907, and a Glimpse at the Life of the Mexican Indian*. New York: G. P. Putnam's Sons, 1909.

Knox, Thomas W. *The Boy Travellers in Mexico*. New York: Harper and Brothers, 1902.

Lester, C. Edwards. *The Mexican Republic*. New York: American News Co., 1878.

Letters by J. A. Zabriskie to the Tucson "Star": Mexico in 1889. San Francisco: n.p., 1889.

Lumholz, Carl. *Unknown Mexico: A Record of Five Years Exploration among the Tribes of the Western Sierra Madre*, 2 vols. Glorieta, N.M.: Rio Grande Press, 1973.

Lummis, Charles F. *The Awakening of a Nation: Mexico of To-day*. New York: Harper and Brothers, 1898.

Martin, Percy Falke. *Mexico of the Twentieth Century*. London: Edward Arnold, 1907.

McCarty, Joseph Hendrickson. *Two Thousand Miles Through the Heart of Mexico*. New York: Phillips and Hunt, 1886.

McClure, Alexander Kelly. *To the Pacific and Mexico*. Philadelphia: J. B. Lippincott, 1901.

McElwin, Henry. *New Orleans Exposition, Texas and Old Mexico, a Series of Letters*. St. Louis: n.p., 1885.

Moses, Jasper T. *Today in the Land of Tomorrow: Sketches of Life in Mexico*. 2nd ed. Indianapolis: Christian Woman's Board of Missions, 1909.

Ober, Frederick A. *Mexican Resources: A Guide Through Mexico*. Boston: Estes and Lavrick, 1884.

————. *Travels in Mexico and Life Among the Mexicans*. Boston: Estes and Lauriat; and San Francisco: J. Dewing, 1884.

Oswald, Felix Leopold. *Summerland Sketches; or, Rambles in the Backwoods of Mexico and Central America*. Philadelphia: J. B. Lippincott and Co., 1880.

Parker, Morris B. *Mules, Mines, and Me, 1895–1932*. Tucson: University of Arizona Press, 1979.

Pastor, M. H. *Impresiones y recuerdos de mis viajes a México*. San Sebastián, Spain: La Voz de Guipúzcoa, 1900.

Payno, Manuel. *Crónicas de viaje*, 2 vols. Mexico City: Consejo Nacional para la Cultura y las Artes, 1996.

Paz, Ireneo. *Nueva Guía de México*. Mexico City: Imprenta de Ireneo Paz, 1882.

Plummer, Mary Wright. *Roy and Ray in Mexico*. New York: Henry Holt and Co., 1907.

Pollard, Hugh Bertie Campbell. *A Busy Time in Mexico: An Unconventional Record of Mexican Incident*. New York: Duffield and Co., 1913.

Prantl, Adolfo. *La ciudad de México, novísima guía universal de la capital de la República Mexicana*. Mexico City: Librería Madrileña, 1901.

Rice, John H. *Mexico Our Neighbor*. New York: J. W. Lovell, 1888.

Rogers, Thomas L. *Mexico? Sí, Señor*. Boston: Collins Press, 1893.

Romero, José. *Guía de la ciudad de México y demás municipalidades del distrito federal*. Mexico City: Librería de Porrúa Hermanos, 1910.

————. *Guía general y descriptiva de la República Mexicana*. Mexico City: n.p., 1899.

Russell, Thomas H. *Mexico in Peace and War*. Chicago: Reilly and Britton Syndicate, 1914.

Sanborn, Helen Josephine. *A Winter in Central America and Mexico*. Boston: Lee and Shepard, 1886.

Schwatka, Frederick. *In the Land of Cave and Cliff Dwellers*. New York: Cassell Pub. Co., 1893.

Sherratt, Harriott Wight. *Mexican Vistas: Seen from Highways and Byways of Travel*. Chicago: Rand McNally and Co., 1899.

Smith, Ann Eliza Brainerd (Mrs. J. Gregory Smith). *Notes of Travel in Mexico and California*. St. Albans, Vt.: Messenger and Advertiser Office, 1886.

Smith, Francis Hopkinson. *A White Umbrella in Mexico*. Boston: Houghton Mifflin and Co., 1889.

Spring, Arthut L. *Beyond the Rio Grande*. Boston: J. S. Adams, 1886.

Stealey, John E., III, ed. *Porte Crayon's Mexico: David Hunter Strother's Diaries in the Early Porfirian Era, 1879–1885*. Kent: Kent State University Press, 2006.

Steele, James William. *To Mexico by Palace Car*. Jansen, McClurg, 1884; Chicago: Rand, McNally and Co., 1886.

Terry, Thomas Philip. *Terry's Mexico: Handbook for Travellers*. Boston: Houghton Mifflin Co., 1909.

Tweedie, Ethel Brilliana Harley (Mrs. Alec). *Mexico as I Saw It*. London: Hurst and Blackett, 1901; New York: Macmillan Co., 1902.

Vaquero. *Adventures in Search of a Living in Spanish-America*. London: J. Bale, Sons and Danielsson, 1911.

Wallace, Dillon. *Beyond the Mexican Sierras*. Chicago: A. C. McClurg and Co., 1910.

Wells, David A. *A Study of Mexico*. New York: D. Appleton and Co., 1887.

Wharton, Joseph. *Mexico*. Philadelphia: Press of J. B. Lippincott Co., 1902.

Wilson, James A. *Bits of Old Mexico*. San Francisco: n.p., 1910.

Winter, Nevin O. *Mexico and Her People of Today*. 1907; rev. ed., Boston: L. C. Page and Co., 1923.

Winton, George Beverly. *Mexico To-day*. New York: Missionary Education Movement of the U.S. and Canada, 1913.

Wright, Marie Robinson. *Picturesque Mexico*. Philadelphia: J. B. Lippincott Co., 1897.

Zabriskie Gray, Albert. *Mexico as it Is: Being Notes of a Recent Tour in that Country*. New York: E. P. Dutton and Co., 1878.

Secondary Sources: Books, Articles, and Unpublished Materials

Adame Goddard, Jorge. *El pensamiento político y social de los católicos mexicanos, 1867–1914.* Mexico City: Universidad Nacional Autónoma de México, 1981.

Adamson, Walter L. *Hegemony and Revolution: A Study of Antonio Gramsci's Political and Cultural Theory.* Berkeley: University of California Press, 1980.

Agostoni, Claudia. *Monuments of Progress: Modernization and Public Health in Mexico City, 1876–1910.* Boulder: University of Colorado Press, 2003.

Alamán, Lucas. *Historia de Méjico desde los primeros movimientos que prepararon su independencia en el año de 1808 hasta la época presente,* 5 vols. Mexico City: Instituto Cultural Hélenico, Fondo de Cultura Económica, 1985.

Alcocer, Alfonso. *La Campana de Dolores.* Mexico City: Departamento del Distrito Federal, 1985.

Alexius, Robert M. "The Army and Politics in Porfirian Mexico." Ph.D. diss., University of Texas at Austin, 1976.

Anderson, Benedict. *Imagined Communities: Reflections on the Origin and Spread of Nationalism.* Rev. ed. London: Verso, 1991.

———. *The Spectre of Comparisons: Nationalism, Southeast Asia and the World.* New York: Verso, 1998.

Anderson, Rodney O. *Outcasts in Their Own Land: Mexican Industrial Workers, 1906–1911.* De Kalb: Northern Illinois University Press, 1976.

Arenas Guzmán, Diego. *Cincuenta retablos de la vida porfiriana.* Mexico City: B. Costa-Amic, 1966.

Ariès, Philippe. *Western Attitudes toward Death: From the Middle Ages to the Present.* Trans. Patricia M. Ranum. Baltimore: Johns Hopkins University Press, 1974.

Arte funerario: Coloquio Internacional de Historia del Arte, 2 vols. Coord. Beatriz de la Fuente. Mexico City: Universidad Nacional Autónoma de México, Instituto de Investigaciones Estéticas, 1987.

Bancroft, Hubert Howe. *History of Mexico,* 6 vols. San Francisco: History Co., 1888.

Bantjes, Adrian. *As if Jesus Walked on Earth: Cardenismo, Sonora, and the Mexican Revolution.* Wilmington, Del.: SR Books, 1998.

Barthes, Roland. *Mythologies.* New York: Noonday Press, 1972.

Bartra, Roger. *The Cage of Melancholy: Identity and Metamorphosis in the Mexican Character.* Trans. Christopher J. Hall. New Brunswick: Rutgers University Press, 1992.

Batres, Leopoldo. *Archaelogical Explorations in Escalerillas Street, City of Mexico, 1900.* Mexico City: J. Aguilar Vera and Co., 1902.

Beals, Carleton. *Porfirio Díaz: Dictator of Mexico.* Philadelphia: J. B. Lippincott, 1932.

Beezley, William H. *Judas at the Jockey Club and Other Episodes of Porfirian Mexico.* Lincoln: University of Nebraska Press, 1987.

———. *Mexican National Identity: Memory, Innuendo, and Popular Culture.* Tucson: University of Arizona Press, 2008.

Beezley, William H., and Linda Curcio-Nagy, eds. *Latin American Popular Culture: An Introduction.* Wilmington, Del.: SR Books, 2000.

Beezley, William H., and David E. Lorey, eds. *Viva Mexico! Viva la Independencia! Celebrations of September 16.* Wilmington, Del.: SR Books, 2001.

Beezley, William H., Cheryl English Martin, and William E. French, eds. *Rituals of Rule, Rituals of Resistance: Public Celebrations and Popular Culture in Mexico.* Wilmington, Del.: SR Books, 1994.

Ben-Amos, Avner. *Funerals, Politics, and Memory in Modern France, 1789–1996.* New York: Oxford University Press, 2000.

———. "Molding the National Memory: The State Funerals of the French Third Republic." Ph.D. diss., University of California, Berkeley, 1988.

———. "The Other World of Memory: State Funerals of the French Third Republic as Rites of Commemoration." *History and Memory* 1 (1989): 85–108.

———. "The Sacred Center of Power: Paris and Republican State Funerals." *Journal of Interdisciplinary History* 22, no. 1 (Summer 1991): 27–48.

Benjamin, Thomas. *La Revolución: Mexico's Great Revolution as Memory, Myth, and History.* Austin: University of Texas Press, 2001.

Benjamin, Thomas, and Marcial Ocasio-Melendez. "Organizing the Memory of Modern Mexico: Porfirian Historiography in Perspective, 1880s–1980s." *Hispanic American Historical Review* 64, no. 2 (May 1984): 323–64.

Berdecio, Roberto, and Stanley Applebaum, eds. *Posada's Popular Mexican Prints.* New York: Dover Publications, 1972.

Bethell, Leslie, ed. *Cambridge History of Latin America.* New York: Cambridge University Press, 1986.

Biografía del señor Gral. José Vicente Villada, gobernador constitucional del Estado de Michoacán. Toluca: Tipografía del Gobierno en la Escuela de Artes, 1895.

Bland, Olivia. *The Royal Way of Death.* London: Constable, 1986.

Bonnell, Victoria E., and Lynn Hunt, eds. *Beyond the Cultural Turn: New Directions in the Study of Society and Culture.* Berkeley: University of California Press, 1999.

Bourdieu, Pierre. *Outline of a Theory of Practice.* Trans. Richard Nice. New York: Cambridge University Press, 1977.

Brown, James. *Heriberto Frías.* Boston: Twayne Publishers, 1978.

Buffington, Robert, and Pablo Piccato. "Tales of Two Women: The Narrative Construal of Porfirian Reality." *The Americas* 55, no. 3 (January 1999): 391–424.

Bulnes, Francisco. *Francisco Bulnes.* Comp. Norma de los Rios. Mexico City: Senado de la República, 1987.

———. *Las grandes mentiras de nuestra historia: La nación y el ejército en las guerras extranjeras.* Paris: La vda. de C. Bouret, 1904.

———. *Los grandes problemas de México.* Mexico City: SRA-CEHAM, 1981.

———. *El verdadero Díaz y la Revolución.* Mexico City: Editora Nacional, 1960.

———. *El verdadero Juárez y la verdad sobre la Intervention y el Imperio.* Mexico City: La viuda de C. Bouret, 1904.

———. *The Whole Truth about Mexico: President Wilson's Responsibility.* Trans. Dora Scott. New York: M. Bulnes, 1916.

Bunker, Stephen B. "Making the Good Old Days: Invented Tradition and Civic Ritual in Northern Mexico, 1880–1910." Honors thesis, University of British Columbia, 1993.

Burke, Peter. *Popular Culture in Early Modern Europe.* New York: New York University Press, 1978.

Bustamante, Carlos María de. *Cuadro histórico de la revolución mexicana,* 3 vols. Reprint ed. Mexico City: Ediciones de la Comisión Nacional para la Celebración del Sesquicentanario de la Proclamación de la Independencia Nacional y del Cinquentenario de la Revolución Mexicana, 1961.

Cabrera, Daniel, ed. *Liberales Ilustres Mexicanos de la Reforma y la Intervención.* Mexico City: Imprenta del "Hijo del Ahuizote," 1890–93.

Cadenhead, Ivie E., Jr. *Jesús González Ortega and Mexican National Politics.* Fort Worth: Texas Christian University Press, 1972.

Cahill, David. "Popular Religion and Appropriation: The Example of Corpus Christi in Eighteenth-Century Cuzco." *Latin American Research Review* 31, no. 2 (1996): 79–81.

Calderón de la Barca, Frances. *Life in Mexico.* Intro. by Woodrow Borah. Berkeley: University of California Press, 1982.

Carreño, Alberto María. *Los españoles en el México independiente (un siglo de beneficiencia).* Mexico City: Imprenta M. L. Sanchez, 1942.

Carreño, Manuel. *Manual de urbanidad y buenas maneras.* New York: Appleton, 1857.

Caruso, John Anthony. *The Liberators of Mexico.* Glouchester, Mass.: Peter Smith, 1967.

Casasola, Gustavo. *Efemérides Ilustradas del México de ayer,* 5 vols. Mexico City: Ediciones Archivo Casasola, n.d.

Castro-Klarén, Sara, and John Charles Chasteen, eds. *Beyond Imagined Communities: Reading and Writing the Nation in Nineteenth-Century Latin America.* Baltimore: Johns Hopkins University Press, 2004.

Chassen-López, Francie R. "A Patron of Progress: Juana Catarina Romero, the Nineteenth-Century Cacica of Tehuantepec." *Hispanic American Historical Review* 88, no. 3 (2008): 393–426.

Chasteen, John Charles. *Born in Blood and Fire: A Concise History of Latin America*. New York: W. W. Norton, 2001.

Clendinnen, Inga. *Aztecs: An Interpretation*. New York: Cambridge University Press, 1991.

Coatsworth, John H. *Growth against Development: The Economic Impact of Railroads in Porfirian Mexico*. DeKalb: Northern Illinois University Press, 1981.

———. "Obstacles to Economic Growth in Nineteenth Century Mexico." *American Historical Review* 83, no. 1 (February 1978): 80–100.

Cockcroft, James D. *Intellectual Precursors of the Mexican Revolution, 1900–1913*. Austin: Institute of Latin American Studies, University of Texas Press, 1968.

Coerver, Don M. "From Confrontation to Conciliation: Church–State Relations in Mexico, 1867–1884." *Journal of Church and State* 32, no. 1 (Winter 1990): 65–80.

———. *The Porfirian Interregnum: The Presidency of Manuel González of Mexico, 1880–1884*. Fort Worth: Texas Christian University Press, 1979.

Cole, Garold L. *American Travelers to Mexico, 1821–1972: A Descriptive Bibliography*. Troy, N.Y.: Whitston Pub. Co., 1978.

Colín Sánchez, Guillermo. *Ignacio Zaragoza: Evocación de un héroe*. Mexico City: Editorial Porrúa, 1963.

Conger, Robert. "Porfirio Díaz and the Church Hierarchy, 1876–1911." Ph.D. diss., University of New Mexico, 1985.

Corrigan, Phillip, and Derek Sayer. *The Great Arch: English State Formation as Cultural Revolution*. Oxford: Basil Blackwell, 1985.

Cosío Villegas, Daniel. *The United States versus Porfirio Díaz*. Trans. Nettie Lee Benson. Lincoln: University of Nebraska Press, 1963.

———, ed. *Historia Moderna de México*, 9 vols. Mexico City: Editorial Hermes, 1955–72.

Cosmes, Francisco. *El verdadero Bulnes y su falso Juárez*. Mexico City: Talleres de Tipografía, 1904.

Costeloe, Michael P. *The Central Republic in Mexico, 1835–1846: Hombres de Bien in the Age of Santa Anna*. Cambridge: Cambridge University Press, 1993.

Covarrubias, Ricardo. *Hombres de la Reforma*. Monterrey: Orven, 1987.

Creelman, James. *Porfirio Díaz, Master of Mexico*. New York: Appleton, 1911.

Crehan, Kate. *Gramsci, Culture and Anthropology*. Berkeley: University of California Press, 2002.

Curl, James Stevens. *The Victorian Celebration of Death*. London: David and Charles, 1972.

da Matta, Roberto. *Carnivals, Rogues, and Heroes: An Interpretation of the Brazilian Dilemma*. Trans. John Drury. Notre Dame: University of Notre Dame Press, 1991.

Darnton, Robert. *The Great Cat Massacre and Other Episodes in French Cultural History*. New York: Basic Books, 1984.

de Gortari Rabiela, Hira, and Regina Hernández Franyuti, eds. *Memoria y encuentros: La ciudad de México y el Distrito Federal (1824–1928)*, 3 vols. Mexico City: Departamento del Distrito Federal, Instituto de Investigaciones Dr. José María Luís Mora, 1988.

De Palma, Anthony. "New Battles Erupt Over Conflicting Interpretations of Mexico's Painful Past." *New York Times*, 29 August 1993.

Desentis M., Alfredo. *Rotonda de los Hombres Ilustres*. Mexico City: Departamento del Distrito Federal, 1985.

Díaz, Arlene J. "Women, Order, and Progress in Guzmán Blanco's Venezuela, 1870–1888." In *Crime and Punishment in Latin America: Law and Society since Late Colonial Times*, ed. Ricardo D. Salvatore, Carlos Aguirre, and Gilbert M. Joseph, 56–82. Durham: Duke University Press, 2001.

Díaz de Ovando, Clementina. *Las fiestas pátrias en el México hace un siglo, 1883*. Mexico City: Centro de Estudios de Historia de México Condumex, 1984.

———. *Memoria de un debate, 1880*. Mexico City: Instituto de Estudios Estéticas, Universidad Nacional Autonóma de México, 1990.

———. *Vicente Riva Palacio y la identidad nacional: Discurso*. Mexico City: Dirección General de Publicaciones, Universidad Nacional Autonóma de México, 1985.

Diccionario Porrúa de Historia, Biografía y Geografía de México, 3 vols. Mexico City: Editorial Porrúa, 2nd ed., 1964; 3rd ed., 1967.

Dirks, Nicholas B., Geoff Eley, and Sherry B. Ortner, eds. *Culture/Power/History: A Reader in Contemporary Social Theory*. Princeton: Princeton University Press, 1994.

Duncan, Robert H. "Embracing a Suitable Past: Independence Celebrations under Mexico's Second Empire, 1864–66." *Journal of Latin American Studies* 30, no. 2 (May 1998): 249–78.
———. "Political Legitimation and Maximilian's Second Empire in Mexico, 1864–1867." *Mexican Studies/Estudios Mexicanos* 12, no. 1 (Winter 1996): 27–66.
Durkheim, Émile. *The Elementary Forms of the Religious Life*. Trans. Joseph Ward Swain. Glencoe, Ill.: Free Press, 1954.
Earle, Rebecca. "'Padres de la Patria' and the Ancestral Past: Commemorations of Independence in Nineteenth-Century Spanish America." *Journal of Latin American Studies* 34, no. 4 (November 2002): 775–805.
Eley, Geoff, and Ronald Grigor Suny, eds. *Becoming National: A Reader*. New York: Oxford University Press, 1996.
Escobedo, Helen. *Mexican Monuments: Strange Encounters*. Photographs by Paolo Gori. Essays by Nestor García Canclini et al. New York: Abbeville Press, 1989.
Femia, Joseph V. *Gramsci's Political Thought: Hegemony, Consciousness, and the Revolutionary Process*. New York: Oxford University Press, 1981.
Florescano, Enrique. *Memory, Myth, and Time: From the Aztecs to Independence*. Trans. Albert G. Bork. Austin: University of Texas Press, 1994.
Forment, Carlos. *Democracy in Latin America, 1760–1900, vol. 1: Civic Selfhood and Public Life in Mexico and Peru*. Chicago: University of Chicago Press, 2003.
Franco, Jean. *Plotting Women: Gender and Representation in Mexico*. New York: Columbia University Press, 1989.
Frank, Patrick. *Posada's Broadsheets: Mexican Popular Imagery, 1890–1910*. Albuquerque: University of New Mexico Press, 1998.
French, William E. "Imagining and the Cultural History of Nineteenth-Century Mexico." *Hispanic American Historical Review* 79, no. 2 (1999): 249–68.
———. *A Peaceful and Working People: Manners, Morals, and Class Formation in Northern Mexico*. Albuquerque: University of New Mexico Press, 1996.
———. "Prostitutes and Guardian Angels: Women, Work, and the Family in Porfirian Mexico." *Hispanic American Historical Review* 72, no. 4 (1992): 529–33.
French, William E., and Katherine Elaine Bliss, eds. *Gender, Sexuality, and Power in Latin America since Independence*. Wilmington, Del.: Rowman and Littlefield, 2007.
Fuentes Mares, José. *Juárez: El imperio y la república*. Mexico City: Editorial Grijalbo, 1983.
Gal, Susan. "Bartok's Funeral: Representations of Europe in Hungarian Political Rhetoric." *American Ethnologist* 18, no. 3 (August 1991): 440–59.
Galindo y Villa, Jesús. *Historia sumaria de la ciudad de México*. Mexico City: Editorial Cultura, 1925.
———. *Reseña histórico-descriptiva de la Ciudad de México*. Mexico City: Imprenta Díaz de León, 1911.
García, Genaro. *Leona Vicario, heroína insurgente*. Mexico City: Secretaría de Educación Pública, 1945.
García Cubas, Antonio. *El libro de mis recuerdos; Narraciones históricas, anecdóticas y de costumbres mexicanas anteriores al actual estado social*. Mexico City: Impr. de A. García Cubas, hermanos sucesores, 1904.
García Granados, Ricardo. *Historia de México desde la restauración de la República en 1867, hasta la caída de Huerta*, 2 vols. Mexico City: Editorial Jus, 1956.
García Luna, Margarita. *Toluca en el Porfiriato*. Toluca: Gobierno del Estado de Mexico, Secretaria de Educación, Cultura y Bienestar Social, Dirección de Patrimonio Cultural; Ayuntamiento de Toluca, 1986.
Gardiner, Clinton Harvey. "Foreign Travelers' Accounts of Mexico, 1810–1910." *The Americas* 8 (1952): 321–51.
Garner, Paul. *Porfirio Díaz*. New York: Longman, 2001.
Garza, James Alex. *The Imagined Underworld: Sex, Crime, and Vice in Porfirian Mexico City*. Lincoln: University of Nebraska Press, 2007.
Geertz, Clifford. *The Interpretation of Cultures: Selected Essays*. New York: Basic Books, 1973.
———. *Local Knowledge: Further Essays in Interpretive Anthropology*. New York: Basic Books, 1983.

———. *Negara: The Theatre State in Nineteenth-Century Bali.* Princeton: Princeton University Press, 1980.

Giesey, Ralph E. *The Royal Funeral Ceremony in Renaissance France.* Geneva: E. Droz, 1960.

Gillis, John R., ed. *Commemorations: The Politics of National Identity.* Princeton: Princeton University Press, 1994.

Gittings, Clare. *Death, Burial and the Individual in Early Modern England.* London: Croom Helm, 1984.

Glantz, Margo, coor. *Del fistol a la linterna: Homenaje a José Tomás de Cuéllar y Manuel Payno en el centenario de su muerte, 1994.* Mexico City: Universidad Nacional Autónoma de México, Coordinación de Humanidades, Dirección General de Publicaciones, 1997.

Godoy, José F. *Porfirio Díaz.* New York: G. P. Putnam's Sons, 1910.

Gómez-Quiñones, Juan. "Social Change and Intellectual Discontent: The Growth of Mexican Nationalism, 1890–1911." Ph.D. diss., University of California, Los Angeles, 1972.

González Navarro, Moisés. *Estadísticas económicas del Porfiriato: Comercio exterior de México, 1877–1911.* Mexico City: El Colegio de México, 1960.

———. *Estadísticas sociales del Porfiriato, 1877–1910.* Mexico City: Dirección General de Estadística, 1956.

———. *Sociedad y cultura en el porfiriato.* Mexico City: Consejo Nacional para la Cultura y las Artes, 1994.

González Obregón, Luis. *México viejo y anecdótico.* 3rd ed. Mexico City: Espasa-Calpe Mexicana, 1966.

González y González, Luis. *San José de Gracia: Mexican Village in Transition.* Trans. John Upton. Austin: University of Texas Press, 1974.

Gorostiza, José. *Death without End.* Trans. Laura Villaseñor. Austin: University of Texas Press, 1969.

Greenleigh, John. *The Days of the Dead: Mexico's Festival of Communion with the Departed.* San Francisco: Collins, 1991.

Guardino, Peter. "Peasants, Politics, and State Formation in 19th Century Mexico: Guerrero, 1800–1857." Ph.D. diss., University of Chicago, 1992.

———. *The Time of Liberty: Popular Political Culture in Oaxaca, 1750–1850.* Durham: Duke University Press, 2005.

Guerra, François-Xavier. *México, del antigua régimen a la revolución,* 2 vols. Trans. Sergio Fernández Bravo. Mexico City: Fondo de Cultura Económica, 1995.

Gunn, Drewey Wayne. *American and British Writers in Mexico, 1556–1973.* Austin: University of Texas Press, 1974.

———. *Mexico in American and British Letters: A Bibliography of Travel Books, Citing Original Editions.* Metuchen, N.J.: Scarecrow Press, 1974.

Guzmán, Martín Luis. *Muertes históricas.* Mexico City: Consejo Nacional para la Cultura y las Artes, Dirección General de Publicaciones, 1990.

Habenstein, Robert Wesley. *Funeral Customs the World Over.* Rev. ed. Milwaukee: Bulfin Printer, 1974.

Haber, Stephen H. "Assessing the Obstacles to Industrialization: The Mexican Economy, 1830–1940." *Journal of Latin American Studies* 24, no. 1 (February 1992): 10–26.

———. *Industry and Underdevelopment: The Industrialization of Mexico.* Stanford: Stanford University Press, 1989.

Halbwachs, Maurice. *On Collective Memory.* Ed. and trans. Lewis A. Coser. Chicago: University of Chicago Press, 1992.

Hale, Charles A. *Mexican Liberalism in the Age of Mora, 1821–1853.* New Haven: Yale University Press, 1968.

———. *The Transformation of Liberalism in Late Nineteenth-Century Mexico.* Princeton: Princeton University Press, 1989.

Hall, Stuart, Dorothy Hobson, Andrew Lowe, and Paul Willis, eds. *Culture, Media, Language.* London: Hutchinson and Co., 1980.

Hamill, Hugh M., Jr. *The Hidalgo Revolt: Prelude to Mexican Independence.* Gainesville: University of Florida Press, 1966.

Hannay, David. *Díaz.* Fort Washington, N.Y.: Kennikat Press, 1970.

Hansen, Roger. *The Politics of Mexican Development*. Baltimore: Johns Hopkins University Press, 1971.

Hanson, Randall S. "The Day of Ideals: Catholic Social Action in the Age of the Mexican Revolution, 1867–1929." Ph.D. diss., Indiana University, 1994.

Hart, John M. *Anarchism and the Mexican Working Class, 1860–1931*. Austin: University of Texas Press, 1978.

Hobsbawm, Eric J. *The Age of Capital, 1848–1875*. New York: Scribner's Sons, 1975.

———. *The Age of Empire, 1875–1914*. London: Weidenfeld and Nicolson, 1987.

Hobsbawm, Eric J., and Terence Ranger, eds. *The Invention of Tradition*. Cambridge: Cambridge University Press, 1983.

Holden, Robert H. *Mexico and the Survey of Public Lands: The Management of Modernization, 1876–1911*. DeKalb: Northern Illinois University Press, 1994.

Hunt, Lynn. *Politics, Culture, and Class in the French Revolution*. Berkeley: University of California Press, 1984.

———, ed. *The New Cultural History*. Berkeley: University of California Press, 1989.

Iturriaga de la Fuente, José. *Anecdotario de viajeros extranjeros en México: Siglos XVI–XX*, 3 vols. Mexico City: Fondo de Cultura Económica, 1988–92.

Iturribarría, Jorge Fernando. "La política de la conciliación del general Díaz y el arzobispo Gillow." *Historia Mexicana* 14, no. 53 (July–September 1974): 81–101.

———. *Porfirio Díaz ante la historia*. Mexico City: Unión Gráfica, 1967.

Johns, Michael. *The City of Mexico in the Age of Díaz*. Austin: University of Texas Press, 1997.

Johnson, Lyman L., ed. *Body Politics: Death, Dismemberment, and Memory in Latin America*. Albuquerque: University of New Mexico Press, 2004.

Joseph, Gilbert M., and Daniel Nugent, eds. *Everyday Forms of State Formation: Revolution and the Negotiation of Rule in Modern Mexico*. Durham: Duke University Press, 1994.

Kammen, Michael. *Mystic Chords of Memory: The Transformation of Tradition in American Culture*. New York: Knopf, 1991.

Kantz, Barbara Lee. "A Social History of the Urban Working Class in Mexico City, 1882–1910." Ph.D. diss., State University of New York at Stony Brook, 1988.

Knapp, Frank A., Jr. *The Life of Sebastián Lerdo de Tejada, 1823–1889: A Study of Influence and Obscurity*. Austin: University of Texas Press, 1951.

Knight, Alan. "*Caciquisimo* in Twentieth-Century Mexico." In *Caciquismo in Twentieth-Century Mexico*, ed. Alan Knight and Wil Pansters, 1–11. London: Institute for the Study of the Americas, 2005.

———. *The Mexican Revolution*, 2 vols. Lincoln: University of Nebraska Press, 1986.

———. "The Mexican Revolution: Bourgeois? Nationalist? Or Just a 'Great Rebellion'?" *Bulletin of Latin American Research* 4, no. 2 (1985): 1–37.

———. "Populism and Neo-populism in Latin America, Especially Mexico." *Journal of Latin American Studies* 30, no. 2 (May 1998): 223–48.

Koselleck, Reinhart. *The Practice of Conceptual History: Timing History, Spacing Concepts*. Trans. Todd Samuel Presner, Kerstin Behnke, and Jobst Welge. Foreword by Hayden White. Stanford: Stanford University Press, 2002.

Krantz, Frederick, ed. *History from Below: Studies in Popular Protest and Popular Ideology*. Oxford: Basil Blackwell, 1988.

Krauze, Enrique. *Mexico: Biography of Power, a History of Modern Mexico, 1810–1996*. Trans. Hank Heifetz. New York: Harper Collins, 1996.

———. *Porfirio Díaz: Místico de la autoridad*. Mexico City: Fonda de Cultura Economica, 1987.

Kselman, Thomas A. *Death and the Afterlife in Modern France*. Princeton: Princeton University Press, 1993.

Lafaye, Jacques. *Quetzalcoatl and Guadalupe: The Formation of Mexican National Consciousness, 1531–1813*. Trans. Benjamin Keen. Chicago: University of Chicago Press, 1976.

Lear, John Robert. "Workers, *Vecinos* and Citizens: The Revolution in Mexico City, 1909–1917." Ph.D. diss., University of California, Berkeley, 1993.

Lears, T. J. Jackson. "The Concept of Cultural Hegemony: Problems and Possibilities." *American Historical Review* 90 (June 1985): 567–93.

Lehning, James R. "Gossiping about Gambetta: Contested Memories in the Early Third Republic." *French Historical Studies* 18, no. 1 (Spring 1993): 237–54.

Lemoine Villicaña, Ernesto. *Morelos, su vida revolucionaria a través de sus escritos y de otros testimonios de la época*. Mexico City: Universidad Nacional Autónoma de México, 1965.

Lloyd, Jane-Dale. *El proceso de modernización del noroeste de Chihuahua, 1880–1910*. Mexico City: Universidad Iberoamericana, 1987.

Lomnitz, Claudio. *Death and the Idea of Mexico*. New York: Zone Books, 2005.

——. *Deep Mexico, Silent Mexico: An Anthropology of Nationalism*. Minneapolis: University of Minnesota Press, 2001.

Lomnitz-Adler, Claudio. *Exits from the Labyrinth: Culture and Ideology in the Mexican National Space*. Berkeley: University of California Press, 1992.

López, Amanda. "In Search of a 'Dignified Necropolis': Liberalism, Public Welfare, and the Panteón de Dolores, 1875–1879." Paper presented at the annual meeting of the Rocky Mountain Council for Latin American Studies, Flagstaff, Ariz., April 9–12, 2008.

López Gutiérrez, Gustavo. *Escobedo: Repúblicano Democrática Benemérito de Chiapas, 1826–1902*. Tuxtla Gutiérrez, Chiapas: n.p., 1968.

López-Portillo y Rojas, José. *Elevación y caída de Porfirio Díaz*. Mexico City: Librería Española, 1921.

López Rosado, Diego G. *La burocracia en México, vol. 3: Mexico Independiente, 1821–1910*. Mexico City: Secretaría de Comercio, 1980.

——. *Los servicios públicos de la ciudad de México*. Mexico City: Editorial Porrúa, 1976.

Loraux, Nicole. *The Invention of Athens: The Funeral Oration in the Classical City*. Cambridge: Harvard University Press, 1986.

Macías, Victor. "Mexicans 'of the Better Class': The Elite Culture and Ideology of Porfirian Chihuahua and Its Influence on the Mexican American Generation, 1876–1936." M.A. thesis, University of Texas, El Paso, 1994.

Maciel, David. *Ignacio Ramírez, ideólogo del liberalismo social en México*. Mexico City: Universidad Nacional Autónoma de México, 1980.

MacLachlan, Colin M., and William H. Beezley. *El Gran Pueblo: A History of Greater Mexico*. New York: Prentice Hall, 1994.

Mandel, Oscar, ed. *The Theatre of Don Juan: A Collection of Plays and View, 1630–1963*. Lincoln: University of Nebraska Press, 1963.

Marroqui, Jose Maria. *La ciudad de Mexico*, 3 vols. 2nd ed. Mexico City: Jesus Medina, 1969.

Maza, Francisco de la. *Las piras funerarias en la historia y en el arte de México: Grabados, litografías y documentos del siglo XVI al XIX*. Mexico City: Universidad Nacional Autonóma de México–Instituto de Investigaciones Estéticas, 1946.

——. "Los restos de Hernán Cortés." *Cuadernos Americanos* 32 (1947): 153–74.

McManners, John. *Death and the Enlightenment: Changing Attitudes to Death among Christians and Unbelievers in Eighteenth-Century France*. New York: Oxford University Press, 1981.

McNamara, Patrick J. *Sons of the Sierra: Juárez, Díaz, and the People of Ixtlán, Oaxaca, 1855–1920*. Chapel Hill: University of North Carolina Press, 2006.

Meinwald, Dan. "*Memento Mori*: Death in Nineteenth Century Photography." *California Museum of Photography Bulletin* 9, no. (1990): 1–7.

Los mexicanos pintados por sí mismos. Tipos y costumbres nacionales. Mexico City: Mungía Press, 1854.

Meyer, Michael C., and William H. Beezley, eds. *The Oxford History of Mexico*. New York: Oxford University Press, 2000.

Meyer, Michael C., William L. Sherman, and Susan M. Deeds. *The Course of Mexican History*. 4th, 6th, and 8th eds. New York: Oxford University Press, 1991, 1999, 2007.

Middleton, David, and Derek Edwards, eds. *Collective Remembering*. London: Sage, 1990.

Molina Enríquez, Andrés. *Los grandes problemas nacionales*. Mexico City: Carranza e Hijos, 1909.

Montellano, Francisco, comp. *C. B. Waite, Fotógrafo: Una mirada diversa sobre el México de principios del siglo XX*. Presented by Aurelio de los Reyes. Mexico City: Grijalbo, 1994.

Mora, José María Luís. *México y sus revoluciones*. 2nd ed. Mexico City: Editorial Porrúa, 1950.

Needell, Jeffrey. *A Tropical Belle Epoque: Elite Culture and Society in Turn-of-the-Century Rio de Janeiro*. New York: Cambridge University Press, 1987.

Nora, Pierre. "Between Memory and History: *Les Liéux des Mémoire.*" *Representations* 26 (Spring 1989): 7–25.

———. *Realms of Memory: Rethinking the French Past*, 3 vols. Ed. and foreword by Lawrence D. Kritzman. Trans. Arthur Goldhammer. New York: Columbia University Press, 1996–98.

Novo, Salvador. *Los paseos de la ciudad de México*. Mexico City: Fondo de la Cultura Económica, 1984.

Olavarría y Ferrari, Enrique de. *Reseña histórica del teatro en México, 1538–1911*, 5 vols. 3rd ed. Prologue by Salvador Novo. Mexico City: Editorial Porrúa, 1961.

O'Malley, Ilene V. *The Myth of the Revolution: Hero Cults and the Institutionalization of the Mexican State, 1920–1940*. New York: Greenwood Press, 1986.

Ozouf, Mona. *Festivals and the French Revolution*. Trans. Alan Sheridan. Cambridge: Harvard University Press, 1988.

Palmer, Stephen. "Getting to Know the Unknown Soldier: Official Nationalism in Liberal Costa Rica, 1880–1900." *Journal of Latin American Studies* 25, no. 1 (February 1993): 45–72.

Payno, Manuel. *Obras completas*, 5 vols. Mexico City: Consejo Nacional para la Cultura y las Artes, 1996–98.

Paz, Ireneo. *Los hombres prominentes de México*. Mexico City: "La Patria," 1888.

Paz, Octavio. *The Labyrinth of Solitude*. New York: Grove Press, 1985.

Peloso, Vincent C., and Barbara A. Tenenbaum, eds. *Liberals, Politics, and Power: State Formation in Nineteenth-Century Latin America*. Athens: University of Georgia Press, 1996.

Pérez-Rayon E., Nora. "La sociología de lo cotidiano. Discursos y fiestas cívicas en el México de 1900. La historia en la conformación de la identidad nacional." *Sociológica* 8, no. 23 (September–December 1993): 171–98.

Perry, Laurens Ballard. *Juárez and Díaz: Machine Politics in Mexico*. DeKalb: Northern Illinois University Press, 1978.

Piccato, Pablo. *City of Suspects: Crime in Mexico City, 1900–1931*. Durham: Duke University Press, 2001.

———. "*Cuidado con los Rateros:* The Making of Criminals in Modern Mexico City." In *Crime and Punishment in Latin America: Law and Society since Late Colonial Times*, ed. Ricardo D. Salvatore, Carlos Aguirre, and Gilbert M. Joseph, 233–72. Durham: Duke University Press, 2001.

Pilcher, Jeffrey. *Que Vivan los Tamales! Food and the Making of Mexican Identity*. Albuquerque: University of New Mexico Press, 1998.

Platt, Tristan. "Simón Bolívar, the Sun of Justice and the Amerindian Virgin: Andean Conceptions of the Patria in Nineteenth-Century Potosí." *Journal of Latin American Studies* 25 (1993): 159–85.

Pratt, Mary Louise. *Imperial Eyes: Travel Writing and Transculturation*. New York: Routledge, 1992.

Prida, Ramón. *De la dictadura al la anarquia. Apuntes para la historia política de México durante la última cuarenta y tres años*, 2 vols. El Paso: Imprenta de "El Paso del Norte," 1914.

Prieto, Guillermo. *Memorias de mis tiempos, 1828–1853*. Puebla: Editorial J. M. Cajica Jr., 1970.

Raat, Dirk W., ed. *Mexico from Independence to Revolution, 1810–1910*. Lincoln: University of Nebraska Press, 1982.

Rabasa, Emilio. *La evolución histórica de México*. Mexico City: Librería de la viuda de Ch. Bouret, Imprenta Franco-Mexicana, 1920.

Radcliffe, Sarah, and Sallie Westwood. *Remaking the Nation: Place, Identity, and Politics in Latin America*. New York: Routledge, 1996.

Ramos, Julio. *Desencuentros de la modernidad en América Latina: Literatura y política en el siglo XIX*. Mexico City: Fondo de Cultura Económica, 1989.

Ramos, Samuel. *Profile of Man and Culture in Mexico*. Trans. Peter G. Earle. Austin: University of Texas Press, 1973.

Rangel Gaspar, Eliseo. *Jesús González Ortega (Caudillo de la Reforma)*. Prologue by Agustín Cue Canovas. Mexico City: Gráficos Galeza, 1960.

Reese, Thomas F., and Carol McMichael Reese. "Revolutionary Urban Legacies: Porfirio Díaz's Celebrations of the Centennial of Mexican Independence in 1910." In *Arte, historia e identidad en América: Visiones comparativas*, ed. Gustavo Curiel, Renato González Mello, and Juana Gutiérrez Haces, 361–73. Mexico City: Universidad Nacional Autónoma de México Instituto de Investigaciones Estéticas, 1994.

Reis, João José. *Death Is a Festival: Funeral Rites and Rebellion in Nineteenth-Century Brazil*. Trans. H. Sabrina Gledhill. Chapel Hill: University of North Carolina Press, 2003.

Rendón Garcini, Ricardo. *El prosperato: Tlaxcala de 1885 a 1911.* Mexico City: Universidad Iberoamericana/Siglo Veintiuno Editores, 1993.

Reyes, Aurelio de los. *Cine y sociedad en México, 1896–1930.* Mexico City: Universidad Nacional Autónoma de México, Cineteca Nacional, 1981.

Riva Palacio, Vicente, Alfredo Chavero, Julio Zárate, Enrique Olavarría y Ferrari, and José María Vigil. *México a través de los siglos,* 5 vols. Barcelona: Espasa y companía, 1886–89.

Rivera Cambas, Manuel. *México pintoresco, artístico y monumental,* 3 vols. Mexico City: Editorial del Valle de México, 1972.

Rivero, Morelos. *Porfirio Díaz: Un Estadista y un regimen mal juzgado por la Revolución.* Mexico City: n.p., 1946.

Roach, Joseph. *Cities of the Dead: Circum-Atlantic Performance.* New York: Columbia University Press, 1996.

Rodríguez Barragán, Nereo. *El General Dn. Mariano Arista (en el centenario de su muerte).* San Luís Potosí: Universitaria, 1955.

Rodríguez Kuri, Ariel. *La experiencia olvidada. El Ayuntamiento de México: Política y gobierno, 1876–1912.* Mexico City: El Colegio de México, Centro de Estudios Históricos, Universidad Autónoma Metropolitana, Atzcapotzalco, 1996.

Roseberry, William. *Anthropologies and Histories: Essays in Culture, History, and Political Economy.* New Brunswick: Rutgers University Press, 1989.

Rubenstein, Anne. *Bad Language, Naked Ladies, and Other Threats to the Nation: A Political History of Comic Books in Mexico.* Durham: Duke University Press, 1998.

Rudé, George. *Ideology and Popular Protest.* New York: Pantheon, 1980.

Rugeley, Terry. *Yucatán's Maya Peasantry and the Origins of the Caste War.* Austin: University of Texas Press, 1996.

Ruiz, Ramón Eduardo. *Triumphs and Tragedy: A History of the Mexican People.* New York: W. W. Norton and Co., 1992.

Rydell, Robert W. *All the World's a Fair: Visions of Empire at American International Expositions, 1876–1916.* Chicago: University of Chicago Press, 1984.

Salado Alvarez, Victoriano. *Porfirio Díaz; Ramón Corona.* Mexico City: n.p., 1985.

Salvatore, Ricardo D., Carlos Aguirre, and Gilbert M. Joseph, eds. *Crime and Punishment in Latin America: Law and Society since Late Colonial Times.* Durham: Duke University Press, 2001.

Santoni, Pedro. "The Failure of Mobilization: The Civic Militia of Mexico in 1846." *Mexican Studies/Estudios Mexicanos* 12, no. 2 (Summer 1996): 169–94.

———. *Mexicans at Arms: Puro Federalists and the Politics of War, 1845–1848.* Fort Worth: Texas Christian University Press, 1996.

———. "'Where Did the Other Heroes Go?' Exalting the 'Polko' National Guard Battalions in Nineteenth-Century Mexico." *Journal of Latin American Studies* 34, no. 4 (November 2002): 807–44.

Schmitt, Karl M. "The Mexican Positivists and the Church–State Question, 1876–1911." *Journal of Church and State* 8, no. 2 (Spring 1966): 200–13.

Schneider, Robert A. *The Ceremonial City: Toulouse Observed, 1738–1780.* Princeton: Princeton University Press, 1995.

Schwartz, Barry. "Mourning and the Making of a Sacred Symbol: Durkheim and the Lincoln Assassination." *Social Forces* 70, no. 2 (December 1991): 343–64.

Scott, James C. *Domination and the Arts of Resistance: Hidden Transcripts.* New Haven: Yale University Press, 1990.

———. *Seeing like a State: How Certain Schemes to Improve the Human Condition Have Failed.* New Haven: Yale University Press, 1998.

———. *Weapons of the Weak: Everyday Forms of Peasant Resistance.* New Haven: Yale University Press, 1985.

Selections from the Prison Notebooks of Antonio Gramsci. Ed. and intro. by Quintin Hoare and Geoffrey Nowell-Smith. New York: International Publishers, 1971.

Semo, Enrique. *Historia Méxicana: Economía y lucha de clases.* Mexico City: Ediciones Era, 1979.

Serrano Migallon, Fernando. *El Grito de Independencia: Historia de una pasión nacional.* Prologue by Andrés Henestrosa. Mexico City: Miguel Angel Porrúa, 1988.

Seward, John E. "The Veracruz Massacre of 1879." *The Americas* 32, no. 4 (April 1976): 585–96.

Sierra, Justo. *Juárez: Su obra y su tiempo*. Intro. by Agustín Yáñez. Mexico City: Editorial Porrúa, 1989.

———. *Obras Completas*, 14 vols. Ed. Agustín Yáñez. Mexico City: Universidad Nacional Autónoma de México, 1948–49.

———. *The Political Evolution of the Mexican People*. Trans. Charles Ramsdell. Austin: University of Texas Press, 1969.

Simpson, Lesley Byrd. *Many Mexicos*. 4th ed. Berkeley: University of California Press, 1966.

Sinkin, Richard N. *The Mexican Reform, 1855–1876: A Study in Liberal Nation-Building*. Austin: Institute of Latin American Studies, University of Texas at Austin, 1979.

Solís, Manuel de J. *Historia de la Bandera, Himno, Escudo y Calendario Cívico Nacionales*. Mexico City: n.p., 1940.

Sommer, Doris. *Foundational Fictions*. Berkeley: University of California Press, 1992.

Sosa, Francisco. *Las estatuas de la Reforma*. Mexico City: Colección Metropolitana, 1974.

Sotomayor, Arturo. *La Rotonda de los Hombres Ilustres*. Mexico City: Colección Metropolitana, 1976.

Sprague, William Forrest. *Vicente Guerrero, Mexican Liberator: A Study in Patriotism*. Chicago: R. R. Donnelley and Sons, 1939.

Staples, Anne. "La lucha por los muertos." *Diálogos* 13, no. 5 (1977): 15–20.

Stephen, Lynn. *Zapata Lives! Histories and Cultural Politics in Southern Mexico*. Berkeley: University of California Press, 2002.

Stevens, Donald Fithian. *Origins of Instability in Early Republican Mexico*. Durham: Duke University Press, 1991.

Strocchia, Sharon T. *Death and Ritual in Renaissance Florence*. Baltimore: Johns Hopkins University Press, 1992.

Taylor, Lawrence J. "*Bás In Eirinn*: Cultural Constructions of Death in Ireland." *Anthropological Quarterly* 62, no. 4 (October 1989): 175–87.

———. "Introduction: The Uses of Death in Europe." *Anthropological Quarterly* 62, no. 4 (October 1989): 149–54.

Tello Díaz, Carlos. *El exilio: Un relato de familia*. Mexico City: Cal y Arena, 1993.

Tenorio-Trillo, Mauricio. "1910 Mexico City: Space and Nation in the City of the Centenario," *Journal of Latin American Studies* 21, no. 1 (1996): 75–104.

———. *Mexico at the World's Fairs: Crafting a Modern Nation*. Berkeley: University of California Press, 1996.

TePaske, John J. "Funerals and Fiestas in Early-Eighteenth Century St. Augustine." *Florida Historical Quarterly* 44 (July 1965–April 1966): 97–104.

Thompson, E. P. *Customs in Common*. New York: New Press, 1991.

———. "The Moral Economy of the English Crowd in the Eighteenth Century." *Past and Present* 50 (February 1971): 76–136.

Timmons, Wilbert H. *Morelos: Priest, Soldier, Statesman of Mexico*. El Paso: Texas Western College Press, 1963.

Tinker, Edward Larocque. *Corridos and Calaveras*. Austin: University of Texas Press, 1961.

Tinker Salas, Miguel. *In the Shadow of the Eagles: Sonora and the Transformation of the Border during the Porfiriato*. Berkeley: University of California Press, 1997.

Tomás de Cuéllar, José. *The Magic Lantern. Having a Ball and Christmas Eve*. Ed. and intro. by Margo Glantz, trans. Margaret Carson. New York: Oxford University Press, 2000.

Tumarkin, Nina. *Lenin Lives! The Lenin Cult in Soviet Russia*. Cambridge: Harvard University Press, 1983.

———. *The Living and the Dead: The Rise and Fall of the Cult of World War II in Russia*. New York: Basic Books, 1994.

Turner, Victor W. *The Ritual Process: Structure and Antistructure*. Ithaca: Cornell University Press, 1985.

Tweedie, Ethel Brilliana Harley (Mrs. Alec). *The Maker of Modern México: Porfirio Díaz*. New York: John Lane Co., 1906.

———. *Porfirio Díaz. Seven Times President of México*. London: Hurst and Blackett, 1906.

Valadés, José C. *El Porfirismo: Historia de un régimen, el crecimiento*, 2 vols. Mexico City: Universidad Autónoma de México, 1977.

———. *El Porfirismo: Historia de un régimen, el nacimiento (1876–1884)*. Mexico City: Antigua Librería Robredo, de José Porrua e hijos, 1941.

Vanderwood, Paul J. *Disorder and Progress: Bandits, Police, and Mexican Development*. Wilmington, Del.: Scholarly Resources, 1992.

———. *The Power of God against the Guns of Government: Religious Upheaval in Mexico at the Turn of the Nineteenth Century*. Stanford: Stanford University Press, 1998.

Vaughan, Mary Kay. *The State, Education, and Social Class in Mexico, 1880–1928*. DeKalb: Northern Illinois University Press, 1982.

Vázquez de Knauth, Josefina. *Nacionalismo y educación en México*. Mexico City: Colegio de México, 1970.

Verdery, Katherine. *The Political Lives of Dead Bodies: Reburial and Postsocialist Change*. New York: Columbia University Press, 1999.

Villoro, Luis. *Los grandes momentos del indigenismo en Mexico*. Mexico City: Ediciones de la Casa Chata, 1979.

Viqueira Albán, Juan Pedro. *Propriety and Permissiveness in Bourbon Mexico*. Trans. Sonya Lipsett-Rivera and Sergio Rivera Ayala. Wilmington, Del.: SR Books, 1999.

Voekel, Pamela. *Alone before God: The Religious Origins of Modernity in Mexico*. Durham: Duke University Press, 2002.

Vovelle, Michel. *Ideologies and Mentalities*. Trans. Eamon O'Flaherty. Chicago: University of Chicago Press, 1990.

Wasserman, Mark. *Capitalists, Caciques, and Revolution: The Native Elite and Foreign Enterprise in Chihuahua, Mexico, 1854–1911*. Chapel Hill: University of North Carolina Press, 1984.

———. *Everyday Life and Politics in Nineteenth Century Mexico: Men, Women, and War*. Albuquerque: University of New Mexico Press, 2001.

———. *Persistant Oligarchs: Elites and Politics in Chihuahua, Mexico, 1910–1940*. Durham: Duke University Press, 1993.

Weber, Eugen. *France, Fin de Siècle*. Cambridge: Harvard University Press, 1986.

———. *Peasants into Frenchmen: The Modernization of Rural France, 1870–1914*. Stanford: Stanford University Press, 1976.

Weeks, Charles A. *The Juárez Myth in Mexico*. Tuscaloosa: University of Alabama Press, 1987.

Wells, Allen. "Out from the Shadows: Recent Scholarship on Late-Nineteenth-Century Mexico." *Latin American Research Review* 35, no. 1 (2000): 172–86.

Wells, Allen, and Gilbert M. Joseph. "Modernizing Visions, Chilango Blueprints, and Provincial Growing Pains: Merida at the Turn of the Century." *Estudios Mexicanos/Mexican Studies* 8, no. 2 (Summer 1992): 167–215.

———. *Summer of Discontent, Seasons of Upheaval: Elite Politics and Rural Insurgency in Yucatán, 1876–1915*. Stanford: Stanford University Press, 1996.

Wilentz, Sean, ed. *Rites of Power: Symbolism, Ritual, and Politics since the Middle Ages*. Philadelphia: University of Pennsylvania Press, 1985.

Wilkie, James W., and Paul D. Wilkins. "Quantifying the Class Structure of Mexico, 1895–1970." In *Statistical Abstract of Latin America*, ed. James W. Wilkie, Paul D. Wilkins, and Stephen Haber, 577–90. Los Angeles: University of California–Los Angeles Latin American Center Publications, 1981.

Williams, Raymond. *Keywords*. New York: Oxford University Press, 1976.

———. *Marxism and Literature*. Oxford: Oxford University Press, 1977.

Wood, Andrew. *Revolution in the Street: Women, Workers, and Urban Protest in Veracruz, 1870–1927*. Wilmington, Del.: Scholarly Resources, 2001.

Yeager, Gene. "Porfirian Commercial Propaganda: Mexico in World Expositions." *The Americas* 34 (October 1977): 230–43.

Zabre, Alfonso Teja. *Vida de Morelos*. Mexico City: Universidad Nacional Autonóma de México, 1959.

Zafra, Emilio. "La elegancia del arte funerario en la ciudad de México, 1850–1930." *México Desconocido* 15, no. 182 (April 1992): 46–50.

Zayas Enríquez, Rafael de. *Porfirio Díaz, la evolución de su vida*. New York: D. Appleton and Co., 1908.

Zolov, Eric. *Refried Elvis: The Rise of the Mexican Counterculture*. Berkeley: University of California Press, 1999.

Index